OXFORD HISTORICAL SOCIETY
General Editor: Alan Crossley

REGISTRUM ANNALIUM COLLEGII MERTONENSIS 1603–1660

Oxford Historical Society
NEW SERIES, VOL. XLI

REGISTRUM ANNALIUM COLLEGII MERTONENSIS 1603–1660

Edited by
J. R. L. HIGHFIELD
Emeritus Fellow of Merton College

THE BOYDELL PRESS

OXFORD HISTORICAL SOCIETY
MMVI (*for* MMII–MMIII)

First published 2006

An Oxford Historical Society publication
Published by The Boydell Press
an imprint of Boydell & Brewer Ltd
PO Box 9, Woodbridge, Suffolk IP12 3DF, UK
and of Boydell & Brewer Inc.
668 Mt Hope Avenue, Rochester, NY 14620, USA
website: www.boydellandbrewer.com

ISBN 0 904107 20 5

A CiP catalogue record for this book is available from the British Library

This publication is printed on acid-free paper

Typeset by Anne Joshua, Oxford
Printed in Great Britain by
Print Wright Ltd., Ipswich

PREFACE

My thanks are due to Pauline Fletcher, Dr John Fletcher's widow, for providing me with photostats of Register I.3 and other materials, also to Dr T. Reinhardt of Somerville College and to Messrs Samuel Eidinow and T. F. R. G. Braun, both of Merton College, for much valuable help with the Latin of the text. Doctors Julian Walworth and Julian Reid, respectively Librarian and Archivist of Merton College, made the Register readily available to me on many occasions. Judith Kirby, the Fellows' Secretary, frequently helped me with typing and photocopying. Dr Steven Gunn read over the Introduction and kindly made helpful suggestions. The General Editor of the Oxford Historical Society, Alan Crossley, gave freely of his time and expertise in checking the text and helping to compile the index.

J. R. L. Highfield, Merton College, July 2006

Oxford Historical Society, New Series, Vol. XLI: Erratum
Preface (page v), line 5: *for* Julian Walworth *read* Julia Walworth

The Oxford Historical Society records its gratitude to the Warden and Fellows of Merton College for a most generous grant towards the publication of this edition.

CONTENTS

ABBREVIATIONS

Bendall, Brooke and Collinson	Bendall, S., Brooke, C. and Collinson, P., *A History of Emmanuel College, Cambridge* (1999)
BL	British Library, London
Bodl.	Bodleian Library, Oxford
Brodrick, *Memorials*	Brodrick, Hon. G. C., *Memorials of Merton College* (OHS iv, 1885)
Coxe	Coxe, H. O., *Catalogus Codicum MSS. qui in Collegiis aulisque Oxoniensibus hodie adservantur* (2 vols, 1852)
Garrod and Allen, *Merton Mun.*	*Merton Muniments*, ed. H. W. Garrod and P.. S. Allen (OHS lxxxvi, 1928)
HUO, iii	*History of the University of Oxford, iii: the Collegiate University*, ed. J. McConica (1986)
HUO, iv	*History of the University of Oxford, iv: Seventeenth-Century Oxford*, ed. N. Tyacke (1997)
Martin and Highfield	Martin, G. H. and Highfield, J. R. L., *A History of Merton College (1997)*
MCR	*Merton College Record*
ODNB	*Oxford Dictionary of National Biography*, ed. H. C. G. Matthew, B. Harrison (2005)
OHS	Oxford Historical Society.
Powicke, *Medieval Books*	Powicke, F. M., *Medieval Books of Merton College, Oxford* (1931)
Reg. Annalium, 1483–1521	*Reg Annalium Collegii Mertonensis, 1483–1521*, ed. H. E. Salter (OHS lxxvi, 1921)
Reg. Annalium, 1521–67	*Reg Annalium Collegii Mertonensis, 1521–67*, ed. J. M. Fletcher (OHS n.s. xxiii, 1974)
Reg. Annalium, 1567–1603	*Reg. Annalium Collegii Mertonensis, 1567–1603*, ed. J. M. Fletcher (OHS n.s. xxiv, 1976)
Wood, *Athenae*	Wood, A., *Athenae Oxonienses*, ed. P. Bliss (4 vols. 1813–20
Wood, *Hist Univ.*	Wood, A., *The History and Antiquities of the University of Oxford*, ed. J. Gutch (2 vols in 3, 1792–6)
Wood, *Life and Times*	*The Life and Times of Anthony Wood*, ed. A. Clark (OHS xix, xxi, xxvi, xxx, 1891–5)

INTRODUCTION

In his introduction to the first published part of the second Merton register, the editor, the late Dr J. M. Fletcher, stated that the full manuscript volume contains the record of college business from 1567 to 1730. He himself refrained from taking his edition to the death of Warden Savile in 1622, because that would have produced a volume of impossible length. He said that he hoped 'at some future date to present to the Oxford Historical Society an edition of the Register from 1603 until 1660' which would 'add the remaining material associated with Savile's wardenship and carry the transcript to a more suitable terminating date'.[1] This promise Dr Fletcher did not live to fulfil. The present edition is intended to make good his promise. The general principles of editing are those used by Dr Fletcher.[2]

The handwriting of the register for the years 1607–13 is that of the then subwarden, Nathaniel Brent. For the years 1633–7 and 1646–55 it is that of the subwarden Alexander Fisher. Fisher always puts a full point in the middle of capital letters such as D.

THE WARDENSHIP OF HENRY SAVILE

The register opens with the death of Queen Elizabeth. Warden Savile had just asserted himself after the *émeute* of 1598. He had been marginally associated with the rebellion of the earl of Essex.[3] The last nineteen years of his wardenship saw three of his major achievements. As one of the members of the Second Oxford Company he participated in the translation of the King James Bible. He supervised the building of Fellows' Quadrangle and completed his edition of the works of St John Chrysostom, though it is true that this last took place at Eton. In the university he founded the Savilian chairs of Geometry and Astronomy and himself gave the first lectures on geometry in 1620. He also took forward the work of his friend, Sir Thomas Bodley, to complete Arts End and the Schools Quadrangle at the east end of the Bodleian Library. The register carefully records Thomas Ravis, dean of Christ Church, as the director of the Fifth (or

[1] *Reg. Annalium, 1567–1603*, p. xi. The manuscript is Merton Coll. Mun., Reg. 1.3.

[2] *Reg. Annalium, 1521–67*, p. xi; cf. below, Editorial Note.

[3] Martin and Highfield, 173–7.

Second) Oxford Company and that three of Savile's fellow translators of the King James Bible borrowed books from Merton Library. They were George Abbott, dean of Winchester, Giles Thompson, dean of Windsor, and Richard Edes, dean of Worcester, though the titles of the books they borrowed are not recorded. Since Fellows' Quadrangle had not yet been built we must suppose that any of the work of translation done in Merton will have taken place in what is now the Breakfast Room and then was part of Savile's Lodgings. The three deans and Ravis were joined by Doctors John Aglionby and John Perne, and by Leonard Hutton, canon of Christ Church. They worked on the Gospels, the Acts of the Apostles and the Book of Revelation. There is no evidence that the warden took part in the committee of twelve revisers which met in Stationers' Hall in 1611.[1]

The story of the building of Fellows' Quadrangle has been told elsewhere.[2] Here it is only necessary to add that in October 1609 the college paid George Brome, the lord of Headington, £15 a year for stone during the construction of the quadrangle.[3] Though the first stone was laid on 13 September 1608 there was a delay until the Yorkshire masons John Ackroyde of Halifax and John Bentley could arrive. The building evidently gave satisfaction since Ackroyde was not only paid £570 but an additional £20 when it was finished,[4] and the carpenter, Thomas Holt, who had been paid £430, was found lodgings in Holywell.[5] Those who first occupied the new rooms were, on releasing them, to leave the utensils which the college had provided or £3 in cash.[6]

The quadrangle provided nine sets of rooms on the first floor for the M.A. fellows. On the east side above three masters' sets the second floor formed a gallery, eventually part of the warden's house. On the south side there were four sets of rooms for M.A. fellows and four above them on the second floor, including one great chamber on the south west looking out over the Meadow. On the west side the two-storey medieval kitchen was incorporated. This still left room for five fellows' sets on the second and third floors.[7] On the ground floor of the eastern

[1] Below, 27–8. A. Nicolson, *Power and Glory. Jacobean England and the making of the King James Bible* (New York, 2003), 154–72. Cf. Martin and Highfield, 181–2; W. C. Costin, *Hist. of St John's College, Oxford* (O.H.S. n.s. xii), 25.

[2] *HUO*, iv. 148–9.

[3] Below, 54.

[4] Below, 50, 67.

[5] Below, 51, 116. He was granted a 40-year lease in Holywell, 16 March 1621.

[6] Below, 62.

[7] Three of these were on the sites of the present New Common Room, Upper Bursary and Old Common Room. There was also a set over the Hall Porch.

and southern sides were rooms for the postmasters nominated by the M.A. fellows who lived above them.[1]

Two of Savile's helpers with his edition of Chrysostom are glimpsed in the register. One, Thomas Allen, fellow, was given permission in April 1603 to make notes in the margin of copies of Latin editions of Chrysostom.[2] Seven years later John Hales, fellow, was allowed in April 1610 to retain all his allocations except commons, so long as he remained at Eton working on the great edition with Savile.[3] Two years later the work was finished and began to be published at Eton; but copies did not sell readily, and in August 1632 those which remained were to be divided among the fellows, who, if they themselves distributed their copies, were to pay £5 to the college for each copy thus disposed of.[4]

In 1597 Savile had shown himself keen to reorganize the theological disputations held in chapel on Fridays at 5 p. m.[5] They were to be held by masters two years after inception; they were to be paid for by the college and defaulters fined. In 1604 he further decreed that the disputes were not to exceed an hour, at the end of which the senior master present was to force a conclusion. No doubt to help towards this the opponent was not to use a preface. Those disputing masters who resided for the greater part of the year and were of two years' standing could share in £60. The topics for debate proposed for Michaelmas 1604 show their highly topical nature. Thus Slade was to respond and Brent oppose on 'whether the pope together with the council is judge of the scriptures', and Yate was to respond and Brent oppose on 'whether the whole of doctrine necessary for salvation is contained in the Scriptures'; Lee was to respond and King oppose on 'whether the pope is the visible monarch of the church', King to respond and Lee to oppose on 'whether it falls to the Roman pontiff to call general councils'.[6]

Theologically Savile seems to have shared the Calvinist position of the visitor, Archbishop Abbot, to judge from the fact that in 1618 he edited the Augustinian *magnum opus* of Abbot's predecessor and the Mertonian fellow, Thomas Bradwardine; he dedicated his edition to the archbishop.[7] In addition to theological disputations both bachelor and master fellows were expected to give philosophical discourses in

[1] Cf. Merton Coll. Mun., Reg.1.6, p. 72; Martin and Highfield, 254.
[2] Below, 1.
[3] Below, 55.
[4] Below, 205.
[5] *Reg. Annalium, 1567–1603*, 324.
[6] Below, 22–3. For 1606 cf. below, 38.
[7] Martin and Highfield, 186.

college known as 'variations'. To 'vary' was to affirm or deny three propositions drawn from the works of Aristotle. In 1624 bachelor fellows had their attention specifically drawn to the second book of the *Physics* and the last two books of *De Anima*, i.e. sources for Natural Philosophy.[1] On another occasion the last two books of *De Anima*, the *Ethics* and the *De Generatione Animalium* were mentioned as sources, and in 1628 the *Physics*, *Moralia*, *Politics*, and *Rhetoric* were specified.[2] Thus key texts on Natural and Moral Philosophy were used. The propositions were to be responded to by the three deans. Variations were held twice a week, either at 8 a.m. or in the afternoons. In 1625, when the regent masters varied in the Hall on themes from Aristotle's *Rhetoric*, the postmasters were to be present to benefit. When variations could not be held because of timetabling difficulties dispensations were freely given.[3]

Savile had claimed in 1598 that the college under his rule had supported 'neare twyse as many felowes as usually it hath done in our memory'.[4] This was to exaggerate. When he was appointed fellow in 1565 the number of masters and bachelors including probationers was eighteen. If in 1577 it had, unusually, fallen to fourteen, in 1597 the number was twenty-six, so there had been an increase, but in most of the previous years of his wardenship the number had hovered around twenty. It is true that between 1603 and 1622 Savile continuously sustained the number of fellows. There were more than twenty fellows in all years except one (nineteen in 1619) and on two occasions (in 1608 and 1609) the number had reached twenty-eight.

In his later years Savile made two benefactions to the college. In June 1616 he gave £100 after his annual visit to his lodgings,[5] and in 1620 he gave to the library books to be selected by the subwarden and senior dean to replace some of those of which it had been deprived.[6] But the final matter on his mind in his last year was the great Malden lawsuit over which he had persuaded the visitor, Archbishop Abbot, to intervene. The warden feared that the college might not be sufficiently appreciative of the archbishop's efforts, and, writing from Eton in January 1622, he urged that a letter be framed and sent to the archbishop to inform him of the value which the college set on his efforts.[7]

[1] Below, 152. For B.A.s in their probationary year along with the *Physics*.

[2] Below, 152, 179.

[3] Cf. *HUO*, iv. 396.

[4] Martin and Highfield, 177.

[5] Below, 92.

[6] Below, 111.

[7] Below, 120. For the Malden lease see N. Jones, 'Long Leases and the Feudal Revenue in the Court of Wards, 1540–1645', *Legal History*, 19 (1), April 1998, 1–22, and especially n. 14.

THE COLLEGE ESTATES

Unlike New College and Magdalen, Merton had no reserve fund with which to deal with the problem of inflation. Already in the fourteenth and fifteenth centuries provision had been made for extra allowances for the fellows. Now Savile increased the income from the estates by the purchase in 1599 of an additional manor at Gamlingay, Cambridgeshire,[1] where the college had held land since the thirteenth century. In 1603 one of Savile's servants, Francis Temple, was made bailiff at an annual stipend of £6 13s. 4d. and he was given £60 with which to stock the newly acquired property.[2] A topographical survey was commissioned from Mr Landon at a cost of £12. This formed part of the survey of several of the estates which took place under Savile.[3] In 1604 the rent of Gamlingay Avenells was set at £60 a year,[4] to be delivered by Temple on 24 June annually and distributed as 'dividend' between the college, the warden and fellows 'in the same way as the dividend was distributed on other college fines'.[5] Another addition to the estates occurred when Beilby was bought out of the £1,000 left by Savile's Yorkshire contemporary, John Chamber. He had specified that the land should be in Yorkshire and go to pay for two new Eton postmasters.[6] In 1621 the college recognized that it was impractical to expect the bailiff to bring the rents to Oxford twice a year as originally envisaged. He was to make one annual journey.[7]

The college estates like those of many other colleges had been run in the sixteenth century on the system of beneficial leases issued for terms of 40 years or less and the payment of entry fines.[8] Among the earliest Merton entry fines were those of William Clare, butcher, who paid

Cf. BL Add. MS. 25246, ff. 73r–74v., 'Doctor Brent's case. Warden of Merton Colledge in the Chancery'. The letter seems to contradict the assertion that Savile 'would not sue for it to oppose Attye who made him warden'.

[1] Cf. *Reg. Annalium, 1567–1603*, p. xxii.

[2] Below, 2, 10.

[3] Below, 5. Malden was surveyed in 1610.

[4] Below, 21. Aylmer records (*HUO*, iii. 528) that usually half the fine went to the college, as was certainly stipulated in injunction 9 in 1638 (below, 250), but in 1632 a fine on the Essex estate of Thracies and Thrognalls was divided between the college (£100) and the fellows (£200): below, 203, 206. For the beginnings of renewal fines for Merton leases see M. S. Saunders, 'The development of the Merton College manorial estate, *c.* 1483–1521', M. Stud. thesis, 1999.

[5] Below, 132.

[6] Below, 19, 20; Martin and Highfield, 189. But in 1641 the possibility of selling Bielby was raised, if another less troublesome manor could be found: below, 273.

[7] Below, 117.

[8] For this system see Bendall, Brooke and Collinson, *A History of Emmanuel College, Cambridge* (1999), 129–30.

£10 in 1501 to secure the lease of Holywell and Wolvercote for 31 years, and the £2 paid by John Croke in 1516 to secure the lease of the much less valuable manor of Ibstone for 20 years at an annual rent of £3 6s. 8d.[1] In 1558 a representative of the same family, Edmund Croke, was paying the same rent and was allowed to spread the payment of an entry fine of £6 13s. 4d. over seven years.[2]

The system was modified by important statutory legislation. First, Acts of 1571 and 1572 guaranteed to colleges a regular and relatively frequent chance to renew their leases and revise their rents; the limit for agricultural leases now was 21 years, for urban property 40 years. Then, by the Corn Rent Act of 1576 'one third of the existing rent was to be reserved and paid in a combination of wheat and malt barley, or in cash equivalent, using the current market price for corn at Cambridge, Oxford or Winchester'.[3] This act proved a very useful way of hedging against inflation.

Merton entry fines were steadily levied in the early seventeenth century. That for Elham rectory paid by Henry Nevill in 1611 for 21 years was £200 and if extended for a further three years would cost him £100 more.[4] That for the manor of Farleigh, Surrey, paid by the lessee, Stephen Heath, in 1614 for 21 years, was 200 marks.[5] The Essex manor of Canes was let to R. Spranger in 1616 for 21 years on payment of a fine for £160,[6] and the neighbouring manor of Norton Mandeville on a fine of £120 for a lease of 21 years to W. Storne.[7] A larger fine was that of £300 paid by Mr Napper for the lease of Holywell Mill for 40 years in 1617.[8] If a tenant resigned 37 years of an old 40-year lease on a Holywell house he might be let off with a fine on the new lease of as little as 20s.[9] By contrast if a fine was exacted towards the end of a lease it might be as large as the £600 paid by the executors of Elizabeth Sedley for the renewal of a lease of the rectory of Elham in 1649.[10] In the case of Thracies and Thrognells in Essex a fine might be shared between the college and the fellows.[11]

A rent as opposed to a fine might also be shared, as in the case of

[1] *Reg. Annalium, 1483–1521*, 252, 461.
[2] Ibid. *1521–67*, 174–8.
[3] Bendall, Brooke and Collinson, 130.
[4] Below, 62–3.
[5] Below, 84.
[6] Below, 91.
[7] Below, 91–2.
[8] Below, 101.
[9] Below, 119 (Thomas Franklin).
[10] Below, 319.
[11] And cf. above, p. xiii, n. 4. One may contrast the proposed practice at Emmanuel College, Cambridge, where soon after 1617 it was decided (but possibly not enacted) that two-thirds of the increase should go to the college and a third be divided among the 'living body, and publicke society': Bendall, Brooke and Collinson, 173.

Gamlingay Avenells, mentioned above, which was shared between the warden and those fellows who had completed two years regency and who had responded and opposed in theological disputations.[1] That an annual surplus might also be shared is shown by what happened when the financial situation had stabilised after the Civil War. In August 1650 we are told that any money left in the treasury by Peter Nicholls, the third bursar, was to be divided between the warden and fellows in the ratio of £30 for the warden and £20 for each fellow.[2] Similarly in August 1651 the total in the treasury (£430) was to be divided in the ratio £30 for the warden and £20 for each fellow, whether master or bachelor, but not among the probationers. Thus fourteen masters and six bachelors benefited.[3]

In the management of its estates Merton on several occasions leased its lands to members of the aristocracy and gentry from whose favour it doubtless hoped to benefit. A most striking case was in 1604 when it let half the value of the lease of its valuable Northumberland livings to Robert Cecil, baron.[4] The same lease had previously been held by Robert, earl of Essex, with whose family Warden Savile had been closely associated.[5] In fact Cecil soon resigned his lease in favour of one of the college's farmers in Northumberland, Richard Read, gentleman, and Read was to farm half of the livings for twenty-one years from 1609.[6] Another aristocrat whose links with the college went back to the time of the Essex rebellion was Sir Henry Neville of Billingbear, Berks., whose family had provided Henry Neville, fellow and diplomat.[7] Sir Henry Neville took over half the lease of Embleton and Ponteland from the earl of Essex in 1603,[8] and confirmed the other half of the revenue of these two parishes to Richard Read for twenty-one years in 1609.[9]

The warden and fellows themselves were not above benefiting from the leasing of college property. Thus Brent in 1622 was lessee of Grantchester Mill for twenty-one years, but soon released it to Richard Beaumont in 1624, when the college agreed to repair it, since it was said to be in a ruinous condition.[10] Brent also held the tithes of Burmington, Warws., in 1622 when he resigned them in favour of the Subwarden, Simonson.[11] This looks like a mark of gratitude to the

[1] Below, 121.
[2] Below, 322.
[3] Below, 327–8.
[4] Below, 14.
[5] Below, 4; *Reg Annalium, 1567–1603*, 350.
[6] Below, 53.
[7] Below, 4.
[8] Ibid.
[9] Below, 53, the fine being £100.
[10] Below, 132, 149.
[11] Below, 133.

subwarden who had recently presided over Brent's own successful election as warden. Later in the seventeenth and eighteenth centuries the tithes of Burmington were regularly granted to the senior fellow.

The ninth injunction issued after the visitation of 1638–9 required that much more precise records be kept of the date of granting leases and of their length. Hence the elaborate table compiled at the end of 1639 and in many subsequent years.[1] If an injunction in the statutes of 1274 had been obeyed the college estates would have been visited by the warden annually.[2] However by the sixteenth century, though progresses had remained regular, they were not necessarily annual and usually concerned a group of manors rather than the whole estate.[3]

CHANGES TO THE CONSTITUTION

In Savile's later years two changes were made to the constitution of the college. As has been seen the number of postmasterships was raised by the foundation in August 1604 of two additional Chamber's postmasterships.[4] They were to be paid for out of the £1,000 left to the college by John Chamber, which was to be invested in lands in Yorkshire. It seemed at one time that the foundation might be wealthy enough to do more, but by 1624 it consisted of two postmasterships held by Etonians and appointed by the provosts of Eton and King's College, Cambridge.[5]

Postmasters were no better protected against the inflation of the sixteenth century than were the fellows. Recognizing this, a former medical fellow, Dr Thomas Jessop, made a grant in 1610 of £17 5s. a year, later to rise to £20 a year, in order to increase the allocations to the twelve postmasters, of whom he himself had been one.[6]

The Bickley lectureship or exhibition had been founded in memory of Warden Bickley (d. 1596), who left £100 to be invested in land to pay for it. By 1604 land bought at Hensington , Oxfordshire, yielded £4 a year. The lectureship was appointed by the warden, and its holder was expected to give a public sermon.[7] One such holder was Griffin

[1] Below, 157.
[2] Garrod and Allen, *Merton Mun.*, 25.
[3] For general progresses see e.g. below, 84, 141, and for progresses to selected groups, below, 146, 361.
[4] Below, 19–20.
[5] Below, 116, 148.
[6] Below, 57–9. Cf. ibid. 83; *MCR* 126 (9 July 1614); F. Maddison, M. Pelling and C. Webster (eds.), *Studies on the life and work of Thomas Linacre 1400–1524*, 237.
[7] Merton Coll. Mun., Reg. 2.2, p. 269; cf. Martin and Highfield, 267. The lecturer also had to give one college sermon: below, 43.

Higgs, fellow, appointed in 1620.[1] Then under Brent a junior Bickley exhibitioner was added in 1627, funded from £100 administered in an original way: the money was entrusted to an Oxford alderman, William Wright, who guaranteed to pay £6 a year to the exhibitioner until the capital ran out. Alexander Fisher, elected in 1628, was expected to give at least one sermon in college and one public sermon.[2]

In 1635 Richard Knightley, of the well-known family from Fawsley, Northamptonshire, gave a rent of £10 a year from land at Badby, Northamptonshire to found a catechetical lectureship so that the junior members might be instructed. Its first holder in 1637 was Edward Corbet, fellow.[3]

THE VISITOR AND VISITATIONS

The role of visitor was notably apparent on the death of Warden Savile. Archbishop Abbot then chose from the three names submitted to him that of Nathaniel Brent. He was to become his vicar-general, a post which he maintained under Archbishop Laud. This did not prevent him from undergoing a visitation in 1638, when grievances against his rule were investigated. The visitation lasted until 1639 and was to be compared in College to the siege of Troy. Its 30 (later 37) injunctions were written into the College Register.[4] After Laud's imprisonment in 1641 his powers were exercised by a parliamentary commission. Under the Commonwealth and Protectorate there were to be three parliamentary Visitations, in 1647–52, June–1 September 1654, and after 2 September 1654. Whether they made much difference to the composition of the College is examined below (pp. xx, xxii)

THE INCOMING OF WARDEN BRENT

The election of Nathaniel Brent brought to the wardenship the expertise of a skilled lawyer and a travelled diplomat. He was unusual in having started life on a Merton estate, Wolford in Warwickshire.[5] It is interesting to consider whether the fact that when Savile died the college was engaged on its single most important piece of litigation – the challenging of the Malden lease[6] – may have affected the decision.

[1] Below, 114.
[2] Below, 172–3.
[3] Below, 225, 234.
[4] Below, 249–52, 256; cf. ibid. 273.
[5] *ODNB*.
[6] See above, p. xii, n. 7.

In any case Brent had been proctor in 1607 and subwarden for six years before he went abroad in 1613–14. His role in smuggling out of Italy Sarpi's *History of the Council of Trent* and the subsequent translation of its Italian text gave him some claim to be considered a scholar.[1] In 1616 he was temporarily in charge of the British diplomatic mission at Spa. When Savile died Brent's was one of the names which the electors sent up to Archbishop Abbot as visitor. The others were those of John King and Thomas Horne. King was a doctor of theology who had disputed before James I in 1603. Horne was another theologian and a canon of Windsor. But Abbot was not tempted by the theologians and chose Brent. Two of the fellows challenged the procedure on the grounds that the election had been hurried and the return of absentees had not been awaited. The archbishop had the objections investigated before setting them aside and choosing Brent as the new warden.[2] Abbot and Brent were to prove as close friends as Abbot and Savile had been.

When he arrived in Oxford he was welcomed by Subwarden Simonson, Dr John Lapworth, John Parker, principal of St Alban Hall, and the new Savilian professor, Bainbridge, among others.[3] He was to be knighted by Charles I in 1629.[4] He was naturally involved in looking after the college's interests in the law courts. When in the autumn of 1641 difficulties arose in cases concerning two lessees, Shires and Holt, these were referred to Brent and Mr Fisher while the question of holding a court baron at Gamlingay was left to the 'prudence' of the warden.[5] In February 1626 his alliance with the visitor had been strengthened by his marriage to the archbishop's niece Martha, daughter of Robert Abbot, bishop of Salisbury.[6]

RELATIONS BETWEEN WARDEN AND FELLOWS

After the excitements of 1598 Savile's relations with the fellows seem to have remained steady until he died, even if after 1607 he was more and more at Eton. His subwarden was Brent (to 1612) and thereafter William Simonson. Gulson, a medical fellow, was fined for striking Blickard, a master fellow, in December 1604.[7] As a result he lost his commons for six weeks and was denied leave of absence for the same period. Blickard seems to have attracted trouble, for in 1607 Philipson

[1] *ODNB*. [2] Below, 126–7. [3] Ibid.
[4] *ODNB*. [5] Below, 272.
[6] Guildhall Library MS. 4449/1, par. reg. of St Stephen's Colman Street. I owe this reference to the kindness of Mr Andrew Hegarty.
[7] Below, 26–7; cf. Maddison, Pelling and Webster, *Linacre Studies*, 241.

publicly called him 'hog and pig' when he himself was applying for permission to advance to the status of master. Savile put the offender out of commons for a month and delayed his magistracy.[1] Then in 1619 Henry Ainscombe, a master, was reprimanded for overfamiliarity with his bachelor fellows and for drinking in the town taverns.[2] In 1638 it was to be complained of Brent that he had been too lenient with offending fellows. He was certainly long-suffering with Humphrey Farrar, one of the two fellows who had challenged the method of the warden's election. Farrar was accused of corrupting the bachelor fellows and spending time frequently in taverns, wineshops and alehouses, into one of which, the King's Head, he retired for five or six days. When he failed to answer a summons in March 1629 he was expelled the following August.[3]

On 9 February 1631 John Holywell, one of the fellows, killed a colleague, George Petty. Holywell was evidently of unsound mind at the time, and though naturally he was deprived of his fellowship he was made an allowance of £20 for two years from the Read and Bodley chests. He had no family or resources of his own.[4]

The overfamiliarity between the master and bachelor fellows and postmasters was an issue which returned to dog Brent, as it had in the cases of Ainscombe and Farrar. It provided the trigger which initiated the Visitation of 1638. The suspect fellow in this case was Mr Nevill senior who was denounced in 1636 with contumelious words by Mr Newman.[5] The warden took this matter in particular to the college meeting of 20 July 1637, and though Mr Nevill's name was to be cleared the topic became the subject of Laud's injunction no. 6.[6]

Brent was notably loyal to his long-serving subwarden, Fisher. For at the Visitation of 1638 Laud secured his dismissal; and, by insisting on future annual subwardenships, indirectly criticized Fisher's overlong exercise of the office.[7] When a dispute ensued in the spring of 1640 between Laud's supporters, John Greaves and Peter Turner, the warden appealed boldly over the head of the visitor to the authority of a committee of the Short Parliament. In the autumn of 1641 Brent associated Fisher with him in settling difficult lawsuits, and in 1646 he re-established him in the face of firm opposition from Turner and Greaves.[8]

[1] Below, 40.
[2] Below, 109–10.
[3] Below, 180–1.
[4] Below, 194–5.
[5] Below, 229.
[6] Below, 235, 250.
[7] Below, 249.
[8] Below, 271, 283, 296, 306, 315.

When Brent was deposed by the king in 1645 and the fellows appointed William Harvey to replace him, Harvey made a disclaimer on entering office.[1] In view of it there seemed to be good prospects of a harmonious relationship developing between the new warden and the fellows. However, on account of the circumstances of the siege of Oxford and the few months in which Harvey had to enjoy his wardenship before the siege was lifted and he judged it wise to leave for London, there was little chance for this new relationship to manifest itself.

FELLOWSHIPS

One of the perquisites of a fellowship was the grant of allowances for up to three years to travel abroad. They were known as 'travellours places'. These allowances which had been so valuable to Bodley and Savile in the sixteenth century continued to be granted in the seventeenth, if at a higher rate of £15, £20, or £30. They were usually taken up to travel in Italy or France, but as will be seen might also take their holder to Ireland, where they could serve as a minor method of subsidising the English government. Isaac Wake was given £15 for three years in February 1612 and went to Italy.[2] Richard Browne followed with £15 in August 1629 and William Berkeley with £15 in February 1630.[3] Wake and Browne were to become diplomats, and Berkeley Governor of Virginia. A link of the fellowship with Ireland had been established when Thomas Gall, fellow in 1615 and an orator, had gone there for his career in 1633 and 1634.[4] The link was notably continued by Hugh Cressy, fellow in 1635, chaplain in succession to Strafford and Falkland.[5] In 1650 it took the form in reverse of appointments by the visitors of Irishmen to Merton fellowships. Thus Clinton Maund, from county Fermanagh, and Charles Willoughby from county Cork and a graduate of Trinity College, Dublin, became fellows.[6] Not surprisingly they both returned to Ireland, where Maund was in 1658.[7] Willoughby took the chance to go via a traveller's place to Padua to take a medical degree before

[1] Cf. Martin and Highfield, 206 and n. 56.

[2] Below, 65, 159.

[3] Below, 184, 187.

[4] Below, 209.

[5] Below, 220, 224.

[6] Below, 320; cf. Maddison, Pelling and Webster, *Linacre Studies*, 252.

[7] Below, 377. For expulsions under the first parliamentary visitation of 1647–52 and replacements in 1648–9, see Martin and Highfield, 211 and n. 90.

becoming a prominent doctor in Dublin.[1] His 'Hortus Siccus' which he gave to Merton Library is the earliest surviving collection of pressed plants from Italy. He became a founding member of the Philosophical Society of Dublin in the reign of Charles II.[2] Robert Whitehall, fellow in 1651 from Christ Church, evidently impressed Henry Cromwell when he appeared in Ireland, for Cromwell seized on the possibility of the traveller's place in order to make good the shortage of good bureaucrats in the Irish capital.[3] As chancellor of Dublin he wrote to the warden and fellows asking that Whitehall should be given a traveller's place. Thus Merton might underwrite the English bureaucracy in Dublin to the tune of £20 a year.

The most outstanding Merton fellow to make an Irish contribution was Robert Huntington, elected fellow in 1658. His tenure as chaplain to the factory at Aleppo for eleven years helped to confirm his oriental interests and enabled him to put together a remarkable collection of oriental manuscripts.[4] When he returned in 1683 he was appointed provost of Trinity College, Dublin, to succeed Narcissus Marsh.[5] In 1692 he became bishop of Lismore and returned to England as a possible candidate for the wardenship of Merton on the death of Sir Thomas Clayton. But when Clayton died that prize went to Richard Lydall, who had been disappointed of it when Clayton had been appointed. Huntington moved from the see of Lismore to that of Raphoe in 1701 and died soon after. He left to Merton a small group of Oriental manuscripts; his great collection was acquired by the Bodleian.[6]

Apart from the possibility of promotion to a college living another valuable asset was the year of grace granted to a fellow on resignation. This varied in value between £15 and £20, though it could be as high as £30 as in the case of Gouldsmith, even if in his case the college stated that it had been generous because of his poor health and need to take an impecunious living as a result.[7] The rates of travel allowance and of the year of grace suggest that a master's fellowship *c.* 1625 was worth £30, though the total would vary according to the number and value of dividends in a given year.[8]

[1] Brodrick, *Memorials*, 291.

[2] Martin and Highfield, 211 n. 90, 220.

[3] Below, 374.

[4] Below, 379. The Levant Company regularly employed chaplains at its Aleppo factory: J. B. Pearson, *A Biographical Sketch of the Chaplains of the Levant Company, 1611–1706* (Cambridge, 1883).

[5] Martin and Highfield, 219–20.

[6] Ibid.

[7] Below, 132–3.

[8] Cf. above, p. xiv, n. 11.

Did the system of visitatorial appointment of fellows between 1642 and 1660 change the nature of the members of the Governing Body? In some sense there was little change: thus in the visitors' choice of medical fellows, like John Arnold, Charles Willoughby and Richard Trevor, the visitors simply continued the tradition of those who had been trained at Padua or Leiden. There were few expulsions under the Visitation of 1647–52. But a distinct novelty was the appointment of undergraduates or graduates of Cambridge. Apart from Warden Harvey himself there seem to have been no previous Cantabrigians; but after 1648 we find Richard Trevor and Joseph Hervey admitted to fellowships (via postmasterships) from Jesus, Cambridge, Nathaniel Sterry from Emmanuel and John Powell from Caius.[1] Edward Roode via an Eton postmastership became a fellow in 1652.[2] Roode was a theologian. The standard of Sterry seems to have been high to judge by his speech at the incoming of Warden Goddard in November 1651. He went on to become a learned theologian and through the patronage of Archbishop Sheldon dean of Bocking in 1674. There was a notable influx under the visitors of men from the Oxford halls as Richard Pavier, Thomas Franke and, via a postmastership, Childe from New Inn Hall and Henry Hurst from Magdalen Hall.[3] A good choice as chaplain was Benjamin Cooper who went on to become an effective registrar of the university.[4] Altogether the chief change was the need for prospective candidates to lobby the visitors, sometimes in London, and the fact that the warden and college lost control of the appointments and of their number.

COLLEGE LECTURERS

There were specific college lecturers in a variety of subjects as Greek, grammar, logic and rhetoric. They were appointed annually. Under Savile the warden seems to have nominated the lecturers in Greek and logic, and the principal of the postmasters. The lectureship in Greek had been initiated by Sir Thomas Bodley who had also been its first holder. The seriousness with which the appointment was regarded by Savile is suggested by the nomination of Isaac Wake for the two years 1605–6 and of John Hales for 1607–8. To have been taught Greek by Hales, the future Regius professor of Greek, or grammar by Thomas Allen (lecturer 1611–12) must have been a privilege. The Greek

[1] Below, 314, 317, 320; Brodrick, *Memorials*, 290.
[2] Below, 346.
[3] Brodrick, *Memorials*, 291, 360.
[4] Ibid. 354.

lecturers were often appointed for four years in succession, as Hugh Ramsden was from 1614–17 or Gouldsmith from 1618–21. This should have made for a valuable continuity.

There should also have been lecturers on classical medicine since two lecturerships, senior and junior, had been founded in 1551 in the name of Thomas Linacre by his executor, Cuthbert Tunstal. They were tied to lecturing on the works of Galen and Hippocrates. By the seventeenth century these authors were becoming outdated. The lecturers were sometimes distinguished physicians like Theodore Gulston (junior Linacre lecturer 1604–11). But whether they actually gave their lectures is hard to determine.[1]

UNDERGRADUATES

The twelve postmasters were the most important of the comparatively small number of undergraduates. As has been seen, to their number were added two new Chamber's postmasterships in 1604. Savile was careful to maintain the standard of the postmasters and in 1609 decreed that any who failed to keep up with their exercises should be expelled.[2] This chimes in with Wood's assertion that he was a 'severe governor and hated by the scholars for his severity'.[3] Under Brent they were instructed in 1625 to attend the regent masters' readings on Aristotle's *Rhetoric* in the Hall. The injunctions of the visitor in 1638 show that they could attend Greek and Grammar lectures given on Tuesdays and Thursdays at 10 a.m. and at 3 in the afternoon. An excellent example of the standard which a postmaster might reach is provided. by Thomas Farnaby, postmaster to John French, a learned fellow and future registrar of the university. Farnaby became an outstanding schoolmaster at Martock in Somerset and later in London. He produced editions of the works of Juvenal, Persius, Lucan, Martial, Virgil, Ovid and Seneca.[4] Though individual postmasters were nominated by individual master fellows, in 1638 we learn that, when Mr Newman was suspended, his postmaster, Mathias Caldecott, was chosen by the warden, the principal of the postmasters and three senior fellows. As has been seen the postmasters' allowances in an age of inflation were the subject of concern to Thomas Jessop, a

[1] Martin and Highfield, 175 n. 120.
[2] Below, 53.
[3] J. Aubrey, *Letters from the Bodleian* (Oxford, 1813), ii. 525 in Wood, *Athenae*, ii. 315.
[4] *HUO*, iv. 262.

doctor of medicine and a former postmaster. He left money to produce an annual income of £17 5s., which eventually was to rise to £20 a year. Here was a practical contribution to allow the bursar to sustain the quality of their food. In August 1625 they each had an allocation of 2s. 4d. a week and in 1627 it was decreed that they should enter the Hall at the same time as the fellows.[1] This was the logical conclusion to bringing them out of Postmasters' Hall. Taken in conjunction with the provision of a new table for the M.A.s this suggests the beginnings of formal hall for the whole college. However, in 1656 it was ordered that commoners of whatever variety should not dine at the masters' table where matters of public college business might be discussed.[2]

Individual commoners to be given special rights first occur in 1595 when Sir Francis Wolley, son of John Wolley, privy councillor, was admitted and granted rooms in the warden's house and the right to dine with the B.A. fellows.[3] Similar privileges were given in 1606 to the nephew of Sir John Fortescue.[4] These instances seem to have stimulated Savile and the college to try out as an experiment in August 1607 the admission of twelve sons of knights and gentlemen 'of great name' as gentlemen commoners. They were to give a piece of silver of at least 10 ounces on admission, pay caution money of 50s. and come under the discipline of the principal of the postmasters.[5] This compares with similar experiments at Lincoln in the previous year, at Balliol (1610) and New College (1677).[6] But by 1616 at Merton the experiment was judged to have failed on the grounds that the newcomers had had a bad effect on the discipline of the other undergraduates, and especially when later they sought degrees.[7] However the admission of well-born individual commoners continued occasionally, as when in April 1639 James Leviston, baronet, was admitted and allowed to join the fellows' table.[8] Interestingly the idea was revived under the Commonwealth when in August 1650 it was agreed that six commoners, sons of knights, the armigerous or noblemen, could be admitted according to seven conditions. Two years later it was decided that the number six need not be strictly adhered to and that those admitted must pay 3d. a week to the principal of the postmasters.[9]

[1] Below, 57–9, 169.
[2] Below, 368.
[3] *Reg. Annalium, 1567–1603*, 317. For a small number of commoners earlier cf. ibid. *1483–1521*, p. xv.
[4] Below, 36.
[5] Below, 44.
[6] *HUO*, iv. 36.
[7] Below, 92.
[8] Below, 255.
[9] Below, 322, 342–3.

Though Savile seems to have been happy with the small number of commoners, he was evidently less so with those who as battelers sought to save money by having their meals direct from the kitchen and not going into Hall, as the example of the Davenport brothers demonstrates.[1]

Servitors, it is clear, were as valuable to the senior fellows, as to their fellow undergraduates. During the plague of 1603 it was ordered that the four *scholares servitores* were to remain in college to wait upon the four senior officers who were also staying in college.[2] Again in March 1631 it was specifically ordered that the four senior officers, the subwarden, dean, senior bursar and principal of the postmasters were entitled to *scholares servientes*; their number was specifically restricted to twelve.[3] In the 18th century they were appointed by the warden.[4]

COLLEGE STAFF

The college staff who were 'on the books' consisted of a butler, an under-butler, a manciple, a senior and junior cook, a porter, a carpenter, a launderer and a groom.[5] The butler's wages were 40s., and the porter's 30s. a year. A new carpenter, called Gollidg, was paid 13s. 4d. a year. A specially important servant during the plague of 1625 was Blackham, one of whose duties was to look after the library and the chapel for 12d. a week. He also became launderer so that the college could avoid anyone with direct contact with the town.[6]

The fact that the college recognized some obligation to its staff is reflected in the fact that we know that several of them were housed in Holywell, and that after their death their widows often continued as college tenants there. This was true of the widow of the senior cook, William Punyard.[7] Retired servants might also live in Holywell, like Thomas Chittenden who had for long been butler and Avice Smith, who, though illiterate, had looked carefully after the warden's belongings during the siege of Oxford.[8]

[1] Martin and Highfield, 195–6.
[2] Below, 7.
[3] Below, 188, 195.
[4] Martin and Highfield, 239, n. 18.
[5] Below, 15, 34, 35, 39, 60, 110, 347.
[6] Below, 8; cf. 157.
[7] Below, 100.
[8] Below, 366. She inscribed her mark at the end of the inventory of Warden Harvey's goods in 1645: ibid. 288.

THE LIBRARY

Following the ordinances which Savile had drawn up for the library in 1586 and the substantial additions of new books bought at Frankfurt or in Italy and by the purchase of the library of John Betts of Trinity Hall, Cambridge,[1] the institution evolved steadily in the seventeenth century. The contributions of newly elected fellows which had started in 1572 continued to provide quite important sums for buying books. Thus in 1613 £18 17s. 4d. was made available and a similar sum in 1616. In 1624 as much as £26 6s. 8d. was raised.[2] The fact that it fell to the subwarden and senior dean in 1620 to make the selection of books from the warden's library for the college library emphasizes that, though there had been two library clerks in 1587, as yet there was no librarian.[3] But librarians were appearing at other colleges, as at St John's in 1603. It may not be a coincidence that when the Merton librarianship was eventually founded on a permanent footing it was funded by a fellow who had been an undergraduate at St John's.[4]

The new Savilian professors were naturally given access to the library in January 1621.[5] The same facility was granted to distinguished outsiders like Matthew Hale and Dr Budden, Professor of Civil Law.[6] Loans of manuscripts and books were sometimes made to outside scholars such as Bodley's Librarian, Thomas James, who was promoting a large project for making available reliable editions by protestant scholars of the works of the patristic fathers. This, it may be assumed, was naturally attractive to the editor of Chrysostom. The library lent five manuscripts of Ambrose to James, but the project was never completed and the manuscripts never returned.[7] Similar permission to borrow individual manuscripts was given to James Usher, archbishop of Armagh. He borrowed a manuscript of Bede and another of William Butler.[8]

In 1623 the south wing of the library was given new seats in the style

[1] *Reg. Annalium, 1567–1603*, p. xx.

[2] Below, 76, 91, 151.

[3] *Reg. Annalium, 1567–1603*, p. 229.

[4] Martin and Highfield, 212; cf. W. C. Costin, *Hist. of St John's College, Oxford*, O.H.S. n.s. xii (1958), 25; *HUO*, iv. 678.

[5] Below, 115.

[6] Below, 46, 53.

[7] Below, 68; Powicke, *Medieval Books*, nos.181, 953, 974, 1188–9, now all Bodleian MSS.

[8] Below, 162. The latter work is Merton Coll. MS. K.2.2 (Cox, 68). Cf. his '*Determinatio*' against the English translation of the Bible: Powicke, *Medieval Books*, p. 207 and M. Deanesly, *The Lollard Bible*, 399–418.

of those already installed in the west, and an empty room at the east end was incorporated.[1] This room had doubtless fallen vacant when Fellows' Quad was built in 1610. The date of its inclusion explains why it is the arms of Archbishop Abbot and Warden Brent which are displayed in the plasterwork. Evidently the opportunity was taken at the same time to place the arms of Archbishop Whitgift and Warden Savile at the north end of the west wing. It seems that the dormer windows which give additional light from the north and east were made at the same time. The library came into its own during the siege of Oxford. Since by then neither the Hall nor the warden's house was available, meetings of the Governing Body such as those presided over by Warden Harvey on 5 August and 27 November 1645, and 6 January 1646, took place in the library, presumably in the vestibule.[2]

In 1653 Griffin Higgs, a former fellow and dean of Lichfield, assigned a debt of his for £1,000 to the college to be invested so that it would produce a revenue of £10 a year, out of which a library keeper was to be paid an annual stipend of the same amount.[3] This benefit did not reach Merton until after Higgs's death in 1659 and the first Higgs' librarian, Robert Huntington, fellow and orientalist, was not appointed until 1667.[4] In the meanwhile on 22 December 1658 an interim librarian, John Wilton, was appointed for life. He had taken his B.A. from Merton in October 1614 and was thus likely to have been born before 1600.[5] Anthony Wood, a friend of his, tells us that he was 'antient chaplain before he went to be vicar of Wolford'. This he had become on 28 June 1616, so his chaplaincy will first presumably have occurred between 1614 and 1616. Wood records that two of his own books were presents from Wilton, a copy of Thomas Becon, *Reliques of Rome* (1563) and another of Lionel Daye, *Concio ad Clerum, Oxon. 1609* (Oxford, 1632). Wood also records that he bought from Wilton his copy of Cay, *Antiquities of Cambridge* (4to, 1574) for 4s. and divers other books of his for £1 4s. Wood borrowed Wilton's copy of Foxe's *Book of Martyrs* (1583) and we know that he also possessed a copy of John of Salisbury, *Policraticus* or *De Nugis Curialium*.[6] In 1627 he became rector of Cornwell, Oxfordshire and took his B.D. in April of the same year. By the time he was appointed librarian he must have been quite senior.

[1] Below, 143.

[2] Below, 293–4, 296. The vestry remained a possible meeting-place.

[3] P. S. Morrish, 'Dr Higgs and Merton College Library', *Leeds Phil. and Lit. Soc.*, Feb. 1988, 63.

[4] Ibid. 43.

[5] Foster, *Alumni Oxonienses, 1500–1714*, 1658.

[6] Wood, *Life and Times*, i. 446; ii. 16, 24, 30, 38–9; iv. 291.

The Restoration brought him a minor canonry of St. Paul's (1660).[1] He was granted a room in college at the north end of the west wing of the library, free victuals and 3s. a week as stipend, not as generous as Huntington was to receive.[2] But it looks as though he resided and resumed his chaplaincy which he held until he died in 1665. He was present at a game of cards when Anthony Wood quarrelled with another player, Roger Brent, who was expelled from college in 1667 as incorrigible.[3]

OTHER COLLEGE BUILDINGS

Just as Brent extended the south wing of the library in 1623, three years later he set about extending the warden's lodgings. It seems that he wished to enhance their standing for receiving important visitors. In 1625 ten chairs and benches of Phrygian work and green and blue cloths were bought for the Lodgings. In July 1626 the warden and fellows agreed to the '*amplificando hospitio suo*' to allow '*num commodi in loco designato aedificium extrui possit*'.[4] Whether any new building was actually contemplated is uncertain, but Brent soon concentrated on the gallery in Fellows' Quad. We know that the gallery existed already from a reference to 'a little chamber by ye gallerie' in the inventory at the incoming of Brent in 1622. It was a bedroom with a bedstead, two pieces of hanging and a warming-pan.[5]

By June 1645 the gallery was regarded as part of the warden's house since at the incoming of Warden Harvey it contained '2 great Turky workd chairs, twelve Turky worked chaires, twelve stooles of ye same, one long drawing table, two side boards and table and one court cupboard'. Did the gallery end in the great bay window looking out over the meadow? It seems likely that it did, while the 'little chamber at ye south end of the gallery was hanged with coarse arras'.[6] Where was this precisely? It sounds like the little chamber present in 1622, perhaps Fellows 3, 7B. What happened in 1627? Changes were made to the central rooms of the Lodgings. The curtains of the '*magna camera*', presumably the present Breakfast Room, were to be repaired and transferred to the '*magnam cameram prope porticum*', perhaps what was until recently the Estates Bursary looking across Fellows' Quad. The '*magna camera*' was to be adorned with wainscotting and ceiled in the

1 Foster, *Alumni Oxonienses, 1500–1714*, 1658.
2 Below, 380.
3 Brodrick, *Memorials*, 286.
4 Below, 163.
5 Below, 138.
6 Below, 290.

upper part of the room, while the old wainscotting was to be transferred to 'Sever's chamber'.[1] That was a room in the older part of the existing house. It faced westwards into Front Quad from the first floor of what is now Front Quad staircase 5. The existing curtains of Sever's chamber were to be fitted up in a new room on the staircase. This staircase must be the new one which Brent had installed and which bears his arms on its panelling. It led from the ground floor up to the entrance to the gallery.

In 1629 came the big moment for the gallery. The college was visited in person by the king and queen on their way back from Woodstock to Abingdon.[2] It was never to see such excitement again. Warden Holland kept books there in the eighteenth century[3] and in the nineteenth it was split up and turned into extra accommodation. Brent's interest in building seems to have been reflected in a variety of other ways. In the chapel it was decided to introduce black and white marble into the floor of the chancel and new seating was installed so that masters might sit more comfortably.[4] Later in 1657, under Goddard, the five bells were recast into eight. They included the great fifth bell given by Warden Abingdon. But the recasting was a failure and needed to be redone in 1680.[5] At the request of Richard Zouche, principal of St Alban Hall and Regius professor of civil law, commoners and lesser scholars of the Hall were given the right of access to the chapel.[6] Brent can be held responsible for the construction of two sets of fellows' rooms in a new staircase to the west of the porter's lodge and east of the graveyard – now Front Quad staircase 1.[7] Though nothing major was done to the Hall, a new table was bought for the masters[8] and a clock set up which must have been a sophisticated affair; at least 30s. was paid to an expert, named Triumph, to look after it for nine months. Later keeping it in order was the task of the new porter.[9] However the Hall had suffered greatly in the siege in the Civil War. By 1645–6 it was '*situ et ruinis squalida*' and unusable for meetings.

[1] Below, 173.
[2] Wood, *Hist. Univ.* ii(1), 367.
[3] Martin and Highfield, 265.
[4] Below, 215, 224, 162.
[5] Below, 370–1; cf. B. Henderson, *Merton College*, 213–14.
[6] Below, 166.
[7] Below, 195.
[8] Below, 162.
[9] Below, 180, 193.

RELIGION

The fact that neither Savile nor Brent was a theologian kept them out of the forefront of the religious disputes of the period. Yet because the visitor of the college was the archbishop of Canterbury religious issues continually impinged on the college, as when Archbishop Abbot tried to prevent the expression in Oxford of the views of John Howson, tried before James I on 10 June 1615.[1] The protestant sympathies of the college were roused by the outbreak of the Thirty Years' War in 1618, but even before that we find grants being made to the city of Geneva because of the poverty in which it found itself as a result of its war with the duke of Savoy.[2] Five refugees from the Palatinate in 1623 were received at the request of the king of Bohemia. Later, in 1629, help was provided for some impoverished doctors coming from Silesia.[3]

Almsgiving was also prompted by regard for those reduced to poverty. Thus in 1632, after a fire in St Ebbe's, 5s. was granted to two men affected by it. Similarly, when a member of staff fell on hard times, college is found granting 5s. to Davis, a former cook, reduced to poverty. The same went for the children of staff such as the daughter of a former porter who was granted 5 marks to relieve poverty in 1632.[4]

Interest was also shown in individual catholics converting to Anglicanism, such as an Italian given 40s. in September 1631.[5] That there was a strong Mertonian tradition of Elizabethan Calvinism in the reigns of her two successors is shown by the careers of Griffin Higgs (fellow 1610–32), who became chaplain to the Winter Queen of Bohemia, Edward Reynolds, Francis Cheynell and Henry Wilkinson, later a member of the Westminster Assembly.[6] In 1629 it is recorded that there was psalm-singing in the Hall. Laud at his trial, when accused of promoting none but his coterie, instanced Griffin Higgs as an example to the contrary, to whom he had granted the living of Cliffe-at-Hoo in Kent[7] and whom he had subsequently supported for the chaplaincy of the Queen of Bohemia and the deanery of Lichfield.

[1] Cf. 'John Howson's answers to Archbishop Abbot's accusations at his trial at Greenwich, 1 June 1615', ed. N. Cranfield and K. Fincham, *Camden Miscellany xxix* (Camd. Soc. 4th ser. xxxiv, 1987).

[2] Below, 17.

[3] Below, 146, 184.

[4] Below, 206.

[5] Below, 199.

[6] *ODNB*.

[7] P. S. Morrish, 'Dr Higgs and Merton College Library', *Leeds Phil. and Lit. Soc.*, Feb. 1988, 142–3.

Cheynell, Reynolds and Wilkinson were all to become commissioners for the university under the Commonwealth.[1] Nevertheless Laud had some supporters in Merton and this is reflected in a skit in which the different colleges were identified with ships in 1636. Here Merton was identified as the Rainbow,[2] because it contained fellows as different as the Laudian, Peter Turner, and Francis Cheynell, a critic of Laud and a moderate presbyterian.

The fact that Brent became vicar-general both to Abbot and, after a period of trial, to Laud put him in a strong ecclesiastical position in the whole of the province of Canterbury. But his relations with Laud remained ambivalent. In 1637 he instructed the fellows to bow to the east when entering or leaving the chapel and he had the High Altar railed off, no doubt in accordance with Laud's wishes.[3] Brent's responsibilities as vicar-general frequently took him away from Oxford as he continued the visitation of the province of Canterbury (1634–6). This was to cost him dear when the visitation of Merton threw into relief his carelessness and negligence of college business. Laud was truer to him than he was to Laud. Wood called him a weathercock and contrasted the warden's instruction of 1637 to bow to the altar with his dismantling of the rich hangings near the High Altar and his criticism of Laud at the archbishop's trial.[4] The warden was not dismissed after the visitation of 1638 and when, in Wood's words, he saw 'the Presbyterians begin to be dominant, he sided with them and because of a pique that had been between the Abbots and Archbishop Laud, he therefore became a frequent witness against the last at his tryal'.[5] Moreover in 1642 he seems to have had no hesitation in leaving Oxford, as did Savile's kinsman, Henry Wilkinson, principal of Magdalen Hall. He took refuge with the parliamentarians in London. Wood therefore had some justification in likening him to M. Varro for his skill in manoeuvring between the opposing parties as Varro had done between Pompey and Caesar.[6]

[1] *ODNB*.

[2] *HUO*, iv. 209. When in 1639 there was a dispute over nominating a subwarden Laud appointed Turner to solve the difficulty: below, 255–6.

[3] Below, 238.

[4] Wood, *Hist. Univ.* ii(2), 615.

[5] Wood, *Athenae*, iii. 334.

[6] Ibid.

ROYAL VISITS

The fact that James I knighted both Bodley and Savile in the opening years of his reign no doubt accounts for the fact that a portrait of the first Stuart for long hung in the warden's lodgings. Nevertheless when James visited Oxford in 1605, though the college sent to the vice-chancellor £6 as a share in the university's expenses,[1] the king did not visit the college. Things were otherwise in 1629. The college took the opportunity of the royal visit to Woodstock to send the warden and subwarden to present a letter of thanks to the king for his confirmation of the college's holding of land in mortmain. Charles received the letter '*sereno vultu*'. Since a similar royal letter was sent to Laud as bishop of London and chancellor of Oxford, it looks as if the confirmation had been secured with the help of the visitor. On the following day (24 August) Merton entertained the ambassadors from France and the Low Countries with a group of councillors and courtiers to an entertainment in the gallery, described by Wood as 'a very sumptuous banquet'. They were addressed by Edward Nevill, fellow. Three days later we are specifically told that 'having received a speech of welcome at the main gate from James Marsh, fellow, the king and queen rested for an hour or so in the warden's gallery, where they were refreshed with fruit and sweetmeats'. Wood exaggerates a little and calls the entertainment 'a rich banquet at the college charges, in honour of their newly knighted warden'.[2]

Relations with Henrietta Maria were involved in 1631 when one Unton used her name in applying for a fellowship for his son at the next vacancy. His letter to the warden was said to be backed by the queen and sealed up. But when the impatient father asked for the letter to be opened without delay, the warden did so and sought to have the application ignored and Unton's calumnies against the college rebutted without offending the queen. This was achieved through the good offices of Edward Sackville, Lord Buckhurst, 4th earl of Dorset.[3]

In 1636 when Laud presided over a much more magnificent royal visit than that of 1629, when the king and queen dined in St John's, at the degree ceremony the warden of Merton presented Prince Rupert and the Elector Palatine for their degrees.[4]

The college was more nearly affected in 1643–6 when, with Charles

[1] Below, 31.
[2] Below, 185; Wood, *Hist. Univ.* ii(1), 367.
[3] Below, 198, 200–1.
[4] Wood, *Hist. Univ.* ii(1), 407–13.

I living at Christ Church, Merton became the headquarters of the queen. She occupied what had been Brent's dining-room and the room over the vault which still bears her name. At one time the two rooms together must have been the 'Queen's rooms'. An entry in the inventory of the incoming warden in 1645 makes it clear that she slept in the warden's dining-room, no doubt in a four-poster bed.[1] She stayed in Merton from 14 July 1643 to 17 April 1644 when she left for France.[2] The college in the meanwhile cooperated in the education of the young duke of York by lending in August 1645 the terrestrial and celestial globes out of the library to Charles Maye, his tutor in Christ Church.[3]

PLAGUE

The college was twice visited by plague under Savile and Brent before the Civil War. In September 1603 in view of danger from plague it was decided to permit a temporary diaspora so that a majority of the college could disperse and go home or remove to the college manor of Cuxham, on the Oxford–Watlington road. Cuxham was to serve as a 'musaeum' where academic exercises could be pursued. William Napper, farmer of Holywell manor, was instructed to send domestic supplies to the college; Blackham was to manage the laundry and to leave his house in town for one in the nearby countryside. Meanwhile a skeleton staff should stay in Oxford consisting of the subwarden, a dean, the present bursar and senior fellow. Four servitors to wait on the masters and one of the warden's servants should join them.[4] When after a respite the plague returned in April 1604 a rudimentary system of quarantine was established. It was decided to close the main gate of the college and to open a smaller gate further east down Merton Street. Double beer was to be drunk and the bursar was to lay in a supply of spices to last for several weeks. When the crisis had passed Blackham was granted 26s. 8d. for having so well looked after the fellows who stayed.[5]

In May 1625 plague was again raging in the capital and arrangements were made for moving the government to Oxford. The plague seems to have arrived in August when a procedure similar to that in 1603 was pursued. A skeleton staff consisting of the subwarden, one

[1] Below, 290.
[2] *ODNB*.
[3] Below, 294.
[4] Below, 6–8.
[5] Below, 8, 22.

dean, one bursar, the principal of the postmasters and six servants remained in college. No one left was to go out without permission of two senior officers. The rest of the college was to retire to Cuxham or elsewhere. B.A. fellows were granted an allowance of 5s. per week and postmasters 2s. 4d. Blackham was to stay and take charge of the laundry which was to be washed nearby. The senior cook also was to stay and obtain a supply of spice. Michaelmas term was delayed until 4 December.[1]

RELATIONS WITH THE UNIVERSITY

Merton continued to cooperate with the university on the occasions when the latter had to raise money for additional facilities. Thus it contributed to the funds needed to sustain a university marshal (to control beggars), and it joined with other colleges and the city in arranging for a regular scavenger.[2] The *pro rata* basis on which it did so had been established before 1603. But much more substantial was the aid which it gave when the old Schools were demolished in 1612.[3] They had long been in need of repair, having been described by Sir Thomas Bodley as 'those ruinous little rooms'. Their demolition and rebuilding became part of the larger plan for the rebuilding of Duke Humfrey's library and the establishment of the Bodleian. Since the college had already shown its strong support for its former fellow's aspiration, it naturally joined in the national appeal made by Sir John Bennett at Bodley's request. It contributed £20 in 1612 and another £20 in 1619 towards an appeal which was to raise over £5,000.[4] As has been observed, the construction of Schools Quadrangle was 'a physical and intellectual extension of the library', and was personally supervised by Warden Savile after Bodley's death.[5] The close link was to be further emphasized when the college lent manuscripts to Thomas James, Bodley's first librarian, to aid protestant patristic research.

Like other colleges Merton provided proctors either under the old arrangements (Christopher Dale in 1603 and Francis Grevil in 1617), or under the new cycle introduced by the king and chancellor at Laud's instigation in 1628 (Doughty and Earle in 1631 and Edward Corbet in 1638). When Laud as chancellor of Oxford and bishop of London asked for funds for rebuilding St Paul's, Merton made a grant of £20

[1] Below, 158–9.
[2] Below, 2; cf. *Reg. Annalium, 1567–1603*, 118.
[3] Below, 79–80; cf. 74–5.
[4] Below, 79–80; cf. 110–11.
[5] Martin and Highfield, 163.

for ten years in March 1632; this might be increased or diminished according to the contributions of other colleges.[1] Merton's grant was relatively cautious when compared with that of St John's at £45.

Merton also helped the university in the support which it was able to give to widening areas of scholarship already initiated in the sixteenth century. Thus in Hebrew studies it found a fellowship for Henry Jacob, a scholar who had worked under Erpenius in the Netherlands and arrived in Oxford in 1628. But after a probationary year as a fellow he left his position. So anxious were his backers and in particular Archbishop Laud to secure his services for Oxford that in 1636 his fellowship was restored and the post of grammar lecturer was made available for him. It did not oblige him to 'carry through the severe exercizes of that society' for which his logic and philosophy were judged inadequate. His backers among the fellows were Peter Turner and Henry Briggs. He was able to compile a catalogue of *Hebraica* for the Bodleian. Archbishop Laud also insisted that he gave a public lecture in Merton Hall weekly 'upon some title of antiquity in which he should compare the Roman, Greek and oriental antiquities one with another'.[2] He was to help Selden with his oriental studies.

In Arabic Merton helped to pay part of the salary of Mathias Pasor, a German. In 1626 a grant of 40s. a year was made for three years and this was increased by 20s. a year in October 1627.[3] Pasor was hoping for the establishment of a chair in Arabic. Like Jacob he had the support of Henry Briggs, who described him as a 'very painfull and diligent reader for Arabicke and Chaldee'.[4] Whether helped by this initiative or not, the Laudian chair of Arabic was founded in 1634. Its first holder was Edward Pococke, a friend of Peter Turner, fellow.

Turner had been appointed Savilian professor of geometry in 1631 in place of Briggs. But his interests were much wider than mathematics. He took a keen interest in oriental studies and supported Henry Jacob's claim for a Merton fellowship in 1636. He was influential with Laud whom he had greatly helped with the compilation of the Laudian Code. As a friend of Pococke he persuaded Laud to let Pococke revisit the Levant in 1637.[5]

A payment of £4 to a certain chemist called Banks in 1632[6] suggests

[1] Below, 201–2: cf. 263.
[2] *HUO*, iv. 457, 483–4.
[3] *HUO*, iv. 479.
[4] Ibid.
[5] Ibid. 481. In 1641 the college bought books in Hebrew, Greek, Latin, Arabic and Persian with money lent by Mr Allen: below, 269. For Turner as Linacre lecturer, see Maddison, Pelling and Webster, *Linacre Studies*, 242.
[6] Below, 203.

that the college was interesting itself in another subject newly explored in the seventeenth century. But this seems to have been an isolated instance.

As we have seen Savile expected the postmasters to take their subjects seriously or leave.[1] That some of them worked to good purpose is best evidenced by the editions of classical authors produced by Thomas Farnaby, already quoted.[2] Whether his editions were made use of by his successors as postmasters cannot be shown.

Though there was no specific lectureship in mathematics we learn that after his appointment as Savilian professor Henry Briggs lectured on Arithmetic 'thrice in a week in Merton College Refectory to the scholars thereof'.[3] There should also have been lectures on classical medicine since two lectureships, senior and junior, had been founded by the executor of Thomas Linacre, Cuthbert Tunstal, in 1551.They were tied to Galen and Hippocrates.[4] But whether because by the seventeenth century these authors were becoming outdated, or for some other reason, these appointments were well on the way to becoming sinecures.

RELATIONS WITH THE CITY

The main bone of contention between Merton and the city was the college's jurisdiction over the manor of Holywell, granted by King Henry III. There was a particular difficulty over the college's ownership of Holywell mill and King's mill, both in the parish. Since the manor had been granted by the Crown, the college, when its rights were challenged, had little difficulty in securing verdicts in its favour in the royal courts (e.g. in January 1605).[5] But there was repeated resistance, as when the townsmen kidnapped the Holywell miller. In July 1605 the college took the matter to the Oxford Assizes and received a favourable ruling from Justice Yelverton, and another before David Williams, justice, in March 1606.[6] Four years later the college was still defending its rights successfully when it gained a favourable King's Bench decision at Serjeant's Inn. A compromise over its privileges was reached in the Easter Term of 1610, although it had to pay costs of £13 6s. 8d.

[1] Below, 53, and see above, Undergraduates.

[2] Martin and Highfield, 195; and see above, Undergraduates.

[3] Martin and Highfield, 188n.

[4] Maddison, Pelling and Webster, *Linacre Studies*, 42–68, 223–49; cf. Martin and Highfield, 154. The assiduity of the lecturers is judged doubtful after 1583.

[5] Below, 28, 30.

[6] Below, 36.

for its success.[1] A regular opponent was Thomas Wentworth, the city recorder, son of the radical M.P. Peter Wentworth (d. 1596) and one of the main opponents of university representation in parliament in 1604.[2] The townsmen wanted the inhabitants of Holywell to be made to grind their corn in the city's Castle Mill rather than at Holywell or King's Mill, and for the citizens to be free to fish in the Cherwell waters adjacent to the mills.

Despite the Holywell dispute there were several signs of friendly relations between the college and the city. Bands made up of musicians from both town and university made regular visits and were given grants, as in March 1604, when they were given 6s 8d., and again in 1609, 1623, and 1624.[3] On the last occasion it was noted that payments were made to 'citharaedi', harpers, presumably musicians playing some kind of lute. Sometimes, too, there were good relations with specific aldermen, as with William Wright, the guarantor for payments to the junior Bickley lecturer. He became a college tenant when he took over Radcliffe's house in the parish of St Martin.[4] Just as there had been appreciation of Robert Brizenden, fellow, in 1598 as the 'publicke and onlie preacher to our citizens',[5] so too there was for Henry Wilkinson the elder, when he preached at the city church, St Martin's,Carfax.

The rapid growth of population in the town is reflected in college leases of Holywell, where there was much house-building in the seventeenth century.[6] Sometimes it is possible to identify roughly the time of the erection of a property, as with the 'recently built house' of John Davies, a Merton cook, who in August 1616 was granted a forty year lease without a fine, or with that of Robert Moore, bedell of theology, who was given the right to build a house on the Holywell waste in August 1626 and had built it by April 1627.[7] John Chandler had built a tenement from its foundations and held it for some years before April 1655, and similarly Francis Sayre, butcher, had built his tenement from its foundations in the two years before August 1655.[8] Sometimes a stable would be rebuilt as a house. Often the college set a minimum cost on the house to be erected (£100 in January 1658).[9] The Holywell waste

[1] Below, 56.
[2] *ODNB*.
[3] Below, 13, 143, 148.
[4] Below, 94, 176.
[5] Martin and Highfield, 174n.
[6] A systematic history of Holywell in the period covered here has yet to be attempted. It will need to draw on Regs. 3.1–3 (Libri rationarii bursariorum, 1585–1677) and Regs. 6.1–3 (lease registers, 1586–1682).
[7] Below, 94, 166, 169.
[8] Below, 359.
[9] Below, 378.

lay on the south side of the street, between it and the city ditch, and also south of St Cross church, between it and Holywell.

The varied nature of the Holywell parishioners is illustrated by Partridge, a stonemason, Isaac Weekes, a chandler from St Clements, and various college staff, not only of Merton but of neighbouring colleges, such as John Couch, a Wadham cook, in 1628 and Abraham Watson, butler of Balliol, who rented part of the town ditch in 1630.[1] The ditch was gradually built over as it came closer to the street at its western end. Plots on the south of the street became more cramped until the last were let in the late 1650s. There were stables such as Smoote's in 1655, barns and another stall which was to be turned into a house costing £100,[2] no doubt much to the relief of its neighbours. A reference in 1626–7 shows that there was an infirmary, perhaps adjacent to St Cross church, for in that year Mr Napper, the farmer of Holywell manor, paid £4 13s. 4d. to the curate who was to make it available for the infirmary. For the church itself a stipend of £10 a year was granted from the college for a preacher, providing that the inhabitants contributed a further £10.[3]

LITIGATION

The long struggle over the college's privileges in Holywell was only one part of a constant battle waged in the law courts to assert Merton's rights. The most important case in this period, that of the long lease of Malden, has already been mentioned. A compromise to settle it by parliamentary verdict was considered in 1624 but rejected in 1627. When the final verdict came it ensured that though the Goode family could retain the manor for three lives its fate thereafter was to return to Merton, which it did in 1707.[4]

Other lawsuits were successfully pursued, as against the mayor and burgesses of Cambridge who were three years in arrears with the rent of the King's mill. Savile took the opportunity to go over himself and to stay at King's College while the matter was decided.[5] An end was also made to the long drawn-out battle with the heirs of Richard Fitzjames over Knowle Park, Somerset. A verdict was obtained from the judges at Chard and a settlement imposed on John Fitzjames of Redlynch.[6] The frequent need for college officers to stay in London led

[1] Below, 175, 189. [2] Below, 359, 378. [3] Below, 169–70, 374–5.
[4] Martin and Highfield, 169 and n. 83. [5] Below, 87–8.
[6] Below, 17–18.

to the acquisition of a house with four or five rooms in Warwick Street, which was furnished in 1626; it had great striped hangings for two chambers.[1] Warden Brent seems to have owned a London house in Aldersgate in Little Britain.[2]

FROM THE CIVIL WAR TO THE RESTORATION

Warden Harvey last appears in the register on 28 March 1646. Thereafter Warden Brent returned but resigned in 1651. He was replaced in 1651 by Cromwell's doctor Jonathan Goddard, who had been his physician on the Scottish campaign. In Goddard the medical tradition was sustained. He was moreover a member of the council of the Royal Society. However, as a member of Cromwell's council and in 1653 of the Barebones Parliament he was closely tied to the business of the capital. His plaintive letter in July 1653[3] explains to the subwarden that in the circumstances he cannot ask to be excused from his responsibilities to the House of Commons in order to come to Oxford to elect college officers. He refers their election to the attention of the five senior fellows, i.e. the subwarden, the three deans and the master of Wylliott's exhibition. This was to prove a characteristic feature of Goddard's wardenship. The college came to be ruled by an oligarchy of the subwarden and the senior fellows. This was not to be the only period when the college was virtually run by an oligarchy of fellows. The same fate befell it in the years leading up to the resignation of Warden Bowman in 1936.[4]

Goddard was present for the election of officers in 1655, 1656 and 1657. But once again he was absent in 1658, and writing from Gresham College he reported that he was 'prevented uppon the account of his Highnesse service, and commands to attend here'.[5] Again the five senior fellows were pressed into service. The register last records Goddard's presence on 3 August 1659. For decisions taken on 7 February and 11 June 1660 he sent his written consent.[6] During the last year of the Interregnum the college seems to have kept its head down. Alexander Fisher as senior fellow survived to see the Restoration, but of his chief critics and rivals Peter Turner had died in 1651 and John Greaves in the following year.

[1] Below, 167.
[2] *ODNB*.
[3] Below, 351; *HUO*, iv. 737.
[4] Martin and Highfield, 330–1.
[5] Below, 379–80.
[6] Below, 365–6.

EDITORIAL NOTE

The text of the Register is reproduced in full with marginalia either printed as italic headings or commented upon in footnotes.

Clerkly corrections in the form of erasures and interlineations have been incorporated without comment except when judged to be possibly significant.

The dating formulae which head most of the manuscript pages have been omitted except when they mark the beginning of a college year.

Contractions have been extended unless there is ambiguity and except for ordinal numbers, fractions and standard abbreviations for coinage.

In English passages the form 'ye', sometimes used in the same sentence as 'the', has been retained.

Capitalization and punctuation in the Latin parts of the Register have been rationalized to some extent, but the capitalization of English passages has been preserved.

The letter 'I' for 'J' in Latin passages has been retained except for proper names such as Jackson.

In certain recurrent entries (annual lists of fellows and officers, records of variations) slight amendments have been made in order to standardize the format. Lists of fellows, for example, have been given numbers whether or not they occur in the manuscript.

Editorial interpolations such as supplied letters are in square brackets.

REGISTRUM ANNALIUM COLLEGII MERTONENSIS

[1603]

Elocatio ventimolae apud Ibston Richardi Lane Reg.I.3, p. 202 (cont.)

Martii 30mo socii consentiunt (cui dominus custos ante assenserat) ut, si Richardus Lane de Turvil aedificaret ventimolam nostram apud Ibston, igne consumta, haberet 12 plaustra ly timber et haberet statum 31 annorum solvendi tantum 25s. 8d. annuatim quas conditiones idem Richardus accepit.

Dominus Philipson admittitur in annum probationis

Eodem tempore dominus Philipson admissus est in annum probationis.

Aprilis 3° socii decernunt ut culina reficeretur. Et ut murus horti domini custodis ex opposito aulae aedificaretur.

Aprilis 10° octo senioribus unanimiter consentientibus venia concessa est magistro Allen vel scribendi, vel notascumque aut characteres faciendi in marginibus voluminum quorundam Chrysostomi quae e libraria nostra eius finem ei in manus tradebantur.

Computus Magistri Dale 2^{di} bursarii

Aprilis 14to magister Dale 2^{dus} bursarius computavit et discessit in aere collegii 19 li. 11s. 4d.

Aprilis 17mo habita est commemoratio pro fundatore, lecta statuta, scrutinium celebratum.

Aprilis 21mo socii unanimi statuerunt consensu ut vicecustos et magister Simonson proficiscerentur Gamelingay qui una cum magistro Clavering, rectore ecclesiae parochialis ibidem, haberet liberam potestatem vel elocandi manerium de Avenels pro reditu 100 li. annuatim, salvis conditionibus de quibus conventum erat, cum magistro Sproxton vel constituendi balivum et ita retinendi in manibus collegii.

Elocatio tenementi ly Falcon et Pocrilston

Eodem tempore consensum est ut tenementum vocatum ly Falcon in Gamelingay dimitteretur Francisco Cockerel pro termino viginti unius annorum. Consentiunt etiam eodem tempore ut tenementum nostrum in Pocrilston elocaretur / pro termino 21 annorum Henrico Irishe p. 203
iuniori.

Franciscus Temple, balivus

Aprilis ultimo vicecustos et magister Simonson qui profecti erant Gamelingay, domum reversuntur et postridie socii conveniunt in vestiario et (quoniam firmarium [*sic*] satis idoneus comparari non possit) unanimiter decernunt ut Franciscus Temple, famulus domini custodis, esset balivus noster manerii de Avenells si hoc a domino custode obtineri posset qui quamvis aeger admodum cavere possit famulo suo, tamen ne ullo modum deesset collegio annuit petitioni nostrae.

Maii 20mo socii consentiunt ut 60 li. mitterentur Gamelingay tradendae Francisco Temple balivo nostro per manus magistri Fforne, insumendae in emendis pecoribus caeterisque rebus quae pertinent ad occupationem meliorationemve praedictis seu manerii de Avenels.

Iunii 9° magister Dale 2^dus^ bursarius solvens pedem computi magistro Slade sequenti bursario, presentibus sociis in alta aula, discessit aeque.

Dispensatio magistri King pro variationibus

Eodem tempore dispensatum est cum magistro Kinge pro secundis variationibus, ante perfectas primas, causa erat huius insolitae festinationis quod magister Kinge plus quam instanter affirmaret se necessario[1] discessurum postridie eius diei quo primo variaturus erat summo mane priusquam seniores convenire possent nec brevi reversurum.

Magister King variat

Iunii 10mo magister King variavit in his quaestionibus:

An { Quidlibet fiat ex quolibet. Affirmat.
Mundus sit animal. Affirmat.
Luna sit habitabilis. Affirmat.

Iunii 20mo socii consentiunt ut collegium contribueret una cum aliis collegiis ad sustentationem mariscallorum quorum officium est ut mendicos et desidiosos tenebriones abigerent.[2]

Eodem tempore consensum est etiam de contributione ad sustentationem ly schavager cuius munus est mundare plateas, ultrisque contributionibus duraturis non in certum aliquem terminum se donec aliter visum fuerit custodi et sociis eaque conditione si reliqui collegii singula contribuerunt pro rata portione terrarum et possessionum.

[1] 'nedum' deleted. [2] 'abadibo' deleted.

Dispensatio magistri Talbot pro variationibus

Iulii 5to dispensatum est cum magistro Talbot pro secundis variationibus, ante perfectas primas variationes nihil reliquum esset temporis in quo, pro secundis iure dispensatio concedi posset.

Magister Talbot variat

Iulii 7mo magister Talbot variavit in his quaestionibus:

An { Fontes et flumina generentur ex aere suterraneo. Negat.
Sit ignis elementum. Negat.
Sol et homo generent hominem. Negat quia sol non generat. }

Computus Iohannis Sherwood

Iulii 13mo Iohannes Sherwood, firmarius et balivus noster manerii nostri de Cantabrigia, computavit et discessit aeque.

Commemoratio

Iulii vicesimo in festo beatae Margaretae habita est commemoratio pro fundatore, lecta statuta, scrutinium celebratum, quod prorogatur in vicesimum diem Augusti et quemlibet diem citra.

Computus magistri Carter

Iulii 20mo magister Carter, firmarius et balivus noster manerii de Callowland, computavit in scaccario.

[*blank*] p. 204

Anno Domini 1603°, regni regis Iacobi 1°, fundati collegii Maldoniae 339°, Oxoniae 333°, Henrici Savile custodis 19°. p. 205

Augustus

Nomina et numerus sociorum:

Magistri in artibus

1. Robertus Brizenden
2. Anthonius Antonye
3. Beniaminus Bentham
4. Samuel Slade
5. Christophorus Dale
6. Richardus Taylor in anno gratuitatis
7. Iohannes Tapsel
8. Thomas Allen
9. Leonardus Yate
10. Nathaniel Brent
11. Edwardus Lee
12. Iohannes Kinge
13. Theodorus Gulson
14. Ioannes Talbot
15. Thomas Horne
16. Stucleius Blickard
17. Gulielmus Simonson
18. Isaacus Wake
19. Edwardus Rogers
20. Georgius Garrard
21. Gulielmus Gale

Bacchalaurei in artibus et in anno probationis

1. Franciscus Greevel
2. Samuel Lane
3. Ioannes Elly
4. Ioannes Philipson

Capellani:

1. Robert Beeseley
2. Iohannes Muddle

Ratiocinia de Gamlingaye Avenels

Primo die Augusti per dominum custodem convocati in scaccarium diluculo convenimus; ubi in primis audita sunt ratiocinia de Gamblingaye Avenels, inducta per magistrum Claveringe et Franciscum Temple, balivum nostrum ibidem, a festo Sancti Michaelis, anno 1602 usque ad festum Sancti Petri ad Vincula, anno 1603.

Arreragia solvenda Temple

Secundo, eodem loco et tempore consentimus de tradendis Temple praedicti manerii balivo quinquaginta libris, et paulo amplius eo, in pecuniis receptis a domino custode pro parte arreragiorum Emildone et Pontelande, de diversis annis antea collegio debitorum.

Dimissio medietatis Emildon et Pontelande Henrico Nevile, militi

Tertio, eisdem loco et tempore unanimiter consensum est, de dimittenda medietate rectoriarum Emildon et Pontelande Henrico Nevile, militi, pro termino unius et viginti annorum, postquam assignatio quaedam de eadem medietate, indentata sigillataque ab honoratissimo viro Roberto Essexiae comite, (cui primo per indenturam dicta medietas concedebatur) et per eum tradita in manus praefati Henrici ad usum suum, fuerat collegio assignata.

Medietas rectoriae de Gamblingaye. Dimittitur Iacobo Claveringe

Quarto ibidem et eodem die similis dimissio facta est Iacobo Claveringe Novocastrensi, medietatis rectoriae de Gamblingaye Merton', pro praedicto termino annorum post redditionem prioris indenturae, factae anno regni reginae Elizabethae 42°.

Electio officiariorum

Secundo die Augusti in altam aulam conventum est circiter horam nonam ante meridianam, ad eligendos officiarios sequentis anni. Quae electio proxime praecedenti die procul dubio facta fuisset, nisi quod dominus custos illo ipso una cum sociis praedictis collegii negotiis impeditus, necnon in academicis quibusdam occupatus, huic muneri commode vacare non poterat. Postquam igitur socii, viginti unam claves, quas habuerant communis bibliothecae, officiariique suas

similiter, ante oculos domini custodis in publico sigillatim proposuerant, nisi sunt reliqui omnes ad tempus secedere, praeter quinque simpliciter seniores, a quibus et domino custode designantur in hunc annum, novi officiarii isti qui sequuntur:
magister Slade, vicecustos.
magistri Dale, Horne, Rogers, decani.
magistri Brizenden, Brent, Lee, bursarii.
magister Allen principalis portionistarum cui etiam exhibitio capellani Hamsterley assignatur.
magister Gulson eligitur in bursarium Williot.
Praelectores nominati sunt magister Blickerde, linguae Graecae, magister Simonson, grammaticae.
Exhibitio capellani capellae distribuitur a domino custode inter Horne et Rogers iuniores decanos.
Bacchalaureus Williot per principalem portionistarum constituendus iterum relinquitur.

Anno Domini 1603°, regni regis Iacobi 1°, fundati collegii Maldoniae 339°, Oxoniae 333°, Henrici Savile custodis 19°. p. 206

Augus[t]us

Dispensatio magistri Horne
Eodem tempore consensum est, ut prorogentur variationes magistri Horne quia electus est in officium medii decani usque in annum ab hoc revoluto, proxime sequentem.

Codex topographicus[1]
Item provisum est officiariis, ut paciscerentur cum magistro Langdon pro tabulis topographicis quas de terris nostris Gamblingaiensibus pulcherrime descripserat quo paulo post peracto, tradiderunt ei isto nomine duodecim libras.

Litterae attornatus factae bursariis
Tertio die consensum est in scaccario de litera attornatus tribus bursariis concedenda; qua uti possent, ut instrumento legitimo (si opus esset) ad recuperanda singula huius saltem anni debita collegii vel e redditibus terrarum, vel obligationibus etc. Haec non multo post perlecta fuit coram sociis sigillataque.

[1] Merton Coll. Reg. 6.17.

Centum marcae solvendae duobus St Georges, et sub qua conditione

Ibidem eodemque tempore consensum est ut e publico aerario centum marcae solverentur domino St George armigero filioque eius natu maximo, sub ea conditione, ut manerium nostrum de Gamblingaye Avenels, non ita pridem antea collegii pecuniis coemptum factumque hereditarium, ab omnibus clamoribus, vendicationibus, querelis et quibuscunque tandem litibus liberarent, factumque tectum conservarent, adeoque ea de causa sursum traderent in manus nostras singula scripta, indenturas, syngraphas, quotquot aut ipsi haberent, aut aliunde comparare possent, ius proprium vel aliorum titulos in praedictis possessionibus aut circiter earum immunitates et privilegia, quovismodo demonstrantes; ut sic inposterum securius, quod ad hoc negotium spectat, perpetuo conquiescamus.

Reditus unius anni pro medietate rectoriae de Gamblingaye solvendus Temple balivo

Item consensum est ibidem, eodemque tempore ut superioris anni reditus pro medietate rectoriae de Gamblingaye, illic Temple balivo nostro solveretur quem deinceps iste, in usus necessarios villae seu manerii nostri de Avenels erogaret.

Indentura de medietate Emildone et Pontelande facta Henrico Nevile militi sigillatur

Augusti 19° Indentura de medietate rectoriarum Emildon et Pontelande, superius concessa domino Henrico Nevile, militi, postquam exemplar eius, publico dimissarum terrarum registro mandatum fuerat, coram sociis in alta aula perlecta est, eodemque die sigillata.

Computus Slade tertii bursarii superioris anni

Die 26° Doctor Slade tertius bursarius superioris anni, computavit in scaccario, et discessit in aere collegii 7s. 9d. Quam summam postea solvit magistro Lee, primo bursario, et sic aeque.

September

Decreta tempore pestis

Septembris 2°, consensum est per dominum custodem et socios in alta aula, ut aliquot e scholaribus nostris pauperioribus quorum praesentia commode carere poteramus, ob metum pestis ingravescentis in oppido, e collegio ad tempus saltem amandarentur.

Septembris sexto, dominus custos omnesque socii domi tunc existentes, in altam aulam convenerunt: ubi, quia pestis iam in oppido disseminata latius plus virium, in dies grassando per populum[1] comparaverat, ita ut academicis quoque magnum tacessere periculum videretur, unanimi consensu statuta sunt ista, quae sequuntur.

Primo, ut singuli magistri, bacchalaurei, servi collegii, portionistae, aliique scholares ad unum omnes rus alicubi, aut in patriam suam, se reciperent, tribus exceptis officiariis, vicecustode, decano, praesenti bursario et seniori socio, altero item e clericis, e coquis, ianitore, et quatuor demum e numero scholarium, qui magistris hic commorantibus subserverent, una cum famulo custodis, qui vices obsonatoris gereret, aliasque res nobis necessarias procuraret.

Secundo, dispensatum est cum magistris regentibus pro publicis suis lectionibus, replicationibus, et Augustinensibus, usque ad festum Omnium Sanctorum, sive interea terminus in Academia habeatur, sive minus. Quo festo, si nedum forsan terminus in universitate inchoaret, continuata est haec dispensatio, usque ad inceptionem eiusdem, vel potius usque ad festum Purificationis proxime sequentem. Quo tempore ad summum, si ob pestem adhuc saevientem nondum terminus publice iniretur, decreto cautum est, ut tam magistri regentes, quam reliqui omnes socii, domum reversi, ad manerium nostrum de Cuxham, veluti in commune aliquod musaeum, solitis ingeniorum suorum exercitationibus, studiisque, operam navandi causa, commearent.

Tertio, tutius etiam fore videbatur, ut, pistore, braseatore lanisoque ad tempus valedictis, cum passim oppidum incolerent, Guilielmus Napper, firmarius noster de Holywell rogaretur, quo singula haec alimentaria adiumenta domestica cura et labore suo parata ac confecta quotidie necessitati nostrae communi, assidueque subministraret, quibus ille optatis nostris, paulo post rogatus paratiis suo animo obsecundavit.

Quarto, quo mox abfuturis, proque tempore rus relegandis sociis, aeque atque caeteris istuc commoraturis, aliquot etiam ad victum suum cultumve necessaria, suppeditarentur, communi lege sanciebatur, ut quilibet socius, quicunque praesentibus decretis, dum facta sunt, intererat, pro singulis septimanis, quibus ob pestem / se disiungi p. 207
contigeret, drachmas undecim, e pecunia publica praeciperetur at ne sic sine conditione quidem tot enim drachmas revera habiturus erat, si mercatu proxime praecedente festum Sancti Michaelis mox secuturi, octo modici tritici, tredecim solidis venderentur, sui minoris, decem

[1] MS: 'popellum'.

tantum. Item edictum est ut equiso (qui tempore incola oppidi iussus est abesse a collegio) viginti denarios, et duo coqui, quibus ob similem causam in domum intrare non licuit, coniunctim duos solidos, per singulas hebdomadas, et tertius qui in culina eorum munera obiret, famulusque custodis, vicegerens obsonatoris, communias in alta aula inter servientes, postremo quatuor scholares, qui magistris ministrarent, de mensa, quatuor portionistarum, duobus eis insuper additis denariis pro quolibet prandio, per singulos dies septimanae sumptu publico obtinerent.

Quinto, ne lotrices frequenti accessu et recessu suo, periculum aliquod inclusis creare possent, ordinatum est, ut Blackamus solus ingrederetur, omnes pannos lineas importandi, exportandique causa, sub ea lege, si ex oppido cum tota sua familia in domum aliquam rusticam nec istinc adeo remotam quam primum se transferre vellet quod ille fecit libenter.

Sexto et ultimo consensum est, ut neque praefatae allocationes, nec caetera omnia fieri, aut in usu esse, inciperent, ante nonum diem Septembris proxime sequentis qui erat dies veneris, initiumque septimanae, ut iste primus, praedictis decretis, ortus sui animam viresque infunderet.

Quorundam famulorum biberia sublata sunt

Decimo nono Septembris, dominus custos, sociique tunc domi existentes, in altam aulam convenerunt ad ordinarium computum decani, ubi, quorundam a famulis (ut vulgo vocantur biberia), quod neque olim usitata, nec recentius allocata fuerant, e computis septimanae deleverunt, addito insuper mandato a domino custode, ne haec aut huiusmodi in posterum, nullius consensus authoritate, nec antiqua consuetudine munita, in domo fieri permitterentur.

Ordinata et facta tempore pestis

Nihilominus tamen, quod ianitoris et lotricis ministeria, durante hoc tempore ob pestem dissolutionis, collegio utiliora et laboriosiora fore perspiceret, se contentum esse autumabat, ut sua de mensa solita, solitisve auctiora, inter combibendum haberent, quamdiu haec ob commune malum societatis dimissio permaneret.

Eisdem loco et tempore consensum est, ut durante dissolutione, tres tantum denarii in pane pro olla, caeteris vero temporibus sex, et pro lacte et frumento, novem denarii, pro singulis diebus illis quibus haec in usu sunt, allocarentur, item ut potiorem cervisiam, duplam quam vocant birramus, haberemus, solventes pro singulis tonnellis semiquadrantem extra tempora refectionum.

Isto porro consensu, et colloquio initum est consimili, quomodo praefatae allocationes tam pecuniariae quam reliquae, quod prorsus novae et insolitae esse videbantur, in computis nostris digestae essent atque dispensatae satius tandem fore iudicatum est, ut haec ratiocinia, ad imitationem, antea solitorum quam minima fieri posset cum mutatione disponerentur, quod postea debita cum curia diligentiaque factum est, ut videre licet in codicillis septimanae et bursariorum libro pergamentario. Quoniam vero collegii stromatarius erat oppidanus, tutius etiam fore visum est, ut bursarius mature tot aromata coemeret, quot pro pluribus septimanis, usui nostro sufficerent eaque apud se deposita reservaret ne pro qualibet re minutissima, durante peste in urbem mittere[1] cogeremur.

Die vicesimo quarto, dominus custos et quotquot domi relicti erant socii in scaccarium convenerunt, ubi unanimiter decretum est, ut post discessum custodis, quem uno aut altero die post facturus erat, nemo exiret e collegio, sine venia trium officiariorum, et senioris socii supradictorum (quibus solis tota cura et tutela domus tunc temporis commitebatur) prius impetrata, et in quadam schedula chartae cum personae egrestura nomine descripta, et sic ad ianitorem delata, nene ut unus aliquis ex ipsis quatuor viris, sine huiusmodi licentia, a tribus reliquis et concessa oppidum ingredi posset.

Computus generalis, et specialis

Eisdem tempore et loco, habitus est generalis computus de omnibus et omni modis reditibus, aliisque rebus forinsecis, receptis et non receptis, omnique liberatorum genere, per 3 bursarios, ab anno 1601, usque ad annum 1602, ut patet in codice membraneo bursariorum ibidem etiam eodemque consensu, specialis computus factus est unius et alterius septimanae, tempore pestis praeteritae, ut illa methodus, qua in huiusmodi computis, durante dissolutione, utendum esse censuimus praemonstrata facilius deinceps[2] observaretur.

October

Ratiocinia Temple balivi de Gamblingaye Avenels

Nono die Octobris, quotquot domi eramus, in scaccarium convenimus, ubi ratiocinia Temple, balivi nostri de Gamblingaye Avenels,

[1] 'ingredi' deleted. [2] 'et sedulo' deleted.

audivimus ab 18° die maii anno domini 1603, usque ad festum Sancti Michaelis proxime sequentis de dicto manerio continuata, computataque.

Procuratorium de Shaftsburie sigillatur Temple balivo

Postero die ex consensu domini custodis assentis, perlectae sunt coram sociis in alta aula, litterae attornatus, factae Francisco Temple, ad recuperanda areragia, distringendo litesque prosequendo, de Shaftsburye in Dorcestria quarum etiam exemplar in registro describitur, eodemque die communi sigillo fuerunt consignataeque.

Allocatio facta Temple balivo de Avenels, pro victu et stipendio suo ibidem

Eodem loco et tempore, ex voluntate domini custodis absentis, per litteras et sociorum praesentium, viva voce, significata, allocati sunt Temple dicto balivo, pro singulis septimanis, quibus apud manerium
p. 208 nostrum de Avenels, in negotiis collegii occupatus / versaretur, quinque solidi, ob victum quotidianum, et pro annuo stipendio, ob labores, sex librae, tredecim solidi, quatuor denarii.

November

Duae indenturae sigillantur a duobus St Georges et una cum aliis sursum traditae sub collegio. Item una obligatio sigillatur ab eisdem.

Novembris decimo quinto, perlecta est in alta aula in praesentia sociorum, indentura quadam, facta inter nos et dominos St Georges, patrem et filium, in qua illi ambo, omne suum ius, titulum, ac interesse, quod aut ipsi haberent aut habere possent in manerio nostro de Avenels, m[o]lestias a quibuscumque personis, vel quocunque modo, in semet ipsos derivatum pro aliquo termino annorum, collegio resignant ob eamque causam in manus nostras tradiderunt, singula sua scripta, tam propria quam aliena, quotquot acquirere poterant ad hoc negotium spectantia, quae sunt in archivis nostris recordita. Haec omnia nobis concesserunt sub ea conditione, ut pro tali sua resignatione, centum marcas eis solveremus, velut supradictum est. Ibidem eodemque tempore perlecta est altera indentura, seu factum in for[is]facienti concessa a dictis duobus St Georges, quatuor sociis collegii, quorum nomina mihi exprimuntur, pro terris quibusdam nostris in Moresley, intra comitatum Huntingdonensem, iacentibus; ulteriusque indenturos exemplaria, in publico registro dimisserunt praediorum, memoriae mandata sunt. Perlecta porro est obligatio quaedam in qua ambo St Georges steterunt obligati collegio, in ducentis marcis ad singula requisita et pacta perficiendis, prior indentura, sursum redditionis scilicet communi sigillo nostro est sigillata die 17° utraque vero, per magistrum Brent et magistrum Gale, duos de numero infrafatorum ad dictos Sanctos Georgios, apud Gamblingeiam existentes, paulo post delata fuit. Quibus utrisque simulque obligationi, propria illi sigilla opposuerunt, super ea parte fundorum ad quos occupandos atque possidendos in usum collegii, dicti infeodati mittebantur.

December

Cessante peste, incipit terminus in Academia

Decembris quarto iam defervescente (deo gratias) in oppido, sed non prorsus extincta peste publicus in Academia terminus incepit; quo dietam communi, quam primatae dissolutioni finis ultimus imponitur. Nam et alii academici passim e patriis suis ad pristina[m] domiciliam, et nostri collegii socii, ad hoc suum sibi bene rotum musaeum, aut iam redierant, aut in dies magis magisque revertebantur, et antedictas sibi allocatas pecunias, pro absentia, in aerario consequebantur.

Computus Lee 1 bursarii

Die 15to Decembris, magister Lee primus bursarius presentis anni, computum suum fecit in scaccario, et discessit in aere collegii, 13 li. 5s. 10d. quam summam, perlecto computo suo in aula 27° Ianuarii, solvit magistro Brent sequenti bursario, et sic aeque.

Commemoratio pro fundatore

Decembris 17°, qui fuit dies octavus ante natale Christi, circiter horam quartam antemeridianam, habita est commoratio, more solito, pro fundatore, et deinde in aula lecta sunt statuta, et prorogatum est scrutinium in primum diem Ianuarii.

Tres probationarii admittuntur in societatem.

Eisdem loco et tempore, tres bacchalaurei iurati admittuntur in perpetuam societatem huius domus, nominatim, dominus Franciscus Greevel, dominus Samuel Lane, dominus Ioannes Elly. Dedimus etiam potestatem magistro Brent, ligna caesa collegio coemendi, si in aliquot vilioris pretii incidere posset.

Dilatio dimidii debiti Wilmote

Decembris 26°, convenimus in vestiarium ubi ex consensu domini custodis, per literas prius significato, distulimus Richardo Wilmot de Ibstone, dimidiam solutionem quadraginta librarum solvendarum collegio, ultimo huius mensis, 1603, usque ad eundem diem in anno 1604, quo die debet solvere per obligationem suam 20 li.

Scrutinium in vigilia circumcisionis

Ultimo die Decembris, qui erat vigilia circumcisionis, de more habitum est scrutinium, in quo actum est 1° de moribus servientium, et huius articuli moderatio commissa est officiariis; 2°, de numero portionistarum, qui, ut solitus sit, decernitur; 3°, de hortulano, quod officium ad magistrum Lee, et suffragiis eligentium, et iure senioritatis devenerit.

[1604]

Ianuarius

Dimissio manerii nostri de Gamblingaye Avenels pro tribus anni, una cum aliis, quae concessa sunt

Septimo die Ianuarii, in alta aula consensum est, ut manerium nostrum de Gamblingaye Avenels, novo quidem tenenti dimitteretur ita ut possessiones illas non intraret, ante festum Sancti Michaelis proxime sequentis ad habendum sibi, vel assignatis suis, pro termino trium annorum, quo de cursu temporis spatio per novam indenturam factam (si modo vellet) pro termino viginti et unius annorum, denuo ei dictum manerium dimitteretur; item consensum est, ut sumptibus collegii, praedia in campis patentia ararentur, fierentque novalia ante praefatum festum, sub ea tamen conditione, ut ille huiusmodi terras sic aratas cultasque, impensis propriis, tertio illinc anno ante idem festum, relinqueret, nimirum, si firmam tunc omnino deserere, nec iterum eam occupare vellet. Postremo, ita inter nos convenitur ut quamcunque operam illi intranti, famulis et iumentis suis collegium praestaret, eandem ille egrediens sub fine anni tertii, collegio beneficii gratiam referret. Iterum consensum est ut oves aliquot ibidem pascentes venderentur ante festum Annunciacionis Mariae proxime sequentis.

Reparationes decretae

Porro ibidem concessum est, ut ineunte vere, hospitium Sancti Georgiis, et vetusta domus dicti manerii, tantum essent instaurata, quantum necessarium esse videretur.

p. 209 Anno Domini 1603, regni regis Iacobi 1°, fundati collegii Maldoniae 339°, Oxoniae 333°, Henrici Savile custodis 19°.

Probatio cuiusdam chartae immunitatum, quanti valet

Eodem loco et tempore consensum est, ut quaedam charta seu diploma regium cum sigillo complectens immunitates nostri collegii, et firmariorum eiusdem a decimis domino regi solvendis (quae olim ab Henrico Sexto praedecessoribus nostris fuerat concessa)[1] ex archivis in gazophulacio depromeretur; in eum nempe finem, quo, termino proxime sequente, in scaccario Westmonasterii, ex sumptibus dictorum firmariorum, clameum ita vendicationem nostram, eius virtute exhiberemus. Quod paulo post factum est revera, sed nullo cum effectu. Illic enim animadversum est, huiusmodi obcessionem regiam, ab ipsomet rege, qui concesserat, ante obitum suum fuisse revocabatur. Haec chartam postea receptam, in eo loco in quo fuerat primis collocata reposuimus.

Computus cistae Reade

Vicesimo primo Ianuarii, habitus est computus cistae Reade per custodes eiusdem, quia vix commode haberi poterat antea, ob sociorum absentiam tempore pestis, et in pristino statu relinquitur, nec non patera quaedam de annata tradita magistro Brent in pecunias communi extend' anno superiore, etiam est q[uod] penes eundem manet.

Februarius

Dispensatio cum magistris regentibus pro quibusdam lectionibus

Februarii 5[to], convenimus in vestiarium, ibique dispensavimus, cum magistris regentibus, Simonson, Wake, Rogers, Garrard, Gale, pro publicis suis praelectionibus, quolibet die Martis ab illo tempore, usque ad diem sabbati in comitiis proxime futuris idque per singulas septimanas quoties praedicto die Martis circiter horas antemeridianas septimam et octavam in academia concio haberetur.

Concessa musicis

Tunc etiam consensum est ibidem, ut publicis academiae oppidique musicis bursarius sex solidos octo denarios, more solito, elargiretur.

Allocata magistro Bentham societatem relicturo

Decimo nono Februarii, iterum in eundem locum convenimus, ubi ex consensu domini custodis prius per litteras significato, conceditur magistro Bentham, a die matrimonii sui futuri nondum cognito, integer annus gratuitatis, in quo singulis privilegiis, commodisque

[1] MCR 74, letters patent granting immunity from aids, subsidies, etc., 15 Aug. 1444, printed in Garrod and Allen, *Merton Muniments*, 38–9.

domus (suo tantum excepto suffragio) frueretur, idemque liberaturam suam haberet, licet abfuturus esset, per dimidiam partem, vel eo amplius, istius anni. Quae omnia sub hac conditione ei allocata sunt ut si modo diem nominaret, quem ducturus uxorem, non transiliret quo mox ille libenter fecit, festum scilicet Annunciationis beatae Virginis proxime sequentis anno domini 1604 praestituendo.

Literae missae a domino Roberto Cecyll Barone

Die vicesimo tertio, in alta aula literas legimus honoratissimi viri, domini Roberti Cecyll Baronis, et principalis secretarii serenissimi regis nostri Iacobi in quibus rogavit nos, ut medietatem rectoriarum Emildone et Pontelande, quam sibi pro termino viginti et unius annorum concesseramus (sicuti superius memoratum est) Richardo Reade generoso, et priori nostro firmario ibidem, per consimile instrumentum, pro eodem temporis spatio confirmaremus, quod ut legitime a nobis fieret.

Resignatio medietatis Emildon et Ponteland

Miserat etiam eo nomine praefatus Robertus, unam indenturam suo sigillo sigillatam, qua omne ius suum clamum, ac interesse, quod habuit in praedictis rectoriis, virtute superioris suae indenturae, sursum in manus nostras tradidit, atque resignavit. Haec resignatio quoque, coram sociis perlecta est, qui voluntati Baronis illico assentientes, medietatem illam de novo, dicto Richardo qui praesens fuit, et praefatas literas attulerat pro termino viginti annorum ex eo tempore, concesserunt.

Indentura de praedicta medietate facta Magistro Reade, sigillatur

Cuius concessionis indentura, postero die, publice, et ex utraque parte, sigillata fuit.

Caenae quadragesimales concessae

Vicesimo octavo Februarii allocatae sunt sociis caenae quadragesimales, more solito, et forma superioribus annis expressa.

Quaedam concessa loco domini custodis

Ibidem etiam consensum est, ut supellex tam linea, quam lanea, quanta ad usum domini custodis in loco suo, circa mensam, vel lectos, necessaria esse videretur, sumptibus collegii coemeretur, circa idem tempus etiam consensum est, ut domuncula quaedam, quae veluti mandra, muro innixa est in hortulo custodis, diruta transferretur in eum locum, ubi nunc aedificata conspicitur, et ut culina eius, pavimento de ly ragge sterneretur.

Martius. 1604

Electio obsonatoris eiusque auctum stipendium
Martii vicesimo septimo, convenimus in conclave custodis ubi eligitur Richardus Foster, obsonator, eiusque stipendium, facta allocatione 26s. 8d., amplificatum est, ex consensu, usque ad quinque marcas per annum.

Allocationes factae pro tempore pestis
Ibidem etiam eodemque tempore allocantur 7 magistris, et duobus bacchalaureis, pro absentia tempore pestis, 40s. pro singulis tametsi supradicto decreto, cum primum fieret non intererant. Item allocantur Maurice, ianitori illo tempore existenti 6s. 8d.

Sigillatio indenturae de medietate rectoriae de Gambling[aye].
Die vicesimo octavo, in alta aula coram sociis perlecta, et cum registro collata est nova indentura, facta magistro Claveringe Novocastrensi, eodemque die, communi sigillo consignatur.

Commemoratio pro fundatore
Ultimo Martii, hora 8va antemeridiana, celebrata est commemoratio fundatoris in templo, nona, lecta sunt statuta, et postea habitum est scrutinium, quod prorogatum est, in decimum quintum Aprilis et in quemlibet diem citra.

Aprilis

Unus probationarius admittitur in societatem
Aprilis 2°, dominus Iohannes Philipson iuratus, unanimi consensu 13^{m} sociorum admittitur in perpetuam societatem huius domus, quo tempore admissus est etiam Israel Tho[mas] White [?] in clericum iuniorem, prius exhibito ei iuramento, quod donum domus tunc videbitur.

Allocatio quorundam in hortulo custodis
Ibidem etiam consensum est ut fenestra musaei proprii, hortum minorem domini custodis, a tergo domus prospiciens, in latus ex opposita parte, alteri respondente transferretur, et ut foramen sive ostium in dorso muri ly storehouse, caementis et lapidibus obstrueretur, quae non multo post[e]a facta su[nt].

p. 210 Anno Domini 1604, regni regis Iacobi 2°, Henrici Savile custodis 19°.

Instrumentum procuratorium de 2 Gamblingayes conceditur Temple

Aprilis 26to, convenimus in vestiarium, et concessimus Temple balivo, ut haberet instrumentum sub sigillo publico, ad colligendos reditus, et ad distringendum, et ad reliqua huiusce officii munera obeunda, in duobus maneriis nostris de Gamblingayes, Merton, et Avenels.

Dispensatio

Item dispensatum est cum singulis magistris regentibus pro duabus praelectionibus publicis in duobus ultimis terminis insuper cum magistro Wake, pro una aut altera praelectione, necessariis negotiis rus avocato, sed hoc postea factum est.

Computus magistri Brent 2^{i} bursarii.

Die 29° magister Brent secundus bursarius huius anni, computum de administratione sua fecit in scaccario et discessit in aere collegiis 6s. 4d. quam summam non multo post solvit magistro Brisenden sequenti bursario, et sic aeque.

Decreta circa pestem renascentem

Vicesimo die in alta aula consensum est, ut propter pestem pullulantem in parochia Sancti Iohannis, in domo e regione opposita portae ecclesiae nostrae boreali, communis collegii ianua clauderetur, et ut horti ostiolum septentrionale iuxta viam regiam aperiretur, pro duabus saltem septimanis, et ianitori, duo solidi sex denarii, darentur, pro singulis, et ut communarii aulae Albanae, qui intra collegium antea iacuerant, praedictum temporis spatium ex eo non egrederentur, idque ob scholarem quendam de aula Albana, qui ex peste aegrotasse, ferebatur.

Maius

Variationes magistri Gulson

Maii vicesimo quinto, magister Theodorus Gulson, in istis variationibus variavit:

An {
1^{a}. Sapientiores sint, qui experientiam habent, quam qui artem tenentur? Affirmat.
2^{a}. Naturae repugnet, ut sinistra, sit dextra deterior? Affirmat.
3^{a}. Calor primogenius sit caelestis? Negat.
}

Die sequenti, cum eodem dispensatum est, pro secundis suis variationibus.

Iunius

Elemosyna data Genevae

Decimo quarto Iunii, in aula consensum est ut elemosyna de 30s. ex publico aerario, dono daretur civitati Genevae, quae in inopiam ex bello cum duce Sabaudiae, redacta fuerat.

Charta condonata generalis

Circa hoc tempus, a domino nedum rege accepimus condonationem generalem collegii, membrana exaratam, et magno Angliae sigillo consignatam, pretium erat 27s. 8d.

Iulius

Variationes magistri Blickarde

Iulii quarto, magister Stucleius Blickerde, in istis thesibus variavit:

An {
1. Innatum odium, non est causa dissidiorum inter bruta animantia. Contra Aristotelem.[1]
2. Animantes femellae, mitiores non sunt ingenio, quam mares.
3. Melancholici, non sunt prudentissimi.

Die sequenti dispensatum est cum eodem, pro secundis suis variationibus.

Dimissio medietatis sylvarum Farleighe

Iulii decimo tertio convenimus in conclave domini custodis, ubi consensum est, ut altera medietas sylvarum Farleighe, iusticiario Fenner per indenturam dimitteretur.

Dispensatio cum regentibus pro secundo anno suae regentiae

Ibidem etiam eodemque tempore dispensatum est, per dominum custodem, et octo seniores, cum magistris regentibus, Simonson, Wake, Rogers, Garrarde, Gale, pro publicis suis praelectionibus, replicationibus et Augustinensibus sibi habendis perficiendisque, secundo anno suae regentiae.

Evictio causae contra Fitziames

Eisdem tempore et consensu, ordinatum est ut magister Brent, et Temple, balivus noster de Gamblingayes, Chardum oppidum in comitatu Somerseti, mitterentur ad prosequendam litem super quadam districtione, aliquod iumentorum, in fundis vocatis Knowles Parke existentium, contra magistrum Fitziames generosum coram

[1] These words follow a bracket linking the first two questions, and probably intended to include the third.

iudicibus sessitantibus in comitiis. Haec lis collegio est adiudicata eiusdemque facta est. Aestimatio 16 li. ii s. Postero die perlecta est in aula, sigillataque indentura de Pocrilstone, superiore anno concessa Henrico Irish iuniori.

Generalis acquietantia concessa domino Willughbye baroni

Iulii 16° ex consensu domini custodis et sociorum concessa ac perlecta est in aula, generalis quaedam acquietantia facta honorabili viro, Baroni Willughbye, de Eresbye, de omnibus et omnimodis debitis actionibus ac postulatis ab initio mundi usque ad praesentem illum diem, haec acquietantia communi sigillo est signata, cuius forma in registro videre licet, missa est postea Londini, ut sub ea conditione, dicto Baroni in manus traderetur, quatenus illico solveret collegio, 54 li. eosque paulo amplius.

Commemoratio habita est pro fundatore &c.

Vicesimo Iulii, qui erat festum beatae Margaretae, habita est, hora et loco solitis, commemoratio fundatoris, lecta sunt statuta, scrutinium celebratur, quod in primum Augusti, et quemlibet diem citra prorogatum.

Columbarium extruendum apud Thorncroft

Circa idem tempus, post consensum domini custodis, in literis suis ad socios scriptis significatum, concedimus veniam magistro Gardiner de Thorncroft, columbarium ibidem in usum suum domesticum de novo construendi.

p. 211 Anno Domini 1604, regni regis Iacobi 2°, Henrici Savile custodis vicesimo.

Nomina et numerus sociorum:

Magistri

1. Robertus Brizenden
2. Anthonius Antony
3. Samuel Slade
4. Christophorus Dale
5. Iohannes Tapsell
6. Thomas Allen
7. Leonardus Yate
8. Nathaniel Brent
9. Edwardus Lee
10. Iohannes Kinge
11. Theodorus Gulson
12. Iohannes Talbot
13. Thomas Horne
14. Stucleius Blickarde
15. Guilielmus Simonson
16. Isaacus Wake
17. Edwardus Rogers
18. Georgius Garrard
19. Guilielmus Gale

Bacchalaurei

1. Franciscus Greevil
2. Samuel Lane
3. Iohannes Elly
4. Iohannes Philipson

Primo die Augusti convenerunt omnes socii domi existentes quos vicecustos certiores fecit de literis a domino custode acceptis, quibus significavit se gravioribus negotiis detineri, quo minus hoc tempore adesse possit, ideoque sibi placere ut electio officiariorum in adventum suum differatur quocirca scrutinium prorogatum est in decimum diem huius mensis et quemlibet diem citra.

Magistri Chamberi donum M. librarum

Quinto die Augusti adfuit dominus custos et postridie convocatis sociis in conclave suum exposuit morae suae causam fuisse, studium procurandi collegii negotia et emolumentum quod satis clare constabat ex iis quae retulit nobis de testamento magistri Iohannis Chambers, quondam collegii nostri socii nuperrime defuncti, qui prae amore singulari quo religionem, bonas artes, collegium hoc complexus est moriens mille libras legavit collegio nostro ad eos usus et finem quod ipse praescripsit ut patet ex ea parte testamenti illius in hanc formulam quam dominus custos eodem tempore nobis tradidit.

Conditiones eius

For the farther suppression of wickednes and superstition I also give and bequeath to Merton Colledge in the university of Oxford one thousande pounds to be bestowed upon lands, tenements and hereditaments, within the County and Dioces of Yorke, yf conveniently they may be purchased ther, by the advise and direction of Sir Jhon Savile, knight, Baron of the Excheckuer and Sir Jhon Jackson, Knight, the king's Atturney at Yorke, to this end, intention, and purpose only, and to none other, that out of the yearely profitts of the lands and tenements so to be purchased and assured to the sayd Colledge by advise of learned counsayle, so many schollerships and fellowships may be erected and founded in the sayd Colledg as between mee or my executors of the one party and the sayd Colledg of the other shal be agreed uppon and thought resonable. The sayd schollerships to be supplied and filled out of the schollers of the schoole and foundation of Eaton only, by the nomination and Election of the Provost of the King's Colledg in Cambridge, and the Provost of the King's Colledg at Eaton. And the sayd fellowships to be filled and supplied of such schollers or Bachelours of Art only as formerly have been brought up in the sayd schoole and foundation of Eaton and departed thence uppon honest causes, by the nominacion and Election of the sayd Warden and schollers of Merton Colledge, accordinge to the statutes of that Honourable Foundacion and under such other articles, covenants, and conditions as by mee or my executor of th'on party, and the sayd Warden and schollers of th'other shal be agreed uppon. Haec perfecta schedula proposuit dominus custos placeretne nobis accipere has pecunias in hunc usum nobis datas hiis atque aliis conditionibus de quibus uberius acturi sunt executores magistri Chambers cum collegio qua in re singuli uno consensu demonstrarunt, quam grata esset tanta tam pii viri munificentia.

His ita transactis circa hora decima ante prandium monuit dominus custos ut omnes adessent hora tertia pomeridiana in alta aula quo tempore convenerunt custos et socii in altam aulam, ubi primo dispensatum est cum magistro Allen iam tum elect[o] socio collegii Eatonensis, ut liceret ei se transferre ab hac domo in collegium Eatonense deinde concessimus eidem magistro Allen communias in annum sequentem et usum cubiculi in tres menses et deinceps quam diu eius iustae occasiones postularent necessario.

Officiarii electi sexto die Augusti

Modo non excederet temporis spatium per quod in causis similibus caeteri hoc beneficio uti solent. Tandem vero ubi officiarii claves suas deposuissent et reliqui claves bibliothecae communis protulissent in medium secedentibus caeteris dominus custos et quinque simpliciter seniores designant officiarios hos in annum sequentem videlicet:
magistrum Dale, vicecustodem.
magistros Brent, Lee, Wake, decanos.
magistros Slade, Kinge, Garrard, bursarios.
magistrum Yate, principalem portionistarum.
magistrum Brizenden, bursarium Williott.
magistrum Gulson, capellanum capellae.
Exhibitionem Hamsterly dividunt inter magistrum Brizenden et magistrum Dale; dominus Lane per ipsum dominum custodem designatus est bacchalaureus Williot; claves communis bibliothecae tantum productae sunt, defuerunt vero [*damage*].

Eodem tempore prorogatum est scrutinium in decimum quintum diem Nov[embr]is.

Anno Domini 1604, regis Iacobi 2° Henrici Savile custodis vicesimo. p. 212

Augusti 7° computavit dominus custos, eodem tempore habiti sunt computus generales.

8° die Augusti custos et socii convenientes in conclave custodis decernunt communias sociorum singulis diebus Martis augendas ad summam denarii unius in singulis ferculis ex allocatione pecuniarum magistri Iacobi Leech quas ille in eum usum destinarat et quemadmodum e pecuniis Elae Comitissae singulis diebus iovis ad prandium habemus communias auctiores per denarium in singulis ferculis ita et diebus Martii haberemus easdem e pecuniis quas ille in sociorum communias contulit.

Eodem tempore dominus custos et socii consentiunt sexaginta libras provenientes e reditu Gamblingay Avenels singulis annis in posterum distribuendas inter custodem et socios in festo Sancti Iohannis Baptiste.

Rerum ea lege et socii omnes qui huius quasi novae liberaturae participes esse velint singulis annis post exactum biennium suae regentiae semel respondeant in disputationibus theologicis et semel opponant, de requisitarum [*damage*] disputationum forma et legibus plenius post hac multa (si Deus voluerit) statuemus.

Eodem tempore dispensatum est cum quatuor ex iis sex magistris qui hoc anno variare tenentur dummodo duo variantium munus praestent, reliqui quatuor in annum sequentem distulimus.

Eodem tempore consensum est per custodem et omnes socios domi existentes ut allocatio tritici et hordei ad mensam custodis quae tantum a generali computo in generalem computum durare solet, post hac rata sit nec necessario amplius singulis annis proponantur.[1]

Eodem tempore consensum est per custodem et omnes socios domi existentes ut rata communiarum sociorum permaneat eadem perpetuo in posterum quae iam est, nec proponatur post hac sicut ante solebat, et si quarterium tritici vilius fuerit viginti solidis. Consensum est ibidem per custodem et omnes socios ut caenae sociorum in quadragesima in posterum perpetuo ratae sint, nec post hac petatur consensus pro iisdem et praeterea per eosdem decretum est ut unus denarius adiiciatur ad singula illarum caenarum fercula, ut ita habeant singuli socii post hac duos denarios obolum ad singulas caenas quadragesimales.

[1] 'vide p. 132' in margin, referring to a minute of 1587 now printed in *Reg. Annalium 1567–1603*, 232.

Consensum est eodem tempore per eosdem ut tres solidi, quatuor denarii allocarentur custodi pro singulis caenis tempore quadragesimae et simul ad mensam suam habeat vicecustodem et capellanum.

Eodem tempore dominus custos et socii allocarunt viginti sex solidos octo denarios Iohanni Blackam qui sedulo subministrarat sociis domi manentibus tempore pestis. Eodem tempore placuit domino custodi ut praelectores grammaticae et linguae Graecae iidem manerent qui fuerant anno superiore quamdiu ipsi custodi videretur aequum.

14° Augusti, viz. die martis, habuerunt socii communias auctiores ex allocatione trium solidorum pecuniarum magistri Leech quos per singulas septimanas posthac voluit ille conferri ad augendum communias sociorum ad summam unius denarii in singulis ferculis.

16° Augusti, habitus est computus cistae Reade per custodes eiusdem et in statu pristino relinquitur.

17° Augusti, magister Brizenden tertius bursarius superioris anni computavit et discessit in pede computi 8 li. 18s. 5d.

Septembris quarto, convenientibus domino custode et sociis in conclave domini custodis visum est iis aequum, allocare solidos magistro French pro laboribus quos ille susceperat in quibusdam collegii negotiis.

Eodem tempore consenserunt dominus custos et socii ut per quatuor menses viz. Novembrem, Decembrem, Ianuarium et Februarium socii omnes in alta aula ad caenam et prandium haberent potum mixtum e sumptibus collegii, extra aulam vero solverent tres partes quadrantis pro singulis ly tunnes eiusdem, necnon ut vicecustos eodem uteretur emolumento, eodem tempore ex communi consensu domini custodis et sociorum. Reverendi quidam viri ad translationem prioris partis Novi Testamenti per regiam maiestatem designati, mutuo acceperunt e communi collegii nostri bibliotheca hos libros sequentes viz. [*none named*]

p. 213 Anno Domini 1604, regis Iacobi 2°, Henrici Savile custodis 20.

Disputationum theologicarum ratio singulis terminis huius anni observanda.

Septembris 5° convenientibus domino custode et sociis in conclave domini custodis censuerunt dominus custos et octo seniores hanc rationem ineundam esse pro theologicis disputationibus habendis in annum sequentem et singulis (hoc ipso tempore) assignarentur.

Quaestiones in quibus responderent et opponerent diebus destinatis uniuscuiusque termini viz.

Termino Michaelis[1]

ut[2] secundo die sabbati termini Michaelis responderet vicecustos, opponente magistro Slade, in hac quaestione: An pontifex cum concilio sit iudex scripturarum?

4° vero die sabbati eiusdem termini responderet magister Slade, opponente vicecustode, in hac quaestione: An sacra scriptura sit per se sufficiens ad decidendas fidei controversias absque autoritate ecclesiae.

6° vero die sabbati eiusdem termini ut responderet magister Yate, opponente magistro Brent, in hac quaestione: An omnis doctrina ad salutem necessaria contineatur in scripturis?

Termini vero Hilarii

Secundo die sabbati ut responderet magister Brent, opponente magistro Yate, in hac quaestione: An papa sit visibilis monarch ecclesiae.

4° autem die sabbati eiusdem termini, ut responderet magister Lee, opponente magistro Kinge: An sit penes pontificem Romanum convocare concilia generalia iisdemque praeesse?

6° die sabbati eiusdem termini responderet magister Kinge, opponente magistro Lee: An ecclesia possit errare?

Termini vero Paschae

2° die sabbati ut responderet magister Gulson, opponente magistro Horne in hac quaestione: An verae notae ecclesiae sint sincera verbi praedicatio, et administratio sacramentorum?

4° die eiusdem termini ut responderet magister Horne, opponente magistro Gulson: An ministri ecclesiae sint ad caelibem vitam obligandi.

Termini vero Sanctae Trinitatis

2° die sabbati responderet magister Blickarde in hac quaestione. An monachatus pontificius tribus votis obligatus sit cultus Deo acceptus. Cui magister Blickard quoniam pari destituebatur quem opponens tenebatur disputare[3] bis in aliorum disputationibus loco secundo, vel tertio. Magistro Brizenden hanc provinciam imposuerunt dominus

[1] This sub-heading is in margin, its successors in the body of the text.
[2] *Margin*, '2°'.
[3] 'replicare' deleted.

custos et seniores ut loco respondendi et opponendi, bis concionaretur in celebratione Eucharistiae, videlicet semel in festo Omnium Sanctorum et iterum in festo Nativitatis domini.

Et quo disputationes istae facilius procederent et studiose magis instituerentur statuerunt dominus custos et 8 seniores has conditiones observandas:

1^{am}. Disputationes durare debent ad unius tantum horae spatium,
2^{am}. Suppositiones esse quam brevissimas.
3^{am}. Opponenti non licere praefatione uti.
4^{am}. Seniorem magistrorum praesentium exacto horae spatio finem imponere disputationibus.
5^{am}. Neminem participem posse illarum sexaginta librarum quae inter disputantes dividendae sunt, etsi responderit et opposuerit, nisi per maiorem partem anni preaesentis in collegio commoratus fuerit. Praeterea statuerunt istas sexaginta libras in usum domini custodis et disputantium destinatas in festo Sancti Iohannis Baptistae distribui oportere quo tempore liberatura solet solvi.

Septembris 6°, convenimus in conclave domini custodis quo tempore propter nonnulla incommoda ingruentia per nonullos scholares et graduatos in collegio degentes absque speciali venia a domino custode prius impetrata, dominus custos mandavit ut omnes eiusmodi qui non sunt membra collegii ante festum Sancti Michaelis proxime sequens [*sic*] discederent e collegio.

Eodem tempore dimisimus hospitium vocatum ly Faulcon in Gamblingay Francisco Cockrel ad spatium 20 annorum.

Eodem tempore consensum est progressum suscipiendum per vicecustodem et bursarium ad maneria de Cuxam, Ibston et Gamblingay et curias ibidem tenendas etc.

Septembris 10, convenerunt omnes socii domi existentes in altam aulam ubi significavit vicecustos placere domino custodi ut vicecustos et bursarius reliqua maneria inviserent.

Septembris 20, convenientibus omnibus sociis domi existentibus (domini custodis consensu primo significato) decretum est literas atturnatus bursariis sigillandas esse. Ibidem magister Brizenden 3us bursarius anni superioris solvit 8 li. 18s. 5d. pro pede computi sui magistro Blickard loco Garrard, primi bursarii. Et sic discessit aeque.

Eodem die sigillatae sunt indenturae Iusticiario Fenner pro altera medietate sylvarum Farleigh, atque etiam indenturae Francisci Cockrel pro ly Faulcon in Gamblingay sigillatae sunt, ex consensu domini custodis et sociorum.

Eodem die vicecustos et magistri Yate et Brent iter susceperunt ad visitanda maneria.

Septembris vicesimo primo, dominus custos creatus quid [*blank*].

Octobris 12 computavit Robertus Mayne firmarius de Chedington et balivus ibidem.

Octobris 18 reversi sunt vicecustos et bursarius a progressu et significarunt in quo statu reperissent singula maneria.

Octobris 19, computavit Gulielmus Nevvil, firmarius de Barkby et balivus ibidem, et discessit aeque.

Octobris 20, viz. 2° die sabbati termini Michaelis respondit vicecustos, opponente magistro Slade in disputationibus theologicis.

Eodem die computavit Richard Wilmot, firmarius de Ibston et balivus ibidem.

Octobris 26, Doctor Barnes superior praelector Linacri moritur postquam eum locum tenuriae per 46 annos.

Novembris 3° habitae sunt disputationes theologicae,[1] respondente magistro Slade, opponente vicecustode.

Novembris 4, Doctor Dotchen electus est superior praelector Linacri per dominum custodem et octo seniores socios collegii.

Anno Domini 1604, regis Iacobi 2°, domini Henrici Savile custodis 20. p. 214

Novembris 9°, magister Theodorus Gulson electus est inferior praelector Linacri per dominum custodem et septem seniores.

Novembris 18° habitae sunt disputationes theologicae, respondente magistro Yate, opponente magistro Brent per dispensationem custodis et sociorum quia illae disputationes habendae fuissent postridie viz. 6° die sabbati termini Michaelis.

Eodem die profectus est magister Brent versus Londinum ad persequendum lites adversus oppidanos qui nuper violarunt libertates Collegii Holywell.

Novembris 19, dominus custos et quidam e senioribus audiverunt computum quorundam arreragiorum pro quibusdam partibus residuum

[1] *Margin*, 'Terminus Michaelis 2° die sabbati'.

rectoriarum de Emildon et Ponteland. Et computatis computandis tam collegio quam firmariis satisfactum est abunde et utraeque partes discesserunt aeque.

Eodem die computavit Edmundus Gregory firmarius de Cuxam.

Novembris 28, computavit Richardus Lane pro sylvis venditis apud Ibston.

Novembris 29, computavit Guilelmus Napper balivus pro tenementis Oxon', Holywell, Witney, London, a festo Sancti Michaelis in 43° regni Elizabethae usque ad idem festum in anno regis Iacobi 2° et sic per tres annos. Et clare debuit 56 li. xis.

Decembris 1°, sigillata est indentura Spranger pro Canes in Essex.

Eodem die sigillata est indentura Stanes pro Norton Mandevile in eodem comitatu.

Commemoratio

Decembris 18°, habita est commemoratio fundatoris eodemque die celebravimus scrutinium in quo magister Blickard proposuit quaedam adversus magistrum Gulson quoniam pleniorem examinationem distulit dominus custos in diem sequentem.

Decembris 20, computavit magister Garrard primus bursarius.

Decembris 21, convenientibus domino custode et 7 senioribus in aulam altam magister Blickard querelam suam exposuit viz. quod gravem percussionem passus esset in carnem propria[m] a magistro Gulson, magistro vero Gulson pernegante se gravem aliquam percussionem intulisse magistro Blickarde sed latente iurgium inter eos ex improviso exortum quoniam nec magister Blickarde testem aliquem oculatum protulit nec ullo modo constabat domino custodi et senioribus gravem aliquam percussionem factam fuisse. Censuerunt dominus custos et seniores hanc qualem insolentiam hoc modo castigandam, viz. ut magister Gulson privaretur communiis et reliquis collegii allocationibus ad sex septimanas.

Mulctatur Gulson

Ipse vero dominus custos praeteraea dedit magistro Gulson primam monitionem secundum statuta fundatoris in causis similibus edita ut ita postea se intra modestiae et concordiae limites contineret. Insuper iniunxit eidem dominus custos ut durante sex septimanarum extra academiam non proficisceretur nisi venia prius impetrata ab ipso domino custode. Et quum urgentibus suis gravioribus negotiis, magister Gulson saepius petiisset a domino custodi ut liceret et Londinum proficisci, repulsam passus est.

Decembris ultimo (qui erat vigilia circumcisionis) de more habitum est scrutinium in quo magister Kinge designatur hortulanus, numerus portionistarum solitus confirmatur. Et ad mores servientium reformandos detentae sunt claves coquorum quod placitum domini custodis.

[1605]

Ianuarii 7°, sigillata est indentura Thomson pro Hampton Powell.

Ianuarii 9°, sigillata est indentura Lane pro molendino de Ibston.

19 Ianuarii, sigillata est indentura doctoris Atkins pro Callowlande sigillata est ex consensu domini custodis et sociorum.[1]

12° Ianuarii computavit Gulielmus Savile, firmarius de Kibworth et balivus ibidem pro tribus annis.

Eodem tempore allocantur 40s. Ambrosio Sanders per dominum custodem et socios pro laboribus quos impenderat ille saepius in negotiis collegii procurandis.

Eodem tempore dominus custos assidentibus sibi decanis et bursariis inivit rationes redigendi reditus firmariorum omnium et maneriorum in certiorem formam et magis expeditam.

Eodem tempore Ambrosius Sanders constitutus est balivus sylvarum apud Ibston per dominum custodem et socios.

21° Ianuarii profectus est vicecustos versus Londinum ad prosequendum litem contra oppidanos circa libertates manerii nostri de Holywell.

Ianuarii 26°, disputationes theologicae habitae sunt,[2] respondente magistro Brent, opponente magistro Yate.

Ianuarii 29, Doctor Dotchyn superioris lecturae Linacri praelector moritur.

Februarii 13, in hospitium domini custodis convenerunt ex mandato regio dominus Henricus Savile custos collegii nostri, D. Abbots, decanus Winton', D. Tompson, decanus Windsor, aliique gravissimi viri ad translationem prioris partis novi testamenti.

[1] 'custodis et sociorum' deleted, probably in error, to accommodate next entry.
[2] *Margin*, '2° die sabbati termini Hilarii'.

Febuarii 9. In theologicis disputationibus[1] respondit magister Lee, opponente magistro Kinge.

Februarii [*blank*] Doctor Bust electus est in superiorem praelectorem Linacri per custodem et seniores.

Februarii 23°, respondit magister Kinge, opponente magistro Lee, in theologicis disputationibus.[2]

Martii 23°, habita est commemoratio fundatoris et scrutinium celebratum in quo lotrici allocantur. Prorogatum est scrutinium in [*blank*].

Translatio, nova Biblia

Februarii 13. Libri collegii (quos mutuo acceperent e communi bibliotheca collegii reverendi decani Winton', Windsor et Wigorniensis), reducuntur ad hospitium domini custodis ubi ipse dominus custos et D. Abbots, decanus Wintoniensis, doctor Tomson, decanus Windsor', doctor Harmar, custos collegii Wintoniensis, D. Eaglionbee, D. Perin et D. Hatton saepius multum operae posuerunt in translatione prioris partis novi testamenti ab ipsa regia maiestate ad hoc egregium opus designati.

p. 215 Anno Domini 1605, regis Iacobi 3°, domini Henrici Savile 21.

Aprilis 12°, vicecustos et magister Yate profecti sunt versus Kibworth et Barkby ad tenendum curias in ambobus illis maneriis, ex assignatione domini custodis et sociorum.

Aprilis 18°, computavit magister Kinge 2^{dus} bursarius.

Aprilis 20°, viz. die sabbati 2° termini Paschae magister Gulson lapso ab equo adesse non potuit ut munus respondentis vice sua sustineret.

Maii 4°, viz. die sabbati quarto termini Paschae respondit magister Horne in disputationibus theologicis, magistro Gulson opponente.

Eodem die convenientibus domino custode et sociis consensuerunt omnes plenam potestatem dandam domino custodi ad persequendum lites cum oppidanis circa molendinum de Holywell. Et ut ipse dominus custos vel componeret vel persequeretur lites in causa libertatum manerii de Holywell.

Maii 9°, de novo sigillatae sunt indenturae Spranger et Stanes pro Canes et Norton Mandevill.

[1] *Margin*, '4° die sabbati termini Hilarii'.
[2] *Margin*, '6° die sabbati termini Hilarii'.

Maii 12°, magistro Slade concessa est praesentatio ad vicariam Emildon eademque sigillata est postridie.

Maii 17°, variavit magister Horne in his quaestionibus:

An
1. Recte, Hippodamus statuerit honore afficiendos esse legum novarum inventores? E lib. 2° Polit., cap. 6°.
2. Materia 1ª, Aristotelica alicuius generationis sit subiecta? De Generatione, lib. 1, 3° cap.
3. Recte Lycurgus magistratu dignos eundem petere iusserit? Lib. 2, Pol. cap. 7°.

18 Maii, cum eodem dispensatum est per 8 seniores pro secundis variationibus.

Oppidani

Iunii 5°, consensuerunt omnes socii e re collegii futurum si dominus custos proficisceretur ad villam Sancti Albani in comitatu Hartford ad inspiciendum quasdam terras collegii per quorundam fraudem vocatas in controversiam, atque etiam ut Londinum iter faceret ad promovendum causam collegii contra oppidanos quocirca ut iterumque faceret petierunt ab eo per literas vicecustodis ad eum datas.

Iunii 8°, magister Blickard respondit in theologicis disputationibus,[1] magistro Gulson opponente, eodem die permissum est magistro Gulson ut responderet etsi extra ordinem praescriptam. Eodem die consensu omnium sociorum domi existentium transmisimus quendam librum pergamentarium continentem exemplaria diversarum evidentiarum collegii ad dominum custodem quem ab eo recepimus Iunii 28°.

Iunii 23° respondit magister Gulson in theologicis disputationibus, opponente magistro Horne.

Iunii 26° variavit magister Rogers in his quaestionibus:

An
1. Virtutes insint nobis a natura? Affirmat. E lib. 2 Ethic. cap. 1°.
2. Aliquid fiat a fortuna? Negat. E 2 Physicorum cap. 7°.
3. In recte instituta reipublica vitae feminis sint leges ponendae? Negat.

Postridie cum eodem dispensatum est pro secundis variationibus.

Iunii 28° quoniam certiores nos fecit magister Slade vicariam de Emildon litigiosam esse, nec sibi animum esse persequi litem propriis impensis ideoqe se libenter cedere eo iure quod collegium ei

[1] *Margin*, '2° die sabbati termini Trinitatis'.

concesserat, placuit domino custodi et sociis omnibus ad ipsum per literas significant[es] domi existentibus praesentare magistrum Antonium Walker ad eandem vicariam ea conditione ut is remitteret et resignaret quemcunque alium titulum per quem in praedicta vicaria tanquam in lapsu existente ius aliquod prius praetendisset atque ita sigillata est praesentatio magistri Walker.

Iulii 13°, computavit Sherwoode firmarius de Cantabrigia.

Iulii 13°, dominus custos presens in vestiario significavit se nullo modo adesse posse ad primum diem Augusti quo saepius solent officiarii in annum sequentem eligi, ideoque proposuit ut magister Horne a die veneris proximo ante primum Augusti exequeretur officium bursarii usque ad adventum suum, huius subrogatio placuit omnibus senioribus.

2, eodem tempore placuit domino custodi et sociis omnibus domi existentibus impendere quinque literas ad restaurandum monumentum fundatoris in ecclesia cathedrali Roffensi.

3, tum etiam haec gratia facta est viduae doctoris Ellis ut a festo Michaelis proxime sequenti usque ad festum Annuntiationis proxime sequens uteretur domo collegii in Salisbury Ally London[1] absque solutione alicuius reditus pro illorum sex mensium spatio ut ad festum Annuntiationis prorsus discederet. Et interim permittat domino custodi et sociis usum quorundam cubiculorum prout eorum occasiones postularent.

4, consensum est quoque aliquas impensas faciendas ad reparandum collegium in adventu regis ad academiam.

5, itemque visum est domino custodi et sociis allocare aliquas pecunias magistro Napper qui in causa molendinorum Holywell solet magnam pecuniae summam expendere in litibus prosequendis.

Molendini causa

Iulii 15° causa molendinarii de Holywell tractata est coram iusticiario Yelverton in magnis sessionibus pro comitatu Oxoniensi adversus oppidanos. Et de tritico [*sic*] vi a molendinario nostro de Holywell erepto per officiarios oppidanorum per duodecim viros iuratos damnati sunt oppidani.[2]

[1] Given to the college by will of Warden Sever (d. 1471).
[2] *Margin,* 'sed illud factum iam negantes'.

Anno Domini 1605, regni regis Iacobi 3°, domini Henrici Savile custodis 21. p. 216

Vicesimo die Iulii (qui erat festum beatae Margaretae) habita est commemoratio fundatoris. Et lectis statutis celebravimus scrutinium in quo admoniti sunt omnes qui habent aliquem librum collegii in sua privata custodia virtute iuramenti collegio praestiti proferrent omnes et singulos huiusmodi libros ante proximam electionem officiariorum. Eodem tempore admoniti etiam omnes sunt maiore post hac uti cura in claudendis libris existentibus in communi bibliotheca collegii.

Quaedam proposita sunt contra portionistas viz. quod exciderant arborem in sylvula collegii sine venia impetrata, quorum hac in causa examinatio et castigatio principali commissa est.

Atque etiam quaedam obiecta sunt contra coquum inferiorem quod negligens esset et in conservandis et in aliis officii sui partibus praestandis huius reformationem ab officiariis[1] omnes efflagitabant.

Tonsoris quoque negligentiam taxarunt quidam e magistris.

Regis Oxoniam Adventus

Eodem tempore consenserunt omnes collegium nostrum ad excipiendam Regiam Maiestatem publice ab Academia exhibere (quod reliqua collegia fecerant) iuxta proportionem antiqui annui reditus pro quolibet centenario librarum triginta solidos. Census collegii nostri iam delatus ad vicecancellarium erat 400 li. iuxta quam summam bursarius collegii liberavit domino vicecancellario sex libras. His tandem peractis prorogatum est scrutinium usque in primum diem Novembris et quemlibet diem citra.

24°, convocatis omnibus sociis domi commorantibus perlectae sunt quaedam leges et cautiones quas dominus vicecancellarius voluit a singulis Academicis observari (sub poena satis gravi infligenda) quamdiu regia maiestas moram faciet in Academia.

[*rest of p. 216 blank*]

[1] 'demandata est' deleted.

p. 217 Anno Domini 1605, regni regis Iacobi 3°, domini Henrici Savile custodis 21.

Augustus

Magistri in artibus

1. Robertus Brizendine
2. Antonius Antonie
3. Samuel Slade
4. Christophorus Dale
5. Iohannes Tapsel
6. Leonardus Yate
7. Nathanael Brent
8. Edovardus Lee
9. Iohannes King
10. Theodorus Gulson
11. Iohannes Talbot
12. Thomas Horne
13. Stucleius Blickard
14. Gulielmus[1] Simonson
15. Isaacus Wake
16. Edovardus Rogers
17. Georgius Garrard
18. Gulielmus Gale

Baccalaurei in artibus

1. Franciscus Grevil
2. Samuel Lane
3. Iohannes Elly
4. Iohannes Philipson

Officiarii anni praesentis

magister Brent, vicecustos.
magister Yate, magister Gulson, magister Blickard, decani.
magister Slade, magister Horne, magister Simonson, bursarii.
magister Brizendine, primarius portionistarum.
magister Dale, bursarius Williott; exhibitiones capellani capellae et Hamsterly assignatae sunt magistro Yate; praelector Graecae linguae, magister Wake; rhetoricae, magister Rogers, logicae dominus Lane.

Decretum de pistrionibus et braseatoribus

Augusti 23° decretum est per custodem et socios ne liceat ulli officiariorum pistorem admittere vel braseatorem nisi qui frumentum moleret apud nostra molendina quibus oppidani iniuriam conantur.

Regis adventus

Augusti 27mo Oxonium venit potentissimus rex noster Iacobus comitante serenissima regina, filio Walliae principe caetuque heroum spectabili. Quem quibus ceremoniis excepit academia si qui quaerat liber elaboratissimus declarabit quem brevi existurum speravimus. Fecerunt collegia duas contributiones, singulis contribuerunt 30s. pro quolibet centenario reditus antiqui.

[1] partly deleted.

Electio
Septembris 2do electi sunt Iohannes Hales et Iohannes Morly. Decretumque ut admittantur in annum probationis in initio termini proxime sequentis.

Eodem tempore consenserunt custos et socii ut ostenderentur magistro Good terraria et rotuli curiarum et alia quecumque munimenta quibus facilius terras de Maldon a falsis quorundam titulis et vendicationibus seu clameis vindicaret.

Computus Temple
September 3° computavit Franciscus Temple balivus de Gamelingay Avenels.

Anno Domini 1605, regni regis Iacobi 3°, domini Henrici Savil custodis 21. p. 218

Balivatus Savil et Ray
Septembris 7mo sigillatae sunt literae attornalitiae Willelmo Savil et Richardo Ray ad recipiendos reditus manerii de Kibworth.

Admissio probationistorum
Octobris 9° Iohannes Hales et Iohannes Morly admissi sunt in annum probationis.

Literae procuratoriae bursariorum
Eodem die sigillatae sunt literae procuratoriae bursariis ad recipiendos omnes proventus et reditus collegii tam ordinarios quam extraordinarios.

Indentura Salesbury Ally
Octobris 12mo sigillata est indentura magistro Trafford ad experiendum in iure cum vidua Ellis pro domo in Salisbury ally, London, et literae attornalitiae magistro Master ad deliberandam possessionem.

Eodem die magister Slade solvit pedem sui computi et discessit aeque.

Augusti ultimo (ut rem repet[it]am per oblivionem praetermissam) decretum est per custodem et socios ut disputationes eodem modo habeantur quo anno precedenti. Quaestiones autem haec fuerunt:[1]

Subwarden 1. An clerici sint exempti a iudicio secularis potestatis?
Slade 2. An lex civilis non minus obliget in conscientia quam lex Dei?
Dale 3. An liceat magistratui civili iudicare in causa religionis?

[1] 'An lex civilis non minus obliget in' deleted.

Yate 4. An sit purgatorium pontificium? Et an indulgentiae prosint defunctis?

Lee 5. An sancti sint religioso cultu adorandi?

King 6. An imagines dei, sanctorum et angelorum colendae sint cultu religioso?

Gulson 7. An sacramenta ex opere operato conferant gratiam?

Horne 8. An sint duo tantum sacramenta?

Blickard 9. An baptismus praecise et simpliciter sit necessarius ad salutem?

Simonson 10. Corpus et[1] sanguis domini corporaliter sint in cena domini?

Wake 11. An missa sit sacrificium propitiatorium pro vivis et defunctis?

Rogers 12. An auricularis confessio sit ex iure divino?

Gale 13. An remisa culpa maneat reatus operibus quibusdam redimendus?

Computus custodis

Eodem die computavit dominus custos et computatis computandis et allocatis allocandis discessit aeque.

Decretum de biberiis et stipendio equisonis

Eodem tempore decretum est ut equiso haberet singulis septimanis quatuor denarios in promptuario pro biberiis. Et ut stipendium eius annuatim sit 40s.

Decretum de biberiis ianitoris

Atque ut ianitoris biberiis singulis septimanis 2d. qua adderetur.

Dimissio tenementi in Sancto Albano

Novembris 2° sigillata est indentura tenementi in Sancto Albano Iohanni Clarke et literae attornalitiae Francisco Temple ad deliberandum possessionem. Et quoniam iure certandum erat de hoc tenemento decretum est ut impensae litis a collegio solverentur.

Tollitur lis de tenemento in Sancto Albano

Novembris 4° Londinum profectus est vicecustos in negotiis collegii, ubi omnem illam de tenemento in Sancto Albano controversiam sine sumptu sedavit et sustulit, ea conditione ut Iohannes Iennings equus auratus illud tenementum occuparet per nostram indenturam Iohanne
p. 219 Clerk libentissime / consentiente.

[1] 'et' repeated.

Finis impositus litibus cum Fitziames

Finem etiam imposuit litibus cum Iohanne Fitziames de Redlinch armigero, adduxitque secum in gazophylacium reposuit cum evidentiis pro quieto reditu de Knowle Park duo ly writs super duobus iudiciis, quibus ius nostrum in illo reditu maxime roboratur, viaque munitur ad arreragias (si quae forte futurae sint) sumptis perexiguis recuperandas.

Nova dimissio tenementi in Sancto Albano

Decembris 9° consentientibus domino custode et sociis sigillata est indentura tenementi in Sancto Albano Iohanni Iennings equiti aurato.

Commemoratio

Decembris 18° habita est commemoratio pro fundatore lectisque statutis celebratum est scrutinium.

Computus Simonson

Eodem die et sequenti computavit magister Simonson primus bursarius de administratione sua, et discessit in aere collegii 17 li. 13s. 8d. quam summam paulo post solvit sequenti bursario et sic aeque.

Scrutinium servientium. Punitur coquus inferiorus

Ultimo Decembris post cenam celebravimus de more scrutinium. In quo electus in hortulanum magister Gulson, decretum [est] ut numerus portionistarum sit solitus, ut deque moribus servientium videant officiarii, excepto quod[1] coquus inferior multatus est amissione stipendii huius quarterii ob contumaciam et alia graviora et privatus omni emolumento domus, donec officarius in iis quae obiicerentur aliquo modo satisfaceret.

Eodem tempore decretum est ut penula sumptibus collegii emeretur equisoni.

Novus Servus

Et ut quendam Gollidg fabrum lignarum servum collegii admitteremus, et annuum ei stipendium daremus 13s. 4d., consentiente postea domino custode. Cui rei causam dedit nova incorporatio quorundam manuariorum vix ferenda.

[1] 'iunior' deleted.

[1606]

Consensus de communario

Ianuario 19mo convenimus in vestiario post preces vespertinas, ibi decretum ut nepos domini Iohannis Fortescue equitis aurati et regi a consiliis sit communiarius inter socios, ut antea dominus Franciscus Wolley.

Pecuniae Chambers

Eodem tempore decretum est ut cista ferrea induceretur in thesaurarium et nominaretur parva cista iocalium, et servaret pecunias Chambers quas dedit collegio ac ut sufficeret executoribus Chambers si pecunias illas solverent Londoni, et non tenerentur ad collegia [*sic*] perferre.

Lis cum magistro Machil

Eodem etiam tempore decretum est ut si custodi videretur iure certaremus cum magistro Machil qui visum franci plegii vendicat apud Gamelingay, et nostris ibi tenentibus molestiam afferet.

Libertates Holiw'

Martii, obtinuimus causam contra oppidanos pro libertatibus in Holiwel coram domino Davide Williams iusticiario assisae.

Commemoratio

Aprilis 13mo habuimus commemorationem pro fundatore et benefactoribus nostris. Die sequenti lecta sunt statuta, et scrutinium celebratum quod prorogavimus in 10^{mum} diem Maii.

Computus 2^{di} bursarii

Aprilis 17mo computavit magister Horne secundus bursarius de administratione sua. Et discessit in aere collegii 28 li. 9s. 10d. quam summam paulo post solvit sequenti bursario et sic aeque.

Maii 28vo magister Napper firmarius de Holiwel computavit in scaccario pro duobus annis. Et idem balivus de Holiwel computavit pro uno anno.

p. 220 *Variationes*

Iunii 6to magister Wake variavit in his quaestionibus:

An {
Aristotelis obscuritas in disciplina physica tradenda est vituperanda.
Caelum non agit in inferiora motu vel lumine sed tantum influentia.
Vir non est perfectior faemina.
}

Die sequenti dispensavimus pro secundis eius variationibus.

Variationes

Iulii 4° variavit magister Simonson in his quaestionibus:

An { Faelicitas Aristotelis nulla.
Cor non est principium aut primo sensitivum.
Nobilitas non est maiorum dignitas.

Die sequenti dispensavimus pro secundis eius variationibus.

Computus

Iulii 7mo computavit Iohannes Sherwood firmarius de Cambridg.

Computus

Iulii 10mo computavit Henricus Atkins doctor in medicina firmarius de Callowland.

Computus

Iulii ultimo computavit Stephanus Heath firmarius de Farleigh.

[*rest of p. 220 blank*]

Anno Domini 1606, regni regis Iacobi 4to, domini Henrici Savil custodis 22°. p. 221

Augustus

Magistri in artibus

1. Robertus Brizendine
2. Antonius Anthonie
3. Samuel Slade
4. Iohannes Tapsel
5. Leonardus Yate
6. Nathanael Brent
7. Edovardus Lee
8. Theodorus Gulson
9. Iohannes Talbot
10. Thomas Horne
11. Stucleius Blickard
12. Gulielmus Simonson
13. Isaacus Wake
14. Edoardus Rogers
15. Georgius Garrard

Baccalaurei in artibus[1]

1. Franciscus Grevil
2. Samuel Lane
3. Iohannes Elly
4. Iohannes Philipson

In anno probationis

1. Iohannes Hales
2. Iohannes Morly

[1] This group is also marked 'socii'.

Officiarii anni praesentis
magister Brent, vicecustos.
magister Horne, magister Simonson, magister Rogers, decani.
magister Lee, magister Blickard, magister Wake, bursarii.
magister Gulson primarius portionistarum; magister Brizendine, bursarius Williot; exhibitio Hamsterly assignatur magistro Yate. Exhibitio capellani capellae dividitur inter magistrum Brizendine et magistrum Yate. Praelector Graecae linguae, magister Wake; rhetoricae, magister Simonson; logices dominus Hales.

Augusti 5to per dominum custodem et socios decretum est ut disputationes theologicae eo modo haberentur hoc anno sequenti quo aliquot retro annis habitae fuerunt. Electae sunt hae questiones:

Vicecustos. Yate.	An sit aliquod peccatum ex sua natura veniale? An concupiscentia iuvenalis sit proprie peccatum?
Lee Gulson.	An sufficiens gratia ad salutem aliquando et ad evitandum peccatum semper adsit omnibus hominibus? An post naturae corruptionem sit ulla vis liberi arbitrii ad opera pietatis?
Horne. Blickard.	An fides iustificans sit fiducia in speciali dei misericordia? An fides sola iustificet?
Simonson. Wake.	An electi certitudine fidei possent esse certi de sua salute? An renati possint perfecte implere legem die?
Rogers.	An bona opera renatorum sint meritoria vitae eternae?

p. 222 Anno Domini 1606, regni Iacobi 4°, domini Henrici Savil, custodis 22do.

Balivi constituti
Augusti septimo literae attornatitiae concessae sunt balivis diversorum maneriorum, videlicet Iohanni Sherwood de Cambridg; Abrahamo Iacob, et Ambrosio Saunders de Gamelingay; et Henrico Saer de Barkby.

Progressus
Eodem tempore consenserunt custos et socii de progressu et ut quinque librae darentur pro feodo magistro Denham, senescallo in eodem progressu.

Admissio servientium

Eodem etiam tempore Gulielmus Punyarde admissus est in locum senioris coqui, et [*blank*] Winder in locum ianitoris.

Decretum de electione facienda

Augusti nono convenerunt dominus custos et socii in conclavi custodis et decreverunt electionem sociorum faciendam.

Indentura renovata

Eodem tempore dimiserunt Matthaeo Udal domum suam in Holiwel pro termino viginti unius annorum.

Computus custodis

Eodem etiam tempore dominus custos computavit et discessit in plussagio.

Renovatio indenturae

Augusti 12mo dominus custos et socii dimiserunt viduae Turly tenementum suum in Holywel pro termino 21 annorum.

Allocatio pecuniarum facta magistro Slade

Eodem etiam tempore consenserunt ut quindecim librae annuatim pro tribus annis darentur magistro Slade peregre profecturo.

Electio

Augusti 13mo elegimus in socios futuros Timotheum Hawkesworth, Georgium Pettie, Danielem Iames, Thomam Allen in artibus bacalaureos. Decrevimusque ut admitterentur circa festum Omnium Sanctorum proximum. Insuper statuimus ut dominus Haukesworth et dominus Allen solverent in usum bibliothecae singuli 20s., dominus Petti et dominus Iames 3 li. 6s. 8d. singuli.

Admissio

Octobris 12mo convenientibus sociis in alta aula dominus Hales et dominus Morly admissi sunt in perpetuam societatem huius domus.

Whitlocke senescallus

Eodem tempore consenserunt socii ut magister Whitlock esset senescallus manerii nostri de Holiwel per literas nostras patentes durante bene placito, et feodum haberet annuatim 20s.

Consensus de litibus persequendis

Eodem etiam tempore consenserunt ut in iure prosequeremur liberos quosdam tenentes manerii nostri de Thracies et Thrognols qui reditus suos cum arreragiis solvere recusarent. His omnibus dominus custos antea consensum profuerat.

Admissio

Novembris 6to dominus Hawkesworth, dominus Pettie, dominus Allen, dominus Iames admissi sunt in annum probationis.

Computus firmariorum

Novembris 4to Henricus Saer firmarius de Barkby computavit in scaccario et discessit aeque.

Novembris 19mo habuimus in scaccario computum generalem.

Novembris 25to Richardus Wilmot de Ibston firmarius computavit in scaccario, et discessit aeque.

Novembris 28vo Edmundus Gregorie firmarius de Cuxam computavit in scaccario, et discessit aeque.

Commemoratio

Decembris decimo octavo[1] habuimus commemorationem pro fundatore, celebravimus scrutinium idque prorogavimus in primum diem Ianuarii et quemlibet diem citra.

p. 223 Anno Domini 1606, regni regis Iacobi 4to, domini Henrici Savil custodis 22do.

Scrutinium

Decembris ultimo celebravimus scrutinium pro servientibus in quo elegimus magistrum Talbot in hortulanum.

[1607]

Commemoratio

Martii 29° habuimus commemorationem pro fundatore, et sequenti celebravimus scrutinium, idque protulimus in primum diem Maii.

Querela

Aprilis 2do magister Blickard querelam detulit publicam contra dominum Philipson (cui tempus tum primum venerat ut cooptaretur in numerum magistrorum) quod inter bacalaureos eum appellare soleret suem, seu porcum, Anglice Hog et Pig. Custos eum multavit amissione communiarum pro uno mense, et decrevit ne ascenderet ad gradum magisterii durante beneplacito suo.

[1] 'vicesimo primo' deleted.

Nisi Prius

Circa hoc tempus scilicet ad assisas in Oxon' ventilata est inter nos et opidanos quaedam iuris actio vocata Nisi Prius. Caput et summa erat controversiae: an omnes qui infra praecinctus civitatis Oxon' habitarent, sive essent privilegiatae personae, sive non, tenerentur grana sua ferre ad molendinum opidanorum subtus castrum Oxon'. Re audita 12 iuratores pro nobis pronunciarunt, scilicet non teneri: et sic veredictum (ut appelunt) retulerunt. Opidani, qui animum obstinarant in hac re, quosdam qui grana sua portarant ad nostra molendina, citarunt ad comparendum coram baronibus de scaccario in hospitio vocato Serieants Inne. Socii igitur de consensu domini custodis decreverunt ut vicecustos Londinum proficisceretur ad has lites prosequendas termino sequenti, scilicet Paschatis. Causa audita non est, quod summus Angliae thesaurarius, honoratissimus noster cancellarius (a quo academia obtinuerat scriptis ad eum literis et per oratorem suum publicum missis ut videret ne quid ipsa detrimenti caperet, re scilicet ad personas privilegiatas pertinente) nec adesse posset die statuto. Nec alium certum praestituere prae negotiorum quibus distinebatur multitudine. Causa igitur adhuc pendet. Obtinuimus tamen iudicium super veredictum praenominatum in curia regia vocata the King's Bench et 13 li. 6s. 6d.[1] pro expensis in iure prout in exemplari sub sigillo plenius continetur.

Obsonator

Aprilis 4to Iohannes Olive admissus est in locum obsonatoris.

Eodem tempore firma de Barkby dimissa est Henrico Saer pro termino viginti unius annorum, a festo Michaelis proxime praeterito. Cum additamento copiae cuiusdam continentis tres quartos virgae antea in possessione cuiusdam Allot.

Renovatio indenturae

Eodem tempore renovata est indentura magistri Faunt pro molendinis Grancester, et tres anni ei gratis concessi sunt.

Computus

Aprilis 8vo computarunt magister Savil et magister Ray firmarii de Kibworth pro duobus annis. Et computatis computandis et solutis solvendis discesserunt aeque.

Aprilis 9° magister Blickard secundus bursarius computavit et discessit in aere collegii 39 li. 11s. 7d. ob. qua. Quam summam solvit Iunii nono magistro Lee tertio bursario, et sic aeque.

[1] The shape of the '6' shows that '8' was intended.

Dispensatio

Eodem tempore dispensatum est cum magistro Garrard pro variationibus suis donec maneat et communias capiat in collegio per spatium unius mensis continue.

p. 224 Anno Domini 1607.

Imparcatio

Eodem tempore decretum est ut magister Wake Londinum proficisceretur et assisteret domino custodi in negotiis collegii pertinentibus ad imparcationem quarundem terrarum in manerio de Maldon. Quae res quomodo sit transacta apparet in actis ultimae sessionis parliamenti.

Renovatio indenturarum

Iunii 28vo tenementum quoddam in Ibston dimissum est Edoardo Hal pro termino 21us annorum. Et Thomae Hawkins indentura domus suae in Holiwel renovata est pro eodem termino.

Allocatio facta magistro Simonson

Eodem tempore allocatae sunt magistro Simonson p[er]egre profecturo 10 li. annuatim pro tribus annis.

Computus firmariorum

Iulii nono H. Atkins doctor in medicina firmarius de Watford computavit in scaccario, et discessit aeque.

Iulii 16to Iohannes Sherwood firmarius de Cambridg computavit in scaccario, et discessit aeque.

Iulii 28vo Stephanus Heath firmarius de Farleigh computavit in scaccario et discessit aeque.

[*rest of p. 224 blank*]

p. 225 Anno Domini 1607, regni regis Iacobi 5to, domini Henrici Savil custodis 23.

Augustus

Magistri in artibus[1]

1. Robertus Brizendine
2. Antonius Antonie
3. Samuel Slade
4. Iohannes Tapsel
5. Leonardus Yate
6. Nathanael Brent
7. Edovardus Lee
8. Theodorus Gulson
9. Iohannes Talbot
10. Thomas Horne

[1] Also marked 'socii'.

11. Stuckleius Blickard
12. Gulielmus Simonson
13. Isaacus Wake
14. Edoardus Rogers
15. Georgius Garrard
16. Franciscus Grevil
17. Samuel Lane
18. Iohannes Elly
19. Iohannes Philipson

Baccalaurei

1. Iohannes Hales
2. Iohannes Morly

In anno probationis

2. Timotheus Hauksworth[1]
1. Georgius Pettie
3. Thomas Allen
4. Daniel Iames

Capellani

1. Robertus Beesly
2. [*blank*] Warberton

Augusti quarto electi sunt officiarii hi videlicet:
magister Brent, vicecustos.
magister Lee, magister Wake, magister Lane, decani.
magister Talbot, magister Rogers, magister Grevil, bursarii.
principalis portionistarum, magister Brizendine; bursarius Williot et exhibitionarius Hamsterly, magister Yate; capellanus capellae, magister Horne; praelector grammaticae, magister Elly; praelector Graecae linguae, dominus Hales; praelector logicae, dominus Morly.

Exhibitionarius doctoris Bickly

Eodem tempore magister Horne electus est exhibitionarius doctoris Bickly, decretum ut haberet stipendium pro hac exhibitione 4 li. annuatim quamdiu esset socius ut nominatio huius exhibitionarii semper pertineret ad dominum custodem atque ut praeter concionem publicam habendam in universitate semel ad minimum concionaretur, intra privatos parietes in cena domini capienda.

Gamlingay Avenells Roberto Dickman

Augusti quinto dominus custos et socii unanimi consensu dimiserunt Roberto Dickman manerium de Gamelingay Avenells pro termino viginti unius annorum.

Tenementum in Turvil Edovardo Hal

Eodem tempore dimiserunt tenementum in Turvil Edoardo Hale pro termino viginti unius annorum.

[1] 'Pettie' deleted. Numbers shown as in MS.

Tenementum in Haliwel Thomae Hawkins

Eodem etiam tempore dimiserunt tenementum in Haliwel Thomae Hawkins pro termino etiam 21 annorum.

Electio sociorum

Eodem etiam die deliberarunt custos et socii an numerus sociorum auguri posset necne. Decreverunt habendam esse electionem. Electi autem sunt die octavo huius mensis in socios futuros dominus Turner, dominus Marshe, dominus Dickinson. Admissio in annum probationis dilata est in id tempus quo qui tum erant probationistae admittendi sunt in socios. Decretumque ut solverent bibliothecae singuli 3 li. 6s. 8d.

Computus custodis

Augusti sexto dominus custos computavit. Et computatis computandis et allocatis allocandis discessit in plussagio 9 li. 3s. 10d.

Augusti septimo habitus est computus Read.

p. 226 Anno Domini 1607, regni regis Iacobi 5to, domini Henrici Savil custodis 23.

Domus Noble magistro Man

Augusti 8vo domus in parochia sancti Martini olim vocata domus Nobel unanimi consensus custodis et sociorum dimissa est per indenturam magistro Man. Eodem die concessum est magistro Gardiner de Thornecroft ut mutaret vitam in indentura sua nempe uxorem pro fratre reponeret.

Decretum pro pentionariis

Augusti decimo factum est decretum per dominum custodem et socios de recipiendis in domum communariis sive pentionariis numero duodecim, filiis equitum auratorum vel generosorum magni nominis. Decretum est ut singuli statim post primum adventum darent collegio poculum argenteum quod pondere aequaret decem uncias ad minimum. Eorum regimen commissum est principali portionistarum.

Magister Poultney submersus

Augusti 21mo submersus est in aquis iuxta prata nostra de Haliwel Gabriel Poultney ex aula Albana in artibus magister. Magister Isaac Bartholomeus coronarius pro civitate Oxon' quaestionem de more habuit de eius morte. Nos autem praesente et audiente magna hominum multitudine protestationem eodem tempore fecimus solemnem hoc ei non licuisse unquam nec licere nunc, quod manerium nostrum illud esset de comitatu Oxon' non de civitate.

Protestatio contra oppidanos

Hoc factum est ne oppidani praetextum aliquem hinc arriperent libertates nostras de Haliwel more suo solito invadendi.

Quaestiones theologicae

Quaestiones in disputationibus theologicis discutiendae hae constitutae sunt pro hoc anno:

Vicecustos.	Pontifex Romanus cum concilio non est iudex scripturarum.
Yate.	Sacra scriptura est per se sufficiens ad decidendas fidei controversias absque ecclesiae autoritate et explicatione.
Lee.	Omnis doctrina ad salutem necessaria in scripturis sacris continetur.
Gulson.	Papa non est visibilis monarcha eclesiae, sed potius anti Christus.
Talbot.	Non est penes pontificem Romanum concilia generalia convocare eisque praeesse.

Horne.	Ecclesia potest errare.
Blickard.	Notae ecclesiae sunt sincera verbi dei praedicatio et sacramentorum administratio.
Wake.	Ministri eclesiae non sunt ad celibem vitam obligandi.
Rogers.	Monachatus pontificius tribus votis obligatus non est cultus deo acceptus.

Computus firmariorum

Octobris decimo Robertus Mayne firmarius noster de Chedington computavit in scaccario et discessit aeque.

Octobris vicesimo quarto Richardus Wilmot firmarius de Ibston computavit in scaccario et discessit aeque.

Admissio sociorum

Novembris sexto dominus Petti, dominus Hauksworth, dominus Allen, dominus Iames admissi sunt in perpetuam societatem huius domus.

Admissio probationistarum.

Eodem tempore dominus Turner, dominus Marshe, dominus Dickinson admissi sunt in annum probationis.

Computus firmariorum

Novembris octavo Robertus Ray firmarius de Kibworth computavit in scaccario et discessit aeque.

Novembris nono Edmundus Gregorie firmarius de Cuxam computavit in scaccario et discessit aeque.

p. 227 Anno Domini 1607, regni regis Iacobi 5to, domini Henrici Savil custodis 23.

Computus Saer

Novembris 21mo Henricus Saer firmarius de Barkby computavit in scaccario et discessit aeque.

Computus Napper

Decembris 13to Gulielmus Napper balivus noster de Haliwel computavit in scaccario et discessit in aere collegii 12d.

Computus primi bursarii

Decembris 16to magister Grevil primus bursarius computavit et discessit in aere collegii 38 li. 15s. 11d. Quam summam solvit magistro Rogers sequenti bursario.

Commemoratio

Decembris decimo octavo habuimus commemorationem pro fundatore, legimus statuta, scrutinium celebravimus.

Scrutinium

Decembris ultimi habitum est scrutinium pro servientibus. Electus est magister Horne in hortulanum.

[1608]

Computus Saunders

Ianuarii 16to Ambrosius Sanders balivus pro sylvis Ibston computavit in scaccario.

Commemoratio

Martis 20mo divina fecimus pro fundatore, legimus die crastino statuta et scrutinium habuimus.

Eodem tempore concessimus ut magister Hale admitteretur in librariam nostram, accepto prius iuramento.

Eodem tempore concessimus ut sigillum commune collegii de novo apponeretur indenturae magistri Faunt pro molendinis Grancester, quod sigillum antea apponitum frangebatur. Custos antea per literas concenserat.

Magister Yate rector de Cuxam

Aprilis 8vo rectoria de Cuxam concessa est magistro Yate. Datum est ei spatium deliberandi utrum acceptaret necne usque ad primum diem Ianuarii futurum anno domini 1609.

Flower de lice

Eodem tempore domus sive hospitium vocatum the Flower de lice dimittitur Oram pro termino viginti unius annorum;finis constitutus quinquaginta librae.

Eodem tempore magister Talbot electus est inferior praelector Linacri. Decretum etiam est eodem tempore ut magister Lee mitteretur in comitatum Leycestriae ad lustranda duo maneria nostra de Kibworth et de Barkby ut conficeret librum quemdam campestrem in singulis maneriis vulgo appelatum a feeld booke, et unam mappam generalem coloribus depictam.

Aprilis 10mo custos licentiam dedit magistro Elly intrandi sacros ordines ante finitam regentiam.

Oppidanorum actio pro consuetudine sua molendinaria

Circa hoc tempus oppidani litem nobis de novo intenderunt de consuetudine suo molendinaria, in qua causa saepe antea succumbuerant iam nobiscum iure communi experiretur, vocarunt duos communes pistores Petrum Porie et Alexandrum Hil qui molere apud nostra molendina solent, personas privilegiatas, et molitores praeterea nostros in cameram scaccarii vulgo dictam, sive cameram concilii. Nempe id agebant ut causam stricti iuris, vel potius strictissimi obtinerent in curia aecquitatis. Curiae autem quae tum erat plenissima aequisissimum visum est ut causa referretur ad ius commune. Baronibus autem potestas facta est (nobis consentientibus et oppidanis) ut constituerent statum quaestionis in hac causa, eumque minime captiosum, quo lis ista[1] quae nos exercuit per aliquot annos, nempe oppidanis semper contendentibus nobiscum et semper victis, finem aliquando acciperet.

Commemoratio pro fundatore

Iulii vicesimo, nempe in festo Margaretae habuimus commemorationem pro fundatore, legimus statuta, scrutinium fecimus quod prorogavimus in decimum diem Augusti et quemlibet diem citra.

[1] 'finem aliquando' deleted.

Computus Heath

Iulii ultimo Stephanus Heath firmarius de Farleigh computavit in scaccario et discessit in arreragia 23s. 4d.

p. 228 Anno Domini 1608, regni regis Iacobi 5to, domini Henrici Savil custodis 24.

Magistri in artibus

1. Robertus Brizendine
2. Antonius Antonie
3. Samuel Slade
4. Iohannes Tapsel
5. Leonardus Yate
6. Nathanael Brent
7. Edoardus Lee
8. Theodorus Gulson
9. Iohannes Talbot
10. Thomas Horne
11. Stuckleius Blickard
12. Gulielmus Simonson
13. Isaacus Wake
14. Edoardus Rogers
15. Georgius Garrard
16. Franciscus Grevil
17. Samuel Lane
18. Iohannes Elly
19. Iohannes Philipson

Baccalaurei in artibus

1. Iohannes Hales
2. Iohannes Morly
3. Georgius Pettie
4. Thomas Allen
5. Daniel Iames
6. Timotheus Hauksworth

In anno probationis

1. Petrus Turner
2. Nicolaus Marshe
3. Gulielmus Dickinson

Capellani

1. Robertus Beesly
2. Gulielmus Warberton

Officiarii

Augusti secundo electi sunt officiarii:
magister Brent, vicecustos.
magister Talbot, magister Rogers, magister Philipson, decani.
magister Lee, magister Gulson, magister Wake, bursarii.
primarius portionistarum et exhibitionarius Hamsterly, magister Yate; bursarius Williot, magister Brizendine; exhibitionarius doctoris Bickly et capellanus capellae, magister Horne; praelector grammaticae, magister Lane; praelector Graecae linguae, dominus Hales; praelector logicae dominus Morly.

Gamelingay Merton cum sylvis magistro Iacob
Eodem die renovavimus magistro Iacob indenturam suam pro firma de Gamelingay Merton supplendo tertiam vitam. Et indenturam pro sylvis Mertonage.

Hospitium in Watford cuidam Bruister
Eodem die renovavimus cuidam Bruister indenturam pro hospitio in Watford vocato the rose.

Cranes in Tilburye Francisco Temple
Eodem die dimisimus Francisco Temple tenementum nostrum in West Tilberry vocatum Cranes pro termino 21us annorum.

Rectoria in Gamelingay magistro Clavering
Eodem die renovavimus magistro Clavering indenturam medietatis rectoriae in Gamelingay ad terminum viginti unius annorum.

Dispensationes
Eodem tempore dispensavimus cum magistris regentibus pro lecturis et frequentatione disputationum.

Eodem tempore dispensavimus cum magistro Elly et magistro Philipson pro variationibus suis, eas differendo in annum sequentem.

Computus custodis
Augusti 3^{io} dominus custos computavit et computatis computandis et allocatis allocandis discessit in plusagio 12 li. 3s. 8d.

Tenementum domini Bust
Eodem die renovavimus doctori Bust indenturam suam tenementi in Haliwel pro termino [*blank*].

Tenementum Gulielmi Ranclin[1]
Eodem die renovavimus Gulielmo Ranclin indenturam tenementi sui in Haliwel ad terminum 21us annorum.

Computus bursarii
Augusti 24to, 25to magister Talbot tertius bursarius anni praecedentis computavit et discessit in aere collegii [*blank*] quam summam elapsis octo septimanis solvit magistro Wake, primo bursario.

Initium novi aedeficii
Septembris 13^{io} inter horas octavam et nonam antemeridianas positus est primus et imus lapis fundamentalis novi aedeficii operis certe

[1] The name was more usually Rankin or Rancken, an established Oxford family.

magni quod construere proponimus, quod ut faciamus auspicatum faxit deus.

Indenturae sigillatae

Octobris nono variae indenturae sigillatae sunt, doctori Bust pro tenemento suo in Haliwel, cuidam Bruster pro hospitio ly Rose in Watford, Gulielmo Rankin pro tenemento in Haliwel, magistro Iacob
p. 229 pro firma de / Gamelingay Merton, Francisco Temple pro tenemento in West Tilbury, Richardo Oram pro ly Flower de lis in Oxon'.

Computant firmarii

Octobris 3to magister Napper computavit pro Holiwel et Wolvercot.

Octobris 22do Richardus Wilmot firmarius de Ibston computavit in scaccario.

Novembris 20do [*sic*] Robertus Ray firmarius de Kibworth computavit in scaccario.

Novembris 21mo Henricus Saer computavit, firmarius de Barkby.

Admissio sociorum

Novembris septimo dominus Turner, dominus Marshe, dominus Dickinson admissi sunt in perpetuam societatem huius domus.

Commemoratio

Decembris 17mo divina fecimus pro fundatore, legimus statuta et scrutinium celebravimus. In quo preceptum est decanis et bursariis ut monerent coquos ne permitterent feminas culinam ingredi ad operas aliquas praestandas, tum quia omnia fieri debent per mares, tum quia periculum est ne surripiant utensilia.

Scrutinium

Decembris ultimo habuimus scrutinium de servientibus. In eo coquus inferior acerrime puniendus videbatur. Is enim pessime se gesserat, et quod erat inusitatissimum, non adfuit eo tempore. Socii decreverunt ut vicecustos poenam, quae sibi aequa videretur, infligeret, qui multavit eum viginti solidis cum morbum excussaset et vehementer protestatus fuisset de moribus in posterum emendandis.

[1609]

Faber lapidarius

Ianuarii 28vo consensimus ut quidam Iohannes Acroyde de Halifax, faber, esset lapidarius pro toto aedificio construendo, quod dominus custos paucis post diebus approbavit. Atque ut haberet pro toto hoc opere lapidario summam quingentarum septuaginta librarum praeter expensas itineris.

Wake peregrinatur

Eodem tempore allocavimus magistro Wake peregre profecturo summam 15 librarum pro tribus annis si tam diu peregrinaretur.

Allocationes

Ianuarii 29no allocavimus de more tibicinibus 6s. 8[d].

Eodem tempore allocavimus ly scavengers 13s. 4d. per annum.

Commemoratio

Aprilis nono habuimus commemorationem pro fundatore et die sequenti scrutinium quo tempore consensimus ut arbores emeremus apud sylvam Stow et venderemus apud Ibston et alia loca ubi commode fieri potest.

Faber lignarius

Circa initium Maii decrevimus, domino custode approbante, ut quidam Thomas Holt esset faber lignarius pro toto aedificio construendo. Summa quam ex pacto a nobis recepturus est pro toto opere lignario est 430 li. praeter expensas itineris.

Variationes

Iunii 2do magister Lane variavit in his questionibus:

An {
1. terra moveatur circulariter? Affirmat.
2. Socrates platonicus reprehendus fuerat quod eandem viri et mulieris virtutem esse diceret? Negat.
3. Fortitudo sit virtus moralis? Negat.

Dispensationes

Paulo post cum eo dispensavimus pro secundis variationibus.

Iunii 6to dispensavimus cum magistro Grevil pro variationibus hoc anno, ea conditione ut magister Elly hoc anno variaret.

Variationes

Hic variavit Iulii 7mo in his quaestionibus:

An {
1. Mutili sint exponendi? Negat.
2. Numerus sit aliqua causa rerum? Affirmat.
3. Ex emeritis militibus causidici, ex emeritis causidicis sacerdotes eligi debeant? Negat.

Dispensatio

Iunii 7mo dispensavimus cum magistro Elly pro secundis variationibus.

Commemoratio

Iulii vicesimo habuimus commemorationem pro fundatore, et scrutinium celebravimus, quod prorogavimus usque ad 20mo diem Augusti proxime sequentem.

Computus firmariorum

Iulii vicesimo nono Stephanus Heath firmarius de Farleigh computavit in scaccario.

p. 230 Anno Domini 1609 regni regis Iacobi 6to domini Henrici Savil custodis 25.

Magistri in artibus

1. Robertus Brizendine
2. Antonius Antonie
3. Samuel Slade
4. Iohannes Tapsel
5. Leonardus Yate
6. Nathanael Brent
7. Edovardus Lee
8. Theodorus Gulson
9. Iohannes Talbot
10. Thomas Horne
11. Stucleius Blickard
12. Gulielmus Simonson
13. Isaacus Wake
14. Edovardus Rogers
15. Georgius Garrard
16. Franciscus Grevil
17. Samuel Lane
18. Iohannes Elly
19. Iohannes Philipson
20. Iohannes Hales
21. Iohannes Morly

Baccalaurei

1. Georgius Petty
2. Timotheus Haukesworth
3. Thomas Allen
4. Daniel Iames
5. Petrus Turner
6. Nicolaus Marshe
7. Gulielmus Dickinson

Capellani

1. Robertus Beesly
2. Gulielmus Warberton

Augusti 1mo electi sunt officiarii:
magister Brent, vicecustos.
magister Lee, magister Grevil, magister Elly, decani.
magister Simonson, magister Lane, magister Hales, bursarii.
primarius portionistarum, magister Horne; bursarius Williot, magister Brizendine; exhibitionarius Hamsterly, magister Yate; exhibitionarius

doctoris Bickly, magister Horne; capellanus capellae, magister Blickard; praelector grammaticae, magister Philipson; Graecae linguae, magister Morly; logicae, dominus Hawkesworth.

Dimissiones indenturarum

Eodem die dimisimus magistro Read pro termino 21 annorum medietatem Emildon et Ponteland, 100 li.; magistro Ascough medietatem Stillington et Ceton Carew, 120 li.; et viduae Hartburne alteram medietatem Stillington et Ceton Carew pro eodem termino 21 annorum, 100 li.; domino doctori Atkins manerium de Callowland, 6 li. 13s. 4d.; Gulielmo Parker, terras quasdam apud Kibworth vocatas ly Swathes pro termino 21 annorum, 5 li.[1]

Sigillatio indenturae

Hancque indenturam eodem die sigillavimus.

Socii presentes

Istis concessionibus praeter 7 baccalaureos, interfuerunt magistri Yate, Brent, Lee, Talbot, Horne, Blickard, Simonson, Lane, Elly, Hales, Morly.

Mandatum custodis de exercitiis portionistarum

Eodem tempore dominus custos in mandatis dedit ut vetus decretum de exercitiis per portionistas praestandis executioni mandaretur ut qui non possunt praestare exercitia huius domus post dimidium anni elapsum locis privarentur.

Augusti 20mo venerabilis vir dominus doctor Budden in iure civili professor regius admissus est in bibliothecam nostram prius suscepto iuramento; eodem tempore data est ei clavis.

Anno Domini 1609, regni regis Iacobi 7mo, domini Henrici Savil custodis 25. p. 231

Computus custodis

Augusti decimo quarto dominus custos computavit in scaccario.

Obitus magistri Brizendin

Augusti 16to magister Robertus Brizendine socius huius collegii, vir pietate insignis et concionator optimus, admodum provectus etate, diem clausit extremum. Collegio legavit testamento 5 li.

[1] MS has above fines in a marginal note next to each lease.

Computus bursariorum

Augusti 23^{io} et 24to magister Lee tertius bursarius computavit et reliquit in pede computi 8 li. 10s. 4d. quam summam solvit magistro Hales sequenti bursario.

Praesentatio

Octobris 2do consensimus ut magister Blickard praesentaretur ad rectoriam de Farleigh.

Electio bursarii Williot

Eundemque elegimus in bursarium Williot loco magistri Brizendine defuncti.

Reditus pro lapicidina

Eodem tempore consensimus de dandis 15 li. annuatim magistro Brome, domino manerii de Hedington, pro lapicidina donec constructum esset illud aedificium quod (si deus voluerit) constructuri sumus in collegio nostro.

Literae attornatitiae sigillatae

Consensimus etiam de sigillandis literis attornatitiis Francisco Temple ad distringendum pro reditu de Cranes in West Tilbery.

Computus generalis

Octobris 4to habuimus computum generalem.

Allocatio facta cuidam Dano

Octobris 6to decrevimus (domino custode antea per literas consentiente) ut Danus cuidam nomine Reuter haberet de bonis collegii annuatim 20s. durante beneplacito nostro.

Sigillationes

Eodem die sigillavimus indenturam magistri Ascough, et domini doctoris Atkins.

Computus firmariorum

Octobris 8° Robertus Maine firmarius de Chedington computavit in scaccario.

Octobris 18vo Richardus Wilmot firmarius de Ibston computavit.

Novembris 4to Edmundus Gregorie firmarius de Cuxam computavit.

Novembris 13^{io} Willelmus Napper firmarius de Holiwel et Wolvercot computavit in scaccario.

Novembris 18vo Robertus Ray firmarius de Kibworth computavit.

Decembris 1° Henricus Saer firmarius de Barkby computavit.

Sigillationes
Decembris 3^io^ sigillata est indentura viduae Hartburne et magistri Read.

Decembris 4to sigillavimus praesentationes magistri Blickard ad vicariam de Dodington quam ille obtinuerat a collegio, prius resignata et renunciata rectoria de Farleigh.

Rectoria de Farleigh magistro Slatter
Decembris nono concessimus magistro Slatter praesentationem ad rectoriam de Farleigh quam antea in manus nostras resignaverat magister Blickard, eamque sigillavimus eodem die.

Commemoratio
Decembris 18vo habuimus commemorationem pro fundatore, et scrutinium celebravimus idque prorogavimus in primum diem Ianuarii.

Computus bursarii
Decembris 21mo et 22do magister Hales primus bursarius computavit.

Scrutinium servientium
Decembris ultimo habuimus scrutinium pro servientibus, quo tempore elegimus hortulanum magistrum Simonson.

[1610]

Commemoratio
Aprilis 1mo habuimus commemorationem pro fundatori, et sequenti die scrutinium celebravimus quod prorogavimus in vicesimum diem eiusdem mensis.

Consensus pro conducendis sylvis regiis
Aprilis decimo post preces matutinas convenimus in vestiario ubi consensimus ut conduceremus sylvas regias de Stow et Shotover una cum aliis collegiis pro virili.[1]

Concessio facta magistro Hales
Eodem tempore dispensavimus cum magistro Hales pro ordinariis lectionibus in / scholis et concessimus ei omnes allocationes collegii p. 232
praeter communias quamdiu Aetonae versaretur cum domino custode et operam navaret in editione divi Chrysostomi; his omnibus dominus custos assensum antea praebuerat.

[1] Possibly meaning 'mature wood'.

Compromissum inter nos et oppidanos

Circa hoc tempus inter nos et oppidanos convenit ut domini barones de scaccario privatim audirent veterem illam litem de consuetudine molendaria adhibitis utriusque consiliariis, finemque ei imponerent. Dominus custos et vicecustos termino sequenti scilicet Paschatis una cum magistro Wentworth civitatis, ut appellant, recordario, barones adierunt, petieruntque ut onus hoc in se susciperent, qui et susceperunt, et tempus huic negotio pertractando et peragendo praestituerunt primum diem sabbati termino Michaelis proximo.

Computus bursarii

Aprilis 17mo et 18vo magister Lane secundus bursarius computavit.

Computus firmarii

Iulii sexto Iohannes Hassie novus firmarius de Watforde computavit in scaccario.

Commemoratio

Iulii 20mo in festo Margaretae habuimus commemorationem pro fundatore et scrutinium celebravimus quod prorogavimus in primum diem Septembris proxime.

Computus firmariorum

Iulii 29no Willelmus Napper generosus balivus de Holiwel computavit in scaccario.

Iulii ultimo Stephanus Heath firmarius de Farleigh computavit.

p. 233 Anno Domini 1610, regni regis Iacobi 8vo, domini Henrici Savil custodis 26to.

Magistri in artibus

1. Anthonius Antonie
2. Samuel Slade
3. Iohannes Tapsel
4. Leonardus Yate
5. Nathanael Brent
6. Edovardus Lee
7. Theodorus Gulson
8. Iohannes Talbot
9. Thomas Horne
10. Stukleius Blickard
11. Willelmus Simonson
12. Isaacus Wake
13. Edovardus Rogers
14. Georgius Garrard
15. Franciscus Grevil
16. Samuel Lane
17. Iohannes Elly
18. Iohannes Philipson
19. Iohannes Hales
20. Iohannes Morly

Baccalaurei

1. Georgius Pettie
2. Timotheus Hawkesworth
3. Thomas Allen
4. Daniel Iames
5. Petrus Turner
6. Nicolaus Marsh
7. Willelmus Dickinson

Capellani

1. Robertus Beesly
2. Willelmus Warberton

Literae domini doctoris Iesope

Augusti primo ad horam nonam antemeridianam convenimus in custodis conclavi ubi dominus custos legit literas quas ad nos miserat peregregius vir Thomas Iesope, doctor in medicina, quondam alumnus huius collegii, primum portionista, dein socius. Is habens iam in animo permissum praestare quot aliquot abhinc annis fecerat de communiis portionistarum adaugendis scripsit ad nos ut sequitur:[1]

To the right worshipfull Sir Henrie Savil, knight, warden of Merton colledg in Oxford and to ye fellowes of the said colledg yeve these. Good mr Warden I have bin much sorie that I have bin so long hindered from ye performance of my long entended purpose for ye releef of the poore post-masters of Merton Colledg occasioned by meane of mani great suites in law which I have bin enforced to undergo for the defence not only of the best part of thestate which god hath endowed me withal, but also the better part of thestate of the familie from whence I am descended. Al which now (I most hartely thankk god for it) wel setled I looke back againe to my former intention. The which I purpose, god willing, with as convenient speed as I can to effect, and fully to perfect. In ye meane I have sent to the colledg so much monie as wil suffice to make payment beforehand for on whole yeares allowance to be made by me for the postmasters releife according to the platforme I sent to you and the Colledg long since. The which platforme I have sent at this present to you againe by Ioseph Darbie my servant togeather with the sum of 17 li. 5s. for on yeares allowance from me in the same mentioned. Beseeching you and the rest of the societie of the Colledg to accept thereof, and to be pleased to ad to it yearly such increase to the former allowance in time past made by the Colledg to the post-masters as is in my said platforme set downe. Assuring you, which I do also by this my lettre assume and

[1] *Margin*, in a different hand, 'v. supra, p. 169, 175', referring to register entries now printed in *Reg. Annalium 1567–1603*, 307, 318.

p. 234 promise that until such time so much as I now / send, being 17 li. 5s. shal by me to the warden and scholers of Merton Coll. out of good land be assured for ever. I wil, god willing if I live, make or cause payment of so much to be made in Merton Coll. hale to the Coll. the next tuesday that shal be after the eight of Iulie yearly. And after my death the same sum of 17 li. 5s. shal god willing be made out ful 20 li. per an. (to be[1] imploied by the Coll. to som other purposes) by as good assurance for the true payment thereof yearly, as by the Colledg learned councel at law and mine shal be devised; with a forfeiture or nomine poenae of 10 li. per an. according to the motion you made in your former lettres long since written to me, to be inserted into the said deed which shal be payable to the Coll. if payment shal not be made according to the deed which I purpose shal be made for the assurance of ye yearly rent or payment before mentioned; with a clause of distresse toties quoties as wel for the more sure payment of ye said rent-charg of 20 li. per an. to the said Coll. for ever; as for the said 10 li. nomine poenae as often as the said rent charge shal happen to be unpaid, wherunto the land out of which this yearly rent charg is to be levied shal be ever overt and liable. For the procuring and purchasing whereof, I mean of so much land as may suffice for the maintenance of the former charge I have in readinesse the sum of 800 li. and upwards in monie which I dayly seeke to bestow in land for that purpose, and hope will be shortly effected. Until the accomplishment wherof mine executor shal stand fully charged for ye true performance of ye promises by my last wil and testament as hetherto ever he hath bin charged since my first intention of this good purpose. Most earnestly entreating you good mr Warden and the rest of the incorporation of Merton Coll. for this present to accept not only of this sum of monie now sent and presently to employ the same according to the platforme sent with this lettre, but also to accept this my letter for assurance of my farther intention, until I may make it every way so assured to ye col. as that neyther you, in whom the incorporation of ye same coll. now resteth nor your successors may ever be defrauded therof hereafter. The which (god willing) you shal find I wil dayly hasten: for that (beleeve me) I shall never be quiet in mind until this worke be fully finished. Praying you further that this allowance and new encrease intended for the poore post-masters may begin with this new year now to come which beginneth, as I take it, with Merton

[1] Presumably 'not to be' is intended.

Colledg yearly upon Lammas day the first of August. Written at my house in Gillingham, from whence I verie hartely salute you and al that societie. The 21th [*sic*] of Julie 1610, and do rest a most affectionat welwiller to Merton Coll. and

your ever assured poore frend
Thomas Jesope

Quid autem nos censuimus et statuimus ex literis apparet quas ad eundem scripsimus domino doctori Iesope his verbis:

Literae domini custodis et sociorum
Sir we have receaved your frendly lettre of ye 21th [*sic*] of Julie, and most willingly embrace your liberal offer of 17 li. 5s. per an. to be emploied for the bettering of the post-masters allowance. The platforme of the particulars which you sent we very wel approve, and ar most willing to make that final addition of our owne which you desire we should. And the proportion to be this. For every day in ye yeare not being fast by the lawes of the church we allow in meat 19d., for every dinner when the day is fast 10d., for bread every meal for every post-master ob., and beere as hath bin accustomed. This to continue as long as your allowance of 17 li. 5s. which we make no doubt wil endure to the worlds end. Thus with tender of our love and protestation to requite your great favor don to our poore post-masters in whatsoever we may, earnestly desiring to see so worthi and charitable a gentleman in our colledg, we bid you hartely farewel and rest

your very loving frends

Hisse literis subscripserunt custos et socii.

Dispensatio
Eodem tempore dispensavimus cum magistro Hales pro variationibus suis hoc anno.

Anno Domini 1610, regni regis Iacobi 8vo, domini Henrici Savil custodis 26to. p. 235

Electio officiariorum
Eodem die tempore pomeridiano convenerunt in alta aula custos et socii ubi resignatis de more clavibus electi sunt officiarii:
magister Brent, vicecustos.
magister Simonson, magister Grevill, magister Lane, decani.
magister Horne, magister Philipson, magister Morley, bursarii.

principalis portionistarum, magister Lee; bursarius Williott, magister Hales; exhibitionarius Hamsterly, magister Elly; capellanus capellae, magister Hales; praelector grammaticae, magister Grevil; Graecae linguae, dominus Hawkesworth; logices, dominus Marshe.

Disputationes theologicae

Eodem tempore decretum pro disputationibus in theologia renovatur.

Dimissiones indenturarum

Augusti 2do dimisimus viduae Ewer tenementum apud Callowland pro termino 21us annorum.[1]

Augusti 7mo dimisimus cuidam Crook tenementum apud Ibston vocatum Sunnings pro termino 21us annorum.[2] Et maiori et burgensibus Oxon. parcellam quamdam terrae apud Smithgate, ea conditione si illi nobis renovaverint indenturam pro parte quadam horti nostri. Et cuidam Boulton tenementum in Haliwel nunc in occupatione matris suae. Et Mariae Heathcock filiae Francisci Heathcock tenementum iam in parentum occupatione. Et cuidam Bernard de Kibworth dedimus licentiam alienandi tenementum suum ibidem.

Socii presentes

Istis concessionibus interfuerunt Brent, Lee, Gulson, Talbot, Horne, Blickard, Simonson, Grevil, Lane, Philipson, Morly, Pettie, Hawkesworth, Allen, Iames, Turner, Dickinson.

Eodem tempore dominus custos pronunciavit magistrum Rogers et magistrum Garrard excidisse iure societatis.

Sigillationes

Augusti 11mo sigillavimus indenturam Mariae Heathcocke et indenturam collegii Bayliolensis pro gardino aulae Albanae.

Augusti 12mo sigillavimus licentiam alienationis Willelmo Barnard.

Computus bursarii

Augusti 23^{io} et 24to magister Simonson computavit de administratione sua et pedem computi statim solvit magistro Morly sequenti bursario et sic aeque.

Admissio promi

Septembris 8vo Thomas Chittenden admissus est in promum et iuratus.

[1] *Margin*, '50s.' [2] *Margin*, '5 li.'

Dimissio indenturae

Novembris 1mo dimissimus magistro Mayne de novo firmam de Chedington pro fine sexaginta librarum.[1]

Admissio

Novembris 7mo dominus Pettie, dominus Hawkesworth, dominus Allen, dominus Iames admissi sunt in numerum magistrorum.

Admissio clerici

Novembris 8vo Galle admissus est in clericum.

Resignatio vicarie de Dodington

Decembris 1mo convenientibus sociis in alta aula magister Blickard, vicarius de Doddington palam et publice professus est se vicariam suam in manus diocesani sui resignasse, et resignationem suam solemnem literis comprehensam, et manu signatam publici notarii illis ostendit. Deinde petit ut pristino gauderet iure societatis. Huic petitioni custos tum absens assensu antea praebuerat, socii tunc temporis unanimiter consenserunt.

Commemoratio

Decembris 17mo divina fecimus pro fundatore, legimus statuta, scrutinium celebravimus, quod continuavimus in vigiliam circumcisionis.

Scrutinium servientium

Decembris ultimo habuimus scrutinium pro servientibus, quo tempore tria nobis proposuit bursarius presens, 1um de moribus servientium, quod negotium officiariis committitur, 2^{dum} de numero portionistarum, de quo statuimus ut sit solitus, 3^{ium} de electione hortulani quem constituimus magistrum Grevil.

Anno Domini 1610, regni regis Iacobi 8vo, domini Henrici Savil p. 236
custodis 26°.

Novum aedificium

Hoc anno circa festum Michaelis 1610 imposuimus finem aedificio nostro quadrangulari versus austrum, quod inchoavimus die carnis privii proxime precedente; quo tempore posuimus primum totius structurae lapidem, excepta tantum tertia plus minus fundamenti parte positi a nobis octodecim pene mensibus antequam opus fervere inciperet. Cui cessationi occasio data est quod fabri deessent per

[1] *Margin*, 'magister Yate interf[uit?]', apparently referring to the Cheddington lease.

aliquod temporis spatium quas ad tantum aedificium construendum sufficere arbitrabamur.

[1611]

Computus custodis
Ianuarii 10mo dominus custos computavit de exceptis et allocatis, et discessit in plussagio 29s. 11d.

Commemoratio
Martii 17mo habuimus commemorationem pro fundatore, die proximo legimus statuta et scrutinium fecimus.

Decretum pro communariis
Martii 19° venit ad collegium dominus custos, et die crastino socio vocavit in conclave suum, ubi sic provisum est de indemnitate collegii quod ad communarios attinet ut singuli deponerent in manibus bursarii 50s. quod esset instar cautionis pro solutione batellorum.

Decretum pro cameris novi aedificii
Eodem tempore decretum est unanimi consensu domini custodis et sociorum ut singulis sociis inhabitantibus in novo aedificio versus austrum pro cameris suis instruendis tres librae allocarentur de communi, sed ea conditione ut unusquisque discessurus a camera sua eandem successori reliquat pecuniae summam vel utensilia quae tanti valent, in quo optio erit successoris. Et si forte inter partes oriatur lis ut vicecustos pro tempore existens honorarius esset arbiter et controversiam sopiret.

Magister Simonson inferior praelector Linacri.
Eodem die concessimus inferiorem lecturam Linacri in medicina magistro Simonson pro spatio trium annorum.

Eodem tempore sabbate 20mo die Martii dominus Henricus Nevil eques auratus resignavit in manus nostras totum ius suum et interesse quod habuit in medietate rectoriae de Emildon et Ponteland, quam medietatem statim dimisimus magistro Richardo Read firmario alterius medietatis pro termino 21^{ius} annorum.

Dimissiones indenturarum
Eodem tempore dimisimus domino Henrico Nevil praedicto rectoriam de Elham pro termino 21^{ius} annorum; finis 200 li.[1] Et permittit se

[1] *Margin*, 'Magister Talbot interfuit sigillationi indenturae de Elham'.

daturum 100 li. praeterea si nos deinceps addiderimus huius statui tres annos.

Eodem tempore concessimus magistro Woode aulam portionistarum pro termino quadraginta annorum; finis eius 40 li. Et Gulielmo Meriman domum suam in Holiwel pro termino 40 annorum; finis eius 10 li.[1]

Eodem tempore unanimiter decretum est ut indentura domus Iohannis Stile in Holiwel antea concessae Gulielmo Paynard coquo superiori sigillaretur.

Anno Domini 1611, regni regis Iacobi 8vo, domini Henrici Savil custodis 26to. p. 237

Aprilis 18vo magister Philipson 2^{dus} bursarius de administratione sua computavit in scaccario. Et discessit in aere collegii quod postea solvit sequenti bursario et sic aeque.

Variationes
Maii 10mo magister Philipson variavit in his quaestionibus:

An {
1. Felicitas sit in dormiente. Affirmat.
2. Caelum ab Atlante moveatur. Affirmat.
3. Faeminae sint miliori ingenio quam mares. Negat.

Dispensatio
Maii 11mo dispensatum est cum magistro Philipson pro 2^{dis} variationibus.

Maii 25to omnes socii concesserunt ut dominus Gulson ius retineret in camera sua quamvis abesset usque ad septimum diem Augusti anno domini 1612.

Variationes
Iulii 3to magister Grevil variavit in his quaestionibus:

An {
1. Abortus faciendi ratio non est approbanda propter nimiam liberorum multitudinem.
2. Inter formas politiae deparatas status popularis est deterrimus.
3. Nobilis a generoso non distinguitur.

Dispensatio
Iulii 4to dispensatum est cum magistro Grevil pro 2^{dis} suis variationibus.

[1] *Margin,* notes the fines mentioned in above leases.

Computus firmariorum

Hoc anno hi firmarii computarunt in scaccario 8 balivi, videlicet Iohannes Sherwood de Cambridg, Augusti 13mo; Robertus Maine de Chedington, Octobris 8vo; Richardus Wilmot de Ibston, Octobris 13°; Robertus Ray de Kibworth, Octobris 18vo; Edmundus Gregorie de Cuxham, Novembris 6to; Henricus Saer de Barkby, Novembris 26°; magister Napper firmarius de Holiwel et Wolvercot et balivus de Holiwel, Oxon', Witnie, London, Iulii 18vo.

Litere domini Iesope

Iulii 7mo accepimus literas a viro peregregio domino Thoma Iesope, doctore in medicina, portionistarum benefactore in hanc sententiam:

To my assured good frends ye subwarden & bursar of Merton Coll.
in Oxforde these be delivered.

Good mr Subwarden and mr bursar I direct these my letters to you & the rest of your companie for that I doubt Sir Henry Savil your warden is not at home. To whom I pray you if he be now present or when he shal be at the Colledg, present these my letters with my kindest salutations, as I now do to you & the rest of your societie. And withal thus much; that I have sent by mr Josias Clarke seventeen pounds five shillings in gould fast sealed up in a purse for on yeares payment or exhibition to com from the first day of August next, to be imployed for ye bettering of the poore post-masters commons, much desering to settle and assure it to ye colledg for continuance for ever, according to thefect of my letters written last yeare to mr Warden and the Colledg. For which I am not yet fully readie, but hope shal be ere long. In the
p.238 meane time do / pray you to accept of that which is now sent: and to deliver an acquittance for receipte of the same to mr Clarke, as wel for his discharg as my better satisfaction. And so with my best wishes & continual prayers for ye good estate of that worthie colledg and you al do commit you to god, resting your ever assured poore frend,

Thomas Iesope.

Gillingham this 10th of Julie 1611.

Ad hunc vicecustos statim rescripsit literas gratiarum plenas.

Adventus domini custodis

Iulii vicesimo venit ad collegium dominus custos dieque crastino circa horam octavam matutinam socios omnes domi existentes vocavit in conclave suum.

Curiae tenendae
Quo tempore decretum est curias tenendas esse apud Gamelingay, Kibworth et Barkby.

Supervisorium faciendum
Et supervisorium Anglice a Survey, faciendum esse in manerio nostro novo de Beelby in comitatu Ebor' ad quod negotium peragendum nominati sunt vicecustos et magister Lee.

Literae testimoniales magistro Dixwel
Eodem tempore decretum est ut collegium testimonium praeberet magistro Edwardo Dixwel, vicario de Ponteland pro morum integritate sub sigillo nostro communi.

Promptuarium
Et ut promptuarium ad capiendam cervisiam reficeretur publicis collegii impensis.

Electio
Eodem tempore decrevimus electionem sociorum, facienda et statim publica cepit fieri examinatio.

Eodem die Stephanus Heath firmarius de Farleigh computavit in scaccario, et computatis computandis et allocatis allocandis discessit aeque.

[*rest of p. 238 blank*]

Anno Domini 1611, regni regis Iacobi 9°, domini Henrici Savil custodis p. 239
27mo.

In artibus magistri

1. Anthonius Anthonie
2. Iohannes Tapsel
3. Nathanael Brent
4. Edovardus Lee
5. Theodorus Gulson
6. Iohannes Talbot
7. Thomas Horne
8. Stucleyus Blickard
9. Gulielmus Simonson
10. Isaacus Wake
11. Franciscus Grevil
12. Samuel Lane
13. Iohannes Elly
14. Iohannes Philipson
15. Iohannes Hales
16. Iohannes Morly
17. Georgius Petti
18. Timotheus Hawkesworth
19. Thomas Allen
20. Daniel Iames

Baccalaurei in artibus

1. Petrus Turner
2. Nicolaus Marshe
3. Gulielmus Dickinson

Capellani

1. Robertus Beesly
2. Gulielmus Warberton

Electio sociorum

Augusti 2do ad horam 8^{vam} matutinam convenerunt in conclavi custodis custos et 13 seniores et hos 4^{or} bacalaureos elegerunt in socios futuros, Richardum Hawly, dioceseos Lond', Griffinum Higs, dioceseos Oxon', Willelmum Sellar, dioceseos Bathon', Hugonem Ramsden, dioceseos Ebor'.

Electio officiariorum

Eodem die ad horam 10^{mam} antemeridianam convenimus in alta aula, produximus 21 claves publicae bibliothecae et resignavimus claves officiariorum nostrorum. Dein dominus custos et 5 simpliciter seniores, reliquis ad tempus secedere iussis, elegerunt in officiarios sequentis anni:

vicecustodem, magistrum Brent.

magistrum Blickard, magistrum Philipson, magistrum Hawkesworth, decanos.

magistrum Lee, magistrum Lane, magistrum Hales, bursarios.

principalem portionistarum, magistrum Simonson; bursarium Williot, magistrum Grevil; exhibitionarium Hamsterly, magistrum Elly; capellanum capellae, magistrum Hales; praelectorem Graecae linguae, magistrum Morly; grammaticae, magistrum Allen;[1] praelectorum logices eligendus a principali.

Dispensatio

Eodem tempore dispensatum est cum magistro Hales pro variationibus suis hoc anno.

Dimissiones indenturarum

Augusti 2do convenimus in conclavi domini custodis et dimisimus Richardo Hore domum suam in Holiwel pro termino 21^{ius} annorum pro fine 5 li. et Richardo Iddens domum suam in Holiwel pro termino 21^{ius} annorum pro fine 3 li. 6s. 8d., et Iohanni Sherwood firmam suam de Cambridg pro termino 21^{ius} annorum pro fine 40 li.

[1] 'Hawkesworth' deleted.

Anno Domini 1611, regni regis Iacobi 9no, domini Henrici Savil custodis 27mo. p. 240

Alienationes

Eodem tempore concessimus cuidam Todmorton de Holiwel licentiam alienationis pro ly towne ditche.

Et magistro Ray de Kibworth licentiam alienationis pro 2^{bus} molendinis et cotagio, cui finem statuimus 10s.

Socii presentes

Istis concessionibus interfuerunt magistri Brent, Lee, Gulson, Blickard, Simonson, Grevil, Lane, Ellie, Philipson, Morly, Petti, Hawkesworth, Allen, Iames; bacalaurei, Turner, Marshe, Dickinson.

20 li Iohanni Acroyde

Eodem tempore allocavimus Iohanni Acroide architecto viginti libras praeter alias 20^{ti} quas antea acceperat quod fidelem operam navaverat in constructione novi aedificii quadrangularis.

Camera concessa magistro Warberton

Et concessum magistro Warberton iuniori capellano ut haberet novam cameram derelictam cum probationarii admittendi in initio termini Michaelis proximi elegissent.

Computus firmarii

Augusti 3^{io} Iohannes Sherwood firmarius de Cambridg computavit in scaccario.[1]

Computus custodis

Eodem die dominus custos computavit pro receptis et allocatis et discessit in plussagio 26 li. 4s. 10d. ob.[2]

Sigillationes

Augusti undecimo sigillavimus magistro Edwardo Dixwel literas testimoniales, et Willelmo Todmorton licenciam alienationis.

Admissio probationariorum.

Octobris decimo baccalaurei electi 1mo die Augusti in socios futuros admissi sunt in annum probationis.

[1] Entry deleted and repeated below in *Varii computus.*
[2] Entry deleted and repeated below in *Varii computus.*

Claves librariae

Octobris 29no dominus Hawley et dominus Sellar admissi sunt ad librariam et claves acceperunt.

Magistri facti

Novembris septimo dominus Turner, dominus Marsh, dominus Dickinson admissi sunt in numerum magistrorum huius domus.

Novembris 22do sigillavimus magistro Roberto Ray licentiam alienationis antea ei concessam.

Varii computus

Augusti 3^{io} dominus custos computavit de receptis et allocatis et discessit in plussagio 26 li. 4s. 10d. ob.

Eodem tempore Iohannes Sherwood computavit in scaccario et discessit aeque.

Octobris 19no Richardus Wilmot firmarius et balivus de Ibston computavit in scaccario.

Octobris ultimo Edmundus Gregorie firmarius de Cuxam computavit in scaccario.

Novembris 22do Henricus Saer firmarius et balivus de Barkby et Robertus Ray firmarius et balivus de Kibworth computarunt in scaccario. Iulii ultimo [*blank*] Heath de Farleigh computavit in scaccario.

Commemoratio

Decembris 17mo habuimus commemorationem pro fundatore nostro, legimus statuta, et scrutinium celebravimus; quod prorogavimus in primum diem Ianuarii et quemlibet diem citra.

Scrutinium servientium

Decembris ultimo habuimus scrutinium pro servientibus quo tempore
p. 241 tria nobis proposuit, bursarius presens, / primum de moribus
servientium quos post admonitiones aliquot commisimus officiariis; 2^{dum} de numero portionistarum quem censuimus eundem esse debere qui ante fuit; 3um de electione hortulani quem fecimus magistrum Lane.

[1612]

Ianuarii 12mo beatus Ambrosius MS. incatenatus in communi libraria collegii mutuo datus est ex consensu magistro Iames protobibliothecario.

Allocatio 15 li. magistro Wake

Februarii 16to allocatio facta est magistro Wake quindecim librarum annuatim pro spacio trium annorum si tamdiu moram fecerit in partibus transmarinis.

Dispensatio

Eodem tempore dispensavimus cum magistro Allen magistro regente febricitante pro tot praelectionibus in scholis publicis quot erunt dies legibiles durante febre.

Variationes

Martii 13mo magister Morly variavit in his quaestionibus:

An {
1. Mundus sit aeternus? Negat.
2. Elementa ex principiis aut[1] mista ex elementis coeperint? Negat.
3. Statui monarchico optimatum imperium sit praeferendum? Affirmat.

Martii 15to dispensavimus pro secundis eius variationibus.

Commemoratio

Aprilis quinto divina fecimus pro fundatore nostro, dieque crastino legimus statuta, et habuimus scrutinium quod prorogavimus in primum diem Maii et quemlibet diem citra. Eodem tempore commisimus negotium reparandi vasa stannea vetera et emendi nova, prout usus collegii postularet, bursario praesenti et decano seniori.

Dispensatio

Aprilis 24to dispensavimus cum magistro Iames gravi laborante, qui tum regens erat pro suis praelectionibus in scholis publicis donec convalesceret, et cum reliquis regentibus, videlicet magistris Pettie, Hawkesworth, et Allen pro suis praelectionibus diebus Martis, et quandocunque haberentur conciones ad clerum hoc termino et sequenti.

Obitus magistri Iames

Aprilis penultimo magister Daniel Iames regens magister et socius huius collegii exhalavit animam.

Eodem die dominus custos et socii dimiserunt magistro Brent vicecustodi rectoriam de Burmington pro termino vitae suae naturalis. Indentura autem huius concessionis eodem die sigillata est.

[1] 'principia' deleted.

Eodem etiam tempore concessum est magistris inceptoribus ut acciperent a bursario singuli 6 li. 13s. 4d. pro parte finium debitorum ad sumptus comitiorum sustinendos.

Hoc anno omnes bursarii computarunt et solverunt pedes computorum suorum statutis et consuetis temporibus.

Obitus magistri Marshe

Iulii 13^{io} magister Marshe adolescens optimae spei et indolis, ipso die comitiorum in quibus incepturus erat, summo omnium maerore quibus notus erat e vivis migravit. Legavit autem collegio[1] viginti libras, cistae Reade inferendas, in eundem usum quem prius instituerat vir Clarissimus [*blank*] Reade, Episcopus Cicestrensis.

Commemoratio

Iulii 20mo habuimus commemorationem pro fundatore, legimus statuta et scrutinium fecimus, quod prorogavimus ad 10^{mum} diem Augusti et quemlibet diem citra.

p. 242 Anno Domini 1612, regni regis Iacobi 10mo, domini Henrici Savil custodis 28vo.

Augustus

Magistri in artibus

1. Anthonius Anthonie
2. Iohannes Tapsel
3. Nathanael Brent
4. Edwardus Lee
5. Iohannes Talbot
6. Thomas Horne[2]
7. Gulielmus Simonson
8. Isaacus Wake
9. Franciscus Grevil
10. Samuel Lane
11. Iohannes Elly
12. Iohannes Philipson
13. Iohannes Morly[3]
14. Georgius Petti
15. Timotheus Hawkesworth
16. Thomas Allen
17. Petrus Turner
18. Gulielmus Dickinson

Baccalaurei in artibus

1. Richardus Hawly
2. Gulielmus Sellar
3. Griffinus Higgs
4. Hugo Ramesden

Capellani

1. Robertus Beesly
2. Gulielmus Warberton

[1] The rest of this entry, apparently inserted later, is in a different hand.
[2] Above Horne is 'Gulielmus Simonson', deleted then entered below.
[3] Above Morly is 'Johannes Hales', deleted.

Computus

Augusti primo firmarius de Callowland computavit in scaccario et discessit aeque.

Sigillationes

Augusti 2[do] consenserunt socii in vestiario, ut indenturae Hore, Iddens, Bolton, quae tum legebantur, communi sigillo collegii munirentur.

Adventus domini custodis

Augusti 3[io] venit ad collegium dominus custos, et primo mane una cum quinque senioribus sociis elegit in officiarios huius anni:

Electio officiariorum

vicecustodem, magistrum Brent.
magistrum Lane, magistrum Allen, magistrum Turner, decanos.
magistrum Grevil, magistrum Hales, magistrum Hawkesworth, bursarios.
principalem portionistarum, magistrum Talbot; bursarium Williot et capellanum capellae, magistrum Lee; exhibitionarium Hamsterly, magistrum Elly; praelectorem Graecae linguae nominavit dominus custos magistrum Morly et praelectorem grammaticae magistrum Allen; baccalaureus Williot nominandus a principali.

Mandatum de praesentationibus

Eodem tempore dominus custos dedit in mandatis ut singuli in artibus praesentandi in hac domo solverent seniori decano 2s. 6d. et tantum duobus iunioribus decanis; et ut decani, suo quisque ordine, essent praesentatores si illis placeret forte.

Dispensationes

Eodem tempore dispensavimus ut liceret magistro Hales variare quocunque termino huius anni.

Dispensavimus etiam tunc temporis ut magistri Petti, Hawkesworth, Allen amplius non tenerentur legere ordinarias nec frequentare disputationes baccalaureorum aut Augustinenses. Continuavimus eodem mane allocationem factam non ita pridem portionistis, et disputationes theologicas.

Balivus constitutus

Decrevimus praeterea ut quidam Thomas Dod constitueretur balivus maneriorum nostrorum in Gamelingay sub sigillo communi durante beneplacito.

p. 243 Anno Domini 1612, regni regis Iacobi 10mo, domini Henrici Savile custodis 28vo.

Computus domini custodis

Augusti 4to tempore pomeridiae dominus custos computavit de receptis et allocatis et discessit in plussagio 25 li.

Dimissiones indenturarum

Eodem tempore dimisimus magistro Hopper domum suam quondam magistri Cromwelli Lea, et viduae Davis domum suam pro termino quadraginta annorum.

Eodem etiam tempore concessum est cuidam Iohanni Raw molendinario de Beilby ut indentura molendini sui renovaretur ad terminum viginti unius annorum. Et Roberto Cooke et Iohanni Scot idem concessum de clausura quadam in dicto manerio de Beilby; sed ea conditione ut in posterum uterque reditus haberet ad priorem reditum proportionem sesquialteram.

Augusti 12mo decrevimus ut bursarius equum emeret quod et fecit die sequenti.

Augusti 14to sigillavimus indenturas Richardi Hore, Richardi Iddens, Iohannis Boulton, magistri Hopper, Iocosae Davis, viduae, tenentium in manerio de Holiwel.

Augusti 26to et 27mo magister Lee, tertius bursarius, computavit in scaccario. Quo tempore socii unanimiter concesserunt ut magister Brent, vicecustos peregre profecturus ius haberet retinendi cameram donec rediret.[1]

Augusti 5to habuimus generalem computum in scackario et ut magister Brent vicecustos [2]

Augusti 6to magister Lee tertius bursario [*sic*][3]

Augusti 5to habuimus generalem computum in scaccario.

Eodem tempore decretum est ut magister Brent vicecustos haberet de bonis collegii 15 li. annuatim quamdiu maneret in partibus transmarinis.

Octobris decimo quatuor probationarii videlicet dominus Hawly, dominus Sellar, dominus Higs, dominus Ramsden admissi sunt in perpetuam societatem huius domus.

[1] This sentence is deleted. [2] Entry deleted. [3] Entry deleted.

Anno Domini 1613, anno regni regis Iacobi 11°, domini Henrici Savili custodis 29. p. 244

Computus

Octobris 21 computavit Ricardus Wilmot firmarius et balivus de Ibston et discessit aeque.

Novembris 4to computavit Robertus Ray firmarius de Kibworth et discessit aeque.

Novembris 7° computavit Edmundus Gregorie firmarius de Cuxam et discessit aeque.

Novembris 27 computavit Saer firmarius de Barkby.

Eodem die praesentatio ad medietatem rectoriae de Gamlingay concessa est magistro Lee.

Decembris 5 in vestiario convenientibus una sociis dispensatum est cum magistro Turner pro quibusdam ordinariis lectionibus hoc termino Michaelis habendis.

Eodem die dispensatum est cum magistro Dickenson ut liceret ei pro suo arbitratu ordinaria legere in collegio quia, propter publicam scolarum demolitionem, locus ei ad legendum satis idoneus non dabatur.

Die 17 Decembris celebratum est commemoratio pro fundatore, lecta statuta, initum scrutinium.

Ultimo die Decembris[1] est scrutinium servientium; in quo actum est de electione hortulani, numero portionistarum, et moribus servientium. Hortulanus eligitur magister Philipson, modo fiat sine praeiudicio et iniuria magistri Elly absentis, ad vicariam de Elham praesentati. Numerus portionistarum idem retinetur; servientes si quid delinquerint per officiarios puniendi.

Eodem tempore dispensatum est cum magistro Talbot fracto vel luxato crure laborante ut liceret ei abesse collegio donec commode posset redire.

[1613]

Magister Brent peregrinatur

Maii 5to magister Brent peregre profectus est in Gallias.

[1] *Margin*, 'In vigilia circumcisionis'.

Praesentatio Morly ad rectoriam de Lapworth[1]

Maii 10mo concessa est praesentatio ad rectoriam de Lapworth magistro Morly.

Dispensationes

Eodem tempore dispensatum est cum magistro Hales pro suis variationibus hoc anno. 22° die [? Maii] dispensatio concessa est magistro Petty pro secundis variationibus;[2] variavit in his quaestionibus 21 die Maii idem magister Petty.

Variationes[3]

An {
Senes non sunt timidi; ex Aristotele, 2° Rheto. c. 13°
Nemo natura servus; ex Aristotele, 1° Polit. c. 5°
Habitus magnificentiae oppositi opprobria asserunt; Aristotelis 4 Ethic. c. 2°
}

Obitus et sepultura Thomae Bodleii militis

Ianuarii decimo octavo anno domini 1612, anno regni domini nostri Iacobi Dei gratia Angliae, Franciae, et Hiberniae regis Fidei defensoris etc., decimo, et Scotiae quadragesimo sexto, vir clarissimus Thomas Bodleius eques auratus, sexagesimum septimum aetatis suae agens annum, post fundatum a se et aliqua ex parte extructam, suis suorumque sumptibus magnificentissime instructam Bibliothecam publicam (quam Bodleianam vocant) in hac academia Oxon', in aedibus suis in vico Sancti Bartholomei minoris London', non sine maximo bonarum literarum damno, et literatorum maerore summo diem obiit. Cuius cadaver iuxta tabulas testamenti sui ad collegium hoc nostrum in quo olim diu socius et alumnus vixerat, deferebatur ut in ecclesia dicti collegii, loco aliquo idoneo per custodem et seniores dicti collegii designato, sepeliretur. Funeris vero solemnia talia erant, die lunae 29 die Martii inter horas septimam et octavam antemeridianas anno domini 1613, anno regni domini nostri Iacobi undecimo et Scotiae 46to; corpus omnibus insignibus ad tale funus ornandum requisitis in communi aula dicti collegii ad aliquod tempus collocatur. Adsunt pro more faeciales tres, praecipue Clarencius. Adsunt viri venerabiles inter pullatos primi Laurentius Bodleius, frater senior dicti defuncti (qui summo cum favore totius academiae creatus est doctor seu professor sacrae theologiae), Ioannes Benettus eques auratus legum

[1] 'vicariam' altered to 'rectoriam' in both heading and entry.

[2] 'qui die 21 Maii' deleted.

[3] The entry begins '29', presumably the date [? May].

doctor, curiae praerogativae Cantuariensis iudex, et Gulielmus Hackwell ex hospitio Lincolniensi London' armiger, consanguineus dicti defuncti, duo soli testamenti ultimae voluntatis dicti defuncti executores, una cum Georgio Hackwello, sacrae theologiae professore, fratre Gulielmi Hackwell iuniore et Laurentio Bodleio nepote dicti defuncti, huius collegii portionista; adsunt praeterea Gulielmus Goodwin sacrae theologiae professor, Aedis Christi decanus, concionator, vicecancellarius, procuratores, bedelli singuli, socii omnes huius domus, capellani, portionistae, servientes et de pauperioribus scholaribus per praefectos collegiorum et aularum nominatis septuaginta septem, servi insuper dicti defuncti, multique alii pullis induti vestibus omnes. Mox cadaver dicti defuncti, praesentibus pullatis et subsequentibus necnon et omnibus omnium facultatum doctoribus artium magistris, in artibus bacchalaureis conformi habitu Academico indutis, funus concomitantibus a dicto collegio per Aedes Christi (ut tantae solennitati amplior daretur locus) per latiores plateas civitatis ad scholam theologicam primo deportabatur; ubi magister Corbet academiae orator publicus divertissimam habuit orationem. A schola theologica ad ecclesiam Beatae Mariae, ubi tunc temporis clarissimi Bodleii κενοταφιον erat extructum, defertur, Gulielmo Goodwine sacrae theologicae professore Aedis Christi decano concionante. Tandem ritibus omnibus et ceremoniis hic peractis, oblatis eius insignibus factisque pro more oblationibus ad collegium hoc nostrum reducebatur, ubi post elegantem orationem a Iohanne Halesio habitam in superiori boreali parte cancelli ecclesiae nostrae sepelitur. Sepultura finita lautissimo convivio excipimur omnes in alta aula quo peracto disceditur.

Legavit Thomas Bodleius miles 200 marcas ad cistam

Legavit idem Thomas Bodleius miles tantum pecuniarum universitati Oxon' quantum sufficere possit, ad extruendas summas partes Novarum Scholarum. Dedit collegio ducentas marcas ad cistam ut patebat ex iis quae descripsimus ex testamento dicti Thomae Bodleii.

Anno Domini 1613, anno regni regis Iacobi 11°, domini Henrici Savile custodis 29. p. 245

[*Extract from Sir Thomas Bodley's will relating to Merton College*][1]

[1] Cf. *Trecentale Bodleianum* (Oxford, 1913), pp. 67–86 (will, with minor verbal differences), 87–144 (funeral orations); cf. also Bodl. Wood 460(1), containing *Bodleiomnema* (Oxford, 1613), verses by 31 members of Merton College – 22 in Latin, 4 in Greek, 2 each in Hebrew and Italian, and 1 in English.

p. 246 Anno Domini 1613, regni regis Iacobi 11°, domini Henrici Savil custodis 29°.

Augustus

Magistri in artibus

1. Anthonius Anthoni
2. Iohannes Tapsel
3. Nathanael Brent
4. Edwardus Lee
5. Iohannes Talbot
6. Thomas Horne
7. Guilielmus Simonson
8. Isaacus Wake
9. Franciscus Greevil
10. Samuel Lane
11. Iohannes Elly
12. Iohannes Philipson
13. Iohannes Morly
14. Georgius Petty
15. Thomas Allen[1]
16. Petrus Turner
17. Guilielmus Dickenson

Baccalaurei in artibus

1. Ricardus Hawlye
2. Guilielmus Sellar
3. Griffinus Higgs
4. Hugo Ramsden

Capellani

1. Robertus Beesly
2. Guilielmus Warberton

Scholaris magistri Iohannis Chambers

Augusti 1° venit ad collegium dominus custos ac die crastino circa horam octavam matutinam omnes socios domi existentes in altam aulam convocavit. Quo tempore decretum est per dominum custodem et socios ut pecunia magistri Chambers emptis iam terris ad eos usus, quod praescripsit ipse in testamento (ut superius patet in Registro pag. 211), admitteretur scholaris unus in collegium istud, eligendus semper e collegio Aetonensi et referretur in numerum portionistarum, omnibusque emolumentis et ipsi [*sic*] frueretur ea lege ut tempore refectionum sua vice serviat in promptuario, sicut et iam faciunt alternatim duo praedictorum portionistarum. Ad quod quidem non solum inducti sumus virtute testamenti magistri Chambers sed etiam requisiti per literas a domino Henrico Savile praeposito collegii Eton' et doctore Smith, praeposito Collegii Regalis in universitate Cantabrig', huc transmissas (ad hos enim duos tantum spectat iuxta praescriptum magistri Chambers scholarem praedictum in perpetuum nominare). Admittendus autem hic ad festum Michaelis proxime futurum incipiente termino.

[1] Above Allen is 'Timotheus Hawksworth', deleted.

Indentura doctoris Iesope pro portionistis

Eodem tempore accepimus litteras a domino doctore Iesope una cum indentura quadam anni cuiusdam reditus ad communias portionistarum adaugendas, per quem etiam rogati sumus ut exemplar illius indenturae (quod etiam ipse nobis misit) nos communi collegii sigillo muniremus illudque in manus domini doctoris Clayton medici traderemus, quod etiam paulo post factum est.

Electio officiariorum

Hoc etiam tempore ubi officiarii claves suos deposuissent, ac reliqui claves protulissent in medium bibliothecae communis, secedentibus caeteris, dominus custos et quinque simpliciter seniores designant in hunc annum novos officiarios istos qui sequuntur videlicet:
magistrum Simonson, vicecustodem.
magistrum Grevill, magistrum Morlye, magistrum Dickenson, decanos.
magistrum Philipson, magistrum Petty, magistrum Allen, bursarios.
principalem portionistarum, magistrum Lane; bursarium Williot, magistrum Turner; capellanum capellae, magistrum Lee; exhibitionarium Hamsterly nominatum etiam magistrum Lee; praelectorem Graecae linguae, magistrum Turner et dominum Higgs praelectorem grammaticae nominavit dominus custos; baccalaureus Williot nominandus a principali.

Anno Domini 1613, anno regni regis Iacobi 11°, domini Henrici Savil custodis 29°. p. 247

Electio septem probationariorum

Eodem die deliberarunt dominus custos et socii an sociorum numerum augeri commode posset necne: decreverunt omnes unanimi consensu habendam esse electionem. Electio vero sunt huius mensis die 5to; in socios futuros (lectis prius statutis ad electionem spectantibus ex statuto regni 2° Elizabethae edito) isti septem: Iohannes Gibbs, Humfredus Farrar, Iacobus Marsh, Guilielmus Fettiplace, Henricus Aynscomb, Guilielmus Nevill, Guilielmus Cox. dominus Gibbs, Farrar, Marsh, Fettiplace, qui determinationes suas compleverunt, admittendi in annum probationis in initio termini proxime sequentis. Tres reliqui cum primum in quadragesima determinarint, admittendi. Solvunt in admissione sua ad usum bibliothecae, Gibs 20s., Farrar 3 li. 6s. 8d., Marsh 3 li. 6s. 8d., Fettiplace, 3 li. 6s. 8d., Ainscombe 3 li. 6s. 8d., Nevil 3 li. 6s. 8d., Cox 20s.

Computus domini custodis

Quinto Augusti computavit dominus custos de receptis et allocatis et discessit in plussagio 66 li. 18s. 8d.

Dispensationes

Eodem tempore dispensatum cum magistris Turner et Dickenson ut amplius non tenerentur legere ordinarias nec disputationes baccalaureorum aut Augustinenses frequentare.

Obitus magistri Hawksworth

Augusti septimo magister Hawksworth summae spei iuvenis, huiusque collegii socius, diem obiit.

Computus bursarii

Augusti 26° et 27° magister Greville in scaccario computavit.

Resignatio Morly

Quo tempore magister Morly non ita pridem praesentatus ad rectoriam de Lapwoorth, illam rursus resignavit.

Computus

Septembris 24° computavit Richardus Hodesden firmarius et balivus de Watford et discessit aeque.

Praesentatio Elly ad rectoriam de Lapwoorth

Septembris 29° concessa est et sigillata praesentatio rectoriae de Lapwoorth magistro Elly, una cum indentura quadam cuiusdam terrae vocatae Hains Lese.

Admissio probationariorum

Octobris undecimo quatuor illorum septem baccalaureorum 5to die Augusti in socios futuros electorum admissi sunt (prout in electione constitutum fuerat) in annum probationis.

Computus

Eodem die Mayne firmarius et balivus noster de Chedington computavit in scaccario et discessit aeque.

Varii computus firmariorum

Octobris 23to computavit Richardus Wilmot firmarius et balivus noster de Ibston.

Novembris 6° Edmundus Gregory firmarius et balivus noster de Cuxham computavit in scaccario.

Novembris 9° computavit Robertus Ray firmarius et balivus noster de Kibworth.

Novembris 25° Henricus Saer firmarius et balivus noster de Barkby computavit in scaccario, et in arreragia.

Computus 1^{mi} bursarii
Decembris 16° computavit magister Allen 1us bursarius.

Commemoratio
Decembris 17° divina fecimus pro fundatore, legimus statuta, et scrutinium celebravimus, idque prorogavimus in 1^m diem Ianuarii et quemlibet diem citra.

Scrutinium servientium
Decembris ultimo habuimus scrutinium de servientibus in quo tria nobis proposuit presens bursarius, 1^m de moribus servientium, quod negotium officiariis commissum; 2^m de numero portionistarum de quo decrevimus ut sit idem qui antea, 3^m de electione hortulani quem nominavimus magistrum Petty.

Anno Domini 1613, regni regis Iacobi 11°, domini Henrici Savil custodis 29°. p. 248

[1614]

Computus generalis
Ianuarii 4to habuimus generalem computum in scaccario.

Praesentatio Allen ad vicariam de Elam
Eiusdem mensis 24° die sigillata est praesentatio ad vicariam de Elam magistro Allen.

Adventus custodis. Thracies et Thrognols magistro Taylor dimittitur
Ultimo Februarii advenit dominus custos et postridie convocatis sociis in conclave suum consensum est de dimittendis manerio de Tracies, et firma Thrognols, nuper in possessione magistri Trafford, magistro Taylor infra London marchant taylor pro termino 21 annorum; finis 100 li. Indentura vero sigillata 3° Martii.

Contributio ad constructionem scholarum publicarum
Eodem etiam tempore unanimiter consensum est per dominum custodem et socios de conferendis 20 libris ad structuram scholarum publicarum; de qua summa 20 marcae solvendae de bonis collegii per

bursarium pro tempore existentem, reliquum vero per socios et comminarios contribuendum.

Dimissiones indenturarum

Secundo Martii convenimus in conclave custodis et dimissimus Thomae Seabroke tenementum apud Chedington vocatum Halswick pro termino 21us annorum; finis 20 marcae. Eodem etiam tempore dimissimus Richardo Wilmot firmario nostro de Ibston silvas omnes nostras ibidem pro annuo reditu 32^{rum} librarum.

Doctor Bust superior lectura Linacri, magister Simonson inferior lector

Eodem die concessa est superior lectura Linacri doctori Bust, inferior vero magistro Simonson, utraque pro spatio trium annorum.

Computus bursarii

Aprilis 14° magister Pettye 2us bursarius computavit in scaccario.

Commemoratio

Aprilis 16° divina fecimus pro fundatore, eodem die legimus statuta, et habuimus scrutinium quod prorogavimus in primum diem Iunii et quemlibet diem citra.

Admissio probationorum

Eodem tempore admissi sunt in annum probationis dominus Ainscombe, dominus Neville, dominus Cox, iidemque admissi ad librariam.

Statuta et ordinationes pro cista Bodley in domo sive collegio de Merton in universitate Oxoniensi

Articulus primus

In primis quod singulis annis tempore quo eliguntur vicecustos et alii officiarii domus eligantur tres conservatores cistae Bodley (qui non sunt de bursariis neque custodibus cistae Reade) qui quidem conservatores usque ad proximam electionem anno revoluto conservationi praedictae cistae et incremento eiusdem fideliter intendere teneantur.

Articulus secundus

Item quod eodem tempore eligantur auditores computi trium conservatorum praedictae cistae, qui ratiocinia eorundem una cum custode vel vicecustode, si interesse voluerint, infra mensem proxime sequentem fideliter audiant et finem computo imponant, et indenturam summam praedictam continentem una cum excrescentiis, si quae fuerint, post computum completum et finaliter auditum custodi vel vicecustodi absque dilatione, excusatione, vel fictione quacunque porrigant, et repraesentent securo loco repondendam per quam conservatores eiusdem cistae noviter electi in suo computo poterint onerari.

Articulus tertius p. 249

Item quod conservatores eiusdem cistae administracionem sui officii utiliter gerant, fidelem rationem reddant, cistam indemnem conservent, et quod in omne receptione seu liberatione pecuniae ad minus duo conservatores cistae personaliter sint praesentes si in villa fuerint; et quod circa exactionem debitorum seu insufficientiarum, pro quibus sufficiens cautio non habetur in cista (si contingat, quod absit) solicitem et diligentem curam apponant, et omnia statuta de eadem cista edita cum omnibus suis articulis, quatenus ipso concernunt, observabunt.

Articulus quartus

Item quod collegium si indigeatur duodecim libras, custos octo libras, socius quinque libras poterit licite mutuari super pignore seu cautione reali sufficienti, ita quod singula pignora excedant in aliquo summam pecuniae sic mutuo acceptae, saltem secundum arbitrium conservatorum vel aliorum per quorum notitiam melior inquisitio de pignore poterit haberi. Nec licitum erit dictis conservatoribus quocunque praetextu vel colore quicquam extraneo sive cuicunque personae ultra praefatas mutuo tradere.

Articulus quintus

Item quod cautiones omnes in dicta cista reponantur, et non alibi nisi aliter visum fuerit propter molem cautionis fortasse excessivam, aut aliquam aliam rationabilem causam iudicio omnium conservatorum approbandam; in quo casu tamen dicti conservatores omnes et singuli ad cautionis restitutionem et cistae indemnitatem tenebuntur. Quorum securitati ut melius aliqua saltem ex parte provideatur, ordinatum est ut si quis socius qui per approbationem omnium conservatorum (ut praedictum est) cautionem aliquam aut cautionis particulam in propriis manibus habuerit, collegium reliquerit animo non revertendi infra sex menses, ante discessum suum omnino liberabit in manus dictorum conservatorum integram suam cautionem post 30 dies post expletos sex menses praefatos sine omni contradictione vendendam. Sin collegium reliquerit animo revertendi infra sex menses, nec tamen infra dictum tempus redierit, quod in eo casu ipsius cautio liberabitur in manus conservatorum infra spatium trium mensium immediate sequentium sex illos menses praedictos sine omni contradictione statim vendenda.

Articulus sextus

Item quod nullus conservator cistae praedictae rem venalem illius cistae emat nisi consensu custodis et vicecustodis praedictae domus fideliter aestimetur et plus offerenti detur.

Articulus septimus

Item quod nullus conservator administrationem suam vel claves alicui tradat nisi magistro vel baccalaureo dictae domus.

Articulus octavus

Item quod non licebit conservatoribus praedictis summam aliquam pecuniae ad cistam praedictam pertinentem mutuo tradere alicui socio nisi is qui mutuo accepit duplici iuramento in praesentia conservatorum se obligaverit in haec verba:

1. Iuramentum. Tu iurabis quod omnia statuta et ordinationes pro cista Bodley tu observabis, quatenus te concernunt, sicut Deus te adiuvet et sancta Dei evangelia.

2. Iuramentum. Tu iurabis quod haec cautio tua est, eiusque verus es dominus pro rato, eamque tu servabis quam diu pecuniam iam mutuo acceptam retinebis. Pecuniam quam pro ea recipies ad tuum proprium et nullius alterius singulare commodum mutuaberis cistamque et conservatores eius in hac parte deinceps indemnes conservabis; si autem cautionem istam per te vel per alium nomine tuo emi non contingat venditionem eius nequaquam impedies sed omni iuris remedio ipsam rehabendi renunciabis in hac parte salvis tibi excrescentiis, si quae acciderint, sicut Deus te adiuvet et sancta eius evangelia.

p. 250 Anno Domini 1614, regni regis Iacobi 12, domini Henrici Savil custodis 29°.

Dismissio indenturae de Elam

Vicesimo secundo Aprilis sigillata est domino Henrico Neville et domino Iohanni Iackson indentura rectoriae de Elham pro termino 21us annorum; finis 100 li. Concessa vero haec indentura 2° Martii per dominum custodem et socios unanimi consensu.[1]

[1] Entry deleted and lease later granted on different terms (below, 1 Aug.).

Sigillatio indenturae domini doctoris Iesope pro portionistis

Decimo sexto Iulii accessit ad collegium dominus doctor Iesope insignis medicus ac huiusce collegii quondam socius, secum afferens literas a domino custode quibus monemur communi collegii sigillo munire indenturam quandam tripartitam inter collegium ex una parte, reverendissimum in Christo patrem Georgium archiepiscopum Cantuariensem ex secunda parte, et praefatum dominum doctorem Iesope ex tertia parte, circa confirmationem annuam cuiusdam eleemosynae 17 librarum 5 solidorum in perpetuum allocatae per praedictum dominum doctorem Iesope in usum portionistarum. De qua re plura habentur in hoc registro anno domini 1610, indentura vero die sequenti in altam aulam convocatis omnibus sociis domi existentibus lecta, et statim postea sigillata.

Allocatio 10 li. magistro Horne

Eodem tempore facta est allocatio magistro Horne decem librarum annuatim pro spacio trium annorum si tam diu contigerit eum in partibus transmarinis commorari.

Computus firmariorum

Iulii 18 Iohannes Sherwood computavit in scaccario.

Eodem etiam die magister Napper ballivus de Holliwell, Oxon', Witny, London computavit in scaccario.

Sigillatio

Primo die Augusti sigillata est indentura domino Henrico Nevill et domino Iohanni Iackson rectoriae de Elam pro termino vitae naturalis dominae Margaretae Savill, magistri Iohannis Sydley, et Elizabethae Sydley uxoris eius; finis 100 li.

[*rest of p. 250 blank*]

Anno Domini 1614, regni regis Iacobi 12, domini Henrici Savil p. 251
custodis 30.

Augus[tus]

Magistri in artibus

1. Nathanael Brent
2. Iohannes Talbot
3. Thomas Horne
4. Guilielmus Simonson
5. Isaacus Wake
6. Franciscus Greevil
7. Samuel Lane
8. Iohannes Philipson
9. Georgius Pettye
10. Thomas Allen
11. Petrus Turner
12. Guilielmus Dickenson

Baccalaurei et socii

1. Richardus Hawly
2. Gulielmus Sellar
3. Griffinus Higgs
4. Hugo Ramsden

In anno probationis

1. Iohannes Gibs
2. Humfredus Farrar
3. Iacobus Marsh
4. Henricus Ainscomb[1]
5. Guilielmus Nevil
6. Guilielmus Cox

Capellani

1. Robertus Basly
2. Guilielmus Warberton

Computus custodis

Primo die Augusti ad horam octavam matutinam convenerunt in conclavi custodis custos et omnes socii tunc domi existentes ubi in praesentia omnium computavit dominus custos de receptis et allocatis et discessit in plussagio 57 li. 8s. 9d.

Progressus

Eodem tempore instituit dominus custos ex consensu sociorum progressum causa visitationis maneriorum, cui assignatur loco bursarii magister Simonson.

Dimissiones indenturarum

Eodem etiam tempore concessimus Heath manerium nostrum de Farleigh pro termino 21us annorum; finis 200 marks.

Eodem tempore dimissimus manerium nostrum de Ibston Richardo Wilmot firmario ibidem pro termino 21us annorum; finis 50 li.

Eodem tempore renovavimus Guilelmo Temple indenturam suam de Basingstoke pro termino 21us annorum; finis 50 li.

Electio officiariorum

Eodem die hora 3^{tia} pomeridiana convenimus in alta aula ubi productis clavibus bibliothecae publice et resignatis clavibus officiariorum nostrorum dominus custos et 5 simpliciter seniores, reliquis ad tempus secedentibus, elegerunt in officiarios anni sequentis:
vice-custodem magistrum Simonson.
magistrum Philipson, magistrum Pettye, magistrum Allen, decanos.
magistrum Greevil, magistrum Turner, magistrum Dickenson, bursarios.
principalem portionistarum, magistrum Lane; stipendium bursarii

[1] Above Ainscomb is 'Guilielmus Fettiplace', deleted.

Williot inter duos seniores decanos; capellanum capellae magistrum Simonson; exhibitionarium Hamsterley magistrum Lane; praelectorem grammaticae dominum Hawly; praelectorem linguae Graecae dominum Ramsden; baccalaureus Williot nominandus a principali.

Sigillationes

Eodem tempore dimisimus Iohanni Chandler tenementum in Holliwell nuper in occupatione viduae Davies pro termino quadraginta annorum sursum reddidit 38 annos; finis 20s. Ista indentura una cum altera cuiusdam partis terrae antea concessa Richardo Holdernes ad extruendam domum in Holliwell infra spatium 3um annorum est sigillata 6to Augusti.

Anno Domini 1614, regni regis Iacobi 12°, domini Henrici Saville p. 252
custodis 30°.

Computus bursarii

Augusti 24° et 25° magister Philipson 3^{ius} bursarius computavit in scaccario de administracione sua.

Admissio sociorum

Octobris undecimo dominus Gibs, dominus Farrar, dominus Marsh admissi sunt in perpetuam societatem huius domus; dominus Fettiplace una cum iis ante annum admissus ad probationem, eo quod gravi corporis afflictus in valetudine integro fere anno abfuisset a collegio, nec adhuc adierat, in numerum sociorum cum praedictis aliis hoc tempore non relatus est.

Sigillationes

Octobris 8° sigillatae sunt indenturae Guilielmo Temple de Basingstoke, Stephano Heath de Farleigh, utraque concessa 1° Augusti.

Varii Computus

Eodem die Robertus Mayne firmarius noster de Chedington computavit in scaccario.

Octobris 15° Richardus Wilmot firmarius de Ibston computavit in scaccario.

Octobris 18 Richardus Hodsden firmarius de Callowland computavit.

Novembris 4 magister Napper firmarius de Holliwel et Woolvercot computavit.

Novembris 8 computavit Robertus Ray firmarius de Kibworth.

Eodem die computavit Edmundus Gregory firmarius de Cuxam.

Novembris 28° Henricus Saer firmarius de Barkby computavit in scaccario et discessit in arreragia 9 li. 6s. 2d.

Variationes

Decembris 2° magister Allen variavit in his quaestionibus:

An { 1. Recte Hippodamus legem tulerit ut, si quis utile quid reipublicae adeoque novas leges inveniret premio afficiretur?
2. Senes magis quam iuvenes in illud peccent, ne quid nimis?
3. Inaequalitas in statu democratico tollenda sit per ostracismum? }

Tertio Decembris dispensavimus cum eo pro 2^{dis} eius variationibus.

Computus bursarii

Decembris 14° et 15° magister Dickenson 1us bursarius de administratione computavit in scaccario.

Commemoratio

Decembris 18 divina fecimus pro fundatore nostro, eodemque die statuta legimus et habuimus scrutinium quod prorogavimus in 1um diem Ianuarii et quemlibet diem citra.

Sigillatio

Decembris 19 sigillavimus indenturam de Ibston 1° Augusti concessam Richardo Wilmot pro termino 21 annorum.

Scrutinium servientium

Decembris ultimo habitum est scrutinium pro servientibus. Quo tempore tria fuerunt a bursario presente proposita, primum de moribus servientium qui post admonitiones quasdam commissi officiariis; secundum de numero portionistarum quem eundem esse debere qui antea fuit est decretum; tertium de electione hortulani in quod officium nominatus est magister Turner.

[1615]

Commemoratio

Aprilis 1 commemorationem habuimus pro fundatore et eodem die scrutinium quod prorogatum est in 20^{m} diem mensis eiusdem.

Anno Domini 1615, regni regis Iacobi 13, domini Henrici Savill custodis 30°. p. 253

Admissio

Aprilis 17 convocatis sociis in altam aulam dominus Ainscomb, dominus Nevill, dominus Cox admissi sunt in perpetuam societatem huius collegii.

Dispensatio

Eodem tempore dispensatum est cum magistro Dickenson pro primis variationibus usque ad terminum Michaelis proxime sequentem.

Magistri facti

Iunii tertio dominus Hawly, dominus Sellar, dominus Higgs, dominus Ramsden admissi in numerum magistrorum, dispensatione prius concessa per dominum custodem pro mediatione.

Praesentatio Lane ad Ibston

Iunii 10° sigillata est praesentatio ad rectoriam de Ibston magistro Lane.

Commemoratio et scrutinium

Vicesimo primo Iulii habita est commemoratio pro fundatore, lecta statuta et scrutinium celebratum, quod prorogatum in decimum diem Augusti et in quemlibet diem citra.

Computus firmarii

Iulii 12° Iohannes Sherwood firmarius de Cantabrigia computavit.

Iulii ultimo Stephanus Heath computavit pro Farleigh.

Finis impositus liti cum maiore et ballivis Cantabrigiae pro retractione redditus 20s.

In progressu superioris anni mense Septembris dominus custos Cantabrigiae existens summoneri fecit maiorem villae Cantabrigiae per breve de subpoena, cum ballivi ante per Iohannem Sherwood firmarium nostrum fuissent summoniti per breve consimile, eo quod dicti maior et ballivi per triennium proxime elapsum retraxissent reditum annualem 20s. nobis debitum, et a tempore cuius contrarium in hominum memoria non existit nobis solutum. Qui quidem maior ita summonitus adiit, dominum custodem tum in hospitio praepositi Collegii Regalis morantem, praefatusque se, ballivos, et burgenses omnes villas libere agnoscere praedictam summam 20s. quotannis nobis rite deberi, convenit se satisfacturum collegio tam pro arreragiis trium annorum quam pro expensis in lite ad summam 30s., neque in posterum defuturos officio suo. Quae etiam summae termino sequenti plene solutae sunt ad manus firmarii nostri, atque ita finis impositus est huic liti.

[*rest of p. 253 blank*]

p. 254 Anno Domini 1615, regni regis Iacobi 13, domini Henrici Savile custodis 31°.

Augustus

Magistri in artibus

1. Nathanael Brent
2. Iohannes Talbot
3. Thomas Horne
4. Guilielmus Simonson
5. Isaack Wake
6. Franciscus Greevill
7. Samuel Lane
8. Iohannes Philipson
9. Georgius Pettye
10. Petrus Turner
11. Guilielmus Dickenson
12. Richardus Hawley
13. Guilielmus Sellar
14. Griffinus Higgs
15. Hugo Ramsden

Bacchalaurei in artibus

1. Iohannes Gibs
2. Umphredus Farrar
3. Iacobus Marsh
4. Henricus Ainscombe
5. Guilielmus Nevill
6. Guilielmus Cox

Capellani

1. Robertus Beesly
2. Guilielmus Warberton

Officiarii

Primo die Augusti ad horam nonam antemeridianam, convocatis in altam aulam omnibus sociis electi sunt per dominum custodem et quinque simpliciter seniores officiarii videlicet:
Guilielmus Simonson, vicecustos.
magistri Lane, Turner, Higs, decani.
magistri Philipson, Pettye, Sellar, bursarii.
magister Horne, principalis portionistarum; magister Greevill, bursarius Williot (cui etiam data est exhibitio capellani capelle); magister Hawly, praelector grammaticae; magister Ramsden, praelector linguae Graecae; magister Lane, capellanus Hamsterley; baccalaureus Williot nominandus a principali.

Dismissio indenturae
Eodem tempore dimissa est domus vocata Leaden Porch Londini viduae Eton pro termino 40 annorum; finis 80 li.

Progressus
Eodem tempore consenserunt dominus custos et socii de progressu et de mittendo magistrum Simonson ad terras collegii dimittendas in agro Eboracensi apud manerium de Beilbye.

Computus custodis
Augusti 3° dominus custos in praesentia sociorum computavit et computatis computandis et allocatis allocandis discessit in plussagio 35 li. 13s. 6d. ob.

Scrutinium prorogatum
Eodem tempore scrutinium antea prorogatum in 10 Augusti iterum prorogatum est in 1^{mum} diem Novembris et quemlibet diem citra.

Admissiones indenturarum
Augusti 5to dimissimus indenturam utriusque medietatis silvarum apud Farleigh magistro Fennar pro tempore 21us annorum; finis 80 li. Eodem tempore dimissum tenementum apud Hampton Powell Iohanni Iohnson pro termino 21us annorum.

Computus generalis
Octobris 6 dimissa est Saer indentura de Barkby una cum particula quadam terrae vocata Furmeston pro termino viginti annorum; finis 6 li. 13s. 4d.

Varii computus firmariorum
Eodem tempore habuimus computum generalem in scaccario. Octobris 9° computavit Saer, firmarius de Barkby; Octobris 7 computavit Mayne, firmarius de Chedington; Octobris 10 computavit Wilmot, firmarius de Ibston; Octobris 12 computavit Hodsden, firmarius de Callowland; Octobris 24 Robertus Ray computavit pro Kibworth; Novembris 7° Edmundus Gregory, firmarius de Cuxam, computavit; Novembris 28° Guilielmus Napper, firmarius de Hollywell et Wolvercot, computavit; 29° idem magister Napper computavit pro tenementis Holiwell, Oxon', Witney, London.

p. 255 Anno Domini 1615, regni regis Iacobi 13, domini Henrici Savilli custodis 31°.

Variationes

Decembris 13° magister Dickenson primo variavit in his quaestionibus:

An { Materia sit principium corruptionis.
Plures possint esse formae in eodem composito.
Materia differat a sua potentia. }

Decembris 16° idem variavit secundo in his quaestionibus:

An { Civitas sit a natura.
Civitas bellicosissima sit optima.
Absolutum unius imperium sit optimum. }

Commemoratio

Decembris 17 divina fecimus pro fundatore, statuta legimus, habuimusque scrutinium, quod prorogatum in 1^{mum} diem Martii et quemlibet diem citra.

Decembris 21 computavit magister Sellar 1us bursarius.

Sigillationes indenturarum

Eodem die sigillatae sunt indenturae horti e regione Aulae Albanae magistro Woode pro termino 30 annorum; finis o.

Eodem etiam die sigillatae indenturae domus in parochia Sanctae Ebbes Price pro termino 40 annorum; finis 40s.

Eodem etiam tempore sigillatae sunt indenturae domus in Pye Lane una cum licentia alienat' magistro Bell pro termino 40 annorum; finis xiii li. vis. viiid.

[1616]

Commemoratio

Vicesimo tertio die Martii habita commemoratio pro fundatore, lecta statuta, et scrutinium celebratum, quod prorogatum erat in V^{tum} diem Iulii.

Commemoratio Iesoppe

Aprilis 11° habuimus commemorationem pro domino doctore Iesop portionistarum benefactore non ita multum antea defuncto.

Electio sociorum.
Eodem die convocatis sociis omnibus in hospitium custodis decretum est unanimi consensu electionem sociorum facere, et die sequenti publica cepit fieri examinatio.

Aprilis 15° convenerunt custos et tredecim seniores in predicto conclavi et examinatione finita, hi septem electi sunt in socios futuros, dominus Feeld, dioceseos Winton', dominus Gouldsmith, dioceseos Cicestrensis inelig',[1] dominus Maycot, dioceseos Cantuariensis, dominus Gall, dioceseos Lincolniensis, dominus Anion, dioceseos Cantuariensis, French et Carpenter, dioceseos Oxoniensis, decretumque est ut tres seniores admitterentur primo die termini Hilarii proxime sequenti, quatuor autem reliqui reiecti sunt ad initium eiusdem termini anno revoluto.

Solvunt in admissione sua ad usum bibliothecae collegii, dominus Feeld 3 li. 6s. 8d., dominus Gouldsmith 20s., dominus Maicot 3 li. 6s. 8d., dominus Gall 20s., dominus Anion 3 li. 6s. 8d. dominus French 3 li. 6s. 8d., dominus Carpenter 3 li. 6s. 8d. Summa 18 li. 13s. 4d.

Computus Petty 2^i bursarii
Aprilis 17 computavit in scaccario magister Petty 2us bursarius.

Medietas rectoriae de Gamblingay magistro Lane
Eodem loco et tempore dominus custos proposuit sociis omnibus ut praesentationem medietatis rectoriae de Gamblingay concederent magistro Lane; cui unanimiter consensum est, sed ea lege, ut rectoriam de Ibston ad quam aliquot ante menses praesentatus erat a collegio resignaret rursus ante finem mensis Septembris hic apud collegium sine dolo malo.

Sigillationes indenturarum
Maii 17° concessa ac eodem etiam die sigillata est indentura de Canes Richardo Spranger pro termino 21us annorum; finis 160 li.

Eodem quoque tempore concessa et sigillata indentura de Norton Mandevill Guilelmo Storne pro eodem termino annorum; finis 120 li.

[1] Eligibility, originally limited to those from Winchester diocese, was later extended to any diocese where the college had property. In 1596 Archbishop Whitgift confirmed that eligibility extended to dioceses 'ubi sua beneficia seu feodalia ac alio suo victui deputata consistant'. The college had no property in Chichester diocese, but Gouldsmith was elected.

p. 256 Anno Domini 1616, regni Iacobi 14°, domini Henrici Saville custodis 31°.

Terrae perquisitae apud Newington

Iunii 26° sigillatae sunt indenturae pro terris nuper perquisitae apud Newington in comitatu Cantii.

Domus domini custodis

Eodem die dominus custos post annuam hic mansionem, iam discessum parans, donavit collegio centum libras quae statim repositae fuerunt in cista.

Praesentatio Wilton ad vicariam de Woolford

Vicesimo octavo Iulii sigillata est praesentatio domini Wilton ad vicariam de Woolfoord tum vacantem.

Sigillatio

Quinto Iulii sigillata est indentura pro parte vasti apud Holliwell dimissa Wiblin, Meriman, et aliis.

Commemoratio

Iulii 20 habitis pro fundatore exequiis, lecta sunt statuta et celebratum scrutinium.

Eodem die monitus est dominus Farrer ut se deinceps a frequentandis popinis abstineret; atqe haec est 2da eius admonitio.

Computus

Vicesimo nono Iulii computavit Heath firmarius noster de Farleigh.

Decretum de communariis 1607,[1] factum maturiori consili, iam oblitum

Iunii 1° visum est custodi et 8 senioribus in vestiario congregatis decretum aliquot ante annos factum de recipiendis cominariis duodecim de filiis nobilium et valentium in posterum esse perpetuo dissolvendum, quod experientia compertum esset rem esse noxiam bonis moribus collegii et ad corrumpendam veterem disciplinam plurimum tendere, praesertim cum dicti comminari ad gradum aliquem promoverentur in universitate.

Vicaria de Woolfoord domino Wilton

Iunii vicesimo nono ex unanimi consensu custodis atque omnium sociorum praesentatio ad vicariam de Woolfoorde in comitatu

[1] *Margin,* refers back to p. 226 of this register.

Wigorniensi non ita multo antea concessa, sigillata est domino Iohanni Wilton.

Anno Domini 1616, anno regni regis Iacobi 14, domini Henrici Savile custodis 32. p. 257

Augustus

Magistri in artibus

1. Nathanael Brent
2. Iohannes Talbot
3. Thomas Horne
4. Guilielmus Simonson
5. Isaack Wake
6. Franciscus Greevill
7. Iohannes Philipson
8. Georgius Pettye
9. Petrus Turner
10. Guilielmus Dickenson
11. Richardus Hawlye
12. Guilielmus Sellar
13. Griffinus Higs
14. Hugo Ramsden

Bacchalaurii in artibus

1. Iohannes Gibs
2. Umphredus Farrar
3. Iacobus Marsh
4. Henricus Ainscombe
5. Guilielmus Neville
6. Guilielmus Coxe

Capellani

1. Robertus Beeslye
2. Robertus Gaylarde

electi in annum probacionis alii septem, de quibus vide p. 255.[1]

Electio officiariorum

Primo die Augusti convocatis pro more sociis omnibus per dominum custodem et quinque seniores designati sunt officiarii in annum sequentem:

Guilielmus Simonson, vicecustos.

magister Dickenson, magister Sellar, magister Ramsden, decani.

magister Turner, magister Hawly, magister Higs, bursarii.

principalis portionistarum, magister Greevil; bursarius Williot, magister Philipson; exhibitionarius Hamsterley, magister Dickenson; capellanus capellae, magister Pettye; praelector Graecae, magister Ramsden; praelector grammaticae, dominus Marsh;[2] custodes cistae Reade, tres decani; conservatores[3] cistae Bodley, magister Greevil, magister Philipson, Pettye.

[1] This note, inserted in a different hand, refers back to the minute of 15 April 1616.

[2] *Margin*, 'Memorandum de tribus auditoribus utriusque cistae in posterum annuatim nominandis tempore electionis officiariorum'.

[3] 'auditores' deleted.

Computus Custodis

Augusti 2° dominus custos computavit in praesentia sociorum et computatis computandis et allocatis allocandis discessit in plussagio 5 li. 13s. 6d. ob.

Indenturae

Decimo quarto die Augusti convenerunt dominus custos et omnes socii in alta aula ubi concesserunt Thomae Kemble et Francisco Kemble indenturam in rectoria de Margaretae Stratton pro termino viginti [et] unius annorum.

Cedit autem de iure Thomae Kemble quod in eadem rectoria habuit pro termino vitae suae; finis 300 li.

Eodem die et tempore concessa est magistro Ratliffe indentura de domo nostra in parrochia Sancti Martini pro termino 40 annorum resignata prius indentura 32 annorum; finis 5 li.

Eodem quoque tempore concessimus Thomae Hales indenturam domus cuiusdam in Holliwell aliquando in tenura Gastelow pro termino 40 annorum; finis 3 li. 6s.

Eodem etiam tempore concessa indentura tenementi in Holliwell Richardo Iddens pro termino 40 annorum; finis 40s.

Dedimus etiam Iohanni Davies indenturam tenementi cuiusdam in Holliwell nuper ab eo constructi pro termino 40 annorum; finis o.

Concessimus etiam Guilelmo Poynard indenturam tenementi in Holliwel pro termino 21 annorum, finis o.

Sigillationes indenturaum

Decimo quinto eiusdem mensis sigillatae sunt indenturae Kemble et Iddens.

Augusti 20° indenturae Ratliffe, Davies, Poynar, Hales sigillantur.

Eodem tempore concessa est Wiblin indentura tenementi in Holliwell pro termino 21 annorum; finis 6 li. 13s. 4d.

Computus bursarii

Eiusdem mensis 21° et 22° computavit magister Philipson 3us bursarius in scaccario.

Anno Domini 1616, anni regni regis Iacobi 14, domini Henrici Savile custodis 32°. p. 258

Computus cistae Read
Vicesimo nono Augusti habitus est computus cistae Reade.

Computus cistae Bodley
Augusti 30° habuimus computum cistae Bodley.

Decretum de computu generali
Eodem die decretum est per dominum custodem et octo seniores ut singulis annis statim et immediate (quantum commode fieri poterit) post computum tertii bursarii finitum fiat computus generalis omnium receptorum, expensorum, arreragiorum illius anni. Hunc autem computum faciet vicecustos, qui pro tempore coram septem vel octo seniores [*sic*], et computo hoc generali finito et in pergameno descripto et non antea, pro laboribus percipiet summam tredecim solidorum et 4 denariorum.

Ly Floure de Lys dimittur magistro Woode[1]
Octavo die Septembris convocatis per dominum custodem sociis omnibus consensum est de dimittenda indentura Hospitii de Ly Flowre de Lys magistro Woode pro termino 40 annorum; ea autem lege concessa est ut sese obliget collegio expendere 100 li. ante festum Sancti Michaelis anno 1617 in reparandis aedibus iam per incuriam priorum tenentium ad ruinam fere tendentibus; finis 30 li.

Praesentatio Lane ad Rectoriam de Gamblingay
Duodecimo Septembris conveniunt dominus custos atque omnes socii domi existentes, hora nona, ac unanimi omnium consensu magistro Lane sigillata fuit praesentatio ad medietatem rectoriae de Gamblingay, resignata prius ac tradita in manus custodis rectoria de Ibston, ad quam ante annum praesentatus fuerat a collegio.

Progressus ad Chedington
Decimo sexto eiusdem mensis dominus custos de consensu sociorum aliquot ante dies habito, progressum iniit una cum magistro Philipson loco bursarii ad visitandum manerium nostrum de Chedington ibique tenendam curiam.

[1] 'Thomas Woode' added, in different hand.

Alienationes

Vicesimo die mensis eiusdem dominus custos retulit sociis omnibus in altam aulam convocatis acta in progressu et curia apud Chedington.

Eodem tempore concessa magistro Woode licentia alienandi hospitium de ly Flower de Lys, et Hales tenementum suum in Holliwell.

Dispensatio

Eodem etiam tempore distulimus variationes magistro Sellar et magistro Ramsden in annum sequentem.

Magister Philipson discedit aeque.

Decimo tertio Octobris magister Philipson 3us bursarius induxit computum in scaccarium et soluto pede computi sui discessit aeque.

Progressus ad Cuxam

Eodem tempore consensum est uti vicecustos et magister Dickenson irent Cuxam ad tenendam curiam atque copias quasdam dimittendas.

Computus

Eisdem etiam tempore et loco computavit Mayne firmarius et ballivus noster de Chedington et discedit aeque.

Sigillationes

Eodem die sigillatae sunt magistro Woode indenturae de hospitio nostro vocato ly Fleur de Lys, una cum licentia idem alienandi; sigillatae etiam Iohanni Langly indenturae tenementi in Holliwell nuper in occupatione Clarke, simul etiam sigillata eidem licentia alienandi, finis 20s.; nec non licentia alienandi concessa Halles et sigillata tenementi sui in Holliwell.

Varii computus

Octobris 16 computavit Hodsden firmarius noster de Callowland et discedit aeque.

Eiusdem mensis 26 Wilmot firmarius noster de Ibston computavit in scaccario et discedit aeque.

Novembris quarto Gregory firmarius de Cuxham computavit in scaccario et discedit aeque.

Anno Domini 1616, anno regni regis Iacobi 14, domini Henrici Savil custodis 32. p. 259

Praesentatio ad Rectoriam de Ibston

Vicesimo die Novembris sigillata est ex consensu sociorum magistro Francisco Ruffin praesentatio rectoriae de Ibston, custodis consensu per litteras prius habito.

Computus bursarii

Decembris 18 computavit magister Higs primus bursarius in scaccario.

Commemoratio

Eodem die habuimus commemorationem pro fundatore et celebravimus scrutinium, quod prorogatum est in primum diem Ianuarii et quemlibet diem citra.

Scrutinium servientium

In vigilia circumscitionis convenientibus pro more in alta aula vicecustode et sociis habitum est scrutinium, in quo de moribus servientium quaesitum est; compertum vero nihil severiori animadversione dignum negligentiae solummodo propositae leviores, de quibus per officiarios admonendi[s]. In numero portionistarum nihil commutari voluerint. In hortulanum elegerunt magistrum Hawlye.

[1617]

Admissio probationariorum

Ianuarii 14 admissi sunt in annum probationis dominus Goldsmith, dominus Maycot, dominus Gaule, dominus Feeld, cum his aliquot ante menses electus atque hoc tempore una admittendus, iure admissionis in annum probationis excidit, quod uberius per mortem patris ei obtigit patrimonium.

Commemorati

Aprilis 12 divina fecimus pro fundatore eodem die legimus statuta, et scrutinium habuimus quod in primum diem Maii prorogatum est et in quemlibet diem citra.

Computus bursarii

Decimo sexto eiusdem mensis computavit magister Hawly 2us bursar[ius] in scaccario.

Doctor Warner superior lector Linacri. magister Simonson inferior lector
Eodem die ex consensu domini custodis et octo seniorum concessa est superior lectura Linacri domino doctori Warner, ac die sequenti inferior magistro Simonson, utraque pro spatio trium annorum.

Magistri facti
Maii 17° dominus Farrar et dominus Marsh venia prius concessa per literas a domino custode pro mediatione admissi sunt in numerum magistrorum.

Resignatio domini Gibs
Iunii 24° tradita est in manus vicecustodis per magistrum Sellar resignatio domini Gibs in hanc formam: Ego Iohannes Gibs socius collegii de Merton ultro ac sponte cedo, renuncio, ipseque memet abdico omni privilegio commoditati emolumento quibus quovismodo in ista domo iure societatis uti, frui aut gaudere possem. In cuius rei testimonium huic presenti chirographo proprium sigillum apposui 17° die Maii, anno domini 1617.

Variationes
Iunii 6° variavit magister Hawly in his quaestionibus:

An {
Urbes manibus expedit muniri? Negat.
Artes recte civitati consuluit qui in ea medicis locum non assignavit? Negat.
Populi Europaei arte et ingenio cedant Asiaticis? Negat.

Eodem tempore dispensatum cum eo est pro secundis eius variationibus.

Iulii 9° magister Higs variavit in his quaestionibus:

An {
E re fuerit litteraria in artis verba iuravisse? Negat.
Civilis disciplina a philosophis potius quam a politicis sit discenda? Negat.
Ephori apud Lacedomonios recte e toto populo creati fuerint? Affirmat.

Iulii 10 cum eo dispensatum pro secundis variationibus.

Commemoratio
Iulii 20. Habita est commemoratio pro fundatore, lecta statuta scrutinium celebratum, quod prorogatum est in 10 [die]m Octobris et quemlibet diem citra.

Anno Domini 1617, anno regni regis Iacobi 15°, domini Henrici Saville custodis 33°. p. 260

Augustus

Magistri in artibus

1. Nathanael Brent
2. Iohannes Talbot
3. Guilielmus Simonson
4. Isac' Wake
5. Franciscus Greevile
6. Iohannes Philipson
7. Georgius Pettye
8. Petrus Turner
9. Guilielmus Dickenson
10. Richardus Hawly
11. Guilielmus Sellar
12. Griffinus Higs
13. Hugo Ramsden
14. Umfredus Farrar
15. Iacobus Marsh

Baccalaurei socii

1. Henricus Ainscomb
2. Guilielmus Nevill
3. Guilielmus Coxe

In anno probationis

1. dominus Gouldsmith
2. dominus Maycot
3. dominus Gale

Capellani

1. Robertus Beeslye
2. Robertus Gaylard

Electi alii tres de quibus vide p. 255.[1]

Electio officiariorum

Augusti duodecimo, convocatis ad horam nonam antemeridianam sociis omnibus in altam aulam, productis clavibus bibliothecae publicae et resignatis clavibus officiariorum, electi sunt a domino custode et quinque simpliciter senioribus (reliquis ad tempus secedentibus) hi officiarii in annum sequentem:
vicecustos, magister Simonson.
magister Turner, magister Higs, magister Marsh, decani.
magister Pettye, magister Ramsden, magister Farrar, bursarii.
principalis portionistarum, magister Philipson; bursarius Williot, magister Dickenson; exhibitionarius Hamsterly, magister Dickenson; capellanus capellae, magister Turner; custodes cistae Reade, 3 decani; conservatores cistae Bodly, magister Greevill, magister Hawly, magister Sellar; auditores cistae Read, 3 bursarii; auditores cistae Bodly, 3 decani;

[1] This refers back to the minute of 15 April 1616.

praelector Graecae, magister Ramsden; praelector grammaticae, magister Marsh.

Computus Custodis

Augusti 14 convenimus in conclave domini custodis, ubi dominus custos in praesentia sociorum computavit, et computatis computandis et allocatis allocandis discessit in plussagio 16 li. 18s. 4d.

Dismissiones indenturarum

Eodem tempore dimissimus magistro Iacob manerium de Gamblingay Avenels pro termino 21us annorum; finis 100 li.

Eidem dimissimus silvas nostras de Merton' pro termino 21us annorum; finis 20 li.

Eodem tempore dimissimus Francisco Cooper tenementum apud Kibworth pro termino 21 annorum; finis 50 li.

Eodem tempore dimissimus Edmundo Gregory manerium de Cuxam pro termino 21us annorum; finis 50 li.

Concessimus eodem tempore magistro Whitton tenementum apud Hensington pro termino 20 annorum; finis 50 li.

Eodem tempore concessimus viduae Poynar tenementum in Holliwel, pro termino 40 [annorum].

Concessimus eodem tempore Iddens licentiam alienandi tenementum in Holliwell.

Computus cistae Read

Eodem die a prandio habitus est computus cistae Reade.

Sigillationes

Augusti 15 sigillavimus indenturas de terris superiore anno perquisitis de magistro Whitton apud Hensington.

Eodem tempore sigillata indenturae viduae Poynar; et licentia alienandi Iddens.

p. 261 Anno Domini 1617, anno regni regis Iacobi 15°, domini Henrici Savill custodis 33°.

Computus bursarii

Augusti vicesimo magister Turner, 3us bursarius computavit in scaccario.

Dimissio indenturae

Eodem die et loco dimisimus Clarke tenementum in Holliwell olim in tenura Udall, pro 21us annorum; finis 4 li.

Computus firmarii

Augusti vicesimo primo computavit Hodsden firmarius noster de Callowland.

Dimissio indenturae

Augusti 22° concessimus indenturam molendinorum de Holliwell et Kings Mill magistro Napper pro termino 40 annorum; finis 300 li.

Sigillationes

Octobris primo sigillavimus indenturam tenementi in Holliwell Thomae Clarke, indenturam tenementi apud Kibworth Francisco Cooper atque etiam licentiam alienandi silvas Farleigh magistro Fennar.

Sigillationes

Octobris 26° sigillavimus indenturam tenementi apud Hensington magistro Whitton, indenturam de Cuxam Edmundo Gregory et licentiam alienandi Thomae Clark pro termino 8 annorum.

Novembris 13° sigillavimus magistro Iacob indenturam de Gamblingay Avenels et de silvis Mertonage ibidem.

Computus generalis

Decembris 13 habuimus computum generalem in scaccario.

Commemoratio

Decembris 16 habita commemoratio, lecta statuta, celebratum scrutinium, quod prorogatum est in primum diem Ianuarii.

Computus 1^{i} bursarii

Eodem die et sequenti magister Farrar primus bursarius computavit in scaccario.

Scrutinium servientium

Ultimo Decembris convocatis in altam aulam sociis tria per bursarium praesentem proposita sunt ipsis consideranda: 1um de moribus servientium quod officiariis commissum; 2um de numero portionistarum, de quo determinatum est ut sit solitus; 3um de electione hortulani quem elegerunt magistrum Sellar. Quibus peractis scrutinium prorogatum in primum diem Februarii.

[1618]

Admissiones

Decimo 4to Ianuarii convenimus in altam aulam, ubi ex consensu custodis et sociorum dominus Gouldsmith in anno probationis constitutus in perpetuam societatem huius collegii admissus est. Admissio autem domini Maycot et domini Gall, id quod in anno probationis non ita bene se gesserant, reiecta et dilata in adventum domini custodis. Cuius sententiae nobis autor fuit ipse dominus custos per literas eodem tempore lectas. Quo etiam loco et tempore ex eodem consensu admissi sunt dominus Anion, dominus French, dominus Carpenter in annum probationis, praestito, ut fieri solet, iuramento consueto.

Sigillationes

Vicesimo tertio die Martii sigillatae sunt indenturae diversarum partium terrae in guasto apud Holliwell magistro Tolderbery, magistro French, Watson, Chaundler, Cooke.

Eodem quoque tempore sigillavimus licentiam alienandi magistro Thorrold pro domo in Salisbury Alley.

Commemoratio pro fundatore

Martii vicesimo octavo habuimus commemorationem pro fundatore, legimus statuta, scrutinium celebravimus quod prorogatum in ultimum Maii et quemlibet diem citra.

Computus bursarii

Aprilis decimo quinto magister Ramsden 2us bursarius computavit in scaccario.

Magistri facti

Maii 21° dominus Ainscomb, dominus Nevill, dominus Cox, admissi sunt ex consensu domini custodis et sociorum in numerum magistrorum.

Dimissio indenturae

Eodem tempore dimissa et sigillata est indentura tenementi in Holliwell Edwar[do] Woorsly et Mariae uxori eius pro termino 40 annorum.

Variationes

Maii 22° magister Sellar variavit in his quaestionibus:

An { Salus Reipublicae pendeat a legibus? Negat.
Data Hypothesi oporteat potius ferre quam inferre iniurias? Negat.
Adultis quam pueris aut senibus faelicior sit memoria? Negat. }

Dispensatio

Eodem die cum eo dispensatum est pro 2[is] variationibus.

Iunii 14 dispensatum est cum magistro Ramsden ut liceat ei variationes hoc anno habendas differre in terminum Michaelis proxime sequentem.

Commemoratio

Iulii 20 habita pro fundatore commemoratione, lecta sunt statuta et celebratu[m] scrutinium.

Anno Domini 1618, regis Iacobi 16, domini Henrici Savile custodis 34°. p. 262

Augustus

Magistri in artibus

1. Nathanael Brent
2. Guilielmus Simonson
3. Isaack Wake
4. Franciscus Greevil
5. Iohannes Philipson
6. Georgius Pettye
7. Petrus Turner
8. Guilielmus Dickinson
9. Richardus Hawlye
10. Guilielmus Sellar
11. Griffinus Higs
12. Hugo Ramsden
13. Umfredus Farrar
14. Iacobus Marsh
15. Henricus Ainscombe
16. Guilielmus Nevill
17. Guilielmus Cox

Baccalaurii socii

1. dominus Gouldsmith

In anno probationis

1. dominus Maycot
2. dominus Gale
3. dominus Anion
4. dominus French
5. dominus Carpenter

Capellani

1. Robertus Beesly
2. Robertus Gaylard

Electio officiariorum

Augusti 4 convenerunt in altam aulam hora 8[a] antemeridiana dominus custos et socii ubi singuli eorum claves bibliothecae ad cameras suas spectantes in conspectum custodis deponunt, ac postea resignatis de

more omnium officiariorum anni praeteriti clavibus, custos et quinque simpliciter seniores, secedentibus aliis sociis, procedunt ad electionem officiariorum a quibus electi sunt in annum sequentem hii:
magister Simonson, vicecustos.
magister Greevill, magister Hawlye, magister Sellar, decani.
magister Turner, magister Higs, magister Marsh, bursarii.
magister Dickenson, principalis portionistariorum; magister Pettye, bursarius Williot; magister Philipson, capellanus capellae; magister Higs, exhibitionarius Hamsterley; magister Sellar, praelector grammaticae; dominus Gouldsmith, praelector Graecae; praelector logicae nominandus a principale; conservatores cistae Bodley, magister Philipson, magister Pettye, magister Farrar; custodes cistae Reade, tres decani.

Scholaris magistri Chambers

Eodem loco et tempore lectae litterae a domino Henrico Savile, praeposito Collegii Eton' et domino doctore Collins, praeposito Collegii Regalis in universitate Cantabrigiae pro admittendo scholari magistri Chambers e schola Eton' in numerum portionistarum secundum formam testamenti magistri Chambers et prout decretum est per custodem et socios, ut patet, in registro pagina 211. Qui quidem scholaris eodem die admissus est a principale.

Dimissio indenturarum

Augusti 6to convenimus in conclave domini custodis ubi ex consensu custodis et sociorum dimissae sunt indenturae de Kibworth magistro Ray pro termino 21 annorum; finis 50 li. De Chedington magistro Mayne pro eodem termino; finis 40 li. De ly Rose in Watford pro eodem termino magistro Gerrye; finis 20 li.

Computus custodis

Eodie convocatis sociis in scaccarium dominus custos computavit, et computatis computandis allocatis allocandis discessit in plussagio 22 li. 2s. 2d.

Computus cistae Bodly et Reade

Eodem etiam die habuimus computum cistae Bodly et cistae Reade.

p. 263 Anno Domini 1618, regis Iacobi 16, domini Henrici Savile custodis 34°.

Computus firmariorum

Augusti 22° Hodsden firmarius noster de Callowland computavit.

Octobris 10° Mayne firmarius de Chedington computavit.

Sigillatio

Eodem die sigillata est ei indentura de Chedington.

Computus firmariorum

Octobris 19° magister Napper firmarius de Holliwell et Wolvercot computavit pro 3us annis.

Octobris 24° computavit Wilmot pro firma de Ibston.

Sigillatio

Octobris 20° sigillatae sunt indenturae magistri Ray et Gerie de Kibworth et Watford.

Computus firmarii

Novembris 1° computavit magister Ray pro firma de Kibworth.

Computus firmarii

Novembris 16 H. Saer computavit pro firma de Barkby.

Computus generalis

Eodem die habitus est in scaccario computus generalis.

Licentia alienandi

Novembris 26 sigillavimus magistro Ray licentiam alienandi partem quandam manerii de Kibworth pro termino 10 annorum atque etiam licentiam alienandi magistro Gerry pro ly Rose in Watford.

Scrutinium

Decembris 16 habuimus commemorationem, statuta legimus et celebravimus scrutinium quod prorogatum est in primum diem Ianuarii et quemlibet diem citra.

Computus bursarii

Decembris 17 magister Marsh 1us bursarius computavit in scaccario.

Admissio

Decembris 18 dominus Galle post aliquod tempus a finito anno probationis ex consensu domini custodis et sociorum admissus est in perpetuam societatem huius domus. Dominus Maycot [*incomplete entry*]

Scrutinium servientium

In vigilia circumcisionis iuxta modum et consuetudinem collegii habito scrutinio magister Higs electus est in hortulanum pro anno sequenti. Numerus portionistarum solitus retinetur, servientium delicta relinquntur officiariis corrigenda.

[1619]

Lites pro silvis Chesterton

Vicesimo quinto Februarii convocatis sociis omnibus in altam aulam decretum est de mittendis magistro Turner et magistro Hawly Cantabrigiam ad lites in comitiis prosequendas contra Batisford pro silvis Chesterton, in quibus ius obtinuit collegium.

Commemoratio

Vicesimo die Martii habita est commemoratio fundatoris, eodemque die lecta statuta et scrutinium celebratum quod prorogatum est in 1um diem Iunii et quemlibet diem citra.

Dispensatio

Aprilis 8° dispensavimus cum magistris regentibus pro sex publicis praelectionibus in duobus ultimis terminis, domino custode assensum per literas praebente.

Eodem tempore dispensatum est cum magistro Marsh pro 2^{is} variationibus, primis antea habitis.

Variationes

Martii 20 praedictus magister Marsh variavit in his quaestionibus:

An {
Ars *χρηματίσηχη* [*sic*] est pars prudentiae oeconomicae.
Servitus et nobilitas non sunt gradus hominum a natura destinati.
Male Aristoteles incusat dictum Biantis Ama tanquam osurus.

Computus bursarii

Aprilis 14 magister Higs 2us bursarius computavit in scaccario de administratione sua.

Variationes

Maii 14 magister Farrar variavit in his quaestionibus:

An {
Mechanicus possit exercere virtutes? Affirmat.
Quae de repente fiant fortitudinem veram magis sapiant quam quae ex proviso? Negat.
Difficilius sit voluptati resistere quam irae? Negat.

Dispensatio

Eodem tempore cum eo pro 2^{is} variationibus.

Magister Higs discedit aeque

Iunii 7° magister Higs, 2us bursarius induxit computum in scaccarium, solvitque pedem et discessit aeque.

Vicecustos Etonam mittitur
Iulii 8° sociis in altam aulam convocatis ac audito dominum custodem febre vale periculosa laborasse, visum est omnibus ut vicecustos statim Etonam proficisceretur ad eum invisendum, et communi sociorum nomine gratulandum quod summo dei erga nos nostrumque collegium beneficio nonnihil iam a morbi discrimine sublevaret, quod quidem officium quam grato exceperit animo dominus custos nobis significavit in reditu vicecustodis et abunde testatus est gratiis quibus potuit maximis nobis actis.

Anno Domini 1619, regis Iacobi 17, domini Henrici Savile custodis 34°. p. 263[1]

Commemoratio
Iulii vicesimo (qui erat festum beatae Margaretae) commemorationem habuimus pro fundatore hora et loco solitam [*sic*], statuta legimus, celebravimus scrutinium quod in primum diem Septembris et quemlibet diem citra prorogavimus.

Computus
Iulii vicesimo secundo computavit Sherwood pro Cantabrigia.

Iulii ultimo Stephanus Heath firmarius de Farleigh computavit in scaccario.

[*rest of page blank*]

Anno Domini 1619, regis Iacobi 17, domini Henrici Savile custodis 35°. p. 264a

Augustus

Magistri in artibus
1. Nathanael Brent
2. Gulielmus Simonson
3. Isaac Wake
4. Franciscus Greevil
5. Iohannes Philipson
6. Georgius Pettye
7. Petrus Turner
8. Guilielmus Dickenson
9. Richardus Hawly
10. Guilielmus Sellar
11. Griffinus Higs
12. Umfredus Farrar
13. Iacobus Marsh
14. Henricus Ainscombe
15. Guilielmus Nevill
16. Guilielmus Coxe

Baccalaurei
1. dominus Gouldsmith
2. dominus Gale
3. dominus French

Capellani
1. Robertus Bessly
2. Robertus Gaylard

[1] In MS this page, the *verso* of p. 263, retained the number 263, while the next two pages were both numbered 264, with 'a' and 'b' added later.

Electio officiariorum

Augusti 9° nona hora ante meridiem convenimus in altam aulam custos et omnes socii domi existentes, ubi resignavimus officiarii anni superioris claves officiorum, claves etiam singuli detulimus ad commune ostium bibliothecae spectantes in custodis conspectum, quo peracto iussi sunt reliqui omnes ad tempus secedere praeter quinque simpliciter seniores, a quibus et domino custode designantur in annum sequentem officiarii hi videlicet:

magister Simonson, vicecustos.

magistri Turner, Higs, Nevill, decani.

magistri Philipson, Hawly, Sellar, bursarii.

magister Greevill, principalis portionistarum; magister Petty, electus in bursarium Williot; magister Dickenson, capellanus capellae; magister Higs, exhibitionarius Hamsterly; praelectores nominati, magister Marsh, grammaticae, dominus Gouldsmith, linguae Graecae; assignatio baccalaurei Williot principali relinquitur portionistarum; custodes cistae Reade, 3 decani; custodes cistae Bodly, Petty, Marsh, Coxe.

Doctor Lapworth superior praelector Linacri

Eodem die doctor Lapworth per custodem et septem seniores designatus est praelector superioris lectionis Linacri.

Eodem tempore deliberandum an numerus sociorum augeri posset necne, decretumque electionem sociorum faciendam ac non ita multo postea publica coepit fieri examinatio.

Admissio

Eodem tempore consensum est ut tenementum nostrum in Pocrilston dimitteretur Henri[co] Irish pro termino 21 annorum; finis 30 li.

Dispensatio

Tunc temporis etiam dispensavimus cum magistris regentibus ut non amplius tenentur legere ordinarias, nec disputationes baccalaureorum vel Augustinenses frequentare.

Eodem tempore consensum [est] ut variationes magistri Nevill iam electi in officium iunioris decani prorogentur in annum ab hoc revoluto proxime sequentem.

Computus custodis

Augusti 10 dominus custos computavit pro receptis et allocatis et discessit in plussagio 30s.

Computus de communiis augendis

Eodem tempore consensum est per dominum custodem et socios ut communiae sociorum quibusdam diebus[1] adaugerentur, ita ut in singulis ferculis percipiant decem denarios singulis septimanis ultra summam communiarum quam ad hoc usque tempus perceperunt. Per eosdem etiam consensum est ut mensae custodis vicecustodis et capellani adderentur pro melioratione communiarum singulis septimanis quinque solidi quatuor denarii.

Dismissio

Eodem tempore dimissimus Edwardo Lenge molendinum nostrum apud Beelby et firmam quandam una cum particula prati vocati Bursedale pro termino 21 annorum quae omnia de nobis antea tenuit.

Balivus

Eodem etiam tempore constitutus est praefatus Edwardus Lenge balivus manerii nostri de Beelby; eidemque allocantur quinque marcae per annum pro collectione et transportatione reddituum eiusdem manerii ad collegium.

Anno Domini 1619, regis Iacobi 17, domini Henrici Savile custodis 35°. p. 264b

Electio sociorum

Augusti 13° convenientes custos et 13 simpliciter seniores in conclave custodis procedunt ad electionem sociorum in qua electi sunt hi 7 baccalaurei: dominus Doubtie, dioceseos Worcestrensis, dominus Fisher, dioceseos Cantuariensis, dominus Heath, dioceseos Londinensis (atque hi tres admittendi ad communias in initio termino Michaelis proxime sequentis), dominus Hinton, dioceseos [Lincolniensis ?],[2] dominus Holliwell, dioceseos Eboracensis, dominus Raynolds, dioceseos Wintoniensis, dominus Darbie, dioceseos Eboracensis, in vero admittendi in initio termini Hilarii anno revoluto. Decretum est per eosdem custodem et 13 seniores ut admissione sua solvant in usum bibliothecae, Doubtye, 50s., Fisher, 50s., Heath, 50s., Hinton, 50s., Holliwell, 30s., Raynolds, 10s., Darbie, 30s.

Admonitio

Augusti 16 monitus est magister Ainscomb ut deinceps abstineret a familiaritate cum baccalaureis multis decretis huius domus expressis prohibita et frequentatione locorum in oppido potatione alae infamiam contra iniunctionem a domino custode olim factam, atque haec

[1] 'in singulis septimanis' deleted. [2] MS damaged.

est secunda eius admonitio. Eodem die monitus est dominus Galle propter consimilem causam, et haec est prima eius admonitio.

Subpromus

Eodem tempore deliberaverunt custos atque omnes socii de subpromo faciendo. Et quia ostensum est negotia in promptuario ab uno aliquo non posse commode administrari, visum est alium qui ipsi promo adiumento esset horis et consuetudine debitis, adiungere loco subpromi, cui ex consensu allocantur loco stipendii communiae qualis et caeteri servientes percipiunt et nihil praeterea.

Admissiones

Eodem tempore dominus French admissus est in perpetuam societatem huius domus.

Octobris 11 convenimus in altam aulam ubi ex consensu domini custodis et sociorum admissi sunt dominus Doubtie, dominus Fisher, dominus Heath in annum probationis.

Varii computus

Augusti 26° Hodsden firmarius noster de Callowland computavit; et [discessit] aeque.

Octobris 11 Robertus Mayne firmarius de Cheddington computavit et discessit aeque.

Octobris 23, Wilmot firmarius de Ibston computavit et discessit aeque.

Eodem tempore H. Saer firmarius de Barkby computavit et discessit aeque.

Novembris 3 Edmundus Gregory firmarius de Cuxam computavit et discessit aeque.

Novembris 13 Robertus Ray firmarius de Kibworth computavit et discessit aeque.

Novembris 16 habuimus computum generalem in scaccario.

Computus bursarii

Decembris 16 magister Sellar 1us bursarius computavit de administratione sua in scaccario.

2um collegii donum ad Scholas Publicas

Novembris 17 convenimus in altam aulam, ibique significatum omnia alia collegia iam iterum pecunias contribuere ad novas scholas publicas perficiendas, et ab omnibus consensum ut ipsi e bonis collegii rursus viginti libras hunc in usum conferemus.

Commemoratio cum scrutinio

Decembris 18 habuimus commemorationem fundatoris, legimus statuta et scrutinium inivimus, quod prorogavimus in vigiliam circumcisionis. Quo tempore convenientibus in altam aulam sociis omnibus domi existentibus habitum et de more scrutinium, in quo de moribus servientium est quaesitum, compertum vero nihil severiori animadversione dignum, quorundam negligentia tantummodo propositae de quibus per officiarios admonendi et puniendi.

In hortulanum electus est magister Farrar; in numero autem portionistarum nihil mutandum censuerunt.

[1620]

Libri e custode domino bibliothecae datae [*sic*]

Martii 5° post preces vespertinas in vestiario convenimus, ubi lectae a domino custode litterae quibus significavit se in animo statuisse libros suos quos habebat omnes bibliothecae nostrae dono dare eamque adirent vicecustos et senior decanus, instructi catalogo librorum omnium quos ipsi hic iam antea habebamus, hunc scilicet in finem ut eos quobus libraria nostra destituta erat, et usui nostro maxime necessarios estimarent, eligerent solos, reliquos vero domino custodi relinquerent disponendos prout ipsi videretur quod non ita multo postea peractum est.

Commemoratio

Aprilis 10 habuimus commemorationem pro fundatore, statuta legimus et inivimus scrutinium quod prorogatum est in 1um diem Maii et quemlibet diem citra.

Anno Domini 1620, regis Iacobi 18, domini Henrici Savile custodis 35°. p. 265

Magister Simonson inferior lector Linacri

Aprilis 16 domini custodis et 7 seniorum consensu electus est magister Simonson praelector inferioris lectionis Linacri pro spatio trium annorum.

Computus bursarii

Aprilis 20° magister Hawly 2us bursarius de administratione sua computavit in scaccario.

Variationes

Iulii 5° magister Cox variavit in his quaestionibus [*blank*]

Commemoratio

Iulii 20 scilicet in festo Margaretae habita est pro more commemoratio fundatoris, lecta statuta, initum scrutinium quod continuatur in

[*rest of p. 265 blank*]

p. 266 Anno Domini 1620, regis Iacobi 18, domini Henrici Savile custodis 36°.

Augustus

Magistri in artibus

1. Nathanael Brent
2. Guilielmus Simonson
3. Isaac Wake
4. Franciscus Greevile
5. Iohannes Philipson
6. Georgius Pettye
7. Petrus Turner
8. Guilielmus Dickenson
9. Richardus Hawlye
10. Guilielmus Sellar
11. Griffinus Higs
12. Umfredus Farrar
13. Iacobus Marsh
14. Guilielmus Nevil
15. Guilielmus Coxe

Baccalaurei socii

1. dominus Gouldsmith
2. dominus Galle
3. dominus French

In anno probationis

1. dominus Dowtye
2. dominus Fisher
3. dominus Heath

Capellani

1. Robertus Beeslye
2. Robertus Gaylard

Electio officiariorum

Augusti 1° circiter horam 2^{am} pomeridianam per dominum custodem convocati sunt in altam aulam omnes socii ad officiarios sequentis anni eligendos, postquam igitur socii claves quas habuerant communis bibliothecae officiariisque superioris anni suas similiter in publico deposuissent, secedentibus caeteris, dominus custos et quinque simpliciter seniores hos designant officiarios in annum sequentem videlicet:

magistrum Simonson, vicecustodem.
magistros Sellar, Marsh, Cox, decanos.
magistros Greevil, Higs, Nevil, bursarios.

magistrum Pettye, principalem portionistarum; magistrum Philipson, bursarium Williot et capellanum capellae; exhibitionarium Hamsterley, magistrum Higs; praelectores nominati, magister Farrar, grammaticae, dominus Gouldsmith, Graecae; praelectus logicae, eligendus a principali portionistarum; custodes cistae Reade, 3 decani; custodes cistae Bodly, magister Pettye, magister Turner, magister Farrar.

Dimissiones indenturarum

Eodem tempore unanimiter consensum est de dimittenda una medietate Stillington et Ceton Carewe magistro Ayscough pro termino viginti unius annorum, resignata prius indentura ei 11 ante annos a collegio facta; finis 133 li. 6s. 8d.

Eodem tempore dimissimus cuidam Howse quasdam clausuras in Criclad nuper in occupatione Knight pro termino 21 annorum, postquam assignatio quaedam de eisdam clausuris indentata sigillataque fuerat nobis demonstrata; finis 40 li.

Eisdem etiam loco et tempore concessae Guilelmo Parker quaedam acrae terrae vocatae ly Swathes cum aliis quibusdam terrae arabilis apud Kibworth pro termino 21 annorum; finis 3 li. 6s. 8d.

Die sequente in hospitio custodis terras dominic' de Beelby quae nobis de manibus magistri Dacres nuperrime divenerant, dimissimus per indenturam magistro Heynslye pro termino 21 annorum, et pro redditu annuali de 50 li.

Ballivus

Eodem die eundem magistrum Heinsley constituimus ballivum totius manerii nostri de Beelby propter discessum Edwardi Lenge superioris ballivi ibidem; eidemque allocavimus 40s. per annum pro collectione et transportatione reddituum eiusdem manerii huc ad collegium.

Computus custodis

Eodem tempore dominus custos computavit de receptis et allocandis et discessit in plussagio 7 li. 19s. 4d.

Anno Domini 1620, regis Iacobi 18, domini Henrici Savile custodis 36°. p. 267

Varii computi

Augusti 24° magister Philipson 3us bursarius computavit de administratione sua in scaccario.

Augusti 27 Hodsden firmarius noster de Callowland computavit in scaccario.

Octobris 1° magister Mayne firmarius noster de Chedington computavit in scaccario et discessit aeque.

Curia apud Cuxam

Eodem tempore consensum est de mittendo vicecustode et bursario ad manerium nostrum de Cuxam ut ibi curiam teneant, faciantque facienda.

Admissio

Octobris 11. Dominus Doubty, dominus Fisher, dominus Heath admissi sunt in perpetuam societatem huius domus.

Varii computi

Octobris 27 habitus est computus generalis in scaccario.

Eodem tempore firmarius Ray de Kibworth computavit.

Eodem etiam die Wilmot firmarius de Ibston computavit.

Dimissio indenturarum

Octobris 19 convocatis sociis omnibus in conclave domini custodis dimissimus magistro Hartburne medietatem manerii de Stillington et Ceton Carew pro termino viginti unius annorum; finis 133 li. 6s. 8d. Indentura vero eiusdem una cum altera magistro Ayscough antea concessa, die sequenti sigillata est.

Novembris 7° dimissa firmario Sherwood de Cantabrigia est indentura eiusdem manerii pro termino 21 annorum; finis 30 li.

Eodem die concessa est Hodsden firmario de Callowland indentura eiusdem manerii pro termino 21 annorum; finis 50 li. Utraque indentura una cum altera superius dimissa cuidam Howse de Criklade die sequenti est sigillata.

Eodem etiam tempore concessa est Rankin tenementum in Holliwell pro termino 21 annorum; finis 50s.

Exhibitionarius Doctoris Bickley

Decembris 5° convocatis sociis omnibus domi existentibus in conclave domini custodis magister Higs a domino custode nominatus est exhibitionarius domini doctoris Bickley, stipendium 4 li., sed ea lege ut conciones habeat sicut superius pag. 225 prescriptum est.

Custodia discorum

Eodem loco et tempore per dominum custodem et socios allocati sunt per annum utrisque coquis coniunctim 40s. pro custodia discorum; sub hac conditione ut eorum curam atque onus ipsi in se recipiant, nec domus ullo omnino discorum aut pretio aut dispendio in posterum gravetur.

Obsonator

Eodem etiam tempore Iohannem Flexon a domino custode nominatus in obsonatorem collegii et approbatus ab iisdem sociis. Et quibus omnibus unanimi consensu eidem allocatae sunt communiae quales caeteri percipiunt servientes, atque ultra communias ut habeat de bonis collegii 5 li. annuatim pro stipendio.

Scrutinium in vigilia circumcisionis

In vigilia circumcisionis habitum est de more scrutinium servientium, in quo de eorum moribus quaesitum est. Maximae proponuntur negligentiae, plurimaque comperta severiori animadversione digna sed totum illud negotium in aliud tempus delatum. In hortulanum electus est magister Marsh. In numero portionistarum nihil immutatum.

[1621]

Stipendium promi et ianitoris

Ianuarii 5° convenimus in conclave domini custodis ubi ab omnibus consensum est ut promus habeat in posterum 40 solidos de bursario collegii annuatim pro stipendio. Ibidem ut ianitor recipiat 30 solidos per annum pro stipendio.

Admissiones

Ianuarii 15° convocatis sociis omnibus hora nona in altam aulam ex consensu domini custodis et sociorum admissus est dominus Gouldsmith triennio, ab admissione sua in societatem iam completo, ad incipiendum in facultate artium proximis comitiis praestito in praesentia sociorum iuramento consueto, et eisdem loco et tempore admittantur in annum probationis dominus Hinton, dominus Holliwell, dominus Raynolds, dominus Erles.

Admissio in libraria

Eodem tempore consensum est de admittendis domino doctore Bainbridge et magistro Brigs, publicis praelectoribus in mathematicis, ad studendum, quando ipsis visum fuerit, in bibliotheca nostra communi.

p. 268 Anno Domini 1620, regis Iacobi 18, Henrici Savile custodis 36°.

Allocationes

Februarii 11 convocatis in vestiarium post preces vespertinas sociis allocavimus de more tibicinibus 6s 8d.

Eodem tempore concessa est Richardo Hodsden, firmario licentia alienandi firmam de Callowland pro tempore annorum.

Admissio

Martii 12° admissus est ex consensu domini custodis et magistrorum dominus Gale ad incipiendum in facultate artium.

Dimissio indenturae

Martii 16° dimissimus tenementum quoddam in Holliwell Thomae Holt, nuper in occupatione viduae Thomas, pro termino 40 annorum; finis 20 li.

Magister Wilkinson reddidit 20 li.

Eodem die magister Henricus Wilkinson reddidit collegio viginti libras quas discedens acceperat pro communiis in anno gratuitatis; has autem 20 li. dominus custos censuit reddendas ne novum apud posteros istius modi allocationis exemplum extaret.

Computus

Martii 17 habiti sunt in praesentia domini custodis et sociorum computus cistae Bodly et cistae Reade.

Commemoratio

Martii 24 habita est commemoratio pro fundatore, lecta statuta et celebratum scrutinium.

Sigillationes

Eodem die sigillata est indentura Holt pro tenemento in Holliwell, atque etiam alia indentura sigillata inter executores magistri Chamber et collegium pro electione unius baccalaurei in societatem et duorum scholarum in numerum portionistarum hunc et illos de fundatione Eton; prout in praedicta indentura uberius est expressum.

Commemoratio

Iulii vicesimo nempe in festo Margaretae habita est commemoratio fundatoris et lectis statutis celebratum est scrutinium quod prorogatum est in 1um diem Septembris et in quemlibet diem citra.

Redditus Beelby semel in anno solvendus
Iulii ultimo convocatis a domino custode omnibus sociis in hospitium ab ipso nobis propositum est ut magister Heynsly, firmarius terrarum dominicalium de Beelby in comitatu Ebor', idemque ballivus manerii ibidem per indenturam ei ante annum concessam obligatus ad redditum firmae persolvendum, reddendamque hic apud collegium bis quotannis (nempe ad festum sancti Martini et Pentecostes) ballivatus sui rationem, iam posthac non teneretur ad illud nisi semel in anno ad festum scilicet Pentecostes praestandum. Quod quidem ei tam propter viae longitutudinem [*sic*], quam etiam incommodam hyeme itinerandi rationem unanimiter ab omnibus concessum est. Insuper eidem magistro Heinsly delegata a collegio potestas autoritasque distringendi si modo tenentes redditum debito tempore solvere recusent.

Progressus
Eodem tempore consenserunt dominus custos et socii de progressu in comitatu Lecestriae faciendo mittendoque vicecustode et magistro Turner ad curiam apud Kibworth et Barkby tenendam.

Locatio tenementi in Holywell
Eodem tempore conceditur Boxly tenementum in Holywell pro termino viginti unius annorum; finis 30 li.

Dispensatio
Eodem etiam loco et tempore dominus custos in praesentia sociorum dispensavit cum magistro Gouldsmith ut sacros ordines intraret etiamsi terminum regentiae suae non compleverat.

Anno Domini 1621, regis Iacobi 19, domini Henrici Savile custodis 37°. p. 269

Augustus

Magistri in artibus
1. Nathanael Brent
2. Guilielmus Simonson
3. Isaack Wake
4. Franciscus Greevill
5. Iohannes Philipson
6. Georgius Pettye
7. Petrus Turner
8. Guilielmus Dickenson
9. Richardus Hawly
10. Guilielmus Sellar
11. Griffinus Higs
12. Umfredus Farrar
13. Iacobus Marsh
14. Guilielmus Cox
15. Iohannes Gouldsmith
16. Thomas Gall

Baccalaurei socii

1. dominus French
2. dominus Doubtye
3. dominus Fisher
4. dominus Heath

In anno probationis

1. dominus Hinton
2. dominus Holliwell
3. dominus Reynolds
4. dominus Earles

Capellani

1. Robertus Bessly
2. Robertus Gaylard

Electio officiariorum

Augusti 1° socii omnes a domino custode in altam aulam circiter horam nonam ante meridianam convocati, claves librariae in conspectum domini custodis detulerunt. Postea resignatis de more officiariorum anni praeteriti omnibus clavibus custos et quinque simpliciter seniores designant in hunc annum novos officiarios istos qui sequuntur:

magistrum Simonson, vicecustodem.

magistros Greevil, Higs, Goldsmith, decanos .

magistros Turner, Sellar, Marsh, bursarios.

magistrum Philipson, principalem portionistarum; magistrum Petty, bursarium Williot; magistrum Higs, exhibitionarium Hamsterley; magistrum Gouldsmith, Graecae linguae praelectorem; magistrum Gall, grammaticae lectorem; praelector logices a principale nominandus; custodes cistae Read, tres decani; custodes cistae Bodly, Philipson, Hawly, Cox.

Dimissio indenturae

Eodem tempore dimisimus indenturam de Ly Woolsack in Breadstreete, London', viduae Dorchester pro termino quadraginta annorum; finis 40 li.

Computus custodis

Eodem die dominus custos computavit ac computatis computandis et allocatis allocandis discessit in plussagio viginti una librae, quindecim solidi, quadrans.

Computi firmariorum

Eodem etiam die Stephanus Heath firmarius noster de Farleigh computavit in scaccario.

Augusti 6° magister Sherwood firmarius et ballivus de Cantabrigia in scaccario computavit.

Augusti 28° Richardus Hodsden firmarius et ballivus de Calloland computavit in scaccario.

Octobris 12 Robertus Mayne firmarius de Chedington in scaccario computavit.

Dispensatio

Eodem tempore dispensavimus cum magistro Gouldsmith gravi infirmitate, iam apud suos rure laborante pro suis praelectionibus in scholis publicis donec in pristinam restitutus sanitatem[1] probe convalescat.

Dimissio indenturae

Eodem tempore renovanda est Thomae Franklin indentura tenementi in Holliwel pro termino 40 annorum. Et quia ei superant 37 anni in veteri indentura nobis resignanda, imposuimus ei pro fine solum modo 20s.

Licentia alienandi

Eodem tempore concessa est viduae Dorchester licentia alienandi tenementum ly Woolsack Londoniis pro termino 12 annorum.

Anno Domini 1621, regis Iacobi 19°, domini Henrici Savil custodis 37°. p. 270

Maldon

Vicesimo die Novembris magister Simonson vicecustos ex decreto domini custodis et sociorum profectus est Londinum ea scilicet intentione uti modis quibus poterat omnibus impedire conaretur confirmationem indenturae manerii nostri de Maldon in Surrey 40 ante annos, Reginae Elizabethae in usum comitis Arundel' dimissae pro termino annorum 5000. Quae quidem indentura ut perfectam plenariamque obtineat confirmationem magister Good eiusdem manerii iam firmarius causae reique suae male metuens coram baronibus in parliamento diu multumque laboravit.

Commemoratio

Decembris 17° habuimus commemorationem pro fundatore cum statutorum lectione et scrutinio quod prorogatum in vigiliam circumcisionis.

Computus bursarii.

Decembris 20° magister Marsh 1us bursarius computavit in scaccario.

[1] 'valetudinem' deleted.

Scrutinium servientium

In vigilia circumcisionis continuatum est scrutinium. In quo numerus portionistarum ut sit solitus constituitur. In hortulanum assignatur magistro Cox. Servientes post aliquas monitiones officiariis remittuntur.

[1622]

Admissio in societatem

14° Ianuarii. Dominus Henricus Hinton, dominus Holliwell, dominus Reynolds, dominus Erles admissi sunt in perpetuam societatem huius [domus].

Literae a domino custode

Decimo quarto Ianuarii a domino custode morbo tum Londoni laborante, literas accessimus nos monentes, de litteris archieiscopi Cantuariensis collegii nomine conscribendis, quibus scilicet pro summo et singulari eius studio et cura in causa nostra Maldon coram baronibus in parliamento habita gratias quantas possemus maxima ageremus. Quod quidem (lectis prius in praesentia sociorum in altam aulam convocatorum literis) die sequenti factum est. Literas vero in haec verba scriptas:

Tenor literarum ad archiepiscopum Cantuariensem in causa Maldon

Quanta paternitatis vestrae (reverendissime archipraesul) in familiam Mertonensem sua fuerit indulgentia res nostras per tot retro annorum spatia probe fluentes, nullisque aut in testinis domi disidiis, aut forensium causarum disceptationibus afflictae satis superque testatum reddiderunt, omnem vero venerationem supergressa est nupera ille in totius regni comitiis non ita pridem habitis clementissima vestra erga nos gratia, qua causam nostram Maldonensem a potenti et pecunioso adversario impugnatam morboque (si ita loqui liceat) comitiali iam fere laborantem solus suscipiebas eiusque infamem ambitum reum agebas ethicissime.[1] Quod vero nos incautos pacique nostros indormientes vater ille litium artifex adortus est, hoc etiam vestri adauget gratiam patrocinii. Cum enim alii imputantibus similes sua expressa potius quam indulta difficultate et mora commendent beneficia, tu ultro provenisti vota, et ne rogari quidam sustinuisti. Nostra nimirum iniuriarum iam diu insolens vestroque beneficio secura nimis tranquillitas non potuit tam impudentem et pertinacem malitiam suspicari,

[1] MS, 'ethnicissimi'.

easdem struentis insidias quas in priori quadam regni conventu frustra fuisse noveramus. Innocentia enim eas quibus ipsa non operatur non metuit artes, eaque magis insidiis opportuna est. Tandem vero insidias eluctata, eo arctius se vinculam fatetur quod absolutam; vestrae sicilicet in aeternum devictam, Paternitati, quae non hominibus tantum sed humano generi nobis nostrosque quicquid adhuc nepotum debetur seculo prospexit, malumque mundo corvum propulsavit. Tam insigni beneficio iniuriam facit qui crediderit satis rependi posse gratiarum, paratiorem tantum speramus veniam, si muneris magnitudo ingratitudinis imponat necessitatem. Cum igitur benignitatis vestrae amplitudo aliam nobis gratias solvendi, non reliquerit rationem, spes nostras iugi illius Maldonensis in posterum forsitan excutiendi vestri solius muneris esse profitemur utque favori vestro addas (quod solum addi potest) perpetuitatem et quae fecisti ames beneficia, quicquid sumus Mertonensium vobis votisque obtestamur.

Clementissimae vestrae paternitati filii humillimi devoti, custos et scholares domus sive collegii scholarium de Merton in universitate Oxon.

Vicecustos Etonam mittitur etc.

Decimo die Februarii tristi accepto nuntio dominum custodem graviter et non sine vitae periculo Londoni morbo laborare, deliberatum et conclusum est ab omnibus sociis post preces vespertinas in vestibulo convocatis de mittendo magistro Simonson ad invisendum dominum custodem, atque omnia ei fausta omnium sociorum nomine comprecandum.

Anno Domini 1621, regis Iacobi 19°, domini Henrici Savile custodis 37°. p. 271

Mors domini Savile custodis

Decimo nono Februarii. Dominus Henricus Savile miles, custos huiusce collegii et praepositus collegii Etonensis iuxta Windsor, musarum patronus, Mecaenas [*sic*] litterarum, fortunarumque Mertonensium vere pater obiit. Qui cum custodiae huius domus per integrum triginta sex annorum spatium summa cura, et diligentia fere plusquam humana per dies et per nox [*sic*] serio invigilasset, plenus annorum, honorum plenus moritur Etonae, et academiae nobisque tristissimum tam chari capitis desiderium reliquit.

Deliberatio circa custodem eligendum

Vicesimo primo Februarii hora octava matutina magister Simonson vicecustos convocavit socios omnes in altam aulam, eosque certiores fecit de domini Henrici Savile nuper custodis obitu per cuius mortem naturalem officium custodis exinde vacans declaravit, eosque omnes consuluit de futuri custodis electione. Quo negotio inter eos summa cura iudicioque sagaciter tractato, in tum tandem finem divertum est, ut plurimis gravissimisque de causis horam eiusdem diei a meridie tertiam pro novi custodis nominatione celebranda, unanimiter omnes constituerent. Ac continuo idem vicecustos hortatus est socios et obnixe rogavit omnes ut in dicta provisione tunc futura, praecipue essent concordes et unanimes, quo nostrae domus nec minueretur fama, nec pax, tranquillitasque inopportuna cuiusquam interpellantis malitiae leveretur. Consequenter etiam statutum illud quod ad futuram spectaret electionem lectum est, videlicet de custode autem cum ibi ponendus fuerit hoc modo provideatur septem de provectioribus et discretioribus dictae domus assignentur ad inquirendum a singulis scholaribus, etc.

Quo quidem statuto lecto et deliberato consilio plenius examinato vicecustos quaesivit a praesentibus an estimarent septem seniores esse assignandos ad inquirendum a singulis aliis quos patrono nominandos iudicarent. Hoc ab omnibus concessum procul dubio atque ita negotium de futuri custodis electione iuxta vim et effectum statutorum peragendum usque ad horam tertiam postmeridianam (ut premittitur) delatum est.

Allocatio facta vicecustodi

Conventum etiam est eodem tempore ut vicecustos, sede vacante septimanatim percipiat integram allocationem mensae dimidiae custodis factam usque ad realem novi custodis inductionem.

Electionem [sic] custodis

Hora igitur eiusdem diei tertia post meridiem sociis omnibus una cum dicto vicecustode capitulariter in altam aulam convenientibus ad electionem futuri custodis iuxta et secundum vim et formam statutorum collegii processum est. Lectis enim et examinatis statutis consuetudinibusque domus nostrae, ac ponderatis et attentis omnibus et singulis in hac parte attendendis et ponderandis, septem de provectioribus et discretioribus dictae domus seniores tum domi existentes assignati sunt, videlicet magister Guilelmus Simonson, vicecustos, magister Brent, magister Philipson, magister Petty, magister Sellar, magister Higgs, magister Marsh ad inquirendum a singulis nostri collegii sociis et scholaribus, si quos in spiritualibus et temporalibus sive de dicta domo sive aliunde discretos et exercitatos noverint, ut ex hiis qui per dictos scholares nominati fuerint aut aliis si eiquid magis expedierit, tres magis idoneos et domui nostrae necessarios intelligerent, patrono nostro nominarent. Quid quidem assignatione habita reliquisque secedentibusque vicecustos septem coram senioribus, omnes et singulos a sociis nominatos recitavit, et praedicti septem pensatis industria, probitate et honestate singulorum quorum meminerant, forma statutorum dictae domus observata, in hos tres providos circumspectos, et discretos viros magistrum Brent, dominum doctorem King, et magistrum Horne nunc vel nuper dicti collegii consocios ex eis qui inter nos consocios et scholares dictae domus nominati fuerint vota sua unanimiter omnes direxerunt atque patrono nostro praesentando nominarunt, ut unus ex illis quem ipse magis idoneum et domui nostrae necessarium estimaret custos nobis et nostrae domui autoritate ipsius praeficiatur. Ad quam quidem nominationem coram patrono nostro reverendissimo in Christo patre archiepiscopo Cantuariensi praesentandam, vicecustos una cum omnibus et singulis deputarunt et assignarunt; hos tres circumspectos viros magistros Sellar 2^{dum} bursarium, Griffinum Higgs 2^{dum} decanum et Iacobum Marshe 1um bursarium in et super hoc negotio nostros legitimos procuratores. Atque hi tres cunctis prius secundum statutorum vim partis cum praedicta nominatione et literis procuratoriis, communi collegii sigillo roboratis, Londinum versus die sequenti profecti sunt. Huius autem praesentationis atque etiam literam procuratoriarum formam cuius erraret facile, modo sequentia legere non recuset.

Tenor instrumenti nominationis

Reverendissimo in Christo patri et domino Georgio dei gratia Cantuariensi archiepiscopo totius Angliae primati et metropolitano domusque nostrae patrono vestri humiles et devoti filii, Guilielmus Simonson, vicecustos et scholares domus sive collegii scholarium de Merton in universitate Oxoniensi obedientiam et omnimodas reverentias tanto reverendissimo patri debitas cum honore vacante nuper officio custodis domus praedictae per mortem naturalem domini Henrici Savile ultimi custodis non simul communiter in dicta domo capitulariter congregati vocatis primitiis et praemonitis omnibus et singulis eiusdem domus consociis, visis et examinatis statutis et consuetudinibus domus praedictae, ac ponderatis et attentis omnibus et singulis in hac parte attendendis et ponderandis die et anno infrascriptis, septem de provectioribus et discretioribus dictae domus nostrae sociis assignavimus, eisque ad inquirendum a singulis eiusdem domus nostrae sociis et scholaribus si quos in spiritualibus et temporalibus sive de dicta domo sive aliunde discretos et exercitatos noverint et ipsis auditis industria, probitate, et honestate singulorum nominandorum pensatis ad nominandos tres quos magis idoneos et domui nostrae necessarios intellexerint, ex his qui per dictos scholares nominati fuerint aut aliis si liquido magis expedierit iuxta nostrae domus statuta plenam in domino dedimus potestatem. Qui quidem septem forma statutorum dictae domus observata, in tres providos circumspectos et discretos viros Nathanaelem Brent, Iohannem King, Thomam Horne nunc vel nuper dictae domus consocios et scholares dictae domus nominati fuerint, magis idoneos, et dicta domui necessarios vota sua unanimiter direxerunt.

p. 272 Anno Domini 1622, regis Iacobi 20 magistri Nathanaelis Brent custodis 1°.

Ac ut unus ex illis tribus per vestram reverendissimam paternitatem in custodem dictae nostrae domus proficeretur eosdem vestrae paternitati nominarunt sicut et nominant per presentes.Quos nos etiam vicecustos et scholares domus praedictae eidem vestrae paternitati reverendissimae iuxta et secundum formam nostrorum statutorum tenore praesentium nominamus, humiliter supplicantes quatenus unum ex eis sic vobis nominatis in custodem dictae domus praeficere, sibique administrationem dictae domus nostrae iuxta statutorum exigentiam plenarie committere dignetur eadem vestra reverendissima paternitas, quam in prosperis diutius conservet altissimus ad salubre regimen gregis sui. In cuius rei testimonium sigillum nostrum commune praesentibus apposuimus. Datum in domo nostra praedicta vicesimo primo die Februarii anno domini 1621.

Tenor instrumenti procuratorii

Pateat universis per presentes quod nos Guilielmus Simonson, vicecustos et scholares domus sive collegii scholarium de Merton in universitate Oxoniensi ad effectum infrascriptum in domo nostra praedicta capitulariter congregati dilectos nobis in Christo Guilielmum Sellar 2um bursarium, Griffinum Higs 2um decanum et Iacobum Marsh, primum bursarium dictae domus consocios coniunctim et eorum quemlibet per se divisim et in solidum nostros veros certos et legitimos et indubitatos procuratores, actores, factores negotiorum nostrorum gestores et nuncios speciales nominamus, ordinamus, facimus et constituimus per presentes, dantes et concedentes eisdem procuratoribus nostris coniunctim et cuilibet eorum per se divisim et insolidum ut prefatum est, potestatem generalem, ac tam generale quam speciale mandatum pro nobis et nomine nostro, et nomine dictae domus scholarium de Merton coram reverendisimo in Christo patre et domino domino Georgio dei gratia Cantuariensi archiepiscopo totius Angliae primate et metropolitano domusque nostrae patronus comparandi ac quandam nominationem trium providorum et circumspectorum virorum Nathanaelis Brent, Iohannis King, et Thomae Horne per septem de provectioribus et discretioribus dictae domus nostrae consociis iuxta et secundum formam et effectum statutorum eiusdem domus nuper in nostra domo factam, eidem reverendissimo patri exhibendi, negotiumque eiusdem nominationis sic factae usque ad finalem expeditionem eiusdem cum omnibus et singulis suis incidentibus, emergentibus, dependentibus, et connexis quibuscumque prosequendi et prosequi procurandi, eidemque reverendissimo patri quatenus unum de prefatis tribus circumspectis viris sic sibi nominatis quem domui nostrae magis utilem intellexerit, eligere et assumere, ac ipsum in nostrum et dictae domus custodem iuxta nostrae domus statuta praeficere eidemque dictae domus administrationem committere dignetur, debite supplicandi cetera quoque omnia et singula faciendi, exercendi et expediendi, eorum aliquo aut citra ea necessaria fuerint, seu quomodolibet opportuna etiam si mandatum de sua natura, magis exigat speciale; et quod nos faceremus seu facere possemus si personaliter interessemus, promittimus insuper ratum, gratum et firmum perpetuo habituros totum et quicquid dicti procuratores nostri vel eorum quilibet nomine nostro ac dictae domus fecerint vel fecerit in praemissis seu aliquo praemissorum per presentes. In cuius rei testimonium sigillum nostrum commune presentibus apposuimus. Datum in domo nostra praedicta 21° die mensis Februarii anno domini 1622.

Hac autem nominatione et literis procuratoriis praesentatis eidem reverendissimo patri ac domino domino archiepiscopo Cantuariensi per prefatos discretos viros magistrum Guilielmum Sellar, Griffinum Higs et Iacobum Marsh, idem reverendissimus pater ac dominus patronus dictae domus nostrae et scholarium de Merton indubitatissimus per aliquot dies deliberandum censuit, ut spatium haberent magistri Grevil et Farrar dicti collegii socii ad proponendas exceptiones suas quas se habere praesse ferebant contra validitatem praefatam electionis in eorum absentia celebratae, diem igitur constituit 13^{m} mensis Martii proxime sequentis huic controversiae solemniter audiendae et terminandae in aedibus suis Lambethae quo quidem loco et tempore auditis et perpensis omnibus exceptionibus allegatis per praedictos magistros Grevil et Farrar, idem reverendissimus pater (assistentibus sibi tribus doctissimis et integerrimis iurisconsultis) confirmavit et ratificavit electionem praenominatam, ut patet per actum iudiciale et solenne factum per magistrum Drake notarium publicum ibidem praesentem et manu eius subscriptum in hac scilicet forma, sequenti pagina, verbatim expressa.

p. 273 Anno Domini 1622, regis Iacobi 20, magistri Nathanaelis Brent custodis 1°.

Actum iudiciale per confirmationem custodis

Decimo tertio die mensis Martii anno domini computationem ecclesiae Angliae millessimo sexcentessimo vicesimo primo, coram reverendo in Christo patre et domino domino Georgio providentia divina Cantuariensi archiepiscopo totius Angliae primate et metropolitano in quadam superiori camera infra manerium suum de Lambehithe etc. assidentibus secum venerabilibus viris domino Willelmo Birde, milite, legum doctore, almae curiae Cantuariensis de Arcubus London' officiali, domino Henrico Marten, milite, legum doctore, reverendi patris domini episcopi London' vicario in spiritualibus generali et officali principali et summae curiae admiralitatis Angliae iudice sive preside, ac domino Thoma Ridley, milite, legum etiam doctore, predicti reverendissimi patris vicario in spiritualibus generali et officiali principali, in praesentia mei Iohannis Drake notarii publici etc.

Negotium concernens electionem custodis domus sive collegii de Merton in universitate Oxoniensi.

Quibus die et loco comparuerunt personaliter magistri Nathanael Brent, Franciscus Greevil, Willelmus Sellar, Griffinus Higgs, Humfredus Farrer et Iacobus Marsh, domus sive collegii de Merton predicti socii in quorum praesentiis prefatus reverendissimus pater certificatorium de et super electione novi et futuri custodis dictae domus sive collegii de Merton habita et facta, sigillo communi dicti collegii (ut apparuit) sigillatum, ac per prenominatos Willelmum Sellar, Griffinum Higgs et Iacobum Marsh vigore procuratorii per vicecustodem et scholares domus sive collegii praedicti eis continuatim et divisim in hac parte facti sigilloque eorum communi (ut apparuit) etiam sigillati eidem reverendissimo patrono traditum publice perlegi mandavit et fecit. Quo quidem certificatorio sic lecto idem reverendissimus pater interrogavit omnes praedictos socios praesentes, an aliquas habeant exceptiones proponendas contra praedictam electionem necne in praesentia prefati magistri Greevil repetentis quasdam exceptiones alias per eum praefato reverendissimo patri traditas, in scriptis, conceptas, quas quidem exceptiones dictus reverendissimus pater similiter publice legi fecit. Quibus sic lectis eisdemque ac responsionibus ad easdem exceptiones et toto processu de et super electione praedicta habito et facto debite et plenarie respective examinatis, discussis, et consideratis, idem reverendissimus pater de et cum maturo, sano et deliberato consilio et iudicio prefatorum venerabilium virorum secum assidentium, praefatam electionem per praenominatos vicecustodem et scholares domus sive collegii de Merton praedictae (ut praefertur) factam, firmam et legitimam, ac statutis dicti collegii consonam fuisse et esse pronunciavit et declaravit, tandemque electionem approbavit, ratificavit et confirmavit. Super quibus omnibus et singulis praemissis dictus reverendissimus pater requesivit me prefatum Iohannem Drake unum vel plura instrumenta publica conficere, testesque praesentes testimonium inde perhibere, praesentibus tunc et ibidem personis supra nominatis necnon magistris Georgio Garret et Samuele Lane nuper dicti collegii sociis et Willelmo Baker generoso et aliis.

Ita testor Iohannes Drake, notarius publicus antedictus
Anno 1621 20° Martii[1]

Adventus custodis

Decimo sexto die eiusdem mensis Martii idem reverendissimus pater et dominus dominus archiepiscopus Cantuariensis custodiam collegii Merton' praedicti dedit magistro Nathanaeli Brent observatis omnibus solennitatibus et circumstantiis in hac causa usitatis, ut patet per duo instrumenta sigillata publico sigillo sedis archiepicopi Cantuariensis. Vicesimo die mensis magister Nathanael Brent ex tribus praedictis unus a nobis antea nominatus, et iam ab archiepiscopo creatus istius collegii custos una cum tribus praefatis nostris procuratoribus summo cum omnium sociorum gaudio rediit ad collegium. Cuius adventus uti gratior sit et celebrior appareret dominus doctor Lapworth in medicina professor, idemque superior lector Linacri apud nos praelector, dominus doctor Parker Aulae Albanae principalis, dominus doctor

[1] This date is in another hand.

Bainbridge publicus in astronomia professor Savilianus, omnes purpurati; socii etiam universi tam magistri quam baccalaurei, una cum omnibus nostrae domus scholaribus paratis inversis solemniter indutis, ad magnam collegii portam congregati, custodis accessum praestolantur. In cuius introitu magister Sellar huiusce negotii procuratorum alter tradidit magistro Simonson vicecustodi duo praedicta instrumenta, magno archiepiscopi sigillo (ut praemittitur) sigillata; quarum proxime sequenti pagina subsequitur forma.

p. 274 Anno Domini 1621 regni Iacobi 20, magistri Nathanaelis Brent custodis 1°.

Tenor instrumenti creationis

Georgius providentis divina Cantuariensis archiepiscopus totius Angliae primas et metropolitanus dilecto nobis in Christo Nathanaeli Brent in artibus magistro salutem et gratiam. Ad custodiam domus sive collegii de Merton in Oxon', nostrorum patronatus et iurisdictionis immediatae, per mortem naturalem domini Henrici Savile, militis, ultimi et immediati custodis eiusdem iam vacantem, ad quam per septem socios provectiores et discretiores dictae domus, iuxta statuta eiusdem assignatos, unus ex tribus personis per eos nobis nominatis existis, te primitus tam de agnoscendo supremam authoritatem regiam in causis ecclesiasticis et temporalibus, ac de renunciando, refutando et recusando omni et omnimodo iurisdictioni, potestati, authoritati et superioritati foraneis et extraneis iuxta vim, formam, et effectum statuti parliamenti, huius inclyti regni Angliae in ea parte editi et provisi, quam de observando statuta et ordinaciones dicti collegii iuxta fundacionem eiusdem ad sancta dei evangelia rite iuratum, admittimus teque custodem collegii praedicti praeficimus et constituimus cum suis iuribus et pertinenciis universis, curamque, regimen, et administrationem tam spiritualium quam temporalium, eiusdem domus sive collegii, iuxta statutorum exigentiam, tibi in domino plenarie committimus per praesentes, mandantes et firmiter iniungentes vicecustodi, omnibusque et singulis dictae domus sive collegii, sociis, scholaribus et ministris, quod te in custodem praedictae domus sive collegii benigne admittant, ac tibi pareant et obediant ut custodi eiusdem in omnibus et per omnia iuxta fundationem et statuta collegii praedicti: iuribus nostris archiepiscopalibus et ecclesiae nostrae metropoliticae Christi Cantuariensis dignitate et honore in omnibus semper salvis. In cuius rei testimonium sigillum nostrum presentibus est appensum. Datum in manerio nostro de Lambehith decimo sexto die mensis Martii anno domini iuxta computationem ecclesiae Anglicanae millesimo sexcentesimo vicesimo primo. Et nostrae translationis anno undecimo.

Nicolas Weston Registrarius

Tenor instrumenti mandati

Georgius providentia divina Cantuariensis archiepiscopus totius Angliae primas et metropolitanus dilectis nobis in Christo vicecustodi, sociis, fratribus et scholaribus domus sive collegii de Merton in Oxonia nostrorum patronatus et iurisdictionis immediatae salutem et gratiam. Cum nos dilectum nobis in Christo spectabilem virum Nathanielem Brent in artibus magistrum ad custodiam dictae domus sive collegii unum ex tribus providis, circumspectis et discretis viris nobis per vos praesentatis nominatum per mortem naturalem domini Henrici Savile, militis, ultimi et immediati custodis eiusdem dudum vacantem, primitus tam de recognoscendo supremam authoritatem regiam in causis ecclesiasticis et temporalibus, ac de renunciando, refutando ac recusando omni et omnimodo iurisdictioni, potestati, authoritate et superioritati foraneis et extraneis iuxta vim, formam et effectum statuti parliamenti huius inclyti regni Angliae in ea parte editi et provisi, quam de observando statuta et ordinationes dicti collegii iuxta fundacionem eiusdem, ad sancta dei evangelia rite iuratum admiserimus, ipsumque custodem eiusdem collegii praefecerimus et constituerimus cum suis iuribus et pertinenciis debitis, curamque regimen et administrationem tam spiritualium quam temporalium eiusdem domus sive collegii iuxta statutorum exigentiam sibi in domino commiserimus; vobis ergo commitimus et firmiter iniungendo mandamus, quatenus ipsum magistrum Nathanielem Brent in custodem praefatae domus sive collegii benigne et obedienter recipiatis et admittatis pareatisque et obediatis eidem custodi eiusdem in omnibus et per omnia iuxta fundationem et statuta domus sive collegii praedicti sub poena contemptus, iuribus nostris archiepiscopalibus et ecclesiae nostrae metropoliticae Christi Cantuariensis dignitate et genere et honore in omnibus semper salvis. In cuius rei testimonium sigillum nostrum praesentibus apponi fecimus. Datum in manerio nostro de Lambehith decimo sexto die mensis Martii anno domini iuxta computationem ecclesiae Anglicanae millesimo sexcentesimo vicesimo primo et nostrae translationis anno undecimo.

Nicholas Weston registrarius

Quibus quidem instrumentis in magna collegii porta palam et publice a domino vicecustode recitatis obtulit idem vicecustos authoritate qua in hac parte fungitur, librum statutorum et clavem collegii magistro Nathanieli Brent in signum admissionis illius ad custodiam huiusce domus quae cum praefatus magister Nathaniel Brent a vicecustode accepisset continuo magister Gall hanc et ad eum habuit orationem, cuius exemplar habetur paginas sequenti.

p. 275 *Oratio magistri Gall*

Ignosce, quaeso (desideratissime praeses) si continuis profundis que suspiriis exhausta praecordia, vix tantum spiritus linguae suggerant, quantum laeto tempore sufficiat ad gratulandum. Est haec profecto pietatis infirmitas, quod circa defunctum hactenus aegri, erga viventes deficimus, nec mensuram tibi debitae vocis impendimus, cuius auspiciis non impudenter, nec infeliciter spiramus post Savilium. Nonne huc etiam pietas tua et fama virtutis inclinat tanquam ipse eundem intemperantius desideraris, quum ille te semper ut similem complexus sit, illum tu ut semideum suspexeris. Postquam igitur virum illum, numen credi meritum, nimirum nobis necesse fuit scire mortalem, inter preces et lacrymas multum agitati sumus. Dum lacrymae docerent quid precaremur, similem amisso successorem optavimus, magnitudini doloris aequilibre solatium. Exornavere preces, nec voti degener fuit successus. Ecce enim virum, non sorte et vena, quibus merita indiscreta sunt, sed suffragiis hominum ac iudiciis omnia penetrantibus ad ipsorum principatum merito adscitum. En regimen, cui se credidit academiae decus oculi pupilla custodiendam. Si in turba et collusione multorum unus aut alter caeteris praemineret, num ex illa contumelia gloriose excerperetur. At hic e classe procerum exemptus est, quorum vix inter se priorem agnosceres, nec ipsis inter alios secundum. Nonne non adeo sterilis est Mertona mater, quin sobolem agnoscat longe uberrimam, suo lacte et uberibus enutritam. 'Augustus supremis sermonibus quum tractaret, quinam adipisci principem locum suffecturi abnuerent aut impares vellent, vel iidem possent cuperentque M' Lepidum dixerat capacem sed aspernantem, Gallum Asinium avidum et minorem, L. Arruntium non indignum et, si casus daretur, ausurum.'[1] Tres sibi principatu dignos septicollis domina non tulit, et quartum Augustus deterrimum adoptaverat. Frustra Savilius antiquissimam hanc sedem e suis ruderibus marmoriam excitasset in successore degeneraturam. Vidit illa mens multos superesse sibi megistanas, nec, quum plures in iudicio, quem in votis praecipuum habuerit, non liquet. Erant igitur (vir

[1] Tacitus, *Annales*, ed. H. Furneaux, i (1884), p. 176 (I. 13, lines 6–11).

laudissime) quantacunque est praelati gloriam in te recipe, tibi imputa, operibus tuis, et praemiis operum felix. Ingredere iam parentis animo pronos ad aspectum tui parietes ac iuvenili quadam salutantium alacritate vix firma prisco vestigio fundamenta. Gaudent haec omnia gestiuntque non tam in potestatis tuae ditionem redigi, quam in tuo ingenio regi. Praesenti tibi animus, consilium, iustitia superfuit; caeteris obsequii gloria et concordiae fides relinquatur.

Quibus omnibus ad hunc modum pactis dominus custos est amplexus singulos omnesque itidem eum ad hospitium custodis comitati sunt ubi laetitia magna celebrata post symposium dominus custos in suam et in suam quilibet sociorum cameram se gaudentes recipiunt. Eodem tempore attulerunt secum praedicti magistri extracta quaedam e registro principali sedis archiepiscopalis Cantuariensis subscripta manu magistri Iohannis Drake notarii publici, pertinentia ad ius patronatus huius collegii quae praefatus reverendissimus pater dominus dominus archiepiscopus Cantuariensis digna existimavit quae consequentur in hoc registro ad perpetuam rei memoriam.

Extracta e registro archiepiscopi Cantuariensis

Item vicecustos et fratres domus scholarium de Merton in Oxonia vacante dicta domo orationem praesentabunt archiepiscopo Cantuariensi qui pro tempore fuerit, tanquam patrono suo tres socios et scholares iuxta formam statuti dictae domus, de quibus taliter praesentatis, archiepiscopus unum in custodem domus praedictae admittet, acceptabit et in custode praeficiet dictae domus.[1]

Archiepiscopus Cantuariensis habet iurisdictionem in collegio de Merton et approbationem testamentorum inibi morientium.

Item vacante episcopata Roffensi archiepiscopus Cantuariensis tanquam patronus et ordinarius habebit custodiam spiritualitatis et temporalitatis episcopatus praedicti et conferre debet 24 sergantias [?] sive officia in prioratu Roffensi quae ad episcopi loci collationem pertinent, sede plena sicut continetur in registro domini Walteri nuper Cantuariensis archiepiscopi xxv folio a principio memorando etc.

Ita testor Iohannes Drake notarius publicus

Computus domini Henrici Savile custodis

Vicesimo secundo Martis habitus est computus domini Henrici Savile ultimi custodis pro 22 septimanis, qui computatis computandis et

[1] In another hand is 'V. Reg. Bourchier fol. 45a A.D. 1458'. For this see *Reg. Thomae Bourgchier*, ed. F.R. Du Boulay (Cant. and York Soc. liv, 1953), p. 192.

allocatis allocandis discessit moriens in plussagio xvi li. quam summam magister Sellar 2us bursarius statim postea solvit domino Richardo Harrison executorum uni ultimi testamenti praedicti domini Henrici Savile: et sic aeque.

Allocatio liberaturae magistro Gouldsmith

Eodem tempore per dominum custodem et omnes socios domi existentes concessa est integra liberatura magistro Gouldsmith valetudinis ergo tunc absenti etiamsi per dimidium huiusce anni (iuxta decretum in ea parte factum hic apud collegium non mansisset).

p. 276a Anno Domini 1622, regis Iacobi 20, magistri Nathanael Brent custodis 1°.

Admissio

Aprilis 3°. Dominus French admissus est in numerum magistorum.

Augmentatio liberaturae

Eodem tempore consensum est ut 40 li., residuum annui reditus de Gamlingay Avenells dividerentur annuatim inter custodem et socios eodem modo et eisdem legibus quibus dividi solitae sunt, liberatura vetus et nova; et decretum est hanc constitutionem non diutius duraturam esse quam placuerit domino custodi.

Vicaria de Emildon magistro Cox

Aprilis 6° concessa et sigillata est magistro Coxe praesentatio ad vicariam de Emildon in comitatu Northumbriae, et dies et datus ad deliberandum utrum acceptare velit beneficium illud necne, usque ad comitia proxime sequentia.

Dimissio indenturae

Eodem tempore unanimi consensu omnium sociorum concessa est magistro Nathanaeli Brent custodi indentura de molendinis Grancester pro termino 21 annorum. Eodem etiam tempore ac consensu eodem dimissa est magistro Simonson vicecustodi indentura rectoriae de Burmington pro termino vitae suae cuius quidem rectoriae indenturam magister Brent iam custos, coram sociis sponte sua resignaverat.

Commemoratio

Aprilis 13° habita est commemoratio pro fundatore et celebratum scrutinium.

Computus bursarii

Aprilis 18° magister Sellar 2^{dus} bursarius computavit in scaccario.

Allocatio facta magistro Gouldsmith

Aprilis 29° per dominum custodem et omnes socios consensum est ut 30 li. de bonis collegii darentur magistro Gouldsmith loco emolumentorum quos percepturus erat ex anno gratuitatis. Qua quidem liberalitate inusitata usi sunt dominus custos et socii erga magistrum Gouldsmith eo quod sanitatis recuperandae gratia coactus sit collegio se abdicare et acceptare beneficium exigui valoris quod sumptui faciendo vix par sit, ut aere salubriori apud suos frueretur.

Dispensatio

Eodem tempore dispensatum est cum magistro Gall pro 4 lectionibus duobus terminis immediate post sequentibus in scholis publicis habendis.

Commemoratio

Vicesimo die Iulii scilicet in festo Margaretae commemoratio habita est pro fundatore, lecta statuta et scrutinium celebratum quod prorogatum est in Imum diem Augusti et quemlibet diem citra.

Dispensatio

Eodem tempore dispensatum est cum magistro Gall regente pro lecturis publicis et frequentatione disputationum in 2° anno.

Computus

Iulii 23° Iohannes Sherwood, firmarius de Cantebrigia, computavit in scaccario.

Iulii 26[to] sigillatae sunt litterae attornatitiae Richardo Brent et Guilelmo Gardiner in usum magistri Simonson pro rectoria de Burmington.

Computus

Iulii 30 Heath, firmarius noster de Farleigh, computavit in scaccario.

Anno domino 1622 regis Iacobi 20, magistri Nathanaelis Brent, custodis 1°. p. 276b

Nomina sociorum in adventu Brent custodis:

In Artibus Magistri

1. Gulielmus Simonson
2. Isaacus Wake
3. Franciscus Grevil
4. Iohannes Philipson
5. Georgius Pettie
6. Petrus Turner
7. Richardus Hawly
8. Gulielmus Sellar
9. Grifinus Higgs
10. Humfredus Farrar
11. Iacobus Marsh
12. Gulielmus Cox
13. Iohannes Gouldsmithe
14. Thomas Gall

Baccalaurei socii

1. dominus French
2. dominus Dowtie
3. dominus Fisher
4. dominus Heath
5. dominus Hinton
6. dominus Holiwel
7. dominus Reynolds
8. dominus Earles

Capellani

1. Robertus Beesly
2. Robertus Gaylard

In adventu Brent custodis status collegii in praesentia officiariorum inventus est, ut sequitur. In pecuniis numeratis in cista iocalium 1557 li. 9s. 3d. In manibus magistri Sellar bursarii (quas induxit paulo post) 47 li. Summa 1604 li. 9s. 3d.

A note of ye college plate

In domo custodis ut sequitur

One silver salt
One silver beaker, parcel gilt
Two little tunnes, parcel gilt
One bread bowle, plaine
Five spoones

In promptuario ad usum sociorum

One great salt with a cover, double gilt
Two salts, parcel gilt
Foure plaine white salts
Ten great knobbed spoones
Eight smale knobbed spoones
Ten bigger plaine spoones
Eleven smaler playne spoones
Three broad white bowles
p. 277 Nine great white tunnes
Three little tuns, parcel gilt
One bowle given by mr Carew
One bowle given by mr Newton
One bowle given by mr Colepepper
One bowle given by mr Eliot
One bowle given by mr Pettie
One bowle given by mr Betham
One bowle given by mr Guy
One bowle given by mr Harris
One bowle given by mr Jacob

One bowle given by mr Thornton
One pot with eares given by mr Blunt
One pot with eares given by mr Gibs
One[1] pot with eares given by mr Morgans
One colledg pot given by mr Brunkar
One silver tankard given by mr Pen
One bowle double gilt with a cover given by mr Drurie
One bowle with a cover double gilt given by mr Parry
One pot with eares given by mr Hide
One bowle double gilt with a cover given by mr Peter Fretsvile

Plate usually kept in ye Threasor house
A basin and ewer double gilt
A gilt bowle, with this poseie 'Dominus Pauperem facit et ditat'
A gilt bowle coronet
A gilt bowle with eares and percullesses
A gilt bowle pounsed
Two gilt bowles given by mr Trelawnies
Two gilt saltes one great, another little
One gilt sack cup
Six gilt apostle spoones
One gilt lion spoone
Two tavern bowles parcel gilt
One silver salt given by mr Essex
Two silver flacons
Two flat silver wine bowles
One tankard parcel gilt
One gilt pot with a cover

In ye great chest in ye Threasor house without a lock
One faire basin and ewer double gilt
One white silver flacon for ye Communion
One gilt bowle with a cover for ye Communion

Suppelex in domo custodis p. 278
Large diaper table clothes 6
Square diaper table clothes 8
Diaper towels 8
Diaper napkins new & ould 4 dozen & 4
Plaine table clothes 5

[1] 'Colledg' deleted.

Plaine cupbord clothes 6
Plaine napkins 3 dozen & 6
Broad napkins 11
Holland sheets 2 payre
Holland pillow bures 6
Flaxen sheets 7 payre
Sheets of hemp 7 paire
Table clothes for ye hal 6
Plaine square bord clothes 3
Feather beds 9
Feather boulsters ould and new 10
Pillowes 2
Flock beds ould 2
Flock boulsters 2
Mattresses 3
Blankets new & ould 7 payre
Coverlets, ould & new 7
Rugges 3
Green silk quilt 1
Green silke curtaines 5
Green cloth chaires 2
Red leather chaires 2
High stooles covered with red leather 6
High stooles covered with green clothe 3
High wainscot stooles 16
Low wainscot stooles 6
Low stooles covered with greene and embrodered 6
One long green cloth carpet fringed with silke

In ye little parlor
One drawing table
One cupbord with two drawers
One side table
Ould cupboard carpets 3
New cushion[s] of Turkie worke 6
Ould cushions 2
One damaske table cloth
One damaske table cloth
One damask towel
p. 279 Damaske napkins 12

In ye great chamber
Tables 2
One cupbord
One paire of andirons
Fower peeces of Arras hanging

In ye vault chamber
One bedsteed with a cover, vallens & fringe of silke
Three peeces[1] of hangings
One ould cupbord
One ould wiker chaire
One paire of creepers

In ye chamber next ye vault chamber
One bedstead with a cover of ould cope worke and fring[e]
One ould trunk

In Sever's chamber
One bedstead with a cover of ould cope work and fringe
Curtaines of kersie
One round table
One cupbord
One ould trunke and one ould chest
One paire of andirons
Four peeces of hanging

In ye inner chamber
One bedsted without a cover

In ye chamber over ye buttry
Two ould bedsteeds
One ould chest
One standing deske
Two presses
One ould table

In ye hal
One table, one cupbord, one ould presse
Three benches, three formes, one skreene

In ye buttry
One ould bin, two ould coffers
One stone pot, one bucket

[1] 'of silk' deleted.

In ye Lower parlor
One ould table and an ould carpet
One ould chaire, one paire of andirons
p. 280 Foure formes. One ould cupboard

In ye pewter house
Great chargers 3
Platters great and smale 2 dozen & 2
One pewter pye plate
One little pewter dish
One pewter basin and ewer
One pewter deep basin
Little pewter porringers 6
Little saucers 6
Candelstickes of pewter 5
Chamber pots 3
Pewter close stooles 2

Brasse
One pot, one kettle, three little skellets
One candlestick, one chafing dish
One musket,[1] one ould flask, one brown bil
Foure fire shovels. Three paire of tongues
One old iron chafing dish. One payre of bellowes

In ye chamber by ye kitchin
Ould bedsteads 2

In ye little chamber by ye gallerie
One bedstead, two peeces of hangings
One warming pan

In ye Kitchin
Two boards, two shelves

In ye Larder
Three boards, two shelves

Linen in ye buttry
Napkins porrel 12
Diaper napkins 21
p. 281 Ould flaxen napkins
Table clothes 21
Wipers 6

[1] Above this entry is a double line across the page.

Other things in ye buttry
Two stooles, one forme, one table
One candlestick, one chest to keep plate in
One candlestieke, one box to keep napkins in

In ye Colledg Kitchin
Four brasse pots, one kettel, two brasse pans
Two skillets, eleven spits, long and short, one collender
One scumer. one lever, one mincing knife
One silling ladle, one setting peele
One fire shovel, one fire shovel
One new brasse pot, three paire of pothookes
Five pothangers, two trivets
Two friing pans, two gridirons
One salt tub, one safe

In ye vesterie
One table, one chayre, two stooles
One pulpit clothe
One pulpit clothe for ye Communion table
Two long clothes of cope work, ye one white and green intermixt with gould, ye other of blew chamlet wrought with goulden stars
Two shorter clothes of cope work, white and green
Two copes of blew satten
One hearse
Three great velvet cushions
Eight little velvet cushions

In ye Church
Foure bibles fol. six prayer bookes 4to
Ten prayer bookes 8vo, one carpet for ye communion table
Candlesticks of all sortes 25
One lanterne, one hourglasse

p. 282 Anno Domini 1622, regis Iacobi 20°, magistri Nathanaelis Brent custodis 2°.

Augustus

Magistri in artibus

1. Guilelmus Simonson
2. Isaac Wake
3. Franciscus Greevil
4. Iohannes Philipson
5. Georgius Petty
6. Petrus Turner
7. Richardus Hawly
8. Guilelmus Sellar
9. Griffinus Higgs
10. Umfredus Farrar
11. Iacobus Marsh
12. Guilelmus Cox
13. Thomas Gall
14. Iohannes French

Baccalaurei socii

1. dominus Doubtye
2. dominus Fisher
3. dominus Heath
4. dominus Hinton
5. dominus Holliwel
6. dominus Reynolds
7. dominus Earles

Capellani

1. Robertus Beesly
2. Robertus Gaylard

Claves librariae

Augusti 1° hora 9ª antemeridiana in altam aulam convenerunt dominus custos et omnes socii, ubi resignarunt officiarii superioris anni claves officiariorum. Singuli etiam socii detulerunt claves ad commune ostium bibliothecae spectantes in conspectum domini custodis, secedentibus autem aliis sociis dominus custos et quinque simpliciter seniores procedunt ad electionem officiariorum in annum sequentem, ubi electi sunt

Electio Officiariorum

magister Simonson, vicecustos.
magistri Turner, Sellar, Marsh, decani.
magistri Philipson, Pettye, French, bursarii.
principalis portionistarum, magister Higgs; bursarius Williot, magister Gall; exhibitionarius Hamsterlay, magister Higgs; exhibitio capellani capellae, dividenda inter decanos; praelector grammaticae, magister Marsh; praelector Graecae [*blank*]; conservatores cistae Bodly, magistri Higgs, Farrar, Gall; custodes cistae Reade, tres decani.

Dimissio indenturae Gamblingay M.

Eodem tempore indentura de Gamlingay Merton dimittitur magistro Iacobo. Hoc est una vita loco Richardi filii eius nuperrime defuncti; additur duabus aliis, pro fine centum marcarum.

Liberatura magistro Cox

Eodem etiam tempore conceditur magistro Cox praesentat[i]o ad vicariam de Emildon honesta liberatura atque omnes fines, quae ei presenti poterant deberi, etiamsi absens fuerit hoc anno gratuitatis.

Electio socii

Hora 2[a] eiusdem diei conveniunt dominus custos et omnes socii in conclave custodis, ubi dominus custos et 13 simpliciter seniores procedunt ad electionem domini Abbots dioceseos London' in societatem huiusce domus et decretum ut admitteretur ad communias nono huius mensis Augusti.

Progressus

Eodem tempore consenserunt dominus custos et socii de progressu et assignatur domino custodi loco bursarii magister Turner.

Computus custodis

Augusti 2 habiti sunt computus custodum domini Henrici Savile defuncti, et magistri Nathanael Brent, qui computatis computandis et allocatis allocandis discesserunt in plussagio dominus Henricus Savile 16 li. 14s. 9d., magister Brent 22 li. 2s. 1d. ob. quae summae a bursariis solutae et sic aeque.

Lectores Linacri

Eodem tempore dominus doctor Lapworth rursum constitutus est praelector superioris lectionis Linacri pro termino 3[um] annorum, per custodem et 7 seniores.

Eodem tempore magister Hawly eorundem consensu electus est praelector inferioris lectionis Linacri per spontaneam resignationem magistri Simonson iam vacantis idque pro termino trium annorum.

Anno Domini 1622, regis Iacobi 20, magistri Nathanaelis Brent custodis 2°. p. 283

Varii computus

Augusti 5[to] habitis sunt computus cistae Bodley atque etiam cistae Reade praesentibus domino custode et omnes socii domi existentes [*sic*].

Augusti 8° computavit Hodsden, firmarius de Calloland et discessit aeque.

Admissio

Augusti 10 circiter horam nonam sociis omnibus in altam aulam convocatis per dominum custodem admissus est dominus Abbots in annum probationis, ac decretum ut solvat idem in usum bibliothecae quinque marcas.

Varii computus

Augusti 11 Richardus Hodsden, firmarius noster de Callowland, computavit in scaccario.

Augusti 22 magister Turner, 3us bursarius de administratione sua computavit.

Octobris 11 Robertus Mayne, firmarius de Chedington, computavit in scaccario.

Octobris 15 Richardus Wilmot, firmarius de Ibston, computavit.

Octobris 19 Robertus Ray, firmarius de Kibworth, eodem etiam tempore H. Sayre, firmarius de Barkby computaverunt.

Novembris 2 Edmundus Gregory, firmarius de Cuxam, computavit.

Sigillatio

Decembris 4 sigillatae sunt indenturae de Gamblingay Merton et de silvis Mertonage magistro Iacob antea concessae.

Computus 1^i^ bursarii

Decembris 19, magister French, primus bursarius, computavit.

Commemoratio cum scrutinio

Decembris 18 habuimus commemorationem pro fundatore, statuta legimus, inivimus scrutinium, quod in vigiliam Circumcisionis continuavimus.

Scrutinium servientium

Quo tempore in altam aulam omnes convenimus, ubi per bursarium collegii tria proposita fuerunt consideranda ac determinanda, mores servientium qui officiariis committuntur castigandi, deinde numerus portionistarum de quo decretum ut sit solitus; postremo electio hortulani, quem nominavimus magistrum Galle.

[1623]

Obitus magistri Philipson

Februarii 5to magister Philipson socius huiusce collegii diem obiit.

Lis circa Maldon

Martii 3° lectae sunt per vicecustodem (sociis omnibus in altam aulam convocatis) literae a domino custode scriptae hunc in finem, ut consilium ipse ineamus serio de lite ineunda et prosequenda contra magistrum Good, firmarium de Maldon in comitatu Surrey. Existimavit enim dominus custos, idque ex opinione tam iurisperitorum quam aliorum quorundam magnatum iam adesse tempus, quo speremus indenturam illam manerii nostri de Maldon, pro termino 5000 annorum contra ius ac statuta 13° reginae Elizabethae ea in parte factum, prorsus evertere, ac ipso iure nullam reddere. Quapropter re ista inter nos diu multumque agitata tandem unanimiter conclusum est, ut dominus custos sanum consilium caperet Londini, omnemque optimam iniret rationem, ut hoc negotium ad optatum postea exitum produceretur. 3us bursarius electus in locum Philipson 3^{i} bursarii defuncti.

Eodem etiam tempore ac per easdem litteras a domino custode monemur de substituendo 3° bursario, loco magistri Philipson nuperrime defuncti. Secedentibus ergo ad tempus caeteris conveniunt quinque simpliciter seniores, ac per maiorem eorum partem nominatus est magister Higgs in tertium bursarium, modo dominus custos hanc approbaret electionem. Cuius voluntate paucis post diebus interacta, magister Higgs per vicecustodem in alta aula pronunciatur electus in praesentia sociorum, ac claves tertii bursarii eidem traditae.

Vetus libraria: restauratio

Eodem quoque tempore et loco ad maiorem librariae ornatum et commodiorem studentium usum ordinatum est ut sedes in veteri libraria novae fiant et per omnia sedibus in altera parte antea aedificatis reddantur similes. Ibidem insuper consensum est de eadem augmentanda, addendo quandam iam vacuam cameram in orientali librariae parte sitam,

Concessio musicis

Tunc etiam consensum est ut publicis academiae oppidique musicis bursarius sex solidos octo denarios e bonis collegii pro more solito traderet.

p. 284 Anno Domini 1623, regis Iacobi 21, magistri Nathanaelis Brent custodis 2°.

Commemoratio

Aprilis 5to habita est commemoratio fundatoris, statutorum lectio et scrutinium, quod prorogatum in 21um diem Iulii et quemlibet diem citra.

Moritur magister Beesly et dat collegio 5 libras

Eiusdem mensis 11° magister Robertus Beesley senior capellanus ac ecclesiae Sancti Petri in orientale vicarius moritur, et aliquot post dies sepelitur in ecclesia nostra. Legavit autem testamento quinque libras collegio.

Commemoratio pro Iesop

Aprilis 24° habuimus commemorationem pro domino doctore Iesope.

Admissio

Aprilis 16. Dominus Doubtye, dominus Fisher, dominus Heath, admissi sunt in numerum magistrorum huiusce domus.

Variationes

Iulii 9 magister Gale variavit in his quaestionibus:

An {
Homini magis credendum sit quam caeteris animantibus.[1] Negat.
Beatissima sit republica in qua medii plurimum possunt. Negat.
Recte dixerit Aristoteles puerum mathematicum fieri posse sapientem non posse. Negat.
}

Dispensatio

Iulii 10 dispensavimus cum predicto magistro Gale pro 2^dis^ suis variationibus.

Commemoratio

Iulii 21° nempe in festo Margaretae habita est commemoratio pro fundatore, et scrutinium celebratum, quod prorogatum in 10um diem Augusti et quemlibet diem citra.

Lis mota pro bonis cuiusdam uxoris viduae in Holliwel

Hoc anno litem movit collegium Wadhamense pro bonis cuiusdam Wise, qui interfecerat uxorem, et habitavit infra precinctum fratrum Augustinensium in manerio nostro de Holliwel. Sed cum re maturius

[1] For 'animalibus'.

examinata compererint nihil iuris ipsis competere, sponte cesserunt, et nos nostro antiquo iure gavisi sumus.

Anno Domini 1623, regis Iacobi 21, magistri Nathanaelis Brent custodis 30. p. 285

Augustus

Magistri in artibus

1. Guilielmus Simonson
2. Isaac Wake
3. Franciscus Greevile
4. Georgius Pettye
5. Petrus Turner
6. Guilielmus Sellar
7. Griffinus Higgs
8. Umfredus Farrar
9. Iacobus Marsh
10. Thomas Galle
11. Iohannes French
12. Iohannes Doubtye
13. Alexander Fisher
14. Thomas Heath

Baccalaurei in artibus

1. dominus Hinton
2. dominus Holliwell
3. dominus Reynolds
4. dominus Earles
5. dominus Abbotts

Capellani

1. Robertus Gaylard
2. Iohannes Wilton

Dimissiones Indenturarum

Augusti 1° per dominum custodem convocati hora nona antemeridiem convenimus omnes in altam aulam, ubi unanimiter[1] consentimus de renovanda magistro Richardo Gardiner indentura manerii nostri de Thorncroft, una nimirum vita additur duabus aliis. Finis vero impositus 100 marcarum.

Eodem tempore dimisimus Guilelmo Temple indenturam de Basingstoke pro termino xxius annorum, finis 26 li. 13s. 4d. Eodem etiam loco et tempore assignavimus Iohanni Sherwoode indenturam de Merton Hall, Cantabrigia, finis 6 li. 13s. 4d.

Vicaria Sancti Petri in oriente in magistrum Sellar collata

Eodem quoque tempore unanimi consensu custodis et sociorum praesentatio vicariae Sancti Petri in oriente collata est in magistrum Sellar cautumque si, incompatibilis societati decerni eveniret ut integra maniret magistro Sellar pro arbitrio suo vicariae vel societatis optio, modo alteram linquat statum priorem in alia retineat. Duabus

[1] 'in primis' deleted.

obligationibus datis prima ne fraude aut negligentia sua dicta vicaria in alium patronum cadat, alia si quiete beneficio fruatur uberiori cum cura animarum, collegio in manus reddatur, cuicunque custodi cum sociis visum fuerit de novo conferenda.

His ita iam peractis singuli claves ad bibliothecam spectantes deferunt, in conspectum domini custodis. Claves itidem omnium officiarii anni praeteriti resignant, et secedentibus ad tempus aliis custos et quinque simpliciter seniores in annum praesentem officiarios eligunt hos.

Electio officiariorum

magistrum Simonson, vicecustodem,
magistros Pettye, Higgs, Heath, decanos.
magistros Turner, Sellar, Fisher, bursarios.
principalem portionistarum, magistrum Marsh; bursarium Williott, magistrum Gall; exhibitionarium Hamsterlay, magistrum Higgs; exhibitionem capellani capellae dividendam volunt inter tres decanos; conservatores cistae Bodly magistros Farrar, French, Doubtye; custodes cistae Read, tres decanos.

Computus custodis

Augusti 2° computavit in hospitio custodis sociis omnibus ibidem praesentibus dominus custos et discessit in plussagio 12 li. 9s. 4d. ob.

Progressus in partes boreales

Eodem tempore consentiunt omnes ut dominus custos progressum ineat hoc anno in partes boreales ad visitandas terras nostras de Stillington, Ceton Carew, Emildon et Ponteland, atque eodem consensu designatus est magister Higgs ad equitandum cum domino custode.

p. 286 Anno Domini 1623, regis Iacobi 21 magistri Nathanaelis Brent custodis 3°.

Admissio

Augusti 11°. Dominus custos socios in altam aulam convocavit ibidemque ex unanimi omnium consensu admisit dominum Abbots in perpetuam societatem huius domus.

Allocatio 5 Palantinis facta

Eodem tempore allocavimus quinque Palantinis per litteras a serenissimo rege Bohemiae et honoratissimo domino cancellario nostro universitati commendatis sex libras tredecim solidos quatuor denarios per annum in hunc modum solvendos, dominus custos debit duodecim solidos, singuli socii quatuor solidos annuatim, hoc est singulis tribus mensibus duodecim denarios, quod autem restat solvendum per bursarios e bonis collegii.

Magister Napper, ballivus de Holliwell
Eodem tempore consentiunt praedicti custos et socii de litteris patentibus sigillandis magistro Edmundo Napper pro recipiendis redditibus tenementorum Holliwell, Oxon', Witney, London.

Varii computus
Augusti 1° magister Sherwood, firmarius de Camb' computavit in scaccario.

Augusti 4° Heath, firmarius de Farleigh, computavit.

Augusti 9° Richardus Hodsden, firmarius de Callowland, computavit.

Augusti 11 magister Edmundus Napper computavit pro firma de Holliwel atque etiam pro tenementis de Holliwell, Oxon', Witney, London.

Dispensatio
Octobris 8 dispensavimus cum magistro French iam in 2° anno regentiae suae existente ut non amplius teneretur legere ordinarias, nec frequentare disputationes baccalauriorum aut Augustinenses.

Higs 3us bursarius discessit aeque
Octobris 13 magister Higgs 3us bursarius anni praeteriti in praesentia sociorum solvit pedem computi et sic discessit aeque.

Varii computus
Octobris 20 magister Mayne, firmarius de Chedington, computavit in scaccario.

Eodem tempore Richardus Wilmot, firmarius de Ibston, computavit.

Octobris 29 magister Ray, firmarius de Kibworth, computavit.

Novembris 6° magister Gregory, firmarius de Cuxam, computavit.

Commemoratio
Decimo septimo Decembris habita est commemoratio pro fundatore, lecta statuta et scrutinium celebratum quod continuatum est in vigilia circumcisionis.

Scrutinium in vigilia Circumcisionis

Ultimo Decembris qui erat vigilia Circumcisionis de more habitum est scrutinium in quo actum est, 1° de moribus servientium et huius articuli modo ratio officiariis commititur, 2° de numero portionistarum deliberatum qui ut solitus sit decernitur, 3° de hortulano consultatum quod officium in magistrum French collatum est tam suffragiis eligentium, quam etiam iure senioritatis.

[1624]

Magister Greevil peregrinatur

Februarii 28 sociis omnibus in altam aulam convocatis lectae sunt a domino custode litterae in gratiam magistri Greevil peregrinantis scriptae, atque inde unanimi sociorum consensu decretum est ut eidem magistro Greevil in triennium peregre proficiscenti 15 li. quotannis a bursariis collegii nomine, pro communis pro[ro]gentur ac praeterea quicquid ex finibus et liberatura ad socii partem interea temporis accreverit, ut eidem allocetur, eodem consensu ordinatum est.

Concessio musicis

Tunc etiam consensum est ut publicis Academiae oppidique musicis bursarius 6s. 8d. pro more solito soleret.

Scholaris magistri Chambers

Martii 3° ad nos accessit scholaris quidam Etonensis nomine Temple secum afferens litteras a praepositis collegii Regalis Cantabrigiensis et collegii Etonensis iuxta Windsor in suam ipsius gratiam conscriptas, scilicet ut admitteretur prefatus Temple in locum Edvardi Nevil, unius e duobus scholaribus magistri Chambers et ad gradum baccalauriatus iam promoti. Unde statim secundum formam testamenti magistri Chambers in numerum portionistarum admissus est.

p. 287 Anno Domini 1623, regis Iacobi 21, domini doctoris Brent custodis 3°.

Commemoratio

Martii 23° commemorationem habuimus pro fundatore, legimus statuta et scrutinium inivimus quod prorogavimus in 1um diem Maii et quemlibet diem citra.

Dispensatio

Maii 2° dispensatum est cum magistris Doubty, Fisher, Heath, regentibus pro tribus perlectionibus in 2^{dis} ultimis terminis.

Dispensatio cum Spranger pro pecunia usque ad terminum Michaelis.

Iulii 2°. Dominus custos sociis omnibus in conclave suum convocatis significavit Richardum Spranger, firmarium de Canes in comitatu Essexiae, nuper apud eum Londini precibus contendisse ut solutio librarum, quas ipse propter silvas sibi a magistro Turner collegio iam debuerat numerare, bona nostra cum venia differatur ad terminum Sancti Michaelis proxime sequentem nec enim ante illud tempus se dictam pecuniam parare ulla ratione posse. Quae quidem ipsius petitio ab eisdem custode et sociis concessa est.

Dispensatio cum baccalaureis

Eisdem loco et tempore baccalaureis Hinton, Holliwel, Reynolds, Erles, concessimus veniam incipiendi in facultate artium quamvis debitum trium annorum spatium ab admissione in societatem non compleverant atque inde ordinatum est ut 9° huius mensis inmediate a disputationibus baccalaureorum in numerum magistrorum admittantur.

Molendinum de Grancester; reparatio

Eodem tempore atque eadem authoritate conclusum est ut molendina nostra de Grancester iuxta Cantabrigiam nuper domino Richardo Beaumont per indenturam concessa, tam vetustate quam incuria tenentium iam ruinam minitantia collegii sumptibus restaurarentur.

Maldon

Eodem loco et tempore retulit dominus custos quid factum sit in curia cancellariae in lite intentata contra magistrum Good pro recuperatione manerii de Maldon, nimirum dominum custodem magni sigilli obtulisse collegio incrementum reditus triginta librarum annuatim patronatum vicariae ibidem, et summam 50 li. pro expensis, et interdixisse omnibus curiis, excepto Parliamento, ulterius procedendi ut in hac causa, si collegium hanc concordiam non acceptaret. Habita igitur hac de re matura deliberatione statuimus non acceptare hanc concordiam, sed potius expectare sententiam Parliamenti; quia causam hanc non satis ventilatam fuisse iudicavimus in cancellaria audita tantum parte adversa.

Commemoratio

Iulii 20° nempe in festo beatae Margaretae habuimus, hora et loco consuetis, commemorationem fundatoris; legimus etiam statuta, scrutinium celebravimus, quod prorogavimus in 2° [*sic*] diem Augusti et quemlibet diem citra.

Computus custodis

Iulii ultimo convenimus in hospitium custodis ubi dominus custos computavit in praesentia sociorum; et computatis computandis et allocatis allocandis discessit in arreragia 16 li. 18s. 10d. qua.

Dimissio indenturae

Eodem tempore dimisimus indenturam manerii de Farleigh nuper in tenura Heath, cuidam Matthaeo Bedel, Londinensi pro termino 21ius annorum. Finis 51 li.

p. 288 Anno Domini 1624, regis Iacobi 22, domini doctoris Brent custodis 4°.

Augustus

Magistri in artibus

1. Guilielmus Simonson
2. Franciscus Greevile
3. Georgius Pettye
4. Petrus Turner
5. Guilielmus Sellar
6. Griffinus Higgs
7. Umfredus Farrar
8. Iacobus Marsh
9. Thomas Gall
10. Iohannes French
11. Iohannes Doubtye
12. Alexander Fisher
13. Thomas Heath
14. Hinton
15. Holliwell
16. Reynolds
17. Earles

Baccalaurei in artibus

1. dominus Abbots

Capellani

1. Robertus Gaylard
2. Iohannes Wilton

Electio officiariorum

Augusti 2° convocatis in altam aulam sociis omnibus hora nona antemeridiana et resignatis de more clavibus, dominus custos et quinque simpliciter seniores reliquis secedentibus, designant in hunc annum officiarios istos qui sequuntur:

magistrum Simonson, vicecustodem.

magistros Sellar, Doubtye, Hinton, decanos.

magistros Pettye, Gall, Heath, bursarios.

magistrum Higgs, principalem portionistarum, cui etiam exhibitio Hampsterley est assignata; magistrum French, bursarium Williot; magistrum Reynolds, capellanum capellae; custodes cistae Read, tres decanos; conservatores cistae Bodley, magistros Higgs, Fisher, Holliwell; praelector grammaticae nominatus a domino custode, magister Fisher; praelector Graecae linguae, magister Erles.

Dimissio Indenturae

Eodem tempore dimisimus indenturam muri stabuli Smoote magistro Reynolds pro termino 40 annorum, finis o.

Dominus Fouler; praesentatio ad vicariam de Stratton

Eodem etiam tempore praesentationem vicariae de Margareta Stratton per liberam resignationem Guilelmi Fouler iam vacantem, concessimus Lemueli Fouler in artibus baccalaureo quae quidem praesentatio paucis post diebus sigillata est.

Electio sociorum

Eodem quoque tempore consensum est de electione sociorum habenda et ut sese custodis et sociorum examinationi publica submitterent quicunque in hoc negotio sui rationem haberi cuperent. Indicti autem 2, 3, 4 dies in hunc finem.

Augusti 6to hora 9^{a} ante meridiem dominus custos convenire fecit in conclave suum tredecim seniores, ubi, statuto regni 20° Elizabethae edito electiones spectante processerunt ad electionem in qua electi sunt decem baccalaurei, dominus Greaves, dioceseos Winton', dominus Corbet, dioceseos Herifordensis, dominus Wright, dioceseos Salisburiensis, dominus Gibbs, dioceseos Wigornensis, dominus Browne, dioceseos Roffensis, dominus Cressye, dioceseos Eboracensis, dominus Woodcocke, dioceseos Londonensis, dominus Nevil, dioceseos Salisburiensis, dominus Dumvil, dioceseos Cestrensis, dominus Barkley, dioceseos Londonensis.

Pecuniae ad Bibliotecam

Atque ibi ordinatum ut solvant in usum bibliothecae dominus Greaves 3 li. 6s. 8d., dominus Corbet, 20s., dominus Wright, 20s., dominus Gibbs, 3 li. 6s. 8d., dominus Browne, 3 li. 6s. 8d., dominus Cressye, 3 li. 6s. 8d., dominus Woodcock, 3 li. 6s. 8d., dominus Nevil 20s., dominus Dumvil 3 li. 6s. 8d., dominus Barkley 3 li. 6s. 8d.

p. 289 Anno Domini 1624, regis Iacobi 22°, domini doctoris Brent custodis 4to.

Tempus admissionis probatianorum

Eodem tempore atque eadem autoritate ordinatum est ut ex his 10 tunc electis quinque seniores admittantur in annum probationis initio termini proxime sequentis; quatuor alii ad initium termini Hilarii anni 1625, decimus autem nimirum dominus Barkley admittendus in initio termini Michaelis anno 1626.

Decretum pro commentariis baccalaureorum

Eodem etiam tempore decretum est idque plurimis de causis ibidem propositis, ut baccalaurei in anno probationis constituti, haud amplius sicuti mos erat commententur in secundos primos Aristotelis libros Physic' sed ut labores suos post hac impendant in duos ultimos libros Aristotelis de Anima; comprehensis una in ipsorum commentariis etiam definitionibus Animae ab Aristotele libro primo propositis.

Decretum pro ordinariis magistrorum regentium

Eodem quoque loco et tempore magistri hoc anno regentes nobis significarunt sese obnixe sed frustra apud procuratores universitatis egisse uti ipsis copia legendi ordinaria sua in scholis publicis concederetur, nec istud alia conditione obtinere potuisse, nisi ordinarium et suo laboris iure debitum stipendium aliis remitterent. Rogarunt itaque praefati magistri ut ipsorum iuramento quo tenentur ab admissione ad magisterium iam a nobis consulatur. Unde quidem hoc negotio inter nos aliquamdiu tractato, tandem pro hoc anno praesenti nec omnino ulterius decretum est, quod unoquoque termino praedicti magistri singuli singulis septimanis, bis in alta collegii aula virtute iuramenti sicut antea legere teneantur et quod penes quinque simpliciter seniores sit decernere in quaquam artium facultate quos autores et quibus horis legant.

Ordinatio circa bibliothecam

Eodem etiam tempore negotium circa bibliothecam atque omnia alia ibidem ad vicecustodem, seniorem decanum et bursarium presentem referuntur peragenda, atque ut Blackam pro custodienda et mundanda bibliotheca et ecclesia recipiat de bursario collegii septimanatim pro laboribus duodecem denarios.

Variae concessae indenturae

Eodem etiam loco et tempore Iohannes Okley, firmarius de rectoria de Woolford, petiit ut resignata indentura eiusdem rectoriae pro termino vitae Thomae Munday, Annae Munday et Ing' Horsman multos ante annos concessa, iam ei aliam eiusdem concederemus pro termino vitae ipsius nempe Iohannis Okley, Margaretae uxoris, et Edwardi filii eorum, cui dominus custos et socii assenserunt, et eidem nomine finis imposerant centum marcas, quarum dimidiam partem solvere debet ante festum Omnium Sanctorum proxime sequentem, alteram medietatem circa idem tempus anno revoluto.

Eodem tempore dimisimus Richardo Wilmot indenturam de Ibston pro termino 21^{ius} annorum, finis 80 li., quarum 40 librae solvendae ad sigillationem indenturae ante festum Omnium Sanctorum proxime sequentem,[1] viginti librae solvendae eodem tempore anno sequente, et rursus reliquae 20 librae eodem tempore anno 1626. Concessimus etiam Edmundo Gregory indenturam de Cuxam pro termino 21us annorum finis 100 marcae quarum dimidium solvendum quoque ad festum Omnium Sanctorum proximum, reliquum ad festum Annuntiacionis anno 1625. Concessimus etiam viduae Hore tenementum in Holliwell pro termino 40 annorum finis 8 li. Dimisimus etiam Thomae Haukins tenementum in Holliwell pro termino 21^{ius} annorum, finis o.

Probatianorum admissio

Octobris 9 admissi sunt in annum probationis dominus Greaves, dominus Corbet, dominus Wright, dominus Gibbs, dominus Browne, iuramento prius de more praestito.

Varii computus

Eodem tempore Robertus Mayne, firmarius de Chedington, computavit in scaccario.

Octobris [*blank*] Henricus Sayre, firmarius de Barkby, computavit.

Octobris 26° Robertus Ray, firmarius de Kibworth, computavit.

Octobris 28° Richardus Wilmot, firmarius de Ibston, computavit.

Novembris. Edmundus Gregory, firmarius de Cuxam computavit.

[1] 'reliquae 40 librae' deleted.

p. 290 Anno Domini 1624, regis Iacobi 22° domini doctoris Brent custodis 4°.

Computus bursarii

Decembris 16° magister Heath, primus bursarius, computavit in scaccario.

Commemoratio

Decembris 18 habita est commemoratio pro fundatore, lecta statuta, scrutinium celebratum, et prorogatum in ultimum eiusdem mensis diem.

Scrutinium servientium

In vigilia Circumcisionis inito pro more scrutinio actum est de moribus servientium, de numero portionistarum et de electione hortulani servientium mores ad arbitrium officiariorum decernuntur corrigendi, portionistarum numerus constat idem in statu quo. In hortulanum nominatus est magister Doubtye.

[1625]

Rectoria de Gamlingay magistro Higgs

Nono die Martii sociis in altam aulam convenientibus vicecustos literas a domino custode Londino de rectoria apud Gamlingay per mortem nuperam magistri Lane iam vacante missas perlegit; quibus significavit dominus custos se in beneficio illo conferendo maiori sociorum parti consensurum, copiamque collationis communi sigillo muniendae facturum; socii vero eodem tempore rectoriam illam in magistrum Higgs contulerunt.

Commemoratio pro fundatore

Aprilis nono celebravimus commemorationem fundatoris, legimus statuta et scrutinium inivimus, quod prorogatum est in primum diem Maii et quemlibet diem citra.

Rectoria Gamlingay magistro Higgs

Aprilis ultimo medietas rectoriae de Gamlingay sigillata est magistro Higgs.

Vicaria de Stratton

Martii 9° concessimus Lemueli Fowler praesentationem vicariae de Stratton, hunc vero reverendus in Christo pater dominus episcopus Sarum instituere recusavit et nominationem ad eandem vicariam ad se pertinere affirmavit. Nos autem nominationem dicti reverendi episcopi pro ea tantum vice acceptavimus, hac tamen conditione ut dictum

Fouler a nobis antea praesentatum nominaret, idque ob eam tantummodo causam fecimus, quod fortuna eiusdem Fouler adeo tenuis erat, ut eventum litis expectare non posset.

Variae concessiones indenturarum

Aprilis ultimo sociis in scaccarium per dominum custodem convocatis concessa est indentura rectoriae de Stratton Francisco Kemble pro termino 21 annorum. Finis 80 li., cuius media pars solvenda ad festum Omnium Sanctorum proxime sequentem, altera autem medietas 3° Maii anni sequentis solvenda.

Eodem tempore concessimus magistro Sherwood indenturam de Merton Hall, Cantabrigia, pro termino 21^{ius} annorum. Finis 10 li.

Eodem etiam tempore dimissa est indentura tenementi cuiusdam apud Hampton Powel Iohanni Iohnson pro termino 21. Finis duo pares caponum.

Computus Napper

Eodem tempore magister Napper, ballivus de Holliwell, computavit pro tenementis in Holliwel; et discessit in aere collegii 42 li. 16s. 3d. ob.

Admissio

Eodem die a precibus vespertinis dominus custos convocavit socios in vestibulum atque ibidem concessa est domino Abbots venia incipiendi in facultate artium, etiamsi debitum atque ordinarium tempus non compleverat, unde statim eodem loco et tempore a domino custode admissus est in numerum magistrorum.

Anno Domini 1625, regis Caroli 1°, custodis Brent 4°.[1] p. 291

Pestis

Iulii 21°. Circa hoc tempore ingravescente Londini peste, ubi tum regni comitia latabantur, visum est regi, de sententia consilii sedem mutare, et eundem conventum Oxonii agere. Huius consilii literas praenuntias accepit academia ab aliquot discretioribus consilii primariis viris; iubentes insuper, quo commodius in collegiis hospitari possent viri nobiles, et reliqui burgenses, plebem omnem academicam ad tempus ablegari, et ante calendas Augusti urbe excedere. Custos igitur et socii, uti par erat, serenissimi regis iussa capessentes de ea re ita censuerunt. Baccalaurei et portionistae, durante hoc conventu, ablegantur ad unum omnes. Baccalaurei quamdiu, hac causa, urbe

[1] In a different hand, perhaps that of Peter Turner, subwarden. It was in fact the 5th year of Brent's wardenship.

abfuerint in singulas septimanas quinque solidi, portionistae duo solidi quantuor denarii conceduntur.

E servientum numero sex tantum manento [*sic*], qui sex senioribus serviunt: ii etiam reliquis magistris famulantor [*sic*] intra triduum, quoscunque tangit hoc decretum secedunto [*sic*]. Magistri in aream baccalaureorum se recipiunto [*sic*]; ac prout res tulerit, et inter se constituterint cameras, earumque consortes sortiuntor [*sic*].

Eodem etiam tempore decretum antiquitus sancitum ne quis praeter officiarios intret promptuarium renovendum censuerunt.

p. 292 Anno Domini 1625, regis Caroli 1mo, custodis Brent 5to.

Magistri in artibus

1. Guilielmus Simonson
2. Franciscus Grevill
3. Georgius Petty
4. Petrus Turner
5. Guilielmus Sellar
6. Griffinus Higges
7. Humphredus Farrar
8. Iacobus Marsh
9. Thomas Gall

Probationarii

1. Ioannes French
2. Franciscus Doughty
3. Alexander Fisher
4. Thomas Heath
5. Laurentius Hinton
6. Ioannes Holywell
7. Edwardus Rainolds
8. Ioannes Earles
9. Georgius Abbot
10. dominus Ioannes Greeves
11. Edwardus Corbett
12. Robertus Wright
13. Carolus Gibbs
14. Richardus Brown

Capellani

1. Robertus Gaylard
2. Ioannes Wilton

Augusti 2°. In altam aulam conventum est circa horam nonam antemeridianam, ubi resignatis pro more clavibus officiariorum reliquis sociis ad tempus secedere iussis, custos una cum quique simpliciter senioribus, sequentis anni officiarios hunc in modum designavit:

vicecustos, magister Turner.

magistri Higges, Fisher, Rainolds, decani.

magistri Marsh, Doughty, Hinton, bursarii.

bursarius Williott, magister French; lector linguae Graecae, magister Earles; principalis portionistarum, magister Petty; lector grammaticae, magister Abbott; exhibitionarius Hamsterly, magister Marsh; capellanus capellae, magister Sellar; custodes cistae Reade, tres decani; custodes cistae Bodly, magistri Sellar, French, Heath.

Annus gratuitus magistro Simonson ceditur
Eodem tempore concessus est magistro Simonson annus gratuitus

Dilatio variationum
Magistro Fisher data est licentia differendi variationes suas, hoc anno habendas, in annum sequentem, magistro Doughty similiter concessum est ut differat variationes suas usque in finem termini Hilarii.

Lectori Linacri
[Augusti] 3^{tio}. Dominus Lapworth et dominus Hawly iterum renuntiati sunt lectores Linacri.

Lector Bickley
[Augusti] 8°. Dominus custos magistrum Marsh lectorem Bickley designat.

[Augusti] 16° gliscente nunc in dies peste, cum non aliter commode securitati nostra prospici posset, quam per fugam seu recessum a collegio dominus custos et socii de ea re ita censuerunt.

Decreta tempore pestis
Vicecustos, decanus unus, bursarius praesens, principalis portionistarum, aliquisve horum vicesgerens in collegio maneant continuo, quotquot etiam praeterea voluerint. Quotquot urbe excisserint, percipient singulis septimanis quinque solidos usque ad festum Michaelis, ducto initio a die veneris proxime sequenti. Si ultra illud tempus abesse necessum fuerit, quid singuli recepturi sint, ubi collegium redierint custodis et sociorum arbitrio permittitur.

Soli pensionem decretam recipient, quotquot scribendo abfuere, quive postea ad collegium accidentes, iterum recesserint. Eorum qui in collegio morantur nullus domo exeat nisi prius impetrata venia, et sub chirogapho vicecustodis, bursarii, decani, principalis portionistarum horumve duorum quorumlibet, testata. Intraturis collegium serenissima lex esto.

Ioannem Blackam vice omnium lotricum esto, et domum lavandis vestibus opportunam alicubi in vicinia conducat. Coquus senior una cum lixa moretur in collegio, ipse itidem obsonatoris munus obeat, et aromata, aliaque ab aromato petenda in antecessum comparet. Aromatum modulum pro numero praesentium decanus et bursarius moderentur. Decreta ista haec a 17° Augusti vim suam obtineant.

Promus loco movetur

Chittenden promus propter varias infirmitates factus muneri suo impar, loco cedere iussus est; et stipendii loco numerabit ei bursarius, singulis septimanis tres solidos. Qui in locum ipsius succederit duos spectatae fidei viros procurabit qui sub hypotheca sua, ipsius fidem integram, et collegium indemne praestabunt.

Eodem tempore aequum visum est, ut collegium veniret in partem expensarum, quas subierat dominus custos in excipiendo patrono nostro reverendissimo archiepiscopo Cantuariensi, viginti ergo marcas in se recepit collegium.

Computus custodis

Eodem etiam tempore dominus custos computavit et discessit.

Computus 3^ii bursarii differtur

Computus magistri Petty 3^ii bursarii dilatus est in diem iovis post festum Omnium Sanctorum.

Empte hospitio

[Augusti] 17°. Ad instruendum uberius domini custodis hospitium empta est haec suppellex, decem scamni operis phrygii 8s. 6d. in singulum; ad mensarum peristromata, viridis panni 14 ulnae iuxta 13s. 1d. ob. in singulam; decem cathedrae operis eiusdem 14s. 6d. in singulam; caerulei panni 3 y ½ iuxta 10s. in singulam.

[Augusti] 21°. Maior pars sociorum qui domi aderant in apodyterium statim a precibus convocata, quia Blackamo aliter commode prospici non poterat de domo lavandis vestibus opportuna, ipsi una cum filia sua locum in collegio dandum censuit, praesertim cum non abesset exemplum aliorum collegiorum, quae hac ratione securitati suae consultum inerant.

Et symbola eroganda in pauperes etc.

Eodem die accepimus a domino vicecancellario literas symbolam petentes erogandam singulis septimanis in sustentationem pauperum de peste laborantium.

[Augusti] 27°. Maior pars sociorum, qui domi aderant, in aulam convocata, statuit septimanis singulis in die mercurii (quo die ieiunium publica auctoritate indictum fuerat) omnes tam praesentes quam absentes, in libro seneschalli numerandos esse, tanquam si in prandio adessent et, quae exinde praeveniret, summam erogandam esse in aegrotos, egenos, et ad alia Academiae entra [?] supportanda. [*damage*] um numerandos esse, in pecunia praesentaria viginti solidos magistro French, quaestori aerarii Academiae in hunc usum deputato, [*damage*] ul spem faciendam aliorum viginti post festum Michaelis si publica necessitas hoc ipsum efflagitet.

Anno Domini 1625, regis Caroli 1mo, custodis Brent 5to. p. 293

Augusti 27°. Si quid in hac prandiorum symbola superfuerit pro arbitrio custodis et sociorum erogandum; si quid defuerit ulterius deliberandum.

Literae procuratoriae bursariorum

Eodem tempore literae procuratoriae bursariis sigillatae sunt.

Admissio sociorum

Octobris 13°. Ex consensu custodis, significato per literas datas 7^{bris} 21°, et sociorum quotquot domi aderant, cum per duos dies frustra expectati fuissent reliqui socii qui prae metu pestis in confinio oppidi haerebant, admissi sunt in perpetuam societatem huius domus dominus Ioannes Greeves, dominus Edwardus Corbet, dominus Robertus Wright, dominus Carolus Gibbs, dominus Richardus Browne.

Continuatio dismissionis

Eodem tempore visum est dimissionem superius factam ulterius continuare, usque ad diem Veneris inante festum Omnium Sanctorum.

Obitus magistri Grevill

[Octobris] 28°. Nuntius allatus est de morte magistri Grevill in transmarinis partibus agentis, qui Curiae Rhaetorum fatis concessit, in comitatu domini Isaac Wake nuper socii, cui ille legationem apud Venetos obeunti adhaeserat.

Computus 3^{i} bursarii

Novembris 3°. magister Petty bursarius 3us computavit.

Dispensatio cum magistro Abbots

[Novembris] 10°. Cum magistro Abbot dispensatum est, prout superiori anno cum regentibus dispensatum fuerat, ut vice lectionum suarum in Academia habendarum legat Aristotelis rhetorica bis singulis septimanis in quolibet termino, praesentibus portionistis in alta aula.

Dispensatio cum magistro Doughty

Cum magistro Doughty dispensatum est pro variationibus, modo iis defungatur citra discessum magistri Higgs.

Thesaurarii accomodatio

[Novembris] 11°. Socii in altam aulam convocati inter alia negotia censuerunt mensam in thesaurario succedendam et ad sedilium commoditatem demittendam. Sex etiam scamnos, et cathedram pellibus russis incincta ad hunc usum coemenda censuerunt. Ibidem facta est magistro Wilton copia describendi apographum compositionis vicariae de Wolford.

Ieiunium abrumpitur

[Novembris] 23°. Convocatis in altam aulam sociis ieiunium publica auctoritate indictum, et desaeviente iam peste, in plerisque regni locis ommissum, in collegio haud ultra continuandum censuerunt. Ad sustentationem tam infirmorum et pauperum decretum est ut unusquisque singulis septimanis tres denarios contribuat, quamdiu publica necessitas hoc ipsum efflagitat.

Commemoratio

Decembris 17°. Habita est commemoratio fundatoris. Eodem etiam die statuta in alta aula perlecta sunt, et scrutinium habitum ac etiam prorogatum in calendas Ianuarii sequentis.

Lis circa Stonehouse

[Decembris] 25°. Convocatis sociis in apodyterium statim a precibus vespertinis, lectae sunt literae domini custodis de mittendis duobus e sociis Londinum, ad componendam litem cum Harwood circa Stonehouse. Socii consenserunt in magistros Sellar et French, qui etiam in se receperunt.

Scrutinium

[Decembris] 30°. In vigilia Circumcisionis habitum est de more scrutinium, et prorogatum in Kalendas Februarii, magister Fisher, hortulanus.

[1626]

Ianuarii 1°. Convocatis sociis in apodyterium statim a precibus vespertinis, quia magister [*sic*] Sellar et French designati ad componendam litem cum Harwood, ad tempus praestitutum nequaquam defuncti essent [in] provincia, quam in se recepissent, vicecustos una cum magistro Higgs ad hoc idem munus ex consensu sociorum deputati sunt.

[Ianuarii] 16°. Magister Higgs una cum vicecustode retulit sociis in alta aula, qua a se acta fuerant Londini circa Stonehouse.

Admissio in anno probationis

Eodem tempore dominus Hugo Cressey, dominus Ioannes Woodcock, dominus Edwardus Nevill, dominus Ranulphus Domvill, dominus Guilelmus Berkly admissi sunt in annum probationis.

Hinton variationes

Aprilis 1°. Magister Hinton variavit in his quaestionibus:

An {
Praestet in universum legibus subiici quam magistratus sententiae aliquid relinqui. Affirmat contra Aristotelis 1'.3 Polit' c.11.
Maxima ingenia sint minus ad iniuriam perclivia. Affirmat contra Aristotelis Problemata sectio 29^{a}, pr' 7°.
Accuratior stylus sit superfluus, et inefficax ad captandum populum. Negat contra Aristotelis 3 Rhetorica, c.12.

Die sequenti dispensatum est cum magistro Hinton pro secundis suis variationibus.

Commemoratio

Iunii. 1mo eiusdem mensis habita est commemoratio fundatoris, lecta statuta, scrutinium initum et prorogatum.

Dominus Wright moritur

[Iunii] 24°. Dominus Wright optimae spei iuvenis febri correptus obiit.

Doughty variationes

Iulii 7°. Magister Doughty variavit in his quaestionibus:

An {
Efficacius nos ducant rationes quam exempla. Negat contra Aristotelis, Rhetoric' I, c.2.
Magistratus virum iudicet. Negat contra Aristotelis, Ethic' 5, cap' 3.
Par sit meliores nasci ex melioribus. Negat contra Aristotelis Politic' 5.

Finitis variationibus dispensatum est cum magistro Doughty pro secundis variationibus.

Bedae MS. vol. Commentar' dat' Archiepiscopo Armachano[1]

[Iulii] 16°. Convocatis sociis in apodyterium statim a precibus matutinis, significavit iis vicecustos reverendissimum archiepiscopum Armachanum petere ut liceat sibi extra Bibliothecam MS. quodam Bedae volumine commodato uti. Cui petitioni libenter annuerunt.

Commemoratio

[Iulii] 20°. In festo Margaretae habita est commemoratio fundatoris, lecta statuta, initum scrutinium et prorogatum usque ad vigesimum diem Augusti.

Fielding data facultas amplificando domus suae

Eodem die convenientibus sociis in coenaculo custodis data est licentia magistro Fielding, qui cum custode consilium suum de amplificanda domo sua communicaverat, ut lateritiam illam domus suae partem quae in aream preminet, ulterius proiiciat spatio 5 vel 6 pedum.

Butler MS. mutuo data archiepiscopo Armachano.[2]

Ibidem etiam reverendissimo archiepiscopo Armachano ex consensu MS. Butler contra versionem Anglicanam commodato utendum dedimus.

Passer, salarium

[Iulii] 26°. De consensu custodis et sociorum in ipsius hospitio convenientium magistro Passer, Germano, linguam Arabicam publice professuro decreti sunt quadraginta solidi annuatim loco salarii. Haec summa colligenda est hunc in modum. De liberatura singulorum sociorum deducentur quotannis octodecim denarii. Quantum summa inde proveniens aberit a 40s. supplebit de suo dominus custos. Durabit haec exhibitio per triennium.

Sedilia in templo fabricanda

Ibidem etiam decretum est ut plura sedilia in usum templi fabricanda curet bursarius, quo laxius sedeant magistri in concionibus publicis.

Finis magistri Fielding integer ad socios pervenit

Ibidem etiam dominus custos alteram medietatem finis magistri Fielding inter socios dividendam indulsit.

[1] There were five continuations of Bede in the library: cf. Coxe, nos. 176, 180–1, 257, and Powicke, *Medieval Books*, 1069.

[2] Merton Coll. MS. K.2.2 (Coxe, no. 68).

Concessio magistro Leigh facta irrita

Consensum prius factum, de locandis sylvis Farleigh magistro Leigh irritum esse oportere censuerunt, quia ad tempus constitutum rem transigere neglexisset.

Consilium de amplificando hospitium custodis

Dominus custos consilium suum de amplificando hospitio suo sociis approbavit, cuius arbitrio permittunt num commode in loco designato aedificium extrui possit.

Locationes praediorum [? in the college year 1625–6][1] p. 294

Augusti 2° [1625 ?]. Consensum est de locandis sylvis Farleigh magistro Lea. Finis 40 librae.

Augusti 3°. Roberto Mayne praedium de Chedington locatum est. Locatio incipiet a festo Sancti Michaelis. Finis 35 librae.

Augusti 17°. Decretum insuper est, ut eam finis partem, quod ad socios spectat, ad festum Omnium Sanctorum solvat, alteram partem ad Annunciacionem Beatae Mariae et festum Sancti Iohannis Baptistae, aequis portionibus.

9^bris^ 17°. Sigillata est indentura de Chedington Roberto Mayne.

[Novembris] 17°. Magistro Butler praedium de West Tilbury locatum est si modo aedificia curet reparanda, et fundorum terratam conficiat. Locatio incipiet a festo Michaelis proxime sequenti. Finis 35 librae.

Novembris 10°. Locavimus terras qua[s]dam in Kibworth, vocatas Swaiths, Georgio Gage, pro termino 21 annorum. Finis 5 li., 50s. solvendi in ipsa appositione sigilli, 50s. ad festum Annuntiacionis. Locatio incipit a festo Michaelis proxime praeterlapso.

9^bris^ 10°. Sigillata est indentura G. Gage, et soluta prima parte finis, ex consensu sociorum, dilata est solutio residui in festum Pentecostes sequentis.

27° Augusti. Sigillata est indentura domus, cui Falconis insigne in Gamlingay una cum literis attornatus.

5° Augusti. Data est licentia Henrico Brian alienandi unam virgatam terrae de tribus quas tenet per indenturam Roberto Standen.

[1] Such recording of the year's leases becomes usual practice in the register from this point. The fines are listed in the margins of this section.

Novembris 10°. Consenserunt custos et socii ut Ioannes Ihonson [*sic*] libera sit facultas ius suum in Hampton Poyle transferendi ad filium suum, utque ille in posterum Coloni nomine censeatur.

Eodem tempore magistro Okely qui alteram finis partem ad tempus praestitutum haud solverat, praefixum est tempus solvendi citra festum Purificationis proxime futurum, intra quod tempus si minus solverit, renumerandam illi esse eam, quam iam solvit, pecuniam, et concessionem irritam esse oportere censuerunt.

Februarii 24° [1626 ?]. Custos et socii dederunt liberam facultatem Christophoro Ainscough transferendi ius suum in altera medietate Stillington et Seton Carew, ad Christophorum Morpeth, pro residuo termini. Finis 6 librae.

Februarii 25°. Sigillata est indentura.

Iulii 21°. Anno Domini 1625. Altera pars domus vocate Stonehouse in Knightriders street, defuncto iam M. Harwood veteri inquilino et locationis tempore elapso, magistro Feilding locata est, annua pensione 5 li. Finis 100 librae.

Altera pars eiusdem domus locata est Thomae Ridley durante vita naturali, annua pensione 30 librae.

Varii Computus [*? in the college year 1625–6*]

Augusti 5° [1625 ?]. Hensly balivus de Beilby, computavit, et discessit in aere collegii 78 li. 14s.

Augusti 16°. Sherwood computavit pro Cantebrigia et discessit aeque.

Augusti 23°. Hoddesden, firmarius de Callowland, computavit et discessit aeque.

Octobris 26°. Wilmott, firmarius de Ibston, computavit et discessit aeque.

Novembris 5°. Gregorie, firmarius de Cuxham, computavit, et discessit aeque.

Novembris 10°. Raye, firmarius de Kibworth, computavit, et discessit aeque.

Novembris 17°. Mayne, firmarius de Chedington, computavit, et discessit aeque.

Novembris 26°. Sayre, firmarius de Barkby, computavit et discessit in aere collegii, 4 li.

Iulii 13° [1626 ?]. M. Bedell, firmarius de Farleigh, computavit et discessit aeque.

Anno Domini 1626, Regis Caroli 2°, custodis Brent 6to. p. 295

Magistri

1. Guilielmus Simonson
2. Georgius Petty
3. Petrus[1] Turner
4. Guilielmus Sellar
5. Humfredus Farrar
6. Iacobus Marsh
7. Thomas Gall
8. Ioannes French
9. Ioannes Doughtye
10. Alexander Fisher
11. Thomas Heath
12. Laurentius Hinton
13. Ioannes Holliwell
14. Edwardus Reynolds
15. Ioannes Earles
16. Georgius Abbott

Probationarii

1. dominus Greaves
2. dominus Corbett
3. dominus Gibbes
4. dominus Browne
5. dominus Cressy
6. dominus Woodcocke
7. dominus Nevile
8. dominus Donvile
9. dominus Berkley

Capellani

1. Ioannes Wilton
2. Brent

Augusti 1°. In altam aulam pro more conventum est circa horam nonam antemeridianam, ubi resignatis clavibus officiariorum, reliquis sociis ad tempus secedere iussis, custos una cum quinque simpliciter senioribus officiarios sequentis anni designavit:
vicecustos, magister Marsh.
magistri French, Hinton, Abbott, decani.
magistri Petty, Fisher, Reynoldes, bursarii.
bursarius Williott, magister Heath; praelectores, Graecae linguae, magister Earles, grammaticae, magister Holiwell; principalis portionistarum, magister Sellar; exhibitionarius Hamsterley, magister Marsh; capellanus capellae, magister Earles; custodes cistae Reade, tres decani; custodes cistae Bodley, magistri Sellar, Heath, Holiwell.

Progressus

Eodem die decreverunt progressum instituendum, et itineri bursarius designatur magister Farrar.

[Augusti] 3°. Computavit Heinsly, firmarius de Beilby, et discessit in aere collegii 78 li. 14s.

[1] 'Philip' deleted.

Hessey

Remissae sunt Hessey expensae seu damna ex sententia iuris ingruentia, conditione data solvendi totos annuos redditus, et magistro Heinsly xxiid. ad resarciendum ei damnum literarum ante festum Omnium Sanctorum.

Dispensationes

[Augusti] 4°. Dispensatum est cum magistro Abbott pro praelectionibus publicis anno secundo in scholis habendis.

Eodem tempore concessa est dispensatio magistro [*sic*] Earles, Reynolds, Abbot, ut in annum sequentem eorum variationes differri liceat.

Clausura in Holywell

[Augusti] 18°. Concensum est ius aedificandi domum super terras vaistas in Holywell, et includendi partem earum magistro Roberto Moore, bedello inferiori in theologia.

2° aedificia exagenda

Similiter et Partridge lapidario concessum est consimile, pretium cuique impositum 5s. per annum. Et pro termino quadraginta annorum facta est indentura.

Sylvae exscindendae in comitatu Essex

Eodem tempore concessum domino custodi et bursario itinerario ius excidendi sylvas in occupacione tenentium liberaturae nomine satis notorum, et sub hasta pretium questussissimum faciendi.

Littera atturnatus data Heynes

[Augusti] 23°. Concessa est littera atturnatus magistro Heynes de London' ad recuperanda arreragia Whitton pro Hensington.

Potestas data Aulae Albanae commonariis in Templi antica sedendi

Eodem tempore facta est ex consensu potestas (ad petitionem domini principalis) commonariis ex Aula Albana, et inferioribus scholaribus domus introeundi in templi anticam, ibique divinas preces similiter ut portionistis solet audiendi.

[Augusti] 24°. Computavit magister Marsh 3us bursarius et Octobris 23° fecit suum aeque.

Sylvae excisae

Octobris 20. Concessa est tenentibus Essex ius excidendi sylvas inferiores ad pretium 44 li.

Computus Generalis

Decembris 5°. Convenimus in scaccario ubi computus generalis absolutus est.

Domus Londini conducta

Consenserunt socii de domo conducenda in vico Warwecensi apud Londinum, necessariis collegii usibus deputanda, quoties dominum custodem, aut sociorum aliquot res eorum privatae publicaeve et ad collegium pertinentes eo traherent; in cuius consilii gratiam cautum est, unam alteramve cameram ad socios hospitio recipiendos (si commode fieri potuit) seponendam.

Eodem tempore decretum est ut ad praedictam domum instruendam coemeretur subsequens supellex.
1 Bedstead with ye appurtenance.
2 Featherbeds of ye better sort with ye appurtenances.
1 Featherbed for ye servants.
4 payre of blankets and coverlids for servants beds.
6 Backe stooles of Turky-worke and 12 stooles of Turky worke.
Arras Hanginges for 2 little Roomes and 1 Greate.
Stripd Hanginges for 2 chambers.
Pewter and Brasse etc. for ye Kitchin.
Andirons etc. for ye Chimneyes.
Tables and carpets.

[Decembris] 18°. Eodem tempore consenserunt ut bursarius magister Fisher una cum vicecustode in proximo termino Londinum mitteretur ad haec coemenda, ibique expectarent diem iudicii in lite Maldonensi.

[1627]

Commemoratio

Ianuario 3° habita fuit commemoratio et scrutinium celebratum fuit.

Missus magistri Erles Essex'

Consenserunt socii mittendum magistrum Erles una cum vicecustode ad Canes, Essexiae ut illic venderent ly stadles superstites in excisionem inferiorum sylvarum.

5 socii admissi

Ianuarii16°. Admissi sunt in societatem huius domus perpetuam, dominus Hugo Cressy, dominus Ioannes Woodcocke, dominus

Edwardus Nevile, dominus Ranulphus Domvill, dominus Guilielmus Berkely.

[Ianuarii] 20°. Consenserunt socii in magna aula magistrum Reynolds mittendum esse Londinum una cum bursario in loco vicecustodis quia iter illud commode inire non potuit.

Martii 28°. Consenserunt socii in magna aula eosdem magistros Fisher et Reynolds Londinum mittendos ut attenderent liti Maldonensi.

Commemoratio
[April ?] 17°. Habita fuit commemoratio fundatoris, statuta perlecta, scrutinium initum et prorogatum.

Facta fuit magistro Fisher 2do bursario licentia differendi computum ultra solitum tempus, si in negotiis collegii Londini ita forte detineretur.

Maii 3°. Computavit magister Fisher secundus bursarius.

Responsum collegii honoratissimo cancellario circa statum 60 librarum incremento [in l]ite Maldon
Maii 15°. Consenserunt socii in apodyterio post preces, ut magister Reynolds et magister Doughty mitterentur Londinum ad renunciandum honoratissimo cancellario responsum collegii placere nobis propositum ab eo incrementum sexaginta librarum per annum una cum donacione vicariae de Maldon modo nulla ex parte collegii superaddatum prioris indenturae confirmacio.

Iunii

p. 296 *Magister Holywell variabit, dispensaciones*
His tribus quaestionibus:

An { Opera naturae sunt artis et ingenii sint maiori ex parte prava quam bona. Negat contra Aristotelem, Problemata 44°, sectio 10^{a}.
Homines sint nature contumelosi. Negat, contra Aristotelem, Problemata 16, sectio 29.
Acerbi et difficiles sint aptissimi ad imparandum. Negat contra Aristotelem, Ethica 4.11°. }

Dispensatum est cum magistro Holywell pro secundis variationibus.

Dispensatio cum magistro Fisher
Similiter cum magistro Fisher valetudinis causa dispensatum est pro primis variationibus et daretur ei copia differendi eas in proximum terminum scilicet Michaelis.

Aeque magistri Fisher
Fecit magister Fisher suum aeque.

Commemoratio
Iulii 21. Habita fuit commemoratio et divina fecimus pro fundatore. Celebratum fuit scrutinium et in magna aula concessimus magistro Roberto Moore inferiori bedello in theologia additamentum 6 pedum terrae vacivae in Holywell, priori nostrae concessioni quinquaginta pedum.

Computavit dominus custos et discessit in arreragiis 18 li. 14s.

Rectoriae de Emildon et Ponteland decretae suis nobis dominis locandae
Iulii 31°. Convenerunt in hospitio custodis omnes socii, ubi consenserunt in exclusionem magistri Hickson, firmarii sui borealis, e rectoriis Emildon et Ponteland, et decreverunt unam de medietate earum indenturam signandam ad disposicionem domini custodis, cum in triennium suae expiracionis vergeret, quo per leges Angliae collegiis signare licet, alteram videlicet signandam magistro Ogle armigero e comtitatu Northumbriae solvendas, videlicet in usum sociorum in sigillatura primae indenturae 200 librae in sigillatura 2^{ae} 400 librae. Postea videlicet in usum collegii, quia igitur ultra possit aestimatis rite pretiis incrementi apponi.

Portionistis facta copia aulam ingrediendi in caenae principio
Portionistis concessum est intrare in aulam ad communias recipiendas simul cum sociis.

Indentura huius anni [i.e. in the college year August 1626–7][1]
Augusti 1° [1626 ?]. Indenturae huius anni magistro Hooper locata[e] sunt domus in Holywell et horreum ad solutionem, 20 librae pro fine. Et Augusti 24° signata est illius indentura et Ianuarii 20 [1627 ?] facta illi copia alienandi.

Augusti 3°. Magistro Leigh sylvae Farleigh locantur pro fine 40 librarum ita ut indentura illius inchoaret A° 1625. Signata est illius indenturae Augusti 18.

[Augusti 3°]. Magistro Napper facta est copia vitas commutandi, ut filios ei liceat pro fratribus interponere pro qua commutatione decretum est solveret per indenturam 4 li. xiiis. 4d. incrementum in usum atque uberius stipendium curatoris ecclesiae de Holywell.

[1] That these notes of leases are retrospective is shown by reference in Napper's lease below to a first payment in November 1626.

Impositus ei insuper fuit finis 500 librarum solvendus tribus distinctis solutionibus scilicet in festo Omnium Sanctorum A° 1626 250 librae, A° 1627 100 librae et anno 1628 150 librae.

[Augusti 3°]. Magistro Woodes locantur Aula Portionistarum, et hospitium ly Flower de Lyce ad pretium 40 librarum pro fine quarum 20 librae solvendae in festo Michaelis et reliquae 20 librae in festo anni sequentis. Data est simul licentia alienandi.

[Augusti 3°]. *Beilbye indenturae pro spatio 21 annorum.* Iohanni Lieng locata est medietas una, capitalis firmae, ab eo occupatae. Richard[o] Leing locata est altera medietas et messuagium ab eo iam occupatae simul cum uno ly oxegange, cui additum fuit annui reditus incrementum 40s. per annum. Finis his impositus 20 librarum quarum 15 librae solutae sunt in praesenti, pro residuo 5 librae nomina dedere usque ad festum Annunciacionis. Mathew Kilburn locata sunt duo ly oxenganges terrae, pro fine solutae sunt 5 librarum quae ex consensu datae sunt Rogero Moore coquo seniori in praemium honorarium. Iohanni Iackson cottagium elocatum, non ita pridem in occupacione viduae Cade, unum Hempegarth simul cum libertate communii referta insuper annuo reditu 20s. 6d. Edmundo Cooke et Richardo Arthur elocatus est ager dictus Redcarre, olim in occupacione Gualteri Butler, ad solutionem annui reditus vii li. xiis. iiiid.

Augusti 13°. *Hampton Poyle.* Iohn Iohnson concessum est ius suum quae habet in Hampton Poyle in filium transferre.

[Augusti 13° ?]. *Magister Higges. Dodington.* Rectoria de Dodington locata est magistro Higges ad duracionem trium vitarum. Imposita est illi in finem summa 40 librarum quarum 20 libras solvendas decrevimus in festo Omnium Sanctorum A° 1626, residuas videlicet 20 libras in festo Omnium Sanctorum A° 1627. Signata est indentura Februarii 8° [1627 ?].

Augusti 18°.[1] Isaac Weekes candelario de Sancto Clemente concessa est indentura per spatium 40 annorum pro tenemento in Holywell, olim in occupacione Iohannis Davis coqui. Teneamus pro fine illi solvendos censuimus 20 solidos quam summam in premium honorarium concessimus Thomae Chittenden olim promo.

[Augusti 18° ?]. Elocata est domus in Holywell Iohanni Chandler ad pretium 5 librarum pro fine et in terminum 40 annorum.

[1] This marginal date appears to straddle this and the next entry.

Augusti 24°. Signata est indentura Isaac Weekes.

Octobris 30. Signata est indentura magistri Woodes.

Novembris 10. Concessa alienandi copia Isaac Weekes et Novembris 10 signata ei tabula. Signatae sunt indenturae domini Iohannis Botelyer pro Westilbury.

Ianuarii 20 [1627 ?]. Signatae iterum indenturae magistri Napper pro Holywell et Wolvercott: quo tempore decretum est ut incrementum illud 4^{r} librarum 13s. et 4d. in infirmario de novo impositum in usum ecclesiae per manus vicarii solveretur curatori de Holywell.

Martii 29. Signavimus collegio Magdalensi indenturam qua elocatum nobis agnoscimus hortum e regione Aulae Albanae.

Elocavimus[1] Roberto Moore inferiori bedello in theologia tenementum ab ipso nove extructum in Holywell.

Aprilis 12°. Kibworth. Henrico Brian de Kibworth concessum est ius alienandi et transferendi copiam suam Roberto Standyn eiusdem loci, similiter et Roberto Standyn concessum est ius transferendi copiam suam de dimidia terrae virga in proxima curia Henrico Brian. Roberto Standyn per indenturam elocata est copia Henrici Brian pro spatio 21 annorum. Finis ei impositum fuit 20 librarum quarum 10 libras decrevimus solvendas in festo Pentecostes anno 1627, et residuas 10 libras in festo Sancti Iohannis Baptistae anno 1628. Data est item illi libertas alienandi duas virgas terrae Henrico Brian per spatium 5ginta annorum. Concessa est Gulielmo Good alienandi ius et Mariae uxori eius scilicet ut transferre possint unam virgam terrae de copia sua in Henricum Brian et dimidiam virgam terrae in Nicholao Oswine proxima accedente curia.

Fines insoluti hoc anno.
Magister Napper, 250 librae; magister Woodes, 20 librae; Iohannes Leing, 5 librae; magister Higges, 20 librae; Robertus Standyn, 10 librae.

[1] It is uncertain which marginal date (29 March or 12 April) relates to this entry.

p. 297 Anno Domini 1627, regis Caroli 3°, custodis Brent 7°.

Magistri

1. Georgius Petty
2. Petrus Turner
3. Guilelmus Sellar
4. Humfredus Farrar
5. Iacobus Marsh
6. Thomas Gall
7. Iohannes French
8. Iohannes Doughty
9. Alexander Fisher
10. Thomas Heath
11. Lawrentius Hinton
12. Ioannes Holywell
13. Edwardus Reynolds
14. Ioannes Earles
15. Georgius Abbott
16. Greaves
17. Corbett
18. Gibbes

Domini

1. Browne
2. Cressey
3. Woodcocke
4. Nevile
5. Domvile
6. Berkely

Capellani

1. Ioannes Wilton
2. Brent

Augusti 2°. In altam aulam pro more conventum est circa horam nonam antemeridianam ubi resignatis clavibus officiariorum reliquis sociis ad tempus secedere iussis, custos una cum quinque simpliciter senioribus officiariis anni sequentis sic designavit: vicecustos, magister Marsh.
magistri Farrar, Doughty, Earles, decani.
magistri French, Holywell, Abbott, bursarii.
bursarius Williott, capellanus capellae, magister Petty; praelectores Graecae linguae, magister Fisher, grammaticae, magister Hinton; principalis portionistarum, magister Heath; custodes cistae Reade, tres decani; exhibitionarius Hamsterley, magister Marsh; custodes cistae Bodley, magistri Sellar, Gall, Hinton.

Novus exhibitionarius Bickley

Augusti 16°. Consenserunt socii de locandis 100 li. ad novum stipendium conficiendum pro novo exhibitionario Bickley iuxta testamentum eius de duobus exhibitionariis. Deinde

Augusti 27° electus est magister Fisher et constitutus novus hic exhibitionarius.

De modo stipendii eius

Elocatae sunt centum illae librae Aldermanno Wright qui una cum filio eius per obligationem nomen dedit custodi et magistro Fisher de solvendis annuatim sex libras supra sortem in usum praedicti exhibitionarii.

Magister Reynolds annus gratuitus

Magistro Reynolds concessum est annus gratuitus licet nuptias iniret infra annum, et sors insuper illi permissa una cum sociis in finibus de rectoriis de Emildon et Ponteland.

Baccalaureis iniunctum est, ut portionistarum batella examinarent cum computarent remanentias.

Dispensantur variationes

Dispensatum est cum magistro Abbott et magistro Earles de differendis eorum variationibus in annum sequentem.

De instruendo novo aedificio in hospitio

Septembris 3°. Consenserunt socii ut peristromata magnae camerae purgata et refecta transferentur in magnam cameram prope porticum, interim magna camera ornaretur ly wainscott et[1] opere caelato in superiori parte camerae totum insuper illius veteris ly wainscott transferendum censuerunt in cameram Sever, unde peristromata decreverunt auferenda, ad instruendam novam secundae scalae cameram.

Litterae attornatus

Item decretum literas attornatus signandas bursariis collegii.

Passeri salarium augetur

Octobris 6°. Incrementum datum est magistro Passer Arabico professori scilicet ut antiquo salario de 40s. concesso anno 1625 adderentur 20s. de collegii bonis solvendi.

Leges novi exhibitionarii Bickley

Ordinatum est ut iunior exhibitionarius Bickely haberet 2as conciones annuas in variis Eucharistiis intra collegium et unam publicam in vice collegii intra Academiam. Eucharistiae annuae habendae in festo Pentecostes et festo dedicacionis ecclesiae.

Lapicidarum 20 librae

Concessum est ut latomis solverentur 20 librae de summa 33 librarum 1s. quam postulant ultra recepta sua donec severius fieri poterit examen et mensurarum computacio.

[1] 'frett work' deleted.

Magistro Earles absenti concessa liberatura

[Octobris ?] 27°. Concessa magistro Earles ut licet negotiis eum ab academia avocantibus intra collegium per maiorem partem anni residentiam praestare non posset, una tamen cum caeteris sociis sortiretur partem in liberatura omnibusque emolumentis domus inde consequentibus. Idem indulgerunt magistro Marsh Martii 16°.

Vicecustos: Londinum missus

Consensere in missionem vicecustodis ad Londinium ut conclusioni litis Maldonensis attenderet.

Decembris 18. Computus totius anni generalis factus est.

Computus Abbott

Decembris 22°. Computavit magister Hinton loco Abbott, 1^{mi} bursarii.

Scrutinium

Decembris 22°. Divina fecimus pro fundatore et celebratum est scrutinium

Decembris 31°. In vigilio Circumcisionis habitum est de novo scrutinium, ubi famuli claves suas resignarunt in manus domini vicecustodis, et magister Hinton hortulanus nominatus est.

[1628]

Februarii 22°. Magister Hinton loco Abbott 1^{mi} bursarii solvit pedem computus et discessit aeque.

Martii 18° 1628. Consensum est de sigillanda indentura qua Sebastianus Goode iuxta decretum Cancellariae totum ius suum quod in Maldona sibi super futurum est post annum 1707 28° Novembris in manus collegii resignat.

Aprilis 7°. Divina fecimus pro fundatore et celebratum est scrutinium atque in vicesimum diem Martii prorogatum.

Aprilis 17°. Computavit magister Holywell 2^{dus} bursarius.

Baccalaureus ius incipiendi

Seniores baccalaurei facta prius licentia a domino custode ambiendi hanc gratiam consensu sociorum quotquot domi aderant, veniam impetrarunt incipiendi in proximis comitiis, die interim admissionis in coetum magistrorum ad voluntatem domini custodis delato.

Maii 26°. Sociis in altam aulam coeuntibus, lectae sunt literae domini custodis, quibus consensum suum de 4^r^ senioribus baccalaureis in numerum magistrorum admittendis significavit, magistris itidem assentientibus. Dominus Greaves, dominus Corbett, dominus Gibbes, dominus Browne statim admissi sunt in numerum magistrorum.

Iulii 26. Divina fecimus pro fundatore, lecta sunt postero die pro more (ut forte sit) statuta, scrutinium celebratum, et in vicesimo die Augusti prorogatum.

Iulii 10°. Variavit magister Fisher in his quaestionibus:

An {
Inimicos ulcisci, nec reconciliari velle, non est iustitiae aut fortitudinis specimen, contra Aristotelem 1mo Rhetoric', cap. 9, text' 27.
Epitheta, hyperbolica et peregrina non conveniunt pathetice dicenti, contra Aristotelem 3° Rhetoric', c.7 textu 11mo.
Barbari non sunt magis servi quam Graeci, contra Aristotelem 3° Politic', c.10mo.
}

His finitis eam eo dispensatum est pro secundis variationibus.

Indenturae hoc anno concessae, et signatae [*i.e. in the college year August 1627–8*] p. 298

Augusti 2° [1627]. *Stonehouse.* Concessa est domino doctori Hawley pars illa domus nostrae dictae Stonehouse in Knightriders Streete, London, quod nunc occupatur a domino Thoma Ridley militi, pro spatio 40 annorum post mortem eiusdem domini Thomas Ridley quandocunque accederet. Finis illi impositus summa 40 librarum ita ut prima pars scilicet 20 librae solverentur in festo Michaelis proxime succedente, altera pars in obitu domini Thomae Ridley cum tandem domum occuparet.

[Augusti 2°]. *Wiblin.* Elocatum est Guilelmo Wiblin tenementum in Holywell. Finis ei impositus 6 li. 13s. 4d.

[Augusti 2°]. *Couch.* Elocatum est Iohanni Couch, coquo collegii Wadham tenementum in Holywell ut solveret pro fine 20 solidos.

Augusti 4°. *Beilbye.* Thomae Weekes concessa est indentura pro 4^r^ oxeganges in Beilby ad pretium 3 li. 11s. 8d. pro annuo reditu, et pro fine 15 librarum. Ed' Leing concessa est firma sua ibidem ad pretium 10 librarum pro annuo reditu et pro fine 5 librarum. Eidem concessa est etiam indentura pro molendino. Iohanni Ashton concessa sunt 2 oxeganges ad pretium 2 li. 13s. 6d. pro annuo reditu, et pro fine 8 librarum. Roberto Brathwayte concessa sunt 3 oxeganges ad pretium 3 librarum 5s. pro annuo reditu, et pro fine 15 librarum. Iohanni Haslewood elocatus est ager dictus Wye close in possessione magistri Heinsly una cum domo et garth ad pretium 10 librarum 2s. pro annuo reditu et pro fine 30 solidi. Mathaeo Stevenson elocata sunt 2 oxeganges ad pretium 4 librarum pro fine. Hugh' Heinsley elocata est firma principalis.

Augusti 6to signatae sunt hae indenturae.

[Augusti 6to ?]. Signata est alienatio magistro Lee ut transferret ius suum in Farleigh Woodes in magistrum Bedell firmarium de Farleigh. [Signata est alienatio] magistro Gardiner de Thornecroft.

Augusti 12°. *Spranger, Stanes.* Elocatae sunt Spranger et Stanes terrae in comitatu Essex dictae Canes et Norton Mandevile, ita ut solverent in termino Michaelis 260 libras pro fine.

Sayer. Eodem tempore elocatae sunt Sayer terrae de Barkby ad pretium 6 li. 13s. 4d. pro fine.

Ocobris 6to. Signatae sunt indenturae concessae Spranger et Stanes,

Decembris 10°. Sigillata est indentura inter collegium et Iohannem Whistler armigerum qua certas terras ac possessiones suas obligat pro solutione 10 librarum annuatim durante spatio 17° annorum ad solvendam exhibitionem dominae Margaretae Saviliae.

Februarii 16° [1628 ?]. Elocata est per indenturam domus Radcliffe in parochia Sancti Martini domino aldermanno Wright.

March [*sic*] 16. Ex consensu sociorum in apodyterio residuum annorum in tenemento nostro in Salisbury Ally ante undecim annos Ed'o Thorald elocatum, transferetur in Robertum Ramsey cui item alienandi licentiam indulserunt. Et Martii 18° sigillatae sunt indenturae.

18°. Sigillata est alienandi licentia Iacobo Partridge.

Aprilis 25°. Signata est indentura domino doctori Hawley pro parte domus dictae Stonehouse in Knight Riders Streete.

p. 299 Anno 1628, regis Caroli 4°, custodis Brent 8°.

Magistri in artibus

1. Georgius Petty
2. Petrus Turner
3. Guilelmus Sellar
4. Humfredus Farrar
5. Iacobus Marsh
6. Thomas Gall
7. Ioannes French
8. Ioannes Doughty

9. Alexander Fisher
10. Thomas Heath
11. Laurentius Hinton
12. Ioannes Hollywell
13. Ioannes Earles
14. Georgius Abbott
15. Iacobus Greaves
16. Eduardus Corbett
17. Carolus Gibbes
18. Richardus Browne

Baccalaurei in artibus

1. Hugo Cressey
2. Ioannes Woodcocke
3. Eduardus Nevile
4. Ranulphus Domvile
5. Guilelmus Berkeley

Capellani

1. Ioannes Brent
2. Ioannes Reynoldes

Augusti 1. In altam aulam conventum est circa horam nonam antemeridianam ibique resignatis pro more clavibus officiariorum caeteris sociis ad tempus secedere iussis per custodem una cum quinque simpliciter senioribus officiarii in annum sequentem sic designati:
vicecustos, magister Sellar.
magistri Petty, Fisher, Hollywell, decani.
magistri Farrar, Doughty, Earles, bursarii.
bursarius Williott, capellanus capellae, magister Heath;exhibitionarius Hamsterley, magister Marshe; principalis portionistarum, magister Hinton; custodes cistae Reade, tres decani; praelector linguae Graecae, magister Gall; custodes cistae Bodley, magistri Heath, Hinton, Greaves; praelector grammaticae, magister Greaves; praelector logice nominandus a principali.

Magistro Marsh absenti concessa liberatura

Eodem tempore concessa magistro Marsh licentia extra collegium per maiorem anni partem agenti liberatura et omnia emolumenta domus consequentia.

Lectores Linacri

Dominus doctor Lapworth iterum renuntiatus est lector Linacri superior et magister Turner eligitur inferior.

Seabroake

Elocatum est tenementum dictum Halfewiche Seabroake ad pretium 8 li. pro fine.

Holye'

Augusti 27°. Elocata est domus in Holywell Gabrieli Boxeley ad annum reditum 5s.

Consensum est de progressu habendo ad invisendum aliquot maneria, dimittendas copias, reliqua agenda prout opus fuerit, itineri designatur bursarius magister Sellar.

Temple, Basingstoke

Praedium de Basingestoke locatum Temple finis 10 librae cuius per media solvenda ad festum Omnium Sanctorum proxime sequens, reliqua ad festum Annuntiationis sequens.

Turley, Holywell

Tenementum in Holywell locatum est Turley, finis 40s.

Augusti 4°. Consenserunt dominus custos et socii domi existentes in scaccario ibique dominus custos computum habuit de receptis et allocatis suis et discessit aeque.

Computus Heinsley

Computavit Heinsley, firmarius de Beilby et balivus ibidem discessum est in aere collegii pro arreragiis propriis 78 li. 14s. et tenentium 50 li. 16s.

Augusti 6°. Sigillata est indentura Richardi Palmer pro tenemento quodam Bielbiano quod ei locatum fuerat anno precedente, finis 3 li. 6s. 8d.

Kibworth, Ray

Augusti 11°. Praedia aliquot de Kibworth Harcutt concessa sunt firmario Ray finis 50 librarum, dimidium solvatur ad festum Omnium Sanctorum immediatum, reliquum differatur usque ad idem festum anni sequentis.

Vasea argentea in vitio commutanda

In conclavi custodis conventum et consensum est de commutandis poculis, salinis, aliisque vasis argenteis difflatatibus contusis, aut ex quovis alio casu usui ineptis vicecustodi curae sit de pondere et numero, magister Turner et magister Farrar proficiscantur Londinum et de figura et pretio provideant.

Rectoria de Lapworth confiditur fratri magistri Elly

Magistro Elly quondam huius collegii socio resignante et omni de iure suo cedente ad rectoriam de Lapworth unanimi suffragio frater eius etate provectior ad eandem ecclesiam in eius locum praesentandus sufficitur.

Dispensatio magistri Browne
Octobris 7°. Dispensatio concessa magistro Browne que seria ab academia avocabant negotia quod lectiones quas haberet huic regentiae donec rebus suis apositis ad collegium rediret prorogarentur.

Destinabantur magistris regentibus libri quos interpretarentur videlicet Aristotelis Physica, Ethica, Politica, Rhetorica in quibus eligendum cunct' quem obtinerent in societate, observarent ordinem.

Ray, Chaundler haberent [sic] licentias alienandi
Copia facta est firmario Ray quod liceret ei aliquot praediorum alienarum scilicet indultum. Chaundler pro altero tenementorum in Holywell. Sigillata etiam indentura Turly.

Acquietatia Good p. 300
Octobris 23. Sigillata est acquietantia magistro Good pro centum libris per curiam Cancellariae collegio adiudicatis pro expensis ex partibus collegii in lite Maldonensi habitis. Sigillatae etiam indenturae Ray, Temple, Seabroke, Boxely.

Octobris 24. Computarunt in scaccario Ray, Mayne, Gregory pro Kibworth, Chedington, Cuxham.

Computus Generalis
Novembris 13[i]. Convenimus in scaccario et habitus fuit computus generalis et computavit etiam Sayre pro Barkeby.

Praedium locatum magistro Wilton
Consensum etiam quod imponerentur pro annuo reditu terrarum magistro Wilton elocatarum octo solidi in hunc modum distribuendi in pecuniis quinque solidi, quatuor denarii, in tritico unus modius, in braseo tres modii.

Alienacio Chandler
Sigillata est licentia alienationis Chandler pro altero tenementorum in Hollywell.

Dispensacio magistri Gibbes
Dispensatum est cum magistro Gibbes qui de diutino et gravi laboraverat morbo et valetudini qui rus profi[ci]sceretur atque interea ab omnibus collegii exercitiis quibus ex more et iuramento obstrictus tenebatur absolutus.

Decembris 17°. Habita est commemoratio fundatoris, lecta statuta, scrutinium celebratum quod prorogatum est in Ium diem Ianuarii et quemlibet diem citra.

Emildon et Ponteland domino Mauricio Abbot

Magister Earles 1us bursarius computum fecit in scaccario, ibidem et eodem die altera medietas Emildon et Ponteland concessa domino Mauricio Abbott, equiti aurato. Finis 600 librae.

Decembris 22. Conventum in hospitio domini custodis et consensum est de lustratione maneriorum collegii ut in diagramata redigerentur cuius rei cura demandata est domino custodi et magistro Turner quoad virum, negotia, idoneum salarium, reliqua.

Tenementum locantur Ewer et Boxeley

Locatum est tenementum viduae Ewer in Abbotts Langeley; finis 20 solidi, et aliud tenementum in Hollywell Augustini Boxeley. Gratis.

Decembris 31°. In vigiliis Circumcisionis celebratum pro more scrutinium ubi famuli resignarunt claves in manus vicecustodis quas iterum perspecta fidelitate receperunt et magister Holywell in hortulanum electus.

[1629]

Ianuarii 22. Agitatum et consensum est de ponendo horologio in alta aula et quod magister Wilton nullas omnino decimas solveret rectori de Woolford tractus terrarum illi locatarum quamdiu vicarius ibidem permaneret et alienacio concessa firmario Sayre pro tenementis suis in Barkeby.

Februarii 12°. Dispensatum est cum magistro Earles ut aeque suum in duas prorogaret septimanas propter necessariam eius absentiam in collegii negotiis.

Aequi 1^i bursarii

Februarii 26. Aeque suum habuit magister Earles 1us bursarius in alta aula in praesentia sociorum.

Martii 10. Convenerunt in alta aula custos et socii sed magister Farrar sociorum unus non comparuit quem dominus custos diu antea citaverat proprio ore ut responderet quibusdam articulis seu obiectionibus contra eum de loco et specie faciendis. Eo igitur non comparente dominus custos allegavit in hunc, qui sequitur, modum se audivisse fama seu potius infamia deferente hunc magistrum Farrar frequentasse

multis retro hinc annis publica in oppido hospitia, tabernas, vinarias et allarias et baccalaureos collegii socios in eo grave valde corrupisse veraficissimum etiam dum libros suos fere omnes vendidisse et omnis quam habuit eruditionis penitus esse dein oblatum; se igitur cum statuta fundatoris in quias [*sic*] iurati sumus verba caveant ut si quis e sociis recederet a domo aut deferendi studium aut in ipsa domo studere negligeret in suis persona cessaret omnis sua exhibitio. Statuisse expiri an verum hoc esset adhuc eumque monuisse ut compararet in alta aula decimo die martii sequentis ut sibi et sociis de hac re et de aliis satisfaceret. Sed magister Farrar ut dictum est non comparuit, incepit tunc tempus in quodam hospitio publico villae Oxon' vocato Anglice the King' Head, ubi moram traxerat quinque seu sex dies immediate precedentes quo toto spatio nec cameram suam in hoc collegio nec inviserat. Quidam allegarunt eum vi dies aegrotare. Quod cum nullo modo appareret legitime et essent nulla indicia in contraria dominus custos, assedentibus sibi octo de senioribus prout statuta fundatoris postulant, reliquis autem sociis assistentibus pronunciavit eum contumacem, et in poena contumaciae suae huiusmodi privavit eum omni emolumento societatis suo in dicto collegio excepto tantum usu camerae suae et bibliothecae usque ad festum sancti Petri ad vincula. Hoc tantum adhibit' [*damage*] / moderamine ut si interea p. 301
spatio rediret ad collegium et custodi et sociis aliquo modo satisfaceret in obiectis in integrum primo quoque tempore restitueretur.

Eodem tempore custos et quinque seniores eligerunt loco magistri Farrar magistrum French tertium bursarium, ea lege [?] ut si dictus magister Farrar satisfaceret custodi et sociis in iis quae fuerant obiecta contra ipsum, magister French ei restitueret omne emolumentum dicti officii.

Martii 24. Conventum est in hospitio domini custodis et conclusa de electione habenda de evidentiis et instrumentis collegium visendis et transcribendis, inde iam quod vicecustos proficisceretur Cicestriam circa decimas quasdam legatas collegio a magistro Masters aliquantis huic retro annis ibidem socio.

Martii 29. Habita sunt sacra fundatoris.

Electio habita

[Martii] 30. Lecta sunt statuta in alta aula hora octava atque inde examine per aliquot dies antea facto de eruditione competitorum. Dominus custos in conclavi suo cum venire fecit tresdecim simpliciter seniores alii primi, statuto regni 20 Elizabethae edito ad presens institutum spectante lecto, processum est ad electionem in qua 10 baccalaurei et unus scholaris electi, dominus Nevile ex diocesi Sarisburiensi, dominus Hinton, Londinensi, dominus Chennell, Oxoniensi, dominus Wheare, Oxoniensi, dominus Brent, Londinensi, dominus Iacob, Londinensi, dominus Newman, Lincolniensi, dominus Burton, Lincolniensi, dominus Maplisden, Cantuariensi, dominus Hewson, Oxoniensi et scholaris Wright, Lincolniensi, ex quibus electis quinque admittendi initio termini Michaelis immediati, dominus Nevile, dominus Hinton, dominus Chennell, dominus Wheare, dominus Iacob, reliqui sex eodem tempore et terminum anni sequentis dominus Iacob remissum totum quicquid ex more debetur in usum bibliothecae, dominus Newman solvat 20s. et scholaris Wright, filius, 20s., ceteri sigillatim 3 li. 6s. 8d.

Aprilis 8°. Conventum et placitum domino custodi et sociis quod in merendis et biberiis prorsus abstineretur quibusdam de Iunio ad festum Sancti Petri ad Vincula proxime sequentem exceptis solum[m]odo solemnibus merendis post psalmum in aula decantatum et baccalaureorum biberiis in diebus ieiuniorum. Similiter consensum, priore decreto ex parte mutui admittendo prefixo quod dominus Brent una cum primum designatis admitteretur.

Aprilis 11°. Actum est inclusum in apodyterio de perquirendis terris apud Hensington.

Locatum est tenementum in parochia Sancti Martini Aldermanno Wright pro termino 40 annorum resignatis prius annis 28. Finis 13 li. 6s. 8d.

Magister Doughty computavit.

Aprilis 15°. Magister Doughty 2^{dus} bursarius suum habuit computum in scaccario.

Maii 10. Locata fuit tenementum Meade de terris nuper perquisitis apud Hensington ad annum reditum 10 librarum.

Magistri Abbott variationes

Maii 22. Magister Abbott variavit in his quaestionibus:
An { Sit d' reipublicae semestres tantum constitui magistratui. Negat.
Medii cives sint optimi legislatores. Negat.
Vitium sit honores omnino contemnere. Negat. }

Et cum eo dispensatum est pro 2^{dis} variationibus.

Iunii 10. Magister Doughty 2dus bursarius discessit aeque.

Iunii 13°. Sigillatae indenturae Aldermanii Wright et Ewer'.

Iunii 15°. Baccalaurei copia ambiendi prius facta consensu domini custodis per literas significato a sociis impetrarunt ut in proximis comitiis inciperent die tamen quo in ordine magistrorum admitterentur in finem termini delato.

Magister Earles variavit.

Iulii 9. Magister Earles variavit in his quaestionibus:

An { In forma reipublicae exprimenda ponendum sit aliquid imposter [?]. Affirmat,
Molestior' sit animo suus labor quam corpori. Affirmat.
Vanitas et arrogantia cum summo merito consistant. Affirmat. }

Et dispensatum est pro secundis suis variationibus.

Baccalaurei admissi in ordinem magistrorum

Eodem tempore iuxta primam indultam gratiam admissi sunt in coetum magistrorum hi quinque baccalaurei, dominus Cressey, dominus Woodcocke, dominus Nevile, dominus Domvile, dominus Berkeley.

Iulii 20. In festo Sanctae Margaretae habita est commemoratio fundatoris quo die lecta statuta, celebratum scrutinium et prorogatum in 16 diem Augusti.

Anno 1629, regis Caroli 5to, custodis Brent 9°. p. 302

Magistri in artibus

1. Georgius Petty
2. Petrus Turner
3. Guilielmus Sellar
4. Humphredus Farrar
5. Iacobus Marsh
6. Thomas Gall
7. Ioannes French
8. Ioannes Doughty
9. Alexander Fisher
10. Thomas Heath
11. Laurentius Hinton
12. Ioannes Holywell
13. Ioannes Earles
14. Georgius Abbott
15. Ioannes Greaves
16. Edwardus Corbett
17. Carolus Gibbes
18. Richardus Browne
19. Hugho Cressey
20. Ioannes Woodcocke
21. Edwardus Nevile
22. Ranulphus Donvile
23. Guilelmus Berkely

Capellani

1. Ioannes Brent
2. Ioannes Reynolds

Electio officiariorum

In altam aulam pro more conventum est circa horam nonam antemeridianam, ibique resignatis clavibus officiariorum, caeteris sociis ad tempus secedere iussis, per custodem una cum 5^{que} simpliciter senioribus officiarii[s] in annum sequentem sic designati:
vicecustos, magister Marsh.
magistri Sellar, Greaves, Cressey, decani.
magistri Gall, Fisher, Corbett, bursarii.
principalis portionistarum, magister Doughtye; praelector Graecae linguae, magister Earles; praelector grammaticae, magister Gibbes; bursarius Williott et capellanus capellae, magister Petty; exhibitionarius Hamsterley, magister Marsh; custodes cistae Reade, tres decani; custodes cistae Bodley, magistri Doughty, Earles, Donvile.

Magister Hinton liberaturae iuris

Concessum est magistro Hinton ius ad liberaturam licet per maiorem partem anni interesse collegio non posset. Eodem tempore questione orta de concessa priori annos liberaturam magistro Browne absenti, decretum est universo assensu (nisi quod solus magister Holywell renegaret) solvendum ei caeteris liberaturam. Decretum est de mittendis magistro Sellar et magistro French ad Cicester, ut nomine collegii elocarent decimas ex testamento magistri Masters quondam socii, collegio legatas,

Medici e Silesia

Medicis quibusdam e Silesia ad paupertatem reductis, dati ex consensu 15 solidi.

Magister Browne pergrinans

Consensum est ut magister Browne agens in transmarinis partibus cum legato ad ducem Sabaudiae, ex allocacione collegii frueretur 15 libris annuatim per spatium 3^{ium} annorum.

Computus custodis

[Augusti] 4to. Computavit dominus custos et discessit aeque.

Magister Farrar expulsus

[Augusti] 6°. Convenimus in scaccario, ubi dominus custos, quod magister Farrar iuxta tempus 1° Augusti prescriptum non comparuisset intra 5que dies et se examini submisisset, vacuum eius locum pronuntiavit.

Cricklade

[Augusti] 17°. Missi sunt magister Sellar et magister Corbett ad Cricklade, ut interponerent nomine collegii apud officiarios regios de includendis terris vacivis et communibus.

Legati regis Galliae ordinum Belgiae

[Augusti] 24°. Legati ordinum Belgiae, et Regis Galliae, una cum multis e primoribus Angliae, nobilibus et consiliariis, ex sumptibus collegii luculentissimo convivio excepti sunt. Orationem habuit de gratulando eorum adventu magister Nevil.

Rex et Regina

[Augusti] 27°. Rex et regina redeuntes a Woodstockio ad Abindon, invisere collegium, et per spatium horae se reponentes in porticu custodis bellariis et postmeridianis dapibus, ex sumptu collegii laute excepti sunt. Orationem de adventu gratulatoriam habuit magister Marsh.

Computus Beilby

[Augusti] 28. Computavit in scaccario Marmaducus Prickett, vice Heinsly, firmarii de Beilby, et discessit in arreragiis.

Computus magistri French

[Augusti] 31. Computavit magister French 3us prioris anni bursarius in scaccario, ubi consensum est de allocandis priorum conviviorum sumptibus ex thesauro collegii.

Viarum politio

[Septembris, Octobris ?] 11°. Convenimus in magna aula, ubi consensere socii de reparanda via, et septis reficiendis ante collegium. Profectura illius rei delata est magistro Turner, French, Corbett quibus creditum est ne quid collegium damnum admitteret.

Litterae attornatus

Eodem tempore decretum est ut litterae atturnatus signarentur bursariis collegii de reciperandis quibusque arreragiis collegio debitis. Similiter permissum est curiam apud Kibworth habendam in gratiam Henrici Brian ut liceret ei copiam transferre in alium (ad revertim se redigere) modo ad sumptus collegii non fieret.

Admissio 5^{que} electorum in annum probacionis

Octobris 13. Convenerunt in magnam aulam socii et consensu eorum impetrato, admissi sunt in annum probacionis dominus Richardus

Nevile, dominus Edwardus Hinton, dominus Franciscus Cheynell, dominus Gulielmus Wheare, dominus Henricus Iacob.

Dispensatur cum magistria regentibus pro lecturis
[Octobris] 25. Convenimus in alta aula, ubi ex consensu data est magistris regentibus copia legendi intra domum bis in hebdomade ad horam octavam antemeridianam, vel ad postmeridianam, quatenus per mutationem scholarum lectiones publice haberi non poterant. Divisae 5^{que} magistris facultates artium, ita unus in libros de Anima, vel Parva Moralia perlegeret in Philosophia Naturali, alius in libros Ethices, 3us in libros Rhetorices, 4us in Aristotelis Politic', 5us in Metaphysicen vel Mathematica.

Computus generalis
Novembris 18. Convenimus in alta aula, ubi computus generalis totius anni absolutus est.

Computavit item magister Ray, firmarius de Kibworth, magister Gregory, firmarius de Cuxham, magister Wilmott, firmarius de Ibston.

Decembris 17°. Computavit in scaccario magister Corbett 2us bursarius.

Scrutinium servorum
[Decembris] 21°. Celebratum pro more in alta aula scrutinium, ubi famuli resignarunt claves suas in manus vicecustodis et admoniti de officio male gesto, in spe futurae emendationis, restituti sunt quilibet in suum locum.

Magister Earles hortulanus
Magister Earles eodem tempore creatus sequentis anni hortulanus.

[1630]

Dominus Brent
Ianuarii 14. Dominus Brent absentiae condicione incapax admissionis, in qua admissionem quinque baccalaureorum, veniam culpae deprecatus obtinuit et in annum probacionis admissus est.

Porta aedificanda in templo Beati Petri in Oriente
[Ianuarii] 31.[1] Convenimus post preces in Crypti [*damage*] porticu, ubi communi consensu facta est academiae copia portam aperiendi et extruendi in cancellaria Sancti Petri in Oriente, ad meliorem introitum

[1] '29' deleted.

doctorum in tempore quadragesimae, ad conciones quadragesimales audiendas.

[Ianuarii] 24°. Eodem loco agitatum de muro in horto custodis reparando, qui iniuria temporum et coeli deciderat resque delata est ad vicecustodem et 2^{dum} bursarium.

Magister Berkley peregrinatur

Februarii 7. Eodem loco ex consensu permissum est magistro Berkeley, ut in transmarinis partibus agenti solvere ei 15 libras iuxta concessionem superiorem factam magistro Browne, additumque insuper ut totius biennii summam [*damage*] librarum reciperet in antecessum.

1us bursarius aeque p. 303

Convenimus in alta aula, ubi magister Corbet 1us bursarius solutis arreragiis prioris computi discessit aeque.

[Februarii] 21°. Convenimus in apodyterio post preces ubi per literas domini custodis certiores facti de opere magistri Allen collocato apud Thornecroft in manerio illo demetiendo, atque in tabulas descriptorias digerendo, concessimus duplicatum stipendium ut scilicet l^{ae} solucioni de 6 li. 12s. adderentur et aliae 6 li. 12s.

Rectoria Gamlingay

Martii 14. Convenerunt post preces in apodyterio vicecustos, magister Turner, magister Gall, magister Doughtye, magister Heath, magister Abbott, magister Earles, magister Greaves, magister Corbett, magister Cressey, magister Domvile ubi significatione facta per literas domini custodis, quod rectoria de Gamlingay per voluntariam resignationem domini doctoris Higges erat tum vacua ac destituta rectoris sedes unanimi omnium consensu, praedicta rectoria collata est in magistrum Marsh vicecustodem, et communi edicta ius ei presentacionis ad eandem concessum est.

Commemoratio

[Martii 20]. Divina fecimus pro fundatore, convenientes deinde in alta aula, postquam perlecta sunt statuta, celebravimus scrutinium ubi cum circa singulorum mores et conversacionem omnia in tuto esse repertum, prorogatum est scrutinium in primum diem Maii.

Aprilis 15. Computavit magister Fisher 2^{dus} bursarius.

Vicaria Dodington

Maii 2do. Convenimus in apodyterio post preces ubi ex consensu omnium vicaria de Dodington, tum voluntaria concessione domini doctoris Higgs vacua, collata est in magistro Doughtye, iusque ei presentacionis concessum.

[Maii] 19°. Convenimus in hospitio custodis ubi consensimus de numero scholarium servientium reducendo ad duodecem. Item de nova mensa fabricanda pro magistris in alta aula. Item de partienda domo carbonaria ut totius anni allocacio 26 plaustrorum carbonum in antecessum semper reponeretur. Item ut stipendium 40s. per annum allocaretur subpromo curanti horologium, donec mutacio forte ianitoris fieret, cuius erat eiusmodi officium curare, et pro aetate ad illud solvendum minus latebat.

Iunii 9°. Variavit magister Gibbes in has 3[s] theses:

An { Non possunt indocti esse scientibus πρακτικωτεροι contra Aristotelem 6 Ethic', I.7.
Eruditi facilius populo persaudent quam ineruditi, contra Aristotelem 2 Rhetoric', 23.
Populi facilior est corruptio, quam monarchae, contra Aristotelem 3 Politic', 11.

Eodem tempore post finitas disputationes dispensatum est cum eo pro 2[dis] variationibus.

Iulii 9° variavit magister Corbett, defendens has theses contra Aristotelem:

An { Praemia digne constituuntur notum et utile reipublicae invenientibus contra Aristotelem 2, Politic', 6.
Mundus, ut aliae res suam habet senectutem, contra Aristotelem I, de Caelo, 12.
πολυφιλια non est impedimentum faelicitatis contra Aristotelem 9 Ethic', 10.

Eodem tempore dispensatum est cum eo pro secundis variationibus.

[Iulii] 20°. Divina fecimus pro fundatore, et pro more praelecta statuta, et deinde scrutinium celebravimus, prorogatum videlicet est scrutinium in ultimum diem Augusti.

Eodem die signata est per indenturam praesentatio concessa domino doctori Marsh ad rectoriae medietatem de Gamlingay.

Dodyngton

Eodem die cum magister Doughty ius suum defereret, quod per liberam donacionem sociorum ei concessum fuit, Martii 14° ad vicariam de Dodington, eadem vicaria collata est in magistrum

Rodolphum Crokford, non ita pridem baccalaureum in artibus huius collegii et signata est per indenturam praesentatio.

Elocationes tenementorum sive alienaciones factae hoc anno [*i.e. in the college year August 1629–30*]

Augusti 1 [1629]. *Gamlingay magistro Clavering.* Locata est per indenturam magistro Clavering medietas rectoriae de Gamlingay. Finis et impositus 30 librae, simil[iter] etiam concessum ei ius alienandi. Augusti 4. Signata est ei indentura, et alienacio.

[Augusti] 31. *Molendinum Ibston.* Locatum est molendinum de Ibston Iohanni Franklin, et signata indentura.

Octobris 4. *Domus Merriman magistro Wood.* Admissus est magister Wood rector de Magno Milton in tenementum Merriman de Holywell, qui moriens ei illud testamento legaverat. Concessum est, ut ad solutionem 9 librarum pro fine, indentura illi signaretur in nomine magistri Thomae Parsons de eodem Milton, et anni renovarentur in numerum 40. Dein eodem tempore facta est et licentia alienandi.

Ianuarii 31° [1630]. *Alienacio Moore.* Concessa est alienacio magistro Moore inferiori Bedello in Theologia domus suae nuper extructae apud Holywell.

Martii 20. *Boxely.* Concessum est Ralph Boxely ius alienandi per 10° annos.

Maii 19. *Abraham Watson.* Concessimus Watson, promo collegii Balliolensis, ut ad solucionem 5^{que} librarum pro fine elocaretur ei per indenturam ly Towne ditch in Holywell. Et Iunii 20 signata est indentura.

Anno Domini 1630, Regis Caroli 6° Nathanaelis Brent custodis 10°. p. 304

Magistri in artibus

1. Georgius Petty
2. Petrus Turner
3. Guilielmus Sellar

Doctor in theologia

1. Iacobus Marsh

Magistri in artibus

4. Thomas Gall
5. Ioannes French
6. Ioannes Doughty
7. Alexander Fisher
8. Thomas Heath
9. Ioannes Holliwell

10. Ioannes Earles
11. Georgius Abbott
12. Ioannes Greaves
13. Edwardus Corbett
14. Carolus Gibbs
15. Richardus Browne
16. Hugo Cressey
17. Ioannes Woodcocke
18. Edwardus Nevill
19. Ranulphus Domvill
20. Guilelmus Berkeley

Probationarii

1. Richardus Nevill
2. Edwardus Hinton
3. Franciscus Cheynell
4. Guilelmus Wheare
5. Henricus Iacob

Capellani

1. Ioannes Brent
2. Ioannes Reynolds

Electio Officiariorum

Augusto 2°. Conventum est pro more in altam aulam circa horam nonam antemeridianam ibique resignatis clavibus officiariorum, caeteris sociis ad tempus secedere iussis, per dominum custodem una cum 5que senioribus, officiarii electi sunt in annum sequentem:
vicecustos, magister Abbott.
magistri Holliwell, Corbett, Domvill, decani.
magistri Earles, Gibbs, Cressey, bursarii.
principalis portionistarum, magister Greaves; bursarius Williot, magister Petty; capellanus capellae, magister Fisher; exhibitionarius Hamsterly, magister Sellar; praelectores, Graecae linguae, magister Nevill, Rhetorices, magister Woodcocke; custodes cistae Read, 3 decani; custodes cistae Bodley, magistri Sellar, Gall, Woodcocke.

Progressus

Eodem loco et die decrevimus progressum instituendum ad aliquot e maneriis collegii et eidem, caeterisque apud eadem negotiis obeundis designatus est bursarius itinerans magister Fisher.

Literae patentes magistro Ioanni Brent

Item concessimus literas patentes magistro Ioanni Brent seneschallo maneriorum collegii quibus ei munus hoc sive officium confirmatum est, in hanc scilicet legem, quamdiu se bene gesserit, et has literas sigillavimus 27° eiusdem mensis.

Literae atturnatus Marmaduco Prickett

6°. Convenientes in scaccario potestatem concessimus per literas atturnatus Marmaduco Prickett petendi nomine collegii reditus quoscunque non solutos et debitos a tenentibus manerii de Beilby et has literas sigillavimus 18° eiusdem mensis.

Distributio finis magistri Feilding inter Ioannem Blakham et Iacobum Fenton

20°. Consensum est sociis convenientibus in altam aulam, ut finis magistri Feilding 40s. partim concederetur in praemium honorarium Ioanni Blackham, ianitori collegii, partim eleemosynae causa cuidam Iacobo Fenton natione Hiberno, qui desertis partibus pontificiis et exuto monachatu in gremium ecclesiae Anglicanae reversus est. Assignatis scilicet Ioanni Blackham 26s. 8d. et Iacobo Ffenton 13s. 4d. residuo eiusdem finis.

Computus magistri Gall

27°. Computavit magister Gall 3^{ius} bursarius prioris anni in scaccario.

Computus custodis p. 305

30°. Computavit dominus custos in hospitio suo, ubi consensum est ab omnibus tum domi existentibus, ut singulae allocationes tritici et brasei, altera iuxta quarterii, altera iuxta 4/9 quarterii in singulas septimanas, reducerentur ad ½ quarterii in singulas septimanas et sic discessit in plussagio.

Indentura Henrici Cooper deposita apud vicecustodem

Septembis 4°. Deposuit Henricus Cooper apud vicecustodem indenturam suam pro tenemento in Holywell, ea conditione resumendam, si modo solverit custodi 30 li. pro usu Margaretae Speene immediate post obitum Thomae Rankin patris sui, iuxta tenorem obligationis ea de re contracta.

Admissio in numerum sociorum

Octobris 19°. Conventum est in altam aulam ubi finito anno probationis suae admissi sunt in numerum sociorum domini Richardus Nevill, Eduardus Hinton, Franciscus Cheynell, Gulielmus Wheare.

Admissi in annum probationis

Eodem loco et die admissi sunt in annum probationis domini Richardus Newman, Guilelmus Burton, Ioannes Maplisden, Nicholaus Howson, Franciscus Wright.

Aeque. Magister Gall

21°. Magister Gall tertius bursarius superioris anni discessit aeque.

Computus generalis

30°. Computus generalis habitus est sociis convenientibus in scaccarium.

Dominus Gualterus Chetwin in cancellariam vocandus

Eodem loco et die referente domino custode intelleximus dominum doctorem Huicke quondam huius collegii socium, hac conditione praedia quaedam annui valoris 500 li. collegio per substitutionem in testamento suo reliquisse, si modo tres filiae suae nulla relicta prole decederent, quod cum iam pridem evenerit, et haec interim ignoto iure a domino Gualtero Chetwin occupata, collegio delata non fuerint, eundem decrevimus in cancellariam vocandum cogendumque ibidem ius suum, si quod habet, producere.

Allocatio Henrici Sayre pro collectione reditus

Ibidem et eodem tempore ex consensu allocati sunt 6s. 8d. Henrico Sayre, firmario de Barkeby, pro collectione redituum.

Arreragiae recuperandae

Item decrevimus arreragias quasdam tenementi in Shaftesbury et in villa Sancti Albani, et quieti reditus de Knowle Parke actione instituta recuperandas.

Instrumenta manerii de Beilby Londinum transferenda

Item consensimus, ut chartae et alia quaevis instrumenta manerii de Beilby Londinum transferantur in usum domini custodis in lite quadam eidem manerio intentata.

Sylvae Elham excindendae et vendendae

Novembris 20°. Convenimus in apodyterio, ubi decrevimus sylvas Elham, ne alterius in praedam cederent, excindendas et vendendas, cui negotio constitutus est procurator magister Allen, vicarius ibidem.

Reparatio viae iuxta hortum Collegii

Item consensimus in reparationem viae pro muro horti collegii iacentis, quatenus ad nos pertineret, iuxta monitionem per iuratos curiae letae nuper habitae per vicecancellarium et regentes, cui negotio gerendo ordinavimus procuratores decanum seniorem et bursarium tunc existentem.

Computus magistri Cressy

Decembris 15°. Magister Cressy primus bursarius in scaccario computavit.

Commemoratio fundatoris et scrutinium

16°. Divina fecimus in commemorationem fundatoris, et solenniter deinde in alta aula perlecta sunt statuta, scrutiniumque habitum ac prorogatum in Calendas Ianuarii sequentes.

Secunda eleemosyna Iacobi Fenton

22°. Convenimus in altam aulam, ubi certis de causis ibidem propositis indulsimus Iacobo Fenton superius nominato secundam eleemosinam 20s.

30s. Triumph, curatoris horologii

Item concessimus Triumph 30s. in mercedem curationis horologii per annum.

Scrutinium servientium

31°. Celebratum est in alta aula pro more scrutinium servientium, qui singuli admoniti iam de officio suo et diligentia in posterum, claves quas deposuerant coram domino custode, resumpserunt.

Domini Marsh liberaturae facultas

Item concessimus domino doctori Marsh facultatem percipiendi sortem in communi liberatura et aliis emolumentis, quamuis hic per ½ anni interesse non potuerit.

Electio hortulani

Item electus est hortulanus in annum sequentem magister Abbott.

[1631]

Obitus magistri Brigges p. 306

Ianuarii 26°. Obiit apud nos commensalis magister Henricus Brigges, vir quidem moribus ac vita integerrimus, quem in rebus geometricis, quarum studiis primum Cantabrigiae in societate Sancti Ioannis sese a iuventute sua addixerat, deinde publicam praelectionem Londini in collegio Greshamensi multos per annos sustinuerat, omnium sui temporis eruditissimum, dominus Henricus Savilius, ut primi ex fundatione sua Geometriae professoris munere fungeretur, Oxoniam evocavit. Cuius exequias 29 die proxime sequente, concione habita a magistro Sellar, et oratione funebri a magistro Cressy, una cum primoribus Academiae celebravimus.

Obitus magistri Petty

Februarii 9°. Obiit magister Georgius Petty lethali vulnere inflicto a magistro Iohanni Holywell, cui tamen hoc crimen condonari possit, quod mente per furorem alienata, atque adeo impos' [*sic*] sui, nulla quidem malitia provocate, commiserit.

Prorogatio aeque magistri Cresy

10°. Convenimus in alta aula, ubi prorogavimus aeque magistri Cressy in 16 diem proxime sequentem, quod ad idem audiendum constituto die competens numerus haberi non potuerit.

Aeque magistri Cressy

16°. Magister Cressy discessit aeque.

Magister Doughty electus procurator

Martius 2do. Convenimus in altam aulam, ubi magister Doughty unanimiter electus est in procuratorem universitatis, iuxta statuta et ordinationes novissimas a serenissimo rege de electione procuratorum sancitas.

Capellanorum stipendia aucta

Item decretum est ut capellani singuli recipiant a singulis bursariis 40s. annuatim.

Magister Woodcocke decanus electus

Item electus est in decanum loco magistri Holywell magister Woodcocke.

Claves magnae portae in camera vicecustodis hora decima nocturna deferendae

Item decretum est claves magnae portae singulis noctibus hora decima in cameram vicecustodis deferendas, unde tota deinceps nocte a nemine, nisi ob causam vicecustodi approbandam, petantur.

Claves promptuarii bursario interdicta

Item decretum est, ut nulla sit clavis promptuarii penes bursarium, eo quod precatur promptuarium a pluribus, horis illicitis, et non sine damno domus frequentaretur.

Magister Holywell non socius declaratus iuxta statutum de homicidio etc.

12°. Conventum est in caenaculo superiori domini custodis, ubi dominus custos in praesentia seniorum sibi assidentium magistrum Holywell non socium pronunciavit, prout provisum est in statutis de homicidio, de gravi scandalo, et de gravi percussione socii, quibusdam interim dubitantibus, an statuta hoc exigere videantur, quia in conventu assisarum magister Holywell ob mentis furorem, et impotentiam duodecim-virali suffragio, et sententia domini iudicis absolutus fuerat.

Exhibitio concessa magistro Holywell

Item decretum est ut sors magistri Holywell in communi liberatura cedat in solutionem pecuniae mutuatae a cistis Read et Bodley; ipse autem quod nec pecunias, nec amicos habeat unde sibi consulat, in praesenti recipiat a bursario 5 libras atque in posterum a festo Sancti Iohannis Baptistae per biennium 20 libras annuatim, quo termino elapso, si ita visum fuerit, huiusmodi exhibitio de novo incipiat.

Partitio novi aedificii iuxta magnam portam decreta

26°. Convenimus a precibus vespertinis in apodyterio, ubi decrevimus novum aedificium a parte occidentali magnae portae inter duos socios partiendum, in posterum uni e senioribus in solidum cessurum, modo caeteris commodo recipiendis aliae camerae suffecerint.

Recensio scholarium servientium assignata vicecustodi

Item delegata est recensio scholarium servientium vicecustodi, decano et bursariis senioribus, et principali portionistarum, ut si qui inveniantur excedere numerum decreto superioris anni definitum, ne diutius damno et oneri collegio futuri sint, amoveantur.

Commemoratio fundatoris

Aprilis 2°. Commemoratio fundatoris celebrata est, dein in alta aula perlecta sunt statuta, scrutiniumque habitum ac prorogatum in 16 huius mensis.

Magister Woodcocke bursarius Williot electus

Item electus est bursarius Williott magister Woodcocke loco magistri Petty.

Aeque magistri Gibbs

Iunii 8°. Magister Gibbes coram sociis in altam aulam convocatis pedem computus aequavit.

Dispensatio magistri Cressy

11°. Magistro Cressy dispensatio concessa est a sociis in apodyterio coeuntibus differendi variationes suas in annum proxime sequentem.

Dispensatio magistri Greaves p. 307

Iulii 7°. Convenimus in altam aulam, ubi dispensatum est cum magistro Greaves pro variationibus quas cum habuisse anno praesente oportuisset, modo easdem intra annum proxime sequentem absolvat.

Commemoratio

20°. Divina fecimus pro fundatore, et pro more in alta aula perlecta sunt statuta, scrutiniumque habitum, quod prorogatum est in 2 diem Augusti.

Computus custodis

29°. Computavit dominus custos in scaccario et discessit aeque.

Locationes praediorum [*i.e. in the college year August 1630–1*]

Augusti 2° [1630]. Dimisimus per indenturam magistro Iohanni Iacob firmam de Gamlingay Avenells. Finis 80 librae, sigillata est haec indentura 4° 9^{bris}. Item concessa est magistro Iackson per indenturam medietas rectoriae de Gamlingay nullo constituto fine, eo quod unicus tantum annus adderetur. Sigillata est haec indentura 30 9^{bris}. Item locavimus Thomae Clarke tenementum in Holiwell. Finis 50 solidi. Sigillata est indentura huius locationis 30 9^{bris}.

10°. Locavimus per indenturam magistro Georgio Feilding hortulum adiacentem domui vulgo appellatae Stone-house in Knight-riders streete. Reditus annuatim 5 solidi, et finis 40 solidi. Indentura haec sigillata est 14° Aprilis.

Item locavimus Richardo Wilmott sylvas de Ibston ad solutionem consueti reditus annuatim. Indentura huius locationis sigillata est. Item dimisimus per indenturam medietatem manerii de Stillington et Seton Carew Richardo Hartburne. Finis 200 marcae aequis portionibus solvendus, una scilicet quae spectat ad socios in sigillatione indenturae, altera in festo Sancti Thomae anno proxime sequenti. Indentura huius dimissionis sigillata est 27° 9^{bris}.

Item dimisimus alteram medietatem manerii de Stillington et Seton Carew Christophoro Morpeth. Finis idem et eodem modo solvendus, quo superior. Indentura sigillata est 27° 9^{bris}.

Septembris 4°. Locavimus per indenturam Henrico Cowper tenementum in Holiwell. Finis 5 librae itemque eodem tempore sigillata est locatio.

Novembris 27°. Obligationes suas deposuerunt apud vicecustodem Hartburne et Morpeth pro solutiones 2^{dae} portionis finium suorum in festo Sancti Thomae.

Computus firmarii [i.e. in the college year August 1630–1]

Augusti 6°. Computavit in scaccario Prickett, ballivus de Beilby, et discessit aeque. Item computavit Bedell de Farleigh et discessit aeque. 23°. Computavit in scaccario Napper pro Holiwell et Wolvercott et discessit aeque. Item computavit Hogdeden de Callowland, et discessit in arreragiis, 2 li. 4s. 2d.

Octobris 21°. Computavit Ray de Kibworth in scaccario, et discessit aeque. Item computavit Mayne de Chedington, et discessit aeque.

22°. Computavit in scaccario Wilmott de Ibston, et discessit aeque.

29°. Computavit Sayer de Barkeby, et discessit aeque. Item computavit Gregory de Cuxam, et discessit aeque.

Iulii 12° [1631]. Computavit in scaccario Sherwood de Cantabrigia, et discessit aeque.

29. Computavit in scaccario Prickett, firmarius de Beilby, et discessit aeque.

Anno Domini 1631, regis Caroli 7mo, custodis domini Nathanaelis p. 308
Brent X°.

Magistri

1. Petrus Turner
2. Guilelmus Sellar
3. Thomas Gall
4. Ioannes French
5. Ioannes Doughty
6. Alexander Fisher
7. Thomas Heath
8. Ioannes Earles
9. Georgius Abbott
10. Ioannes Greaves
11. Edwardus Corbett
12. Carolus Gibbes
13. Richardus Browne
14. Hugo Cressy
15. Ioannes Woodcock
16. Edwardus Nevill
17. Ranulphus Domvill
18. Guilelmus Berkeley

Baccalaurei socii

1. Richardus Nevill
2. Edmundus Hinton
3. Franciscus Cheynell
4. Guilelmus Wheare

Probationarii

1. Richardus Newman
2. Guilelmus Burton
3. Ioannes Maplesden
4. Nicholas Howson
5. Franciscus Wright

Capellani

1. Ioannes Brent
2. Ioannes Rainolds

Augusti 1mo. In altam aulam pro more conventum est hora nona antemeridiana, ubi post resignatas officiariorum claves reliquis sociis ad tempus secedere iussis, custos una cum quinque simpliciter senioribus, sequentis anni officiarios hunc in modum designavit:
vicecustos, magister Turner.
magistri Earles, Gibbes, Nevill, decani.
magistri Greaves, Woodcock, Domvill, bursarii.
bursarius Williott, magister Gall; bursarius in progressu, magister Abbott; principalis portionistarum, magister Fisher; exhibitionarius Hamsterley, magister Sellar; capellanus capellae, magister Cressey; lectores linguae Graecae, magister Earles, grammaticae, magister Corbett; custodes cistae Reade, tres decani; custodes cistae Bodly, magistri Gall, Fisher, Corbett.

Augusti primo. Magistro Sellar, qui precedentis Iulii 20° institutus, 25° vero inductus fuerat in rectoriam de Stowe cum 9 ecclesiis, in comitatu Northampton, indultum est ne fraudi sit ipsi quoad liberaturam et alia commoda ac emolumenta domus, quae semestrem praesentiam in domo requirunt, si anno sequenti ultra spatium semestre eum absesse contigerit.

Vacante iam vicaria Sancti Petri in Oriente per praesentationem magistri Sellar ad rectoriam de Stowe, magister Gall nominatur in vicariam Sancti Petri sed praesentatio ipsius differtur rogatu magistri Sellar, quamdiu citra collegium preiudicium fieri poterit, ita ut integrum sit magistro Sellar vicariam Sancti Petri resumere si ipsum causa cedere contigerit, in lite quae contra titulum, ipsius mota est.

Untonus quidam, leguleius, qui ante annum penes custodem deposuerat commendatitias quasdam (quas in filii sui gratiam a serenissima regina nostra impetraverat) sub hac conditione, ut quandocunque electio sociorum habenda foret, hae literae tanquam recentes scriptae haberentur. Nunc demum ulterioris morae impatiens, dominum custodem importune urget ut aperiantur literae. Apertis literis et com[muni] [*damage*] conventu sociorum recitatis, invenimus quales in gratiam hominis ignorabilis a serenissima regina scribi par fuit, hoc solum petentes ut in proxima sociorum electione huius iuvenis ratio habeatur; id quod facturos nos recepimus, si merita ipsius suffragentur. Ille contra iusta ut in gratiam filii sui electionem singularem institueremus, factum id ante hac; nunc vero ni faceremus renunciaturum se serenissimae reginae nihil apud nos momenti literas ipsius habuisse, nec ullum se ex iis fructum retulisse. Responsum hoc a nobis tulit. Renunciaret Regina quae vellet; nos serenissimae reginae facilius satisfacturos, quam ipsi. In eum finem serenissimam Reginam per libellum supplicem adiri placuit.

Dominus Lapworth denuo renuntiatur superior Linacri lector. Dominus Bainbridge vero nunc primum in lectorem inferiorem cooptatur.

Quia magistri, qui hoc ipso anno variare tenentur plures erant quam qui commode intra unius anni spatium variare possent, ideo in hunc annum designantur magistri Greaves et Cressy, cum magistris Woodcock, Nevill, Domvill dispensatum est, ne hoc anno variare teneant. Iniunxit etiam dominus custos 3^{tio} bursario superioris anni, ne imaginarias pecuniae summas ad succedentem bursarium transmittat, sed nomina eorum edat, penes quos fuerint aliquae collegii pecuniae.

2°. Musicis quibusdam, quos haud ita pridem ab oppidanis segreges adsciverat academia, et academiae insigni ac titulo gaudere permisserat, xiid. in singulos socios concessi sunt, e proximo fine deducendi.

20°. Dispensatum est cum magistro Earles 3^{tio} bursario, ut computus per eum reddendus 25° Augusti differatur in 1um Septembris, quia illo die commode haberi non potest, prae infrequentia auditorum, dum Woodstockii Rex aget.

30°. Dispensatum est cum magistro Earles, ut computus ipsius differatur a 1° in 8um diem Septembris, quoniam desubito procurator universitatis renuntiatus, variis negotiis adeo destrictus est e[*damage*] ut rationes in eum diem commode expedire non possit.

Septembris 8°. Magister Earles 3tius bursarius computavit.

13°. De consensu custodis et sociorum quotquot domi aderant, Italo cuidam nostrae ecclesiae proselytum prae se ferenti, qui commendatitias ad dominum custodem attulerat, decreti sunt 40s. eleemosynae loco, scilicet, in singulos socios liberaturae participes xiid. Custos ipse contribuit iis. vid. Quantum summa inde proveniens aberit a 40s. supplebit bursarius ex aerario collegii.

Item de sententia custodis et sociorum statutum est quod nulli in posterum bursario licebit in excipiendis collegii firmariis expendere ultra summam praescriptam in antiquo decreto, quod extat in veteri registro fol. 298,[1] nisi custos (vel in eius absentia vicecustos) et 3^{s} seniores qui domi conveniri poterunt, una cum bursario, pro tempore dispensaverint cum eodem decreto.

[1] *Reg. Annalium* 1521–67, 125.

p. 309 MDCXXXI

Septembris 13°. Dominus custos refricandam censuit memoriam duorum antiquorum, quorum 1mo cavetur ne quis ex officiis collegii pecunias cuivis mutuo dare praesumat sub poena periurii. Atque hoc decretum officiarii alteri animos suos demitterent, serio prenuit et obtestatus est. Secundum vero decretum inhibet bursarium, ne in emendo utensilia domus, aut in reparandis domorum ruinis ultra 3s. 4d. expendat, sine consensu custodis (aut in eius absentia vicecustodis) et 4^r^ seniorum. Rogatu magistri Earles quem non ita pridem spes frustranea brevi vacaturae rectoris de Gamlingay sociorum prensationi alioqui praeproperae implicuerat, cum in ea sociorum partem multo maximam sibi favere deprehendisset, et etiam num spes subesset doctorem Marsh brevi rectoriam illam dimissurum, dominus custos sociorum suffragia exquir[er]e contentus fuit, eosque omnes unanimes invenit in deferendo magistro Earles proxima in rectoria de Gamlingay successione quandocunque vacaverit. Custos itidem suum assensum praebuit, sub conditione revocandi siquam magister Fisher (qui tunc temporis aberat) mutandae sententiae rationem affere potuerit.

Octobris 20°. De consensu custodis per literas significat, et sociorum quotquot aderant, admissi sunt in perpetuam societatem huius domus, dominus Richardus Newman, Guilelmus Burton, Ioannes Maplisden, Nicholas Howson, Franciscus Wright.

Decembris 15°. Magister Domvill 1us bursarius computavit.

17°. Commemoratio fundatoris habita est, lecta etiam statuta, ac initum de more scrutinium, quod et continuatum est ad usque pridie Kalendarum Ianuarii.

31°. Habitum est de more scrutinium in quo tria solennia preponebantur, mores servientium, numerum portionistarum et electio hortulani. Mores servientium referuntur ad officiarios, numerum portionistarum eundem qui prius esse oportere censuerunt. Electus est in hortulanum magister Greaves.

Untoni calumniae, quibus collegium oneraverat apud Reginam, depulsae.
Lectae sunt etiam literae domini custodis, quibus nos certiores facit, qualibus calumniis apud serenissimam Reginam Untonus leguleius ille supra memoratus, collegium nostrum onerasset ac quomodo ad regiam aulam eo nomine accersitus serenissimae reginae abunde satisfecerit annitente honoratissimo comite Dorsettiae cui eo nomine plurimum debet collegium nostrum. Ibidem etiam designatus est magister

Greaves ad citandum dominum Gualterum Chetwin per breve regium e cancellaria deprompturn, ut ostendat quo pacto a collegio aversa sit hereditas fundorum doctoris Huicke, olim socii huius collegii quam ad nos pervenisse oportuit ex testamento ipsius, si filia sua sine liberis decederet, id quod factum est.

[1632]

Ianuarii 15°. Cum iam semestre illud tempus appeteret, intra quod presentandus erat aliquis ad vicariam Sancti Petri in Oriente nisi iure nostro cedere vellemus, magister Sellar suspectum sibi esse titulum suum ad rectoriam de Stowe, ideoque se eum resignasse prae se ferens, de consensu custodis et sociorum resumit vicariam Sancti Petri, hac tamen interposita cautione, ne haec interruptio anni gratuiti (cuius iam fere remissum exegerat) fraudi sit magistro Corbet quoad ius portionistae in collegium cooptandi; quin sive in iudicium deducta secundum ipsum pronuntiatum fuerit, procederet porro annus gratuitus, statim a sententia lata computando tempus, quod deest ad complendum integrum annum, numeranti a XX° Iulii ad 15um Ianuarii.

17°. Praesentatio magistri Sellar sigillata est.

Februarii 16°. Accepimus literas a domino custode, quibus significavit placere sibi ut magister Domvill in angustias pecuniarias tum temporis coniectus, differet solutionem pedis computi sui, non tamen ultra spatium unius mensis cui socii eum in apodyterium statim a precibus convocati, consensum suum praebuere.

Ibidem cum graeculo cuidam Christophoro Angelo collata est symbola hebdomadalis in singulos socios qua inchoanda ante duos menses, quia ab eo tempore reliqua eum collegia symbolas suas contribuerant.

Martii 6°. Literae a domino Cancellario, rogantes ut singula collegia et aulas symbolas suas contribuant ad restaurandum domini Pauli fanum iam vetustate fatiscens, pridie huius diei lectae sunt in conventu praefectorum, quid de hac re sic censuerunt. Singulorum collegiorum ac aularum arbitrio permittendum esse, quem contribuendi modum sequi velint, sive ex aerario publico, sive per capita, sive partim ex aerario partim per capita, sive simul ac semel defungi malint, sive charitatem suam in plurium annorum symbolas diffendere placeat: hoc ipso die socii, quotquot domi aderant, per vicecustodem in altam aulam convocati, et rogati sententias suas, tum sibi tum collegio consultius fore indicabant, si annuam symbolam contribueremus. Huc igitur tandem deventum est, ut singulis annis (si custodi tunc absenti, sic visum fuerit) contribueremus ad hoc opus 20 libras sicilicet custodis et sociorum nomine 6 libras e pecuniis Mayne pro 20 ovibus, reliquas 14 libras ex aerario collegii quotannis durante decennio supplendas.

9°. Consultus super hac re dominus custos respondit per literas datas Martii 9° placere hac in re sibi consilium honoratissimi cancellarii nostri scilicet iamdudum x libras per annum ad idem opus contulisse. Annuam igitur symbolam 20 libras subsidere infra proportionem collegii nostri. Si alia collegia ultra hanc proportionem contribuant, posse nos ad libitum augere.

15°. Magister Domvill solvit partem illam pedis computi sui, quae erat in propriis manibus, quod supererat; magister Gall, magister Doughty, magister Brent singuli sub cirographis suis in manibus ipsorum esse, ac a se collegio deberi agnoscunt.

Anno Domini 1632 regis Caroli 7° exeunte, custodis Brent XI° inchoanti.[1]

[Martii]24°. Commemoratio fundatoris habita est initum de more scrutinium, etc. usque ad Kalendas Maii prorogatum. Ibidem post significatum custodis consensum, decretum est unanimi sociorum assensu, decennalem symbolam ad restaurandum fanum domini Pauli, inchoandum esse a festo Annuntiationis 1632, quo tempore bursarius primam solutionem faciet, ita quod postrema facienda erit ad festum Annuntiationis 1[6]41.[2]

p. 310 MDCXXXII

Aprilis 19°. Magister Woodcock 2us bursarius computavit.

Maii 16°. Consensum est de reparationibus quibusdam in campanile faciendis.

Iunii 16°. Magister Cressy variavit in his quaestionibus:

An {
Scepticorum dubitantia preferenda sit peripateticorum thesibus. Affirmat, contra scientiam dem[onstr]ativam [?] Aristotelis.
Anima humana tanquam divinum quiddam θυραθεν adveniat. Negat, contra Aristotelem I.2 de Generatione Animalium c.3°.
Disputatio contentiosa sit utile exercitium ingenii. Negat, contra Aristotelem, Problemata, sectio 18^{a}, quaestiones 2^{a} et 6^{a}.

Finitis variationibus dispensatum est cum eo pro 2^{dis} variationibus.

[1] In a different hand. [2] Corrected from 1541.

18°. Vacante iam rectoria de Gamlingay per resignationem doctoris Marsh, iuxta premissum prius factum 13° Septembris, de consensu custodis per literas significato, assentientibus eum sociis, collata est eadem rectoria in magistrum Earles.

19°. Praesentatio magistri Earles ad medietatem rectoriae de Gamlingay lecta est coram sociis in aulam convocatis, et postmodo sigillata.

Iulii 6°. Magister Greaves variavit in his quaestionibus:

An {
Vultus et lineamenta corporis sicut indicia animi. Negat contra Aristotelem *φυσιογνωμ(ι)αν*.
Mathesis sit scientiarum praestantissima. Affirmat, contra Aristotelem V° Metaphisica, c. 1°.
Somniorum coniectures maxime insaniant. Affirmat contra Aristotelem *περὶ τῆς καθ' ὕπνον μαντικῆς*.
}

Finitis variationibus, sociis per custodem convocatis dispensatum est cum eo pro 2^dis variationibus.

16°. Dominus custos convocatis sociis in hospitium suum, de communi consensu concessit viduae Holt, ut licentia alienandi ante aliquot annos marito ipsius concessa et per errorem admissum frustranea facta emendatior de novo sigillatur.

Consensum est ibidem de donandis 4 libris, seni cuidam chymico, cui nomine Banks, scilicet 40s. in aerario collegii. 40s. e liberatura anni sequentis numerandam esse pecuniam extemplo, et de manu in manum ad 3^ium bursarium anni sequentis transmittendam, qui e liberatura hanc summam deducit.

20°. Habita est commemoratio fundatoris lecta statuta, initum de more scrutinium, et ad usque Kalendas Septembris, et quemlibet diem citra prorogatum.

20°. Manerium de Thracies et Thrognolds exactis iam 18 annis et quod excurrit, a novissima locatione, elocatum est magistro Trafford, filio magistri Trafford, quondam socii huius collegii, a quo quidam Ioannes Taylour ius ac titulum ad hoc manerium dolo malo avertisse ferebatur. Finis 300 librae unde 200 librae inter socios dividenda.

p. 311 Anno Domini MDCXXXII, regis Caroli VIII°, custodis Brent XI°.

Magistri in artibus

1. Petrus Turner
2. Guilelmus Sellar
3. Thomas Gall
4. Ioannes French
5. Ioannes Doughty
6. Alexander Fisher
7. Thomas Heath
8. Ioannes Earles
9. Georgius Abbott
10. Ioannes Greaves
11. Edwardus Corbett
12. Carolus Gibbes
13. Hugo Cressy
14. Ioannes Woodcock
15. Edwardus Nevill
16. Ranulphus Domvill
17. Guilelmus Berkley

Baccalaurei in artibus

1. Richardus Nevill
2. Edwardus Hinton
3. Franciscus Chennell
4. Guilelmus Wheare
5. Richardus Newman
6. Guilelmus Burton
7. Ioannes Maplesden
8. Nicholas Howson
9. Franciscus Wright

Capellani

1. Ioannes Brent
2. Ioannes Rainolds

Augusti 1°, pro more conventum est in magna aula hora nona antemeridiana, ubi post resignatas officiariorum claves, reliquis sociis ad tempus secedere iussis, custos una cum 5^e simpliciter senioribus sequentis anni officiarios hunc in modum designavit:
vicecustos, magister Turner.
magistri Greaves, Corbett, Cressy, decani.
magistri Gall, Fisher, Gibbes, bursarii.
bursarius Williott, magister French; bursarius itinerans, magister Fisher; principalis portionistarum, magister Nevill; exhibitionarius Hamsterly, magister Doughty; capellanus capellae, magister Woodcock; lector linguae Graecae, magister Cressy; lector grammaticae, magister Corbett; custodes cistae Reade, tres decani; custodes cistae Bodley, magistri French, Woodcock, Nevill.

Cum iam nullum subesset periculum, ne rectoria de Stowe excideret magister Sellar, qui, contra quem simulaverat tam e manibus suis nunquam dimiserat, neque vero spes ulla reliqua foret, eum vicariam Sancti Petri in manus collegii resignaturum, quam nuper resumpserat citra conditiones aut pacta quaecunque, quibus tamen prius vinctus tenebatur; dominus custos de sententia longe maioris partis sociorum pronuntiat annum ipsius gratuitum iam inde a XX° Iulii precedentis exactum esse; usque tamen sibi manere integram potestatem ampliandi huius favoris, quoad ipsis visum sit, et usus poscat, modo ille sub hypotheca sua caverit, de resignanda vicaria Sancti Petri in Oriente in manus collegii, quam primum cum adversario suo compositum fuerit, quo res iam spectabat; id quod ille se facturum plane negabat.

Dyrrachii episcopo decreta est symbola xxxs: xvs., e proxima liberatura deducendi, reliquum ex aerario collegii supplendum, Magistro Domvill comuniis interdictum est usque ad festum Omnium Sanctorum, ob mutuo datas collegii pecunias necdum solutum pedem nuperi computus sui.

Chrysostomi exemplaria, quotquot supersunt, inter socios dividenda quoad usque suffecerint; hac tamen cautione quod, si quis librum suum alienaverit, collegio numerabit quinque libras.

Augusti 3°. Magistro Sellar dies datus est, 23 Augusti, ad respondendum utrum obligationem sigillare velit, quali prius tenebatur, de resignanda vicaria Sancti Petri, quam primum cum adversario suo compositum fuerit, an sententiam contra se latam de finito anno ipsius gratuito, subire.

Ne disciplina collegio [*damage*] lius poneretur pretium quam oeconomiae, utne infructiosior foret [*damage*] decani opera, quam bursariis placuit decanorum stipendia augeri hunc in mensem, ita quod senior decanus de singulis bursariis percipiet 4 libras, iuniores autem tres libras, loco stipendii annui.

Magistro Doughty concessae sunt quindecim librae annuae quamdiu sacellani munere fungeretur in aedibus honoratissimi comitis Northumbriae nec beneficiatus fuerit. Pro biennio autem proxime praeterritarum (cuius partem exegit in obsequio honoratissimi comitis praedicti) conceduntur ei quindecim librae, ad dissolvendum eas alienum xxxvi quo se collegio obstrinxerat nuper in pede computus magistri Domvill. Hoc autem in exemplum trahi in posterum districte vetuit dominus custos. Verum apud posteros utrum plus momenti habiturum sit edictum sive exemplum, viderint quorum interest.

13°. De quadraginta libris superius donatis magistro Holywell nuper socio huius domus, quod supererat simul ac semel solvendum de consensu domini custodis et sociorum decernit.

16°. De consensu custodis et sociorum, vice 6s. 8d. quos antiquiter satrapis villae solvere solebant bursarii, nunc citharaedis academiae deinceps xs. numerandi sunt quotannis.

Duobus egenis incendio domuum suarum in paroecia Sanctae Ebbae afflictis, donantur ex consensu vs.

De fine manerii de Tracyes et Thrognolds ducentae librae ex consensu dividendae inter socios, reliquae centum cedunt collegio. Locationem vide paginam precedentem.

27°. Vicecustodis, decani senioris et bursarii arbitrio permittitur ecquid ad sublevandam egestatem filiae nuperi ianitoris a collegio contribuendam sit, hac tamen cautione, ne symbola, si quam decernandam duxerint, summam v marcarum excedat neve in posterum ulteriorem symbolam hoc nomine petant.

Eodem etiam tempore donati sunt vs. cuidam cognomine Davis ad inopiam reducto.

p. 312 Anno Domini MDCXXXII, regis Caroli VIII°, custodis Brent XII°.

Augusti 28°. Quoniam licentiam panis ac potus pro arbitrio sumendi collegio damnosam esse, frequenti experimento deprehensum est, et in tanto publico tanquam alieni, neglectu ac incuria, dispendia isthaec in immensum itura vero simile erat, placuit igitur custodi et sociis periculum facere, verum magis ex usu collegii futurum esset, necne, singulis sociis, servientibus, et portionistis certam pecuniae summam in singulas septimanas allocare, ita quod ipsi suis quisque sumptibus, panem ac potum sibi comparent. Concessi sunt igitur singulis sociis in singulas septimanas v solidi, servientibus duo solidi, portionistis octodecim denarii, vicecustodi et seniori capellano duodecim denarii, iuniori capellano tres solidi quatuor denarii. Simul etiam ad sustinendam hanc impensam iuscula abrogari placuit tum quibus frumentum, tum quibus pruna incoquuntur. Haec allocatio ad eos non extenditur qui peregre agunt. Ideoque, ne qua fraus fiat collegio, tenentur singuli sub chirographo suo diem ac horam exitus ac reditus sui promo significare, qui secus fecerit, privetur unius hebdomadis allocatione.

Absentibus per partem alicuius septimanae, subrahitur. Sociis in singulos dies viii d. iuniori capellano itidem pro rata (i.e. singulis diebus 6d., praeterquam die veneris, pro quo subtrahendi sunt tantum 3 denarii) vicecustodi et seniori capellano, servientibus etiam et portionistis nihil subtrahitur.

Incrementa panis et potus, sicut et decrementa ad promum ex aequo spectabunt, cuius indemnitati ut consulatur, decretum est quod nemo in promptuario aut cella prandeat vel caenet in posterum. Siquis secus fecerit, privetur unius hebdomadis allocatione. Allocatio haec inchoanda est ab ultimo die mensis presentis, et durante beneplacito custodis continuanda.

Octobris 8°. Magister Greaves soluto pede computus sui discessit aeque.

Novembris 28°. De concensu sociorum omnium (exceptis absentibus, Sellar, Doughty, Heath, Greaves, Domvill, Berkley) pecuniae e duabus proximis exequiis redeuntes (scilicet Williotts in festo Innocentium et Bekington Ianuarii 13°) deputatae sunt in minusculas symbolas erogandae, prout vicecustos sub chirographo suo bursario dictaverit. Siquid ex iis superfuerit in fine termini Fisher, ad sequentem bursarium transmittendum esse. Si hae duae exequiae minus sufficerint bursario, qui pro tempore fuerit, alias exequias eidem usui deputare fas erit.

Decembris 17°. Habita est pro more commemoratio fundatoris, lecta statuta et initum scrutinium. Dominus custos Londino reversus convocatis in hospitium suum sociis varia iis negotia proponit. Primo utrum haereditatem fundorum doctoris Huick a collegio nostro dolo aversum iure persequi vellint, cui assensere plerique.

Deinde utrum negotium quoddam arcanae utilitatis, quodque in publicum emanare sine maximo collegii preiudicio non posset, suae ac vicecustodis fidei clanculum administrandum concedere vellent. Huic etiam plerique assensere, ac eum in finem ordinatum est, ut vicecustos custodem ante Natalem domini Londinum comitetur.

Postea singulorum suffragia exquirit utrum magistrum Trafford (cui ante paucos dies elocatum fuerat manerium de Tracies et Thrognolds) acceptare vellent loco tenentis in molendino de Grancestre, quod ante xi annos domino custodi locatum fuerat pro spatio 21 annorum. Assensere omnes, plerique tamen eo animo, ut putarent adhuc sui arbitrii esse cum illo pacisci, quo pretio redempturus esset elapsos illos xi annos. Sed fefellit eos spes sua; nam paullo post sigillata est indentura absque ulteriori propositione aut mentione finis cuiuscunque. Indicerat etiam mentionem vicecustos cxx libras quas collegium in reparando illo molendino ante octo annos erogaverat, rogatu domini custodis, qui eam pecuniam omnem intra breve tempus renumeraturum [*sic*] se receperat. Aequum igitur visum est vicecustodi, ut in translatione huius status, ratio aliqua habeatur collegii, ex pecunia sic impensa collegio renumeretur. Respondet dominus custos, hac de re alias seu posthac se cogitaturum. Ibidem etiam significavit dominus custos, se iampridem domo illa emigrasse, quae ante vi annos in usum collegii conducta fuerat vico Warwicensi; peripetasmata vero pridem in usum illius domus coempta, non posse commode aptari domui quam ipse iam incolit. Se igitur polymitarium accersivisse, qui ipsorum mensuram iniret et pretium iis ponerat. Et pretium quidem ab ipso positum admodum vile esse, ac infra pretium quo empta fuerant. Rogat igitur socios, quid de iis faciendum sit. Vicecustos consulenda censuit bursariorum computa, ut pro ratione sumptus positi in instruenda illa domo (quem paullo infra trecentas libras subsidere constat) pretium huic supellectili poneretur. Respondet dominus custos illius supellectilis partem usu detritam esse, omnem certe factam deteriorem; nullo modo igitur laturum se, ut pro ratione sumptus fact' in instruenda domo illa, pretium huius supellectilis exigatur. Maior pars praesentium ipsius custodis arbitrio permittendum censuit, quid et quando hoc nomine collegio numeraturus esset.

Ibidem etiam dominus custos magistro Sellar, tunc temporis absenti interdixit omnibus domus emolumentis, cum cautione in integrum ipsum restituendi, si causam suam, sibi ac sociis approbaverit.

Consensum etiam est de emendo organo minusculo, quod vulgo portaticum vocant, ad modulandam dissonam chori nostri psalmasdiam.

Domino Balch subrogato in absentia Rainolds iunioris capellani, de [*damage*]untur singula emolumenta ad illud munus spectantia. Decretum sanciendum contra non significantes promo sub chirographis suis horam exitus sui, si quando oppido excedunt ac pariter reditus sui. Promus neminis nomen libro promptuario inscribet sine expressa licentia custodis, aut vicecustodis. Scrutinium prorogatur in antecalendas Ianuarii.

[Decembris] 20°. Magister Gibbes 1us bursarius computavit.

[1633]

Februarii 18°. Dispensatum est cum magistro Gibbes, ut pedem computus sui differat in festum Paschatis, quia mutandus videbatur pes computus propter errorem admissum in summa excess' et tali ratione novae allocationis.

Martii 21°. Dominus custos Londino adveniens exponit quid actum a se sit in negotio apocrypho supra memorato scilicet circa confirmationem fundorum ac possessionum collegii, et ulteriorem licentiam perquirendi, terras ad manum mortuam, quid in negotio fundorum doctoris Huick, quid denique in negotio circa permutatas terras apud Hensington.

Magister Gall tertius bursarius prospiciens brevi iter sibi capessendum in Hiberniam, rogat custodem ut alium loco suo subrogare dignetur qui bursarii munere fungatur. Cuius rogatu magister Woodcock in [*damage*] hoc munus recepit.

Baccalaureorum in collegio hospitantium post completam determinationem xl^{em}, nomina e libro promptuarii expungenda. Magistri Heath etiam, promoti ad cancellariam Petriburgensem, nomen e libro promptuarii expurgendum praecepit dominus custos, magister Sellar (qui saepius clerico quaesitus, intra cubiculum suum tacitus se continebat, quasi videret monitionem ad comparendum coram custode monendus ut compareat coram ipsis die martis [*damage*] ubi iure redierit dominus custos.

Anno Domini MDCXXXIII, regis Caroli IX°, custodis Brent XII°. p. 313

Martii 26°. Convocatis in magnam aulam sociis, cum magister Sellar, tametsi monitus non compareret, dominus custos de sententia sociorum quotquot aderant, pronuntiat annum ipsius gratuitum iam inde a XX° Iulii precedentis exactum esse, adeoque omnibus domus emolumentis eum excidisse, camerae solius beneficium ei usque ad calendas Iulii sequentis reservandum, citra quem diem supellectilem suam si non amoverit, vicecustos amovendam curaret. Portionistae ipsius in collegio nullum amplius ius competere. Ibidem etiam consensum de responso collegii, iuxta decretum chartophylacii, mittendo ad honoratissimum doctorem Iulium Caesarem, supremum chartophylacem, circa permutatos fundos collegii apud Hensington, utrum permutationem illam stare an rescindi magis e re collegii futurum sit.

Magistro Gall in Hiberniam profecturo conceduntur pro biennio 15 librae annuae, modo citra festum Paschatis iter capessat xx librae statim prae manibus numerandae, reliquae x librae cedunt ad dissolvendum aes alienum xxxvi libras quas debet collegio super pede computus magistri Domville.

Aprilis 13°. Habita est commemoratio fundatoris, lecta statuta, et initum de more scrutinium.

18°. Magister Fisher 2us bursarius computavit.

Maii 12°. De consensu custodis per literas significato, assentientibus etiam sociis in apodyterium convocatis statim a precibus vespertinis magistro Greaves iter ad Batavos meditanti conceduntur 20 librae annuae, pro spatio 3 annorum si tam diu eum in partibus transmarinis agere contigerit, xl librae statim prae manibus numerandae, quod si intra biennium ad collegium reversus fuerit, carebit omnibus domus emolumentis quoad biennium completum fuerit, numeranti ab eo die, quo primum ex hoc regno pedem extulit

Iunii 2°. Convocatis in aulam sociis, statim a precibus vespertinis, vicecustos coram iis literas custodis recitavit in quibus intuitu immensi sumptus exhauriendi in reparandis cancello templi apud Gamlingay, et aedificiis ad rectoriam spectantibus (quod onus omnis nostra incuria et oscitantia recidet in caput magistri Earles praesentis rectoris) alterum annum gratiae a 19° Iunii praesentis inchoandum, magistro Earles indulget, socii etiam unanimes assensere.

13°. Oportunisset magistrum Fisher in praesentia sociorum pedem computus sui dissolvere, si a sociis obtineri potuisset ut in magna aula convenirent.

23°. De consensu custodis, per literas significato, ac 7 insuper seniorum, 4 seniores baccalaurei, Nevill, Hinton, Chennell, Wheare, admittuntur in numerum magistrorum.

21°. Convenientibus in scaccarium sociis, habitus est computus generalis superioris anni quo etiam tempore magister Fisher 2^dus^ bursarius, soluto pede computus sui, discessit aeque.

Locationes praediorum [*i.e. in the college year August 1632–3*][1]

Augusti 1° [1632]. Elocatum est novum tenementum Chaundlerari Holywell, Susannae Blith et Roberto Veysey, sine fine. Concessa etiam licentia alienandi.

Tenementum in Holywell, olim Th. Hales, elocatum est viduae Cracknell. Finis 4 librae una cum licentia alienandi.

3°. Tenementum in Gamlingay, cui insigne Galli elocatur Charnock pro [termino] 3 vitarum absque fine. Sigillata est indentura Susannae Blith et Roberti Veysey.[2]

[1] The sums levied for fines in this section are noted in the margin.

[2] *Margin*, in another hand, 'ly Falcon potius vide pag. 326'.

13°. Sigillata est indentura viduae Cracknell et licentia alienationis. Domus Ryme in Holywell elocatur universitati absque fine.

16°. Rectoria de Elam elocatur domino Iohanni Sedley pro termino vitae suae, uxoris suae, et filii natu maximi. Finis 200 librae praeter 20 libras quas animo gratificandi in antecessum obtulerat domino custodi.[1]

Barkby elocatur Ioanni Mennill pro termino 21 annorum inchoandi a festo Michaelis proximo. Finis 13 li. 6s. 8d.

27° Bull Hall in parochia sancti Aldati locatur Ioanni Price, pro termino 40 annorum inchoandi a festo Michaelis proximo. Finis 13 li. 6s. 8d.

VII^{ris} 11°. Doctori Sanders concessa est licentia alienandi tenementi XVII in Holywell.

VIII^{ris} 22°. Sigillata est licentia concessa doctori Sanders, etiam indentura Price et licentia alienationis.

25°. Sigillata est procuratorium Iacobo Ienkins et Danieli Goodwin ad mittendum dominum Ioannem Sedley in possessionem rectoriae de Elam.

IX^{ris} 20°. Indentura domus Ryme sigillata est universitati.

28°. Indentura manerii de Tracyes et Thrognolds sigillata est magistro Trafford.
30°. Indentura manerii de Beilby sigillata est magistro Pricket.

X^{ris} 17°. Elocatum est tenementum Londini in vico sancti Ioannis, cui insigne Albi Leonis, Gulielmo Scudamore, sine fine.

20°. Sigillata est indentura Guilelmi Scudamore.

Sigillata est indentura molendini de Grancestre, magistro Trafford.

Manerium de Cuxham locatur de novo magistro Gregory, cum adhuc superessent 13 anni. Finis 66 li. 13s. 4d.

Ianuarii 19° [1633 ?] sigillata est indentura magistri Gregory.

Anno Domini MDCXXXIII, regis Caroli IX, domini Nathanaelis p. 314
Brent custodis XIII.[2]

1 *Margin*, 'quae 20 librae inter socios divisae sunt'.
2 'XII°' is inserted beneath the XIII in the hand of subwarden Fisher.

Socii

Magistri in artibus

1. Petrus Turner
2. Gulielmus Sellar
3. Thomas Gall
4. Ioannes French
5. Ioannes Doughty
6. Alexander Fisher
7. Thomas Heath
8. Ioannes Earles
9. Georgius Abbott
10. Ioannes Greaves
11. Edwardus Corbett
12. Carolus Gibbes
13. Hugo Cressy
14. Ioannes Woodcocke
15. Edwardus Nevill
16. Ranulphus Domville
17. Gulielmus Berkley
18. Richardus Nevill
19. Edwardus Hinton
20. Franciscus Cheynell
21. Gulielmus Whear

Baccalaurei in artibus

1. Richardus Newman
2. Guilelmus Burton
3. Ioannes Maplisden
4. Nicolas Howson
5. Franciscus Wright

Capellani

1. Ioannes Brent
2. Ioannes Raynolds

Augusti 1°. Pro more conventum est in alta aula, circa horam nonam antemeridianam, ubi resignatis officiariorum clavibus, per dominum custodem et 5 simpliciter seniores (reliquis ad tempus secedentibus) electi sunt in annum sequentem:
vicecustos, magister Fisher.
magistri Corbett, Domvill, Cheynell, decani.
magistri Cressy, Woodcocke, Nevill senior, bursarii.
principalis portionistarum, magister French; exhibitionarius Hamsterley, magister Earles; bursarius Willyott et capellanus capellae, magister Gibbes; praelectores Graecae linguae, magister Whear, grammaticae, magister Nevill iunior; custodes cistae Reade, tres decani; custodes cistae Bodley, magistri French, Gibbes, Nevill iunior.

Eodem tempore magistro Sellar querelam instituente litigium suum circa rectoriam de Stowe vel nondum, vel saltem nuper finitum esse, in quod non mediocres sumptus se fecisse caussabatur, placuit custodi et sociis ei annum gratuitum indulgere, quod initium sumeret a die Ascencionis domini nostri proxime praeteritae quo tempore, vel circiter, eum cum adversario suo composuisse constabat. Ipse interim coram omnibus professus est, se vicariam Sancti Petri in Oriente, quam hactenus variis coloribus quaesitis detinuerat, collegio resignaturum. Cuius verbis cum dominus custos et sociorum multo maxima pars fidem non adhiberent, obligationem propria manu subscriptam et sigillo munitam exhibuit, qua sub centum librarum cautione recepit, se dictam vicariam ante 14^{tum} diem Decembris proxime sequentis, collegio in manus traditurum, atque hoc se bona fide et citra praetextus ulteriores facturum.

Magistro Doughty concessa est rectoria de Lapworth una cum Heinslease per cessionem magistri Elly tunc vacua, eiusdem ante praesentatio die ii Ianuarii sequentis coram sociis lecta et sigillata est. Dominus custos nomen magistri Heath, cancellarii Petriburgensis, libro promptuarii rursus inseri mandavit.

Augusti XXI. Convenimus in hospitio, ubi dominus custos computavit et discessit aeque. Quo tempore magistro Barkley peregre profecturo concessae sunt 20 librae annuae atque haec concessio per biennium duratura erat. Hoc etiam eius gratiae datum est, ut tota summa, nempe 40 librae ei statim numeraretur. Consensum etiam est de stipendio dando Hawkins, ut promo in promptuario inserviret, et quinque librae annuatim ei concessae sunt.

Cum vero serenissimus Rex Carolus in manu-mortua collegio confirmanda et amplianda se nobis ita propitium exhibuisset, idque praecipue interventu reverendissimi in Christo patris Gulielmi episcopi Londinensis, honoratissimi academiae nostrae cancellarii aequum est visum utrique, tum regi tum episcopo, tanti beneficii gratias, collegii nomine, per epistolas exprimere, atque hoc scribendi negotium vicecustodi datum est. Qui dominum custodem comitatus, regem, tunc Woodstokiae commorantem adiit qui gratias hasce sibi a custode exhibitas sereno vultu accepit, alterae vero iampridem episcopo traditae fuerant Londini.

[*A Letter to the King*][1]

Augustissimae maiestati Caroli D.G. magnae Britanniae, Franciae et Hiberniae potentissimi monarchae.

Ea tempora vidimus (optime principum) quibus inverso rerum ordine, recentia venerati sunt homines, veterum incuriosi. Inde basilicae Deo consecratae, inde musis dicati lares antiquae pietatis monimenta stabant quidem, sed ut magni nominis umbrae squalsori [*sic*] ruinaeque

[1] This letter, presumably relating to the entry above, is bound into the register between pp. 313 and 314.

devota stabant, aliis contemptus, aliis praeda. Longa interim academiarum ecclesiarumque oblivio et quamvis in literatissimo saeculo rarus literarum favor, in religiosissima aetate nullus religionis honor, vidit hanc avi sui labem pius pacificus Iacobus magnus antiquitatis vindex, quo iam coelis inserto, non passa est tua divinior indoles (Rex invictissime) rem optimis auspiciis coeptam, vel incuria vanescere, vel sacrilegio opprimi. Itaque ab ineunte regno, paternis vestigiis insistens, nihil habuisti antiquius quam ne quae Deo literisve sacra erant, ab hominibus, Dei literarumque profanis ultra violarentur. Atque hoc in commune praestitit pietas vestra, illud singulare nostraeque felicitatis proprium, quod vetustissimum musarum domicilium, non effectum sed grave senio, benignissime solatus es, et in ulteriorem spem erexisti, eadem opera literarum et antiquitatis patronus. Audivimus principes qui iniuriarum gratias exigerent, nec beneficiorum suorum quae vel nulla erant vel noxia, erubescerent invidia, vestra bonitas (humanissime princeps) munificentiae tantae vix patitur gratias, eoque uberiores et mereris et habes, quas quum verbis non possumus, verecundo silentio, et tacita adoratione solvemus. Hoc si parum sit, crede illos literarum heroas Scotos, Occamos, Bradwardinos, collegii nostri immo Christiani orbis antiqua lumina, se tibi pronos subiicere et solenne illud ingeminare. Vale saeculi tui immortale decus Caroli Auguste, aeternum vale.

Maiestati tuae humillimi devotissimique subditi custos et scholares collegii Mertonensis.[1]

[Augusti] XXII. Dispensatum est cum magistro Woodcocke tertio bursario loco Gall, ut computum suum in unam septimanam differret, qui deinde xxix die Augusti computavit.

Octobris XIII. Sociis post vespertinas preces in apodyterio convenientibus, consensum est de quinque libris in Bohemos quosdam, Moravosque ministros evangelii causa exulantes conferendis, ita ut una pars huius summae ex aerario collegio suppeditaretur, altera per custodem et socios exolveretur, domino custode 5 solidis contribuente. Ibidem etiam (custodis assensu ante impetrato) a quinque senioribus decretum est quos libros et quibus horis magistri regentes in aula collegii publice hoc anno praelegerent. Consensu etiam est de decem libris magistro

[1] Beneath are later pencilled notes, one attributing the hand to Alex. Fisher, another noting that the letter was 'to return thanks for the increased grant of mortmain granted by Chas. ye 1st to Merton Coll. v. Reg. Mert. fol. 314', another adding 'p. 314' and 'note by J R Hope'. On the reverse, in a 17th-century hand, is 'Concerning ye Coll. Visitation'.

Gall ulterius dandis, in biennalis suae peregrinationis supplementum, ut ipsi etiam, quod nuper magistris Greves et Berkley indultum erat, viginti librae annuae concederentur.

XXIII. Magister Woodcocke agnovit se plussagium sibi computi recepisse, et sic discessum est aeque.

Decembris XIIII. Completo iam tempore, quo magister Sellar vicariam Sancti Petri resignare tenebatur, is tamen fidem suam minime liberavit, sed variis ludificationibus usus, loco et iure suo cedere recusavit, frementibus plerisque, et sibi sic impositum esse aegerrime ferentibus.

XVII. Sacra in memoria fundatoris, pro more fecimus et post lecta statuta, et initum scrutinium, quod in ultimum diem Decembris prorogatum est.

XIX. Magister Nevill 1mus bursarius computavit.

Eodem tempore iniecta est mentio de nova baccalaureorum electione, sed quia magistrorum plerique aberant, dilata res est in tempus magis opportunum. p. 315

Custos itidem socios admonuit, ut linguis in posterum temperarent, nec secreta domus, quod quibusdam solenne esse mandierat, ulterius revelarent.

Bursario etiam negotium datum, ut e collegii aerario quatuor libras vicecancellario deferret, ad vias iuxta Holywell sternendas, cui rei collegiorum pleraque iampridem contribuerant.

Decembris XXXI. Habitum est de more scrutinium, praesertim ad inquirendum in mores servientium, qui cum claves suas in manus vicecustodis tradidissent, ab eo, de officio suo prius admoniti, eas sibi decano commissas receperunt. In hortulanum electus est magister Gibbes.

[1634]

Februarii VI. Magister Nevill Imus bursarius suum aeque confecit.

Martii XVIII. Convenimus in hospitio, ubi consensum est de superiore capellae nostrae parte, usque ad imos gradus, marmore albo nigroque concinnanda.

Consensum etiam est in electionem baccalaureorum confestim instituendam. Examine vero candidatorum per tres dies summa cum accuratione facto.

Electio

XX. Rursus in hospitio convenimus, ubi electi sunt undecem baccalaureorum, et scholaris unus. Dominus Brent e diocesi Vigorniensi, dominus Owen, Menevensis, dominus Broade, Vigorniensis, dominus Clearke, Bristoliensis, dominus Allen, Sarum', dominus Scriven, Lincolniensis, dominus Copley, Sarum', dominus Button, Sarum', dominus Priaulx, Vintoniensis, dominus Sayre, Sarum', dominus Foule, Cicestrensis, et scholaris Loveioy, Lincolniensis. Quibus sic electi ulterius decretum est, priores sex in annum probationis admittendos initio termini Michaelis proximo sequentis, sex reliquis reiectis ad idem tempus anni redeuntis.

XXII. Conventu in hospitio denuo habito, quaesitum est quid horum unusquisque de more in usum bibliothecae dependeret, decretumque eorum singulorum 2 li. 6s. 8d. persoluturos exceptis Clearke, Button, Sayre, Loueioy, qui 20 solidos singuli exsolverent. Aequum etiam visum est sex seniores statim in collegium recipiendos, non quo domus emolumentis ante tempus praestitum fruerentur, sed ut collegii ritibus assuescerent, et sub magistrorum oculis adolescerent. Insuper decretum est ut magistro Vernoyle publicae bibliothecae subcustodi longae valetudinis incommoda perpesso, quinque marcae ex aerario darentur.

XXIX. Divina pro fundatore celebrata sunt, lecta statuta, scrutinium initum, et in Kalendas Maii prorogatum.

Aprilis XIV. Post vespertinas preces, convenimus in apodyterio, ubi consensu est in 30s., Gallo cuidam, ut iactabat abbati, religionis causa profugo, dandos, quorum quindecem ex aerario depromerentur, reliqui quindecem e proxima liberatura deciderentur.

XVII. Magister Woodcocke 2^{dus} bursarius computavit.

Iunii XI. Idem in alta aula suum aeque confecit.

XIX. Consensum est de duobus Bohemis ministris evangelii causa iam per decennium et supra exulantibus pecunia sublevandis, et socii quidem undecem solidos de suo exolverunt, aerarium vero suppeditavit 1 libra 5s.vid.

Iulii XI. Magister Cheynell quamvis decanus, magistro Hinton vices eius ea in officio supplente variavit in his quaestionibus:

An { Virtus posita sit in manu nostra. Negat contra Aristotelem, Ethic' lib.3, c.7.
Ratio sit ex se recta. Negat contra Aristotelem, Ethic' libro 1mo, capitulo ultimo.
Litterae omnes divites reddant quos prudentes. Negat contra Aristotelem, Ethic', lib.6, cap.7.

Quibus finitis dispensatum est cum eo pro secundis variationibus.

XX et XXI. Sacra celebravimus in memoria fundatoris, et cum is dies in dominicum incideret, die sequente lecta sunt statuta, et scrutinium initum, quod in vicesimum Augusti prorogatum est.

Tenementa et praedia hoc anno locata [*i.e. in the college year 1633–4*]
Augusti I [1633]. Dimissum est tenementum vocatum Sunnings Adriano Barney pro termino 21 annorum. Finis 2 librae.

Elocatum est tenementum in Hampton Poyle Gulielmo Astill, pro spatio 21 annorum, facta prius a Iohanne Iohnson, priore possessione, iuris sui renunciatione. Finis 8 librae.

Concessa est licentia viduae Dorchester, alienandi in annos 12 proxime sequentes domum suam Ly Woolsack in Bread Street, London'.

Elocatum etiam est Margarett-Stratton Francisco Kemble pro termino 21 annorum. Finis 80 librae, quarum dimidium ad calendas Novembris dissolveretur, reliquum ad calendas Maii proxime sequentes.

Dimissum est Iohanni Lennard tenementum in Watford, cui insigne Rosae, pro termino 21 annorum una cum licentia alienandi. Finis 15 librae.

Concessa etiam est licentia Iohanni Oakeley, ut rectoria de Wolford alienare possit sed in septennium, nec amplius.

Elocatum est manerium nostrum de Mertonhall in Cantabrigia Iohanni Sherwoode pro 21 annorum spatio. Finis 10 librae.

Dimissa est magistro Georgio Abbott utraque medietas rectoriae nostrae de Emildon et Ponteland pro 21 annorum termino, hoc etiam concesso, ut cum duabus indenturis ante hac dispertirentur, iam una comprehenderentur. Finis 0.

Augusti II. Dimisimus magistro Iohanni Bell domum in Py-Lane, pro p. 316
spatio 40 annorum, una cum licentia alienandi. Finis 10 librae.

Augusti XXI. Dimissa est firma nostra de Callow-Land Richardo Hoddesden pro termino 21 annorum. Finis 60 librae, cuius altera pars ad indenturae sigillationem dissolveretur, altera eodem tempore anni sequentis.

Dimisimus Roberto Makin tenementum cui insigne Albi Leonis in vico Sancti Iohannis, London', sine fine.

Octobris XIII. Dimissa est domus in Hollywell Roberto Smith pro 40 annis una cum licentia alienandi, sine fine.

Ianuarii XV [1634]. Dimisimus domum in Hollywell Gabrieli Boxley pro 40 annis, una cum licentia alienandi, sine fine.

Martii XXII. Dimissa est domus in Holywell viduae Iddens pro 40 annorum termino, facta etiam ei potestate alienandi, sine fine. Elocata est domus Thomae Clarke pro annis 21 qua ipse in fundo nostro in Holywell, nobis insciis, saltem non annuentibus extruxerat. Reditus domui impositus 2s. 6d.

Atque haec omnia, suis quaeque temporibus, sigillata sunt.

p. 317 Anno Domini MDCXXXIV, regis Caroli X, domini Nathanaelis Brent custodis XIV.

Magistri in artibus

1. Petrus Turner
2. Thomas Gall
3. Ioannes French
4. Ioannes Doughty
5. Alexander Fisher
6. Thomas Heath
7. Ioannes Earles
8. Ioannes Greaves
9. Eduardus Corbett
10. Carolus Gibbs
11. Hugo Cressy
12. Ioannes Woodcocke
13. Eduardus Nevill
14. Ranulphus Domvill
15. Gulielmus Berkley
16. Richardus Nevill
17. Eduardus Hinton
18. Franciscus Cheynell
19. Ricardus Newman
20. Gulielmus Burton
21. Ioannes Maplisden
22. Nicolaus Howson
23. Franciscus Wright

Probationarii

1. dominus Brent
2. dominus Owen
3. dominus Broade
4. dominus Clarke
5. dominus Allen
6. dominus Scriven

Capellani

1. Iohannes Brent,
2. Ioannes Reynolds

Augusti II. Convenimus pro more in alta aula, hora nona antemeridiana, ubi resignatis officiariorum superioris anni clavibus, a domino custode, et quinque simpliciter seniores, praesentes electi sunt in annum sequentem:
vicecustos, magister Fisher.
magistri Woodcock, Nevill iunior, Whear, decani.
magistri Gibbs, Hinton, Cheynell, bursarii.
principalis portionistarum, magister Corbett; bursarius Williott et capellanus capellae, magister Nevill senior; exhibitionarius Hamsterley, magister Earles; praelectores, grammaticae, magister Newman, Graecae linguae, magister Wright; custodes cistae Reade, tres decani; custodes cistae Bodley, magistri Corbett, Nevill senior, Cheynell; Bursarius itinerans, magister French.

Enacto iam triennio a proxima electione lectorum Linacri, dominus doctor Lapworth rursus superior renunciatur, dominus doctor Bainbridge inferior in aliud triennium. Cum ex cervisia qua hactenus usa est domus, diluta et incocta plurima aegritudinum materias succrescere crederetur, decretum est ut in posterum per hyemem totam potus melioris copia fieret, sub hac tamen cautione ut officiarii providerent ne quis inde a scholaribus male feriatis abusus suboriretur. Magistro Domvill in transmarinas partes profecturo, concessae sunt 20 librae annuae in triennium atque hoc eius gratiae datum est ut tota summa, nempe 60 librae ei statim numeraretur, hac tamen addita cautione, ut si intra spatium praedictum ad collegium reverteretur pecuniam sic concessam pro rata temporis parte, qua moram hic traxerit, refundere teneretur. Cum in allocatione nuper facta, palam sit, vicecustodem deterioris esse condicione, quam sociorum quemlibet alium, adeo ut quidam eius absentis vices supplere recusaverint visum est aequum, ut in posterum perciperet per singulas septimanas 2s. vid. pro allocatione, ut sic caeterorum sociorum emolumenta exaequaret. Eodem decretum est ut magister Hinton hoc anno variaret, et magister etiam Domvill, si eum, ante iter, quod iam meditabatur, ad collegium reverti contigerit sin vero non redierit, cum eo dispensatum est, hac clausula tamen adhibita, ut statim post eius ab itinere reditum ad collegium variare teneretur. Insuper decretum est, ut via regia, qua horto nostro contingua est, sabulo et lapidibus sterneretur, cuius rei cura vicecustodi et bursario demandata est.

Augusti IIII. Convenimus in hospitio, ubi dominus custos, computavit et discessit aeque, ubi etiam dispensatum est cum magistro Cheynell, ut ante biennium completum a suscepto magisterii gradu, sacris ordinibus initiaretur, quod et magistro Nevill iuniori petenti indultum est.

Augusti XI. Dispensatum est cum magistro Woodcocke bursario, loco magistri Cressy, ut ob defectum auditorum computum suum differret in primum diem Iovis termini sequentis. Atque idem computus postea in unam septimanam ulterius dilatus est.

Augusti XXVIII. Sigillata est praesentatio vicariae de Margaret Stratton, vacanti per mortem Lemuelis Fouler, Gualtero Atwood, in artibus magistro, quem collegio nominavit reverendus in Christo pater Ioannes episcopus Sarum qui hoc sui iuris esse contendebat. Cum vero custos, sociique quibus de iure suo, si quod appareret, ne apicem unum remittere constitutum erat, diu haesissent, nec satis se expedire possebit, visum est pro hac vice rem omittere, nec domino episcopo litem ullam intentare praesertim cum sex menses a morte prioris incumbentis iam fere exiissent nec in nominati personam ulla legitima exceptio caderet, ante tamen protestatione [*sic*] per vicecustodem, et duos alios ex sociis facta[m] coram episcopo, hoc quod a se factum erat, sic intelligi debere, ut nullum inde successoribus suis preiudicium crearetur si in posterum appareret, plenum ius tum nominandi tum
p. 318 praesentandi penes collegium esse./Quam protestationem suam in acta curiae Sarum referri petierunt.

VII^{bris} XXI. Magister Whear iunior decanus, summae spei iuvenis, diuturna tabe absumptus, mortalitatem exuit, in cuius locum suffectus est magister Nevill senior de consensu custodis et quinque seniorum domi existentium

VII^{bris} XXII. Custode et sociis in hospitio convenientibus, datum est magistro Cressy, sic per literas petenti, ut, si in Hibernia ubi tunc commorabatur, per anni spatium moram traxerit, ei, ut caeteris sociorum peregrinantibus, viginti librae numerarentur.

VIII^{bris} VIII. Admissi sunt in annum probationis dominus Brent, dominus Owen, dominus Brode, dominus Clarke, dominus Allen, dominus Scriven. Eodem tempore cum curia apud manerium nostrum de Farleigh necessario habenda esset, atque idem dominus custos per literas significasset, destinatus est vicecustos, ut custodi in hoc negotio praesto esset.

VIII^{bris} XX. Admissi sunt de consensu custodis et sociorum, in numerum magistrorum, dominus Newman, dominus Burton, dominus Maplisden, dominus Howson, dominus Wright. Eodem tempore etiam concessum est a sociis custodis assensu ante impetrato, ut sex baccalaurei nondum in annum probationis admissi, in collegium reciperentur, ubi usque ad admissionem suam more commensalium degerent.

VIII^{bris} XXIII. Magister Woodcocke tertius bursarius loco Cressy computavit.

X^{bris} XVII. Divina celebravimus in memoriam fundatoris, et post lecta sunt de more statuta, et scrutinium initum quod in ultimum X^{bris} prorogatum est. Eodem die magister Woodcock tertius bursarius loco Cressy, confecit suum aeque.

X^{bris} XVIII. Magister Cheynell primus bursarius computavit.

X^{bris} XXXI. Initum est de more scrutinium, ut in quo tribus illis solemnibus propositis, de moribus servientium, de numero portionistarum, de hortulano eligendo, electus est hortulanus magister Woodcock, servientes ad officiarios domus remissi sunt, placuitque ut portionistarum numerus idem esset qui prius.

[1635]

Ianuarii IV. Sigillavimus consensu domini custodis prius per literas significato praesentationem vicariae nostrae de Margaret-Stratton iam vacantem per concessionem Walteri Atwoode Christophoro Iole quem nobis nominavit dominus episcopus Sarum quia de iure nostro, an ullum in ea nominatione nobis competeret, nondum liqueret.

Ianuarii XIX. Sociis in aula convenientibus, lectae sunt domini custodis literae, quibus significavit particulam quandam terrae, manerio nostro de Merton Hall Cantabrigiae vicinam prostare, sibique offerri in quam emendam et manerio nostro adiungendam si consenserint, operae pretium fore sociis consentientibus negotium vicecustodi datum est ut Londinum proficisceretur ad hoc et alia collegii negotia procuranda, sed res haec exitu caruit. Eodem etiam tempore consensum est in viginti solidos quibusdam Germano-Palatinis dandos ita ut sociorum singuli sex denarios dependerent reliquum ex aerario suppeditaretur. Concessae etiam sunt, ex consensu domini custodis, alterae viginti librae annuae in biennium magistro Gall tunc in Hibernia commoranti, ita ut tota summa, nempe 40 librae ei statim exolveretur.

Februarii IV. Magister Cheynell confecit suum aeque coram sociis in aula congregatis.

Martii XXI. Habita est commemoratio pro fundatore, lecta statuta, initum scrutinium in quo quaedam allegata sunt contra iniuriam et insolentiam obsonatoris, ob quae dignus habitus est qui ab officii sui executione, ad tempus saltem suspenderetur. Quando etiam proposita emendatione digna in promptuario, de quibus promus admonitus est. Scrutinium postremo in 20um diem Maii prorogatum est.

Aprilis XVII. Magister Hinton 2dus bursarius computavit, quo tempore decretum est, quod vicecustos et magister Gibbs, bursarius, Londinum proficiscerentur ad varias collegii res procurandas.

Maii XXXI. Cum magister Hinton per literas significasset, se ob nuperam matris suae mortem, et alia inde negotia emergentia, sine rerum suarum gravi dispendio ruri ad collegium redire non posse, socios post vespertinas preces in apodyterio convenientibus, consensum est ut variationes eius in annum sequentem differrentur, et ad aeque suum conficiendum non teneretur donec rebus sui confectis commode redire posset.

Iunii VII. Sociis in apodyterio post vespertinas preces convenientibus consensu prius domini custodis per literas significato, concessae sunt magistro Greaves longinquam peregrinationem meditanti in alterum triennium viginti librae annuatim, ita ut ex iis viginti statim numerarentur reliquae quadraginta, suis postea temporibus perciperentur.

Iulii XX. Divina fecimus in memoria fundatoris, post lecta sunt statuta et scrutinium initum, quod in ultimum diem Augusti prorogatum est. Eodem tempore magister Hinton suum aeque confecit in alta aula coram sociis.

Iulii XXVIII. Confectus est generalis computus in scaccario. Quo tempore etiam computavit dominus custos, et discessit in plussagio 15 li. 15s. ob. qua.

p. 319 *Tenementa et praedia hoc anno locata* [*i.e. in the college year 1634–5*]

Augusti II [1634]. Dimisimus manerium nostrum de Elstage in Chedington Roberto Mayne pro 21 annorum spatio. Finis 44 librae quorum una pars solvenda ad sigillationem indenturae, altera eodem tempore anno revoluto.

Elocatum etiam est Pockrilston Iohanni Prattant pro 21 annis, finis 26 librae 13s. 4d. cuius dimidium solvendum cum sigillaretur instrumentum, alteram eodem tempore anni sequentis

Septembris XXII. Concessa est magistro Napper licentia alienacionis, modo non alienaret maiorem firmae suae partem.

Novembris XV. Concessa est indentura manerii nostri de Beilby Marmaduco Prickett pro termino 21 annorum, cum prius se obligasset in summa quingentarum librarum, ne quid damni inde in collegium redundaret, quod factum est ob clausulas quasdam indenturae insertas, quae ut novae erant, sic et collegio fraudi et preiudicio esse posse credebantur. Finis o.

Decembris IV. Dimisimus Gulielmo Bosevile pro termino 21 annorum firmam et molendinum omniaque alia quae Eduardus Leinge, in manerio nostro de Beilby ante possederat, facta prius ab eodem Leinge omnis iuris sui renunciatione. Finis 6 li. 13s. 4d.

Martii XXVIII [1635]. Concessa est Eduardo Turley ut alienare posset domum suam in Holywell.

Eodem tempore concessum est tenementum nostrum in St Albans cum duabus acris et dimidio terrae, domino Iohanni Iennings pro termino 21 annorum. Finis 5 librae.

Atque haec omnia diversis temporibus sigillata sunt.

Annus domini MDCXXXV, regis Caroli XI, domini Nathanaelis Brent p. 320
custodis XV.[1]

Magistri in artibus

1. Petrus Turner
2. Thomas Gall
3. Ioannes French
4. Iohannes Doughty
5. Alexander Fisher
6. Thomas Heath
7. Ioannes Earles
8. Ioannes Greaves
9. Eduardus Corbet
10. Carolus Gibs
11. Hugo Cressy
12. Ioannes Woodcocke
13. Eduardus Nevill
14. Ranulphus Domvill
15. Gulielmus Berkley
16. Richardus Nevill
17. Eduardus Hinton
18. Franciscus Cheynell
19. Ricardus Newman
20. Gulielmus Burton
21. Ioannes Maplisden
22. Nicolas Howson
23. Franciscus Wright

[1] Beneath is 're vera XIV. Est enim error in annorum numero, ab ipso initio praefecturae custodis Brent'. Further down is another marginal insertion, 'Error quem aliis imputatus, a te fluxit. Cum enim exeunt e anno domini 1632, in margine notatus esset annus custodis Brent XII, initium ducens a 20° Martii anno domini 1632, tum Augusto proxime sequente incipis numerare anno custodis XIII qui non inchoatur ante 20^{m} Martii sequentis, exeunte scilicet anno 1633. At error hic non tunc primum irrepsit, sed ab anno 1622 solennis erat.'

Baccalaurei
domini:

1. Brent
2. Owen
3. Brode
4. Clarke
5. Allen
6. Scriven

Probationarii
domini:

1. Copley
2. Button
3. Priaulx
4. Sayre
5. Foule
6. Loveioy

Capellani

1. Ioannes Brent
2. Ioannes Reynolds

Augusti I. Convenimus, pro more in aula, hora nona antemeridiana, ubi resignatis clavibus officiariorum superioris anni, clavibus item bibliothecae coram prolatis, iunioribus secedere iussis per dominum custodem, et quinque simpliciter seniores praesentes electi sunt in annum sequentem:
vicecustos, magister Fisher.
magistri Corbet, Hinton, Newman, decani.
magistri French, Woodcocke, Nevill iunior, bursarii.
principalis portionistarum, magister Gibs; bursarius Williot et capellanus capellae, magister Nevill senior; exhibitionarius Hamsterley, magister Earles; praelectores, grammaticae, magister Howson, Graecae linguae, magister Wright; custodes cistae Reade, tres decani; custodes cistae Bodley, magistri Gibs, Howson, Wright.

Bursarius itinerans, magister Corbet.

Quo tempore consensum est de novo pulvinari ad suggestum novis item pulvillis ad sedilia in templo, aliasque res ad capellam nostram decentius adornandam. Et ut superior chori pars quae orientem spectat, et mensam dominicam marmore sterneretur. Etiam ut nova sera, cum clavibus quot necessariae essent ad ostium bibliothecae pararetur. Insuper donatae sunt famoso illi equorum domitori Bancks, iam ad egetatem redacto 4 librae et viduae Carpenter 2 librae sic ut unam partem aerarium suppeditaret, altera custos cum sociis.

Augusti II. Concessae sunt magistro Cressy in Hibernia agenti alterae viginti librae in annum sequentem.

Augusti V. Decretum est ut senior capellanus in posterum 20 denarios pro hebdomadali allocatione reciperet (cum antea 12 denarios tantum habuissset) ne deteriori loco esset, quam iunior capellanus.

Cum vero Thomas Holt, eques auratus ex agro Warwicensi decimas rectoriae de Lapworth iniuria detineret, nec magister Doughty, rector ibidem, liti cum tam potente adversario par esset, aequum visum est, ut collegium hoc sibi oneris imponeret, et litem contra eundem auspicaretur atque etiam persequeretur, si non longi temporis et multorum sumptuum res appareret. Decretum ergo est, ut litem hanc per annum spatium persequeremur et ultra etiam, si expedire videbitur.

Augusti XVII. Consensum est ut sylvae nostrae apud Canes et Norton Mandevill in comitatu Essex venderentur, cuius rei cura magistris Eduardo et Richardo Nevilliis demandata est, qui earum auctione centum et decem libras confecerunt, quarum septuaginta solvendae in festo Sancti Iohannis Baptistae hoc anno quadraginta reliquae in festo Purificationis anni sequentis.

Quo eodem tempore sigillata est indentura inter collegium et dominum Richardum Knightley de Preston in agro Northamptoniensi, confecta qua vir ille honoratissimus decem libras annuas in perpetuam collegio donavit ex reditibus suis de Badbie in eodem comitatu provenientes ad fundandam et instituendam lectionem catechisticam, qua iuniores in articulis religionis melius instruerentur. Condiciones tum lectorem tum collegium spectantes, ex ipsa donationis charta melius intelligentur.

Octobris VI. Convenientibus in aula sociis a vicecustode aliisque quibus ea res, pro more demandari solet, constitutum est quos libros et quibus horis iuniores magistri praelegerent.

Octobris VIII. Magister Gibbs tertius bursarius (cuius computus in hunc diem ob defectum auditorum prorogatus erat) computavit.

Octobris IX. Dominus Brent, dominus, Owen, dominus Brode, dominus Clarke, dominus Allen, dominus Scriven, anno probationis iam exacto in socios admissi sunt. Quo eodem die dominus Copley, dominus Button, dominus Priaulx, dominus Sayre, dominus Foule, dominus Loveioy admissi sunt in annum probationis.

Quo tempore Ioannem Flexney, obsonatorem ob arrogantiam et verba contumeliosa, praesertim in magistrum Woodcocke, quem indignis conviciis palam prosciderat, facta a domino custode potestate, ut hominem pro merito suo tractarent, vicecustos et seniores ob officiio removendum censuerunt sine spe regressus, nisi forte in posterum melius se gesserit, moresque suos deinceps domino custode et sociis approbaverit.

p. 321 Octobris XVI. Consensum est a sociis (domini custodis voluntate per literas intellecta) ut magistro Richardo Hartburne potestas fieret, curiam tenendi apud manerium nostrum de Stillington, quoties opus esset, et perquisita curiae, caeteraque, quae iure nostro nobis ibi obveniunt in usum collegii colligendi. Atque haec litera, ut vocant atturnatus ei statim sigillata est, hac cautione disertis verbis interposita, ut haec locum haberent [*sic*], donec aliter de voluntate nostra innotesceret.

Decembris IV. Magister Gibbs 3us bursarius coram sociis in aula suum aeque confecit. Quo eodem tempore (domino custode consensum suum prius significante) concessum est ut magister Berkley in alium biennium 40 libras peregrinationis ergo perciperet quae summa a bursario Nevill ei memorata est.

Decembris XVI. Magister Nevill 1^{mus} bursarius computavit.

Decembris XVII. Divina fecimus in memoria fundatoris, dein lecta sunt statuta et initum scrutinium, quod in ultimum diem Decembris prorogatum est.

Decembris XXXI. Habitum est de more scrutinium in quo tria illa solemnia proposita sunt 1, de moribus servientium, 2, de numero portionistarum, 3, de electione hortulani. Et in hortulanum electus est magister Nevill senior, de numero portionistarum consensum est, ut idem remaneat, qui superius, servientes si qua admiserint in posterum castigatione digna ad officiarios remissi sunt, pro eorum arbitrio corrigendi.

[1636]

Februarii XI. Magister Nevill 1^{mus} bursarius confecit suum aeque.

Martii XXV. Magistro Sellar post varias protelationes, tandem vicariam Sancti Petri in Oriente resignante praesentatio eiusdem vicariae vicecustodi sigillata est unanimi sociorum consensu, si custodis voluntate per literas ante significata. Quo etiam tempore sociis significatum est dominum custodem dispensasse cum magistro Burton ut collegii statutis non obstantibus operam iurisprudentiae navare posset, quamvis regentiae suae annos nondum explevisset.

Aprilis IX. Divina fecimus in memoriam fundatoris, dein pro more lecta sunt statuta et scrutinium initum, quod in calendas Maias prorogatum est.

Aprilis XIIII. Magister Woodcock 2^{dus} bursarius computavit.

Maii XXV. Dominus custos iam ad collegium reversus, socios in apodyterio post preces vespertinas convocavit ubi post expositam doctoris Lapworth, sui superioris Linacri lectoris munere functus erat, mortem, unanimi consensu in eundem locum electus est dominus doctor Bainbridge, praelector antea inferior, cui in hac inferiori lectura successor destinatus est doctor Brodbent e collegio Magdalenensi sed eius electio certis de causis ad festum sancti Petri in Vincula dilata est.

Maii XXXI. Sociis a domino custode in aulam convocatis, actum est de causa domini Iacob. Is ante aliquot annos in collegium electus et in annum probationis admissus, in ipso anni initio, litibus, ut aiebat, implicatus, Londinum profectus est, unde nec eo anno, nec sequentibus reversus, iure quod ei ad societatem competebat, prorsus excidisse visus est; adeo ut nec ratio eius nec mentio per annos complures habita sit. Tandem rei familiaris, quem in lites insumptam caussabatur angustia cogente, patronum nostrum, reverendissimum in Christo patrem archiepiscopum Cantuariensem per amicos interpellavit, qui vicem hominis dolens et eruditione in eo haut vulgarem, in linguis praesertim orientalibus perspectam habens, hasce in eius gratias ad collegium literas dedit.

Inscriptio erat:
To my lovinge freindes ye warden and fellowes of Merton College in Oxford, these. S. in Christo.

After, my harty commendations etc. I have beene moved in ye behalfe of one Henry Iacob, chosen some yeares since into your College, and admitted into his yeare of probation (but by his discontinuance from ye college disabled from further admittance into your fellowship in ye ordinary way), and informed that agaynst this incapacity which he hath contracted by his absence and by his not proceedinge in ye usuall course of studyes and discipline there may be opposed an equivalent capacity grounded upon a fundamentall statute of your college which requires that there shall alwayes be in your society 'grammaticus unus qui studio grammaticae totaliter vacet', hereupon I have considered of that statute, and upon mature deliberation conceive ye intention of your Founder in that statute to have beene that besides those which

were to be trayned up in a course of philosophy there should be one, who wholly should include ye study of philology, whereas therefore I am informed concerninge this Iacob's eminent ability in ye way of philology by such persons whose judgments and sincerity I have no reason to distrust, I have thought fit to recommende him unto you, to ye ende that since he hath deserted his first capacity you may be induced out of ye charitable consideration of his abilityes or rather wants to lay hold of his second capacity, and presently admitt him fellowe by vertue of ye aforementioned statute.[1] My meaning is not
p. 322 however that / he shall be admitted absolutely without any condicion, but with this Clogge perpetualle to be annexed to him, and his place that once a weeke during ye University Terme (ye day and Auditors to be appoynted by ye Warden) He shall openly in your College Hall, unto which it shall be lawfull for any of ye University to resort, reade upon some title of Antiquity, in which He shall compare ye Roman, Greeke, and Orientall Antiquities one with another. And further by way of punishment, for his discontinuinge from ye College, I would have him immediately on his beinge admitted Fellowe, notwithstandinge he was Senior to divers, who are now Masters of Arts in that College, to be admitted in Numerum Magistrorum, but Iunior to all those, who are already Masters. I thinke it sufficient barely to express my desires in this businesse, not doubtinge but you will readily comply with them, as being grounded upon ye playne letter of your Statutes, whereof otherwise, were it ambiguous, you knowe your Patrone hath ye power of interpretinge and of exacting Obedience in Conformity to his Interpretation. I thinke it fitt also, that a copy of this my letter be entered into your Register whereby it may appeare unto posterity upon what grounds both you and I proceeded in this businesse. So I leave you all to God's Blessinge and rest,

your lovinge Frende and Visitor W. Cant.

Lambeth May 18 1636.

Quibus perlectis, dominus custos, quamvis in futura perspiciens, exemplum vereretur tamen ut patrono (cui et suo et collegii nomine se plurimum debere professus est) rem gratam faceret, enim in sociorum, atque adeo magistrorum numerum, modo condiciones literis comprehensas expleverit, admittendum censuit. Caeteri rogati in eandem sententiam abierunt.

[1] Cf. Garrod and Allen, *Merton Muniments*, 21, s.v. 1274 Statutes.

Iunii IX. Magister Woodcocke secundus bursarius confecit suum aeque in praesentia sociorum.

Iunii X. Dominus Iacob admissus est primo in numerum sociorum, deinde magistrorum, praestitis utrobique iuramentis consuetis: hac tamen adhibita condicione ut singulis diebus iovis, lecturam philologicam inter horas primam et secundam postmeridianas in aula collegii praelegeret, durante termino. Is autem durare intelligeretur, quamdiu disputationes baccalaureorum, more recepto, haberentur. Praelectio autem ipsa tres horae quadrantes ad minimum absolveret.

Iulii IX. Magister Nevill iunior variavit in hisce quaestionibus:

An {
Poetae sint exterminandi e bene morata republica. Affirmavit contra Aristotelem, Libro 1mo de Poetica.
Detur ars physiognomica. Negavit contra Aristotelem, libro de Physiognomia.
Carne molles sint maxime ingeniosi. Negavit contra Aristotelem, Libro 2do De Anima.

Quibus finitis cum eo dispensatum est pro secundis variationibus.

Iulii XX. Divina fecimus pro fundatore, deinde lectis statutis initum est scrutinium, quod in 10^{mum} diem Septembris prorogatum est. In hoc autem scrutinio magister Nevill qui ante paucos dies variaverat querellam instituit de iniuria sibi a magistro Newman iuniori decano illata, qui in oppositione sua, in magistri variantis personam plurima, ut ille aiebat effutiverat, famam eius et existimationem non mediocriter laesura. Petiit itaque a domino custode ut magistrum Newman orationem illam, ita ut prolata erat, tradere iuberet.

Iulii XXV. Confectus est computus generalis anni superioris.

Tenementa et praedia hoc anno locata [*i.e in the college year 1635–6*]

Augusti 1mo [1635]. Dimissum est magistro Woodes tenementum nostrum cui insigne Flowre-de-Lyce pro termino 40 annorum atque etiam aula portionistarum, una cum alienacione utriusque, finis 30 librae. Eodem etiam dimisimus hortum e regione Aulae Albanae pro termino 27 annorum, finis o.

Dimissae etiam sunt duae virgatae terrae in Hensington magistro Fisher vicecustodi, pro termino 21 annorum, finis o.[1]

[1] 'concessa est etiam ei licentia alienandi' deleted.

Elocatum est manerium nostrum de Ibston Richardo Willmott pro 21 annis, finis 66 li. 13s. 4d. Quarum prior pars solvenda ad festum Sancti Lucae cum indentura sigillaretur, altera eodem tempore anno revoluto.

Elocatum est ly Woolsacke Gulielmo Sherman pro spatio 40 annorum, finis 26 li. 13s. 4d., ita ut dimidium solveretur ad sigillationem indenturae, altera pars primo die Augusti 1636. Permissa etiam illi est licentia alienandi ad annos 12.

Dimissae sunt clausurae nostrae in Cricklade Richardo Robins pro 21 annis, finis 33 li. 6s. 8d. Dimissum est manerium nostrum de Kibworth magistro Ray pro 21 annorum spatio, finis 40 librae quarum viginti solvendae ad sigillationem indenturae, alterae viginti eodem tempore anni redeuntis. Concessa etiam ei est licentia alienandi, una cum iure ballivatus ibidem. Concessa est viduae Williams, ut domum suam in Holywell alienare posset.

p. 323 Augusti III Dimissum est manerium de Barkby Iohanni Mennell pro termino 21 annorum una cum licentia alienandi, finis 0.

Dimisimus Thomas Weekes tenementum et terras quasdam in Beilby pro spatio 21 annorum, finis 5 librae.

Augusti IV. Dimisimus Eduardo Spranger et Gulielmo Stanes maneria nostra de Canes et Norton Mandevill pro termino 21 annorum, finis 220 librae de quibus Spranger solvit 125 libras, Stanes 95 libras.

Augusti XV. Concessa est Thomae Clarke licentia alienandi domum in Holywell cui olim insigne The White Horse.

Iunii IX. Dimisimus Iacobo Partridge domum suam in Holywell, pro 40 annis unum cum licentia alienandi. Finis idcirca non impositus, quia plurimos in domo illa aedificanda et reficiendam sumptus faciens se pene ad egestatem redegisset.

Iulii IV. Elocatum est tenementum in Holywell olim ye White Horse Iohanni Dickenson pro termino 40 annorum, una cum licentia alienandi, finis 20 librae.

Iulii XVI. Dimissa sunt magistro Georgio Butler firma et molendinum in Beilby quae anno superiori dimissa fuerant Gulielmo Boseville qui Georgio Butler sub chirographo suo ius suum eiuraverat, finis 0.

Atque haec omnia variis ut res ferebat, temporibus hoc anno sigillata sunt.

Anno Domini MDCXXXVI, regis Caroli XII, domini Nathanaelis Brent custodis XV. p. 324

Magistri in artibus

1. Petrus Turner
2. Thomas Gall
3. Ioannes French
4. Alexander Fisher
5. Ioannes Earles
6. Ioannes Greaves
7. Eduardus Corbet
8. Carolus Gibbs
9. Hugo Cressy
10. Ioannes Wodcocke
11. Edwardus Nevill
12. Ranulphus Domvill
13. Gulielmus Berckley
14. Richardus Nevill
15. Eduardus Hinton
16. Franciscus Cheynell
17. Ricardus Newman
18. Gulielmus Burton
19. Ioannes Maplisden
20. Nicholaus Houson
21. Franciscus Wright
22. Henricus Iacob

Baccalaurei in artibus

1. Rogerus Brent
2. Gulielmus Owen
3. Franciscus Brode
4. Georgius Clarke
5. Eduardus Allen
6. Ioannes Scriven
7. Eduardus Copley
8. Rodolphus Button
9. Ioannes Priaulx
10. Robertus Sayre
11. Christophorus Foule
12. Georgius Loveioy

Capellani

1. Ioannes Brent
2. Ioannes Reynolds

Augusti primo. Convenimus in aula hora nona antemeridiana ubi, de more resignatis clavibus officiariorum superioris anni, per dominum custodem et quinque simpliciter seniores praesentes, electi sunt in annum sequentem:
magister Fisher, vicecustos.
magister Nevill senior, magister Burton, magister Houson, decani.
magister Woodcocke, magister Maplisden, magister Wright, bursarii.
principalis portionistarum, magister Cheynell; bursarius Williot et capellanus capellae, magister Gibbs; exhibitionarius Hamsterley, magister Earles; praelectores, Graecae linguae, magister Nevill iunior, grammaticae, magister Newman; custodes cistae Reade, tres decani,; custodes cistae Bodley, magister Nevill iunior, magister Hinton, magister Cheynell.

Eodem tempore dominus custos socios graviter admonuit, ut se a verbis contumeliosis abstinerent, praesertim in variationibus, magistro vero Newman, qui in nuperis magistri Nevill variationibus in contumeliosa pleraque et indecora proruperat, peculiarem admonitionem dedit, eique ad unius mensis spatium communiis interdixit, quo tempore cavit, ne oppido exiret.

Eodem die confectus est computus cistae Bodley.

[Augusti] II. Dominus custos computavit et discessit aeque.

IV. Duae exhibitiones doctoris Bickley, olim collegii huius custodis, et dein episcopi Cicestrensis per resignationem magistri Fisher et magistri Cressy, iam vacuae, in magistrum Gibbs et magistrum Nevill seniorem, sed cum usitatis oneribus annexis, collatae sunt.

VII. Socii a domino custode in aula convocati iuramentum praestiterunt bibliothecae secundum formam pag.124 huius registri exhibitam,[1] quod ubi et ipse custos et sociorum singuli, qui aderant suscepissent, nova clavis unicuique tradita est. Decretumque ut nemo in posterum in bibliothecam admitteretur, nisi eodem prius iuramento astrictus.

XXI. Convenimus in apodyterio statim a precibus vespertinis, ubi sociis et scholaribus (omnes enim iussi sunt interesse) praelecta sunt decreta quaedam ab academiae delegatis, sancita, quibuscuiusque officium continebatur, et quomodo se gererent, dum potentissimus rex Carolus cum serenissima regina, qui prope diem expectabantur in academia moram traxerint. Ad eos vero magificentius et pro dignitate excipiendos, cum pecuniae a universis, qui locum vel ius aliquod in academia obtinerent, contribuerentur (servientibus solis exceptis) collegium nostrum viginti libras suppeditavit, idque secundum annum reditum antiquum, qui quadringentarum librarum erat, solvendo quinque libras pro quolibet centenario, quod et a reliquis collegiis praestitum est. Hac tamen summa minore reperta, alias quinque libras postea dedimus, quod ipsum et caetera collegia pro sua proportione fecerunt.

XXV. Magister French 3us bursarius computavit.

XXIX. Ad academiam accesserunt potentissimi monarchae Carolus et Maria una cum serenissimo electore palatino Carolo, eiusque fratre Ruperto, spledidissimoque heroum et heroinarum comitatu, ubi per biduum commorati summa magnificentia et alacritate excepti sunt.

Octobris X. Admissi sunt in perpetuam societatem huius domus dominus Copley, dominus Button, dominus Priaulx, dominus Sayre, dominus Foule, dominus Loveioy.

[1] Printed in *Reg. Annalium 1567–1603*, 215–16.

XI. Confectus est computus generalis, superioris anni.

XIX. Magister French 3us bursarius confecit suum aeque coram sociis in aula.

Decembris XI. Sigillata est praesentatio magistri Woodcocke ad vicariam de Elham vacantem per mortem naturalem magistri Thomae Allen. Eidem etiam dimissa est indentura decimarum eiusdem vicariae, eodem prorsus modo quo antecessori dimissa fuerat. Quaestione vero suborta an vicaria haec uberius beneficium censeri deberet, domino custodi et seniorum plerisque aequum visum est ut anno iam exacto magistro Woodcocke optio daretur, an beneficium hoc an ius ad societatem mallet. Iuniorum vero plerique utroque eum frui posse censuerunt. Iniecta etiam mentio est de iure eius ad portionistam sed subortis difficultatibus nihil hac de re constitutum est. Ipse tamen de iure suo protestatus.

Decembris XIII. Dispensatum est cum magistro Wright 1mo bursario, p. 325
ut computum suum in alteram septimanam differret.

Decembris XVII. Sacra peregimus in memoria fundatoris, dein lecta sunt statuta, et scrutinium de more initum quod in calendas Ianuarii prorogatum est.

Decembris XXII. Magister Wright 1^{mus} bursarius computavit.

Decembris XXXI. In vigilia circumcisionis celebratum est de more scrutinium, in quo servi claves suas resignaverunt, easque mox, sed de officio suo prius per vicecustodem admoniti, et si quid in posterum commiserint castigatione dignum, ad officiarios remissi denuo receperunt. In hortulanum autem electus est magister Nevill iunior.

[1637]

Ianuarii XVIII. Sociis a domino custode in aulam convocatis consensum est, ut quum libros quosdam ex dono viduae doctoris Gulson olim huius collegii socii missos haberemus, quos eosdem prorsus in bibliotheca ante habuimus, pretium hisce poneretur, et in usum bibliothecae divenderentur. Ex quibus sic divenditis confectae sunt quinque librae.

Decretum insuper ut terras nostras apud Hensington, ante viginti annos a Iohanne Whitton collegio venditas, quas dolo malo quidam Simons (a cuius patre idem Whitton easdem terras emerat) avertere satagebat, iure, licitisque modis omnibus assereremus.

Ianuarii XIX. Magister Corbet praelectionem catachistam, nuper ab honoratissimo viro domino Richardo Knightley fundatam, auspicatus est in sacello statim a precibus matutinis.

Februarii XXIII. Magister Wright 1^{mus} bursarius confecit aeque suum coram sociis in aula.

Martii II. Dati sunt ex consensu triginta solidi cuidam qui se nepotem ferebat honoratissimi viri Thomae Bodlaei huius collegii olim socii dignissimi; de qua summa sociorum unusquisque sex denarios exolvit, reliquum suppeditavit collegii aerarium.

Martii XXVII. Cum de morte doctoris Brodbent nuper in lectorem Linacri inferiorem electi nuntius allatus esset, de consensu domini custodis et septem seniorum in eodem munere ei suffectus est in proximum triennium magister Howson collegii socius, consensum etiam est ut ruinae murorum horti praesertim qua in viam regiam prospiciunt, prout res postularet, sarcirentur, cuius rei cura vicecustodi, seniori decano, bursario et hortulano demandata est.

Aprilis II. Divina fecimus in memoria fundatoris, qui dies cum in dominicum incideret scrutinium et lectio statutorum in sequentem dilata sunt; quibus de more peractis, scrutinium in quartum diem Maii prorogatum est. Quo tempore dispensatum est cum magistro Woodcock, bursario loco magistri Maplisden ut computum suum in duas septimanas differre posset.

Aprilis VIII. Convenimus in apodyterio statim a precibus vespertinis, ubi consensum est a domino custode, omnibusque qui aderant, quae longe maior erat sociorum pars, ut magistro Greaves viginti librae annuae in proximum quadriennium numerarentur si peregrinatio, quam in longinquas regiones tum meditabatur tam diu duraret. Hoc etiam praesentibus eius gratiae datum est, ut omnibus collegii emolumentis tam quoad liberaturam quam fines, tanquam praesens esset, frueretur, quam diu peregre ageret. Consensum etiam, ut huius summae pars altera, nempe quadraginta librae ei pro manibus a bursario solveretur.

Maii IV. Magister Woodcocke loco magistri Maplisden 2^{di} bursarii computavit.

Maiii XVIII. Concessa est licentia magistro Trafford ut alienare posset terras in Newington. Ei ante aliquot annos dimissas ad duodecem annos proxime sequentes.

Iunii XXX. Magister Woodcocke loco Maplisden 2^{di} bursarii confecit suum aeque, etiam magister Wright variavit in hisce quaestionibus:

An { Scholares sint ἐυλόχιδοι . Negavit contra Aristotelem 2do Rhetorice, cap. 10mo.
Magistratus debeat esse temporarius. Negavit contra Aristotelem 2do Politicorum cap. 5to.
Agricolae cives esse debeant in optime constituta republica. Affirmavit contra Aristotelem libro 7mo, Politicorum cap. 14to.

Finitis disputationibus, cum eo dispensatum est pro 2^{dis} variationibus.

Iulii VII. Magister Newman variavit in his quaestionibus:

An { Decet philosophia sic ederi ut interim non sit edita. Negavit contra Aristotelem, Epistola ad Alexandrum.
Verecundia deceat senes. Affirmavit contra Aristotelem libro 4to Ethicorum, capitulo 15to.
Melius de diis senserint poetae quam philosophi. Affirmavit contra Aristotelem et caeteros philosophos.

Quibus peractis, dispensatum cum eo est pro 2^{dis} variationibus.

Iulii XIV. Magister Wright unanimi custodis, omniumque magistrorum tum praesentium consensu electus est in praelectorem unius lecturarum Indotatarum in Academia cuius lecturae ius collegio obvenit, ratione muneris procuratorii, quod anno proxime sequente, secundum cycli procuratorii leges in nostrum collegium devolvebatur.

Iulii XX. Divina fecimus in memoriam fundatoris, post lecta sunt statuta et scrutinium initum, quod in calendas Septembris prorogatum est.

In hoc scrutinio dominus custos, fama deferente, sibi innotuisse dixit, p. 326
quosdam e magistris baccalaureorum immo et scholarium consortio liberius quam decuit, uti; nolle se tanti facinoris infamia quenquam onerare, profiteri tamen, si quos huius criminis compertos in posterum invenerit, se in delinquentes severissime vindicaturum.

Eodem tempore consensum est ut antiquum statutorum exemplar accuratissime manu exaratum, quod ante ligneatheca inclusum (sed cuius sera nescio quo male feriato nuper revulsa erat) in bibliotheca asservabatur, in posterum inter collegii munimenta in aerario asservaretur.

Praedia et tenementa hoc anno locata [*i.e. in the college year August 1636–7*]

Augusti I° [1636]. Dimissa est sentina collegio Corporis Christi pro 40 annis sine fine.

Augusti IV. Elocavimus Iohanni Dickenson domum in Holywell nuper in tenuria Eduardi Turley pro 21 annis una cum licentia alienandi, finis 20 solidi.[1]

Dimisimus tenementum in Gamlingaye cui olim insigne erat Falconis Gulielmo Charnock durante naturali vita Christophori Charnock et Hugonis Charnocke filiorum eiusdem Gulielmi, et alterius Hugonis Charnocke eorundem patruelis, finis idcirco nullus, quia eadem concessio eidem ante quadriennium facta fuit, sed nescio quibus de causis non sigillata.

Dimissum est Roberto Atkinson tenementum in Turfield pro spatio 21 anorum. Finis, 5 librae.

Augusti VII. Dimissum est Hawkins tenementum suum in Holywell pro 21 annis, finis o. Dimissa est etiam Iohanni Chandler particula quaedam terrae in Holywell ex adverso domus suae, quam particulam et antea obtinebat, sed virtute indenturae ante viginti annos factae quatuor viris nempe Meriman, Robins, Chandler, Wiblin, quibus plurimas vacivi nostri in Holywell particulas sub quibusdam condicionibus concessimus; quos iam suo iure excidisse a domino custode et sociis pronuntiatum est ob reditum collegio tempore constituto non solutum. Huic autem particulae etiam et aliam adiunximus quod per indenturam a collegio iam ante obtinebat. Utrumque autem dimisimus pro tempore 40 annorum. Finis o. Ita tamen pro priore particula in posterum sex denarios annuatim solveret, pro posteriore vero sicut ante consueverat, id est 12d.

Augusti XI. Dimisimus firmam sive manerium de Basingstoke Thomae Pearse pro 21 annis una cum licentia alienacionis, finis 40 librae, quarum prior pars solvenda ad festum Sancti Michaelis, altera, ad idem festum anno revoluto. Erat autem hic, socer firmariis nostri Gulielmi Temple, firmamque ab eodem leguleio cuidam oppignoratam redemerat, eoque aequum visum est ut ei firma dimitteretur, sed cautione centum librarum prius data ut collegio de arreragiis Temple et damnis ab eodem sylvis nostris illatis, satisfaceret.

[1] *Margin*, 'Consensum erat ut fines Dickenson et Atkinson partim inter socios dividerentur, partim in pios usus reservarentur'.

Dimissum est Thomas Clarke tenementum suum in Holywell pro 40 annis, finis 6 li. 13s. 4d. Dimissum est etiam Iohanni Hawkes tenementum in Holywell quod antea erat Isaaci Weekes pro 40 annis, una cum licentia alienandi, finis 40 solidi.

Martii XXVII. Indentura terrarum quarundem in Hensington ante biennium magistro Fisher dimissa, iam elocata est magistro Woode pro termino viginti et unius annorum, finis o. Quae omnia suis temporibus sigillata sunt.

Anno Domini MDCXXXVII, regis Caroli XIII, domini Nathanielis Brent custodis XVI. p. 327

Magistri in artibus

1. Petrus Turner, D. Med.
2. Thomas Gall
3. Ioannes French
4. Alexander Fisher
5. Ioannes Earles
6. Ioannes Greaves
7. Eduardus Corbet
8. Carolus Gibbs
9. Hugo Cressy
10. Ioannes Woodcocke
11. Eduardus Nevill
12. Ranulphus Domvill
13. Gulielmus Berkley
14. Richardus Nevill
15. Eduardus Hinton
16. Franciscus Cheynell
17. Richardus Newman
18. Gulielmus Burton
19. Nicholas Howson
20. Franciscus Wright
21. Henricus Iacob

In artibus baccalaurei

1. Rogerus Brent
2. Gulielmus Owen
3. Franciscus Broade
4. Georgius Clarke
5. Eduardus Allen
6. Ioannes Scriven
7. Eduardus Copley
8. Rodolphus Button
9. Ioannes Priaulx
10. Robertus Saire
11. Christophorus Fowle
12. Georgius Loveioy

Capellani

1. Ioannes Brent
2. Ioannes Reynolds

Augusti I^{o}. Convenimus pro more in aula, hora nona antemeridiana, ubi resignatis clavibus officiariorum anni superioris per dominum custodem et quinque simpliciter seniores praesentes, electi sunt in annum sequentem:
vicecustos, magister Fisher.
decani, magister Corbet, magister Nevill senior, magister Hinton.

bursarii, magister Gibbs, magister Newman, magister Burton. principalis portionistarum, magister Nevill iunior; bursarius Williot, magister French; exhibitionarius Hamsterley, magister Earles; praelector grammaticae,magister Wright; praelector Graecae linguae, magister Howson; custodes cistae Reade, tres decani; custodes cistae Bodley, magister Nevill iunior, magister Howson, magister Wright; bursarius itinerans, magister Gibbs.

Eodem tempore decretum est ut sylvae apud Newington et Basingstoke divenderentur, cuius rei cura demandata est vicecustodi et magistro French.

Eodem etiam die confectus est computus cistae Bodley.

Augusti II. Dominus custos computavit et discessit aeque.

Augusti XXIII. Magister Woodcocke 3us bursarius computare incoepit.

Septembris XV. Dominus custos a progressu reversus, socios in aulam convocavit ubi adorationem versus orientem, tam in ingressu quam egressa chori, tanquam decentem, antiquum et nunc etiam usu receptum morem, obnixe commendavit, pluribusque verbis, exemplo etiam suo proposito ut consuetudinem hanc universi in posterum observarent, hortatus est.

In mandatis etiam dedit, ut si qui pecunias collegii detinerent vel quicquam collegio deberent, ante proximum bursarii praesentis computum, omnia exolverent, poena suspensionis a communiis in secus facientes proposita.

Eodem tempore consensum est ut vicecustos una cum magistro French Londinum proficiscerentur ad collegii negotia proximo termino procuranda, atque ut curiam haberent apud manerium nostrum de Farleigh, ubi contumacia cuiusdam Dod, necessario revincenda videbatur. Consensum etiam est ut sumptum qui necessario fiebant in lite nostra cum domino Thoma Holt equite aurato, circa rectoriam de Lapworth, dimidiam partem collegium in posterum suppeditaret, alteram magister Doughtie ecclesiae illius rector.

Cum vero dominus custos inaudisset solenne esse bursariis, et principali portionistarum veteres pistores amovere, novosque pro arbitratu suo surrogare, rem hanc et collegio damnosam, et receptae domus consuetudini, atque adeo decretis adversum existimans, ex usu futurum censuit, si cerevisiarius, tum pistores de communi consensu designarentur, quos vel reiicere, nisi officio suo defuissent, vel novos adsciscere bursariis et principali fas non esset. Rem hanc quinque senioribus 1mo die Augusti ante officiariorum electionem communicaverat, quibus omnibus aequissima visa est, et designati sunt in cerevisiarium magister Hanns, in pistores, Whisler, Moore, Philips, sed officiariis iam electis et renunciatis, quum de pistoribus reclamarent iunior bursarius et principalis, hoc tempore negotium retractari placuit. Consensumque est a domino custode sociisque universis qui praesentes aderant, (tribus solummodo refragantibus) ut in posterum hi tres soli, quod ad pinsendi officium domui subservirent, idque aequali iure, et pari emolumento. Quum autem decretum illud, quod supra pag. 217 extat,[1] allegatum esset. De non admittendo pistore vel braseatore, nisi qui frumentum moleret apud molendina nostra de Holywell.

Dominus custos declaravit decretum hoc, si eo nomine censeri deberet, p. 328
temporarium fuisse, et sublata causa ob quam constitutum erat, ante annos complures inductum, non amplius obligare. Eodem etiam die computus magistri Woodcocke 3^{i} bursarii, ad exitum perductus est, qui ob quasdam difficultates hactenus dilatus erat. Cum eo vero tunc absente dispensatum est per dominum custodem et septem seniores, ut summam decreto praescriptam nempe viginti libras excedere posset, decreto non obstante. Etiam cum eodem dispensatum est, ut aeque suum conficeret, post octo septimanas numerandum non a die quo incoepit computare sed a die praesente magister Woodcocke aeque suum confecit in aula coram sociis.

Decembris 17 et 18. Habita est commemoratio fundatoris, quum ante dies ii in dominicum incideret, die sequente lecta sunt statuta et scrutinium initum, quod ad calendas Ianuarii prorogatum est. Quo tempore magister Woodcocke, quum annus a praesentatione sua sigillata ad vicariam de Elham iam exiisset, petitionem suam manu reverendissimi archiepiscopi Cantuariensis signatam in medium protulit, in qua patronus noster longe honoratissimus mandavit ut in alterum annum magister Woodcocke iure suo ad societatem frueretur.

Decembris XIX. Computus generalis superioris anni confectus est.

Decembris XX. Magister Burton 1^{mus} bursarius computavit.

Decembris XXXI. Habitum est de more scrutinium in quo tribus illis solennibus a bursario propositis, 1, de moribus servientium, 2, de numero portionistarum, 3, de electione hortulani; in hortulanum

[1] Printed above, p. 000

electus est magister Hinton; consensum est ut numerus portionistarum idem sit qui prius; cum autem, quaedam in coquum iuniorem et ianitorem allegata essent, eorum castigatio officiariis domus commissa est, ut in eos pro delictorum gravitate animadverterent.

[1638]

Ianuarii XXVII. Sociis in apodyterio convocatis statim a precibus vespertinis, lectisque ibi litteris domini custodis consensum est ut terraria et rentalia, si quae essent, quae ad maneria nostra de Canes et Norton Mandevill spectarent, Londinum mitterentur, quo melius regiis consiliariis, qui loca haec foresta de Waltham comprehendi asserebant satisfaceret, et causa nostra meliorem exitum sortiretur.

Februarii XIIII. Designatus[1] est magister Corbet procurator Academiae consentientibus suffragiis omnium magistrorum in collegio tunc temporis commorantium, cum dominus custos consensum suum ante per literas significasset.

Eodem die sigillata est praesentatio magistri Nevill senioris ad rectoriam de Farleigh tum vacantem per mortem naturalem magistri Slater ultimi incumbentis.

Februarii XV. Magister Burton 1^{mus} bursarius aeque suum confecit.

Februarii XXV. Sociis in apodyterio congregatis post preces vespertinas lecta est resignatio magistri Earles medietatis rectoriae de Gamlingay, qua a sociis intellecta, et interveniente consensu domini custodis per literas significato, universi consenserunt ut magister Gibbs ad eandem rectoriam praesentaretur.

Cum vero in negotio illo de Canes et Norton Mandevill reverendissimus in Christo pater archiepiscopus Cantuariensis patronus noster honoratisimus, adeo se propitium collegio exhibuerit, ut quicquid pecuniae, compositionis iure, vel nomine poenae firmariis nostris irrogatum erat, quod ad quinquaginta et sex libras excrevit, a munificentissimo rege remitti impetraret, aequissimum visum est ut literae, quae gratitudinem nostram prolixe deferrent collegii nomine ad eum mitterentur quarum scribendarum onus magister Wright rogatus libens suscepit.

Martii IV. Sigillata est litera, quam vocant atturnatus, vicecustodi et magistro Gibbs ut iniunctionem in causa nostra de Hensington contra

[1] 'Electus' deleted.

Simons, qui fundum nostrum vi, vel saltem dolo, lite adhuc pendente occupaverat, executioni demandarent.

Martii XVII. Habita sunt sacra in memoriam fundatoris, post lecta sunt statuta et scrutinium initum quod in calendas Maias prorogatum est. Eodem die hanc quae sequitur citationem a reverendissimo archiepiscopo Cantuariensi patrono nostro longe honoratissimo accepimus.

Guilielmus[1] providentia divina Cantuariensis archiepiscopus totius Angliae primas et metropolitanus, dilectis nobis in Christo vicecustodi, seniori socio, et reliquis sociis et caeteris scholaribus, officiariis ac ministris collegii nostri de Merton in Oxon nostrarum patronatus, fundationis[2] et iurisdictionis immediatae, salutem, gratiam et benedictionem. Pastoris sollicita providentia curae sibi traditae sic debet operam impendens ut vitam et mores suae curae commissari[os] notos et perspectos habere valent atque solerti studio prospiciens ut bona piorum locorum quae ad certum destinatumque usum largitione piorum et fidelium hominum fuerunt destinata, ad illu[m] collegium tam in capite quam in membris ad omnipotentis Dei honorem et animarum degentium in eodem salutem dictique collegii utilitatem propediens visitare defectusque quoscunque inibi reperiendos correctione et reformatione dignos (Deo duce) reformare. Ipsumque collegium nostrum in statum decentem reducere magnopere cupientes. Vos mones et singulos dicti coll[egii] nostri socios, scholares et ministros tenere praesentium peremptorie citamus et citari [iubemus] quatenus compareatis et quilibet vestrum per se divisim compareat coram nobis [commissariisve] nostris in hac parte legitime constitutis eorumve uno vel pluribus quocunque vel q[uibuscunque in] ecclesia vestra infra collegium dictum stituata die Iovis vicesimo non videlicet di[e antepenultimo] Martii inter horas nonam et duodecimam ante meridiem eiusdem diei cum commissariis sine / prorogatione p. 329
dierum et horarum ex tunc sequente prout convenit, visitationis nostrae debitum officium humiliter subituros, ulteriusque facturos, recepturos, visuros et audituros quod iustum fuerit in hac parte ac dictae visitationis nostrae natura et qualitas de se exigunt et requirunt. Inhibentes tenore praesentium vobis vicecustodi et sociis et caeteris ministris omnibus et singulis collegii nostri praedicti ne vos aut vestrum aliquis quicquam in huiusmodi nostrae visitationis praeiudicium attemptetis vel attemptet vestrum aliquis faciatisve aut faciant quovis quaesito colore vel ingenio sub poena contemptus. De die vero

[1] In a different hand.

[2] *Margin*, 'quo sensu' [*underlined*].

receptionis praesentium executionis vestrae necnon quid in praemissis feceritis nos aut praedictos commissarios nostros (ut praemittitur) constitutos eorumve aliquem dictis die horis et loco, per literas vestras patentes harum seriem una cum citatorum nominibus et cognominibus in se continentur sigillo vestro communi munitas certiorem facere curetis. In cuius rei testimonium sigillum nostrum praesentibus apponi fecimus. Datum in manerio nostro de Lambeth 13° die mensis Martii anno domini (iuxta computacionem ecclesiae Anglicanae) 1637° et translationis nostrae 5to.

Martii XVIII.[1] Citatio haec valvis ecclesiae, qua austrum spectant, affixa est, quo facto quum dies is dominicus esset, statim a vespertinis precibus socii in apodyterio convenerunt, ubi literae domini custodis lectae sunt, iisque praeuntibus, consensum est ut commissarii, quoscunque huic muneri praeesse patrono nostro honoratissimo placeret, tam pro sua, quam mittentis dignitate, honorifice collegii sumptibus exciperentur.

Martii XXVIII.[2] Sigillatum est certificatorium ad literas illas citatorias, cuius tenor sequitur, Reverendissime in Christo patri ac domino domino Guilielmo providentia divina Cantuariensi archiepiscopo totius Angliae primati et metropolitano et collegii de Merton patrono, aut commissariis vestris legitime constitutis uni vel pluribus sive eorum alicui vestri humiles et devoti Alexander Fisher, vicecustos, socii, scholares, officiarii et ministri collegii vestri de Merton in universitate Oxon' omnimodam reverentiam debitam et condignam, cum honore literas vestras citatorias praesentibus annexas, datas in manerio vestro de Lambeth 13° die mensis Martii anno domini (iuxta computationem ecclesiae Anglicanae) 1637°, tum ea quae decuit reverentia recepimus die Saturni videlicet 17° die Martii anno domini praedicto. Post quarum receptionem ea quae decuit reverentia die dominico immediate sequenti inter horas tertiam et quartam post meridiem eiusdem diei ostio exteriori ecclesiae collegii nostri sito et situato intra collegium praedictum eisdem affiximus ad effectum monendi et citandi peremptorie omnes et singulos socios, scholares officiarios et ministros collegii praedicti, quorum nomina et cognomina in schedula et praesentibus annexa, contenta et specificata sunt, ut compareant, et quilibet eorum compareat coram vobis vestrisve commissariis die loco in eodem mandato expressis, visitationem vestram humiliter subituri, et ulterius facturi, recepturi, visuri, et

[1] Return to first hand. [2] Return to second hand.

audituri quod iusta fuerit in ea parte ac dictae visitationis natura et qualitas exigunt et requirunt. In quorum omnium maiorem fidem et plenius testimonium sigillum nostrum commune praesentibus apponi fecimus. Datum in domo nostra capitulari 28° die mensis Martii anno domini 1638°

Martii XXIX.[1] Ad collegium accesserunt, visitationis ergo, commissarii reverendissimi patroni nostri videlicet doctor Bayly, praeses collegii divi Iohannis Baptistae et vicecancellarius Oxoniensis, reverendus in Christo pater et dominus dominus Iohannes episcopus Oxoniensis, Iohannes Lambe, miles, decanus Almae curiae Cantuariensis de Arcubus, London'.

Doctor Sheldon, custos collegii Omnium Animarum; et doctor Duck, cancellarius Londoniensis, quibus collegium ingressis in ipsis foribus elegantem orationem habuit magister Wright, deinde in ecclesia eruditam concionem Latinam magister Corbet, procurator designatus. His peractis tradita est per vicecustodem in commissariorum manus citatio supradicta, una cum certificatorio, cui annexa erat schedula nomina et cognomina complectens, omnium sociorum, capellanorum, portionistarum, clericorum, et ministrorum quibus ordine recitatis, lecta est commissio, quae authoritatem dictorum commissariorum testatum faciebat. Deinde articuli 30 numero ad disciplinam et oeconomiam domus spectantes propositi sunt, et unusquisque iuramento adactus ad hisce omnibus fideliter respondendum; id quod factum est ab unoquoque, responsione singulorum scripta comprehensa. Cum autem per dies aliquot moram in collegio traxissent et quaedam confestim reformassent, aliis ad reverendissimi patroni cognitionem reservatis iam discessuri commissarii reverendi dignissimique iniunctiones quasdam in posterum observandas proposuerunt, quas scripto comprehensas se mox ad collegium missuros receperunt. p. 330
magistrum vero Newman ob contumelias illas magistro Nevill illatas (de quibus mentio fit anno superiore) communiis ceterisque omnibus domus emolumentis interdixerent, per unius anni spatium, quo tempore eum illius suffragii vel actius vel passius incapacem declaraverunt, donec aliter reverendissimo nostro patrono visum fuerit. Atque his rite dispositis, et visitatione ad quartum diem Octobris prorogata discesserunt.

Aprilis XIX. Magister Newman 2^{dus} bursarius computavit.

[1] Back to first hand.

Aprilis XXI. Sigillata est praesentatio magistri Gibbs ad medietatem rectoriae de Gamlingay.

Aprilis XXVII. Sociis in aulam convocatis literae domini custodis lectae sunt quibus aequum esse censebat, ut cum magister Gardiner, firmarius noster de Thorncroft, reditum collegio debitum iam per duos annos quamvis saepe interpellatus solvere omisisset, manerium illud alteri dimitteretur, consensum ergo est ut magistro Holloway iurisconsulto nova indentura, sed fiduciaria fieret, et littera atturnatus Ioanni Hopkins et Christophoro More, ut eosdem collegii nomine in manerii illius possessionem immitterent. Die autem 2do Maii utraque instrumenta sigillata sunt.

Iunii II. Litteras a reverendissimo archiepiscopo Cantuariensi patrono nostro longe honoratissimo recepimus in hanc verba. Earum inscriptio erat,

To my very lovinge freinde, magister Fisher, subwarden
of Merton College or in his absence to ye senior fellowe there.
Salus in Christo

After my hearty commendacions etc. these are to lett you knowe, that I have nowe called my visitors together and taken into consideration all those things which were complayned of in my late visitation of Merton College, whomsoever they did concerne, exceptinge those things which my visitors ordered upon ye place; and shall hereafter (God willinge) at my first leasure thinke upon such injunctions, as shall be fitt for ye future government and better discipline of that college. But in ye meane time I do hereby require you, that you yeild full and constant obedience to all such orders and iniunctions, as were given by my visitors by worde of mouth, or otherwise at ye time of ye visitation. And because I cannot judge of ye things presented, till I see how they will rise, and be made good by proofe these are to lett you knowe that I have putt of ye full hearinge of this businesse till ye seconde of October next followinge, that so every man, as far forth as he is concernede, may have time to produce his witnesses for ye clearinge of himselfe, or ye makinge good his complaynt against any other. And at that same time (God willinge) I shall not fayle to be at Lambeth, and give hearinge to ye whole businesse and thereupon do, as to justice shall appertayne. And now havinge given you this large and ample warninge, if any that is concearnde shall fayle to make his iust defence in those things which come then to hearinge, and which he shall have notice of, lett him blame himself, for I shall then, God willinge, certaynly proceede, or give further day, as I shall finde cause. And if any parson be concerned in his owne particular, he must attend ye hearinge for himselfe. But for those complaynts which are made concerning ye discipline or thrift of ye house in generall I think it fitt that some two or three fellowes, which are best acquaynted with ye businesse, and ablest to produce ye witnesses, do attende that service in ye name of ye rest. This is all which at present I have to trouble you with, savinge that hereby I do require both warden and fellows, so far forth as they are concernde, to attende at ye time and place abovementioned. Of which presuminge none of you will fayle, I leave you all to God's blessed protection and rest.

Your lovinge freinde and visitor W. Cant.
Lambeth, May 24 1638

I require that these my letters be publickly reade before all ye fellowes that are at home; and after that putt into your Register-booke and so kept.

Iunii III. Has literas doctor Turner (vicecustode tunc absente) sociis statim a precibus matutinis in apodyterium convocatis palam recitavit. Qui quum ad socios retulisset quosnam ad prosequendas querelas de disciplina et oeconomia collegii deputare vellent. Eorum multa maxima pars in magistros Nevill iuniorem, Burton et Howson consenserunt.

Iunii XIIII. Magister Newman 2^{dus} bursarius aeque suum confecit.

Iunii XXI. Alterae litterae a reverendissimo patrono nostro allatae sunt. Quorum inscriptio erat,

To my lovinge freinde, magister Fisher, subwarden of
Merton Coll. or in his absence to ye senior fellowe at home.

Salus in Christo. p. 331

After my hearty commendacions etc. I sent you a letter not longe since in which I gave you notice of ye time which I had prefixde for a full hearinge of all such things, as have beene complaynde of in my late visitation, of that your college, and not allready ordered by my visitors, while they were upon ye place, yet there are some things which must be thought on, before that time; and to give you notice of them is ye occasion of these present letters; first then I am informde that your generall auditt for accounts and choise of newe officers is usually held at ye beginninge of August, these are therefore to require you that so soone as you have finishde your accounts, I may see both ye forme of them by a copy written out, and sent me, and in what state ye college at present is, secondly I do require you, that at your next audit, and so in all times to come, you observe ye course of your statute, for ye manner of ye election of all your officers, and particularly that you do this yeare, and all other years followinge, make choise of a newe subwarden, who shall never beare that office above once in five yeares at ye least. For I finde already that ye continuance of one man in that office (though yearly chosen for fashion) hath beene very praeiudiciall to ye college both in thrift and government. Thirdly I do likewise require you, that since ye brevity of your statutes hath caused you to make many decrees, that there be a copy of them all written out, both that I may view them to ly by me as visitor, and that I may consider of them for my better direction in such injunctions, as I purpose (God willinge) to sende down to ye college. And whereas your statute-booke, and these decrees are kept up so privately that ye fellowes which are to be governde by them, canot take such views of them as is fitt, that thereby they may know how to regulate theire obedience. I do hereby in ye last place require you, that a copie of your statutes and of all such decrees, as you stande bounde unto, be placed openly in your library, that ye fellowes may have accesse to them, as they have cause, and therein reade their duty, if they doubt. And that ye things herein required be performde. I shall not only expect, but call for an account of all and every of you. In ye meane time I leave you to God's blessed protection, and rest.

Your very lovinge freinde and visitor W. Cant.
Lambeth, June 20 1638

I require that these my letters be publickly reade before all ye fellowes that are at home, and after that put into your register-booke and so kept. Atque hae literae postridie a doctore Turner (vicecustos enim domo aberat) sociis in aulam convocatis praelectae sunt.

Iulii VII. Magister Burton variavit in his quaestionibus [*blank*]. Finitis disputationibus, cum eo dispensatum est pro 2^{dis} variationibus.

Iulii XX. Divina fecimus in memoriam fundatoris, post lecta sunt statuta, et scrutinium initum, quod in calendas Septembris prorogatum est.

Quo die, liber statutorum qui anno superiori inter collegii munimenta in aerario repositus erat, inde desumptus est. Consensumque est, ut in libri calce, quotquot inveniri poterant, decreta collegii inscriberentur, utque in bibliotheca collocatus in posterum publici iuris fieret, iuxta reverendissimi patroni mandatum.

Praedia et tenementa hoc anno locata [i.e. in the college year August 1637–8]
Augusti Iº. Dimissae sunt Richardo Burdet terrae in Kibworth, vocatae The Swaythes pro termino viginti et unius annorum. Finis 5 librae. Elocatum est tenementum XXXII in Holywell viduae Moore pro spatio 40 annorum. Finis 0. Concessa etiam eidem licentia alienandi. Elocatum etiam est magistro Richardo Atwoode tenementum in Holywell pro 40 annis una cum licentia alienandi. Finis 20 solidi inter pauperes ut res ferebat dividendi.

Augusti Iº. Dimisimus manerium nostrum de Cuxham Edmundo p. 332
Gregory pro spatio 21 annorum inchoandorum a festo Sancti Michaelis proxime sequenti. Finis 66 li. 13s. 4d., cuius altera pars ad sigillationem indenturae solveretur, altera in festo annunciationis proxime sequenti.

Augusti IIº. Dimissa est medietas rectoriae de Gamlingay magistro Thomae Claveringe pro 21 annis inchoandis a festo Sancti Michaelis proxime sequenti. Finis 30 librae.

Augusti XXIII. Concessum est Gulielmo Wiblin, ut alienare posset domum suam in Holywell.

Septembris XV. Dimissa est Gulielmo Hardinge coquo domus in Holywell pro 40 annis. Finis 3 librae. Atque eidem concessa etiam est licentia alienandi eandem domum.

Februarii XIX [1638]. Domus XXXIII in Holywell quae ante sesquiannum dimissa erat Partridge, iam dimissa est Mariae Olive, filiae Richardi Olive qui eam a Partridge redemerat pro termino 40 annorum. Finis 0. Sub hac tamen condictione, ut nisi intra septennium proximum, reliqua quae nondum exstructa erant aedificari curaret, haec concessio irrita esset. Eidem etiam concessa est licentia alienandi. Atque haec omnia suis temporibus sigillata sunt.

Anno Domini MDCXXXVIII, regis Caroli XIIII, domini Nathanielis p. 333
Brent custodis XVI.[1]

Magistri in artibus
1. Petrus Turner, D.Med.
2. Thomas Gall
3. Ioannes French
4. Alexander Fisher
5. Ioannes Earles
6. Ioannes Greaves
7. Eduardus Corbet
8. Carolus Gibbes
9. Hugo Cressey
10. Ioannes Woodcock
11. Eduardus Nevill
12. Ranulphus Domvill

[1] In the hand of subwarden Gibbes?

13. Gulielmus Berkley
14. Richardus Nevill
15. Eduardus Hinton
16. Franciscus Cheynell
17. Richardus Newman
18. Gulielmus Burton
19. Nicolas Howson
20. Franciscus Wright
21. Henricus Iacob

In artibus baccalaurei

1. Roger Brent
2. Gulielmus Owen
3. Franciscus Broad
4. Georgius Clarke
5. Eduardus Allen
6. Ioannes Scriven
7. Eduardus Copley
8. Rodolphus Button
9. Ioannes Priaulx
10. Robertus Sayre
11. Christophorus Fowle
12. Georgius Loveioy

Capellani

1. Ioannes Brent
2. Ioannes Reynolds

August 1°. Convenimus pro more in aula hora nona antemeridiana, ubi resignatis clavibus officiariorum anni superioris, per dominum custodem et quinque simpliciter seniores praesentes, electi sunt in annum sequentem,
vicecustos, magister Gibbes,
decani, magister French, magister Howson, magister Wright.
bursarii, magister Fisher, magister Nevill senior, magister Hinton.
principalis portionistarum, magister Corbet; bursarius Williot, magister Cheynel; capellanus capellae, magister Iacob; exhibitionarius Hamsterley, magister Earles; praelectores, linguae Graecae, magister Iacob, grammaticae [*blank*]; custodes cistae Read, tres decani; custodes cistae Bodley, magister Corbet, magister Gibbes, magister Cheynel.

Augusti 1°. Eodem tempore consensum est ut decreta collegii a vicecustode superioris anni collecta ad reverendissimum patronum nostrum mitterentur. Consensum etiam est ut magistro Domvill in transmarinas partes profecturo sexaginta librae concederentur in triennium proximum; de qua summa statim viginti libras reciperet hac conditione adiecta ut has viginti libras magister Gibbes collegio renumeraret, modo magister Domwill vere non peregrineretur. Datae sunt 8 arbores magistro Gibbes arbitrio suo eligendae ad reparandam domum suam apud Gamlingay cuius ecclesiae rector ille erat.

Augusti 6. Dominus custos computavit, et discessit aeque.

Augusti 23. Computavit magister Gibbes tertius bursarius, aeque suum confecit.

Septembris 20. Magister Gibbes 3[ius] bursarius aeque suum confecit.

Septembris 21. Consensum est per dominum custodem et socios in hospitio convenientes ut mortuamanus ante aliquot annos collegio a serenissimo rege Carolo concessa dimittatur et in cista iocalium asservaretur; atque ut libri quibus maneria collegii describuntur in aerario reponerentur.

Magister Howson et magister Iacob hoc anno variari tenerentur. Decretum etiam est ut novi asseres ad stabula reparanda parerentur.

Octobris 12. Convenientibus in altam aulam sociis hora nona matutina, doctor Turner in absentia vicecustodis senior socius significavit ipsis, placerit reverendissimo patrono nostro ut in munus magistri French senioris decani alius subrogetur, resignatis igitur a magistro French officii sui insignibus. Registro scilicet decani, et clavi cistae iocalium reliquisque sociis praeter 5 seniores ad tempus secedere iussis, communibus omnium suffragiis magister Burton electus est in seniorem decanum, prius / autem dominus custos in eam se consentire p. 334
declaraverat, quem tres e senioribus concordibus votis designarent. Post preces vespertinas, convenientibus in apodyterio sociis, doctor Turner (in absentia vicecustodis) de mandato reverendissimi patroni in literis ad se privatim datis, edicta quaedam sive ordinationes ipsius patroni publicavit, singulosque quorum interesset iussu ipsius monuit, ut hisce edictis conformes et morigeros se praestarent, interim dum iniunctiones (post haec mittendae) adomantur.

1. The warden, fellowes and schollars to be in their surplices and hoods on sundayes, and holy dayes and the vigills. And on all other dayes the masters under two yeares standinge, bachelours and schollers to be in the morninge at prayers from the beginninge to the end. And to demeane themselves reverently in time of divine service, and at the entrance and departure out of the chappell. And the principall and commoners of Alban Hall to come into the quire in surplisses and hoods.

2. Divinity disputationes to be held once every weeke in terme, the subwarden to be moderator, or in his absence one of the senior masters to be procured by him. The stipend to be 10 librae per annum, every master after two yeares standinge to answere and oppose in his turne.

3. A new subwarden to be yearly chosen.

4. Noe fellowe or scholler to lye out of the college within the university and the gates to be shutt at nyne, and the keyes brought up within half an hower at the farthest.
5. Noe fellowe or scholler to dyne out of the hall. The subwarden in the warden's absence to take his meales in the hall of the allowance of the warden, and a chapter to be read in the midst of dinner out of the gospells in Latine by one of the schollers to be appointed by the senior deane.
6. Masters of arts not to converse with bachelors or schollers within the university, excepting in the hall and chappell of the colledge.
7. The fellowes and schollers to speak latine within ye colledge at all times exceptinge publick meetings for the colledge affaires.
8. Noe fellow to be absent from the colledge above 3 months in ye yeare, without cause allowed by the warden or subwarden and five seniors. And in these 3 months none to go out of the towne without leave of the warden or subwarden. and none duringe absence to have any profitt of the college but such as have leave to travell. And a booke to be kept to register the tyme of any going out of towne.[1]
9. No leases to be lett but within a fortnight after Our Lady Day and a fortnight after Lammas. And each tennent shall at least one daye before the proposition of renewinge his lease repaire to every fellow then in the college and make knowne his desire to have his lease renew'd. All leases to be brought to 21 yeares, and halfe the money of leases to goe to the college.
10. Noe election of fellows to be made above the number of five or under three in one yeare.
11. All arrerages to ye college are to be satisfyed before All-Hallows tyde next, and a schedule of them to be sent to my Lord's Grace.
12. Fellowes presented by the college to benefices shall have their places in the coll' within the yeare. Only the fellows that stand presented shall have power before Our Lady-Day next to leave the benefices, but after that they are precluded, and shall not permute or exchange but freely leave them. And a fellow instituted into a benefice of the presentation of any other patron to the value of 8 librae per annum and any secular preferment or yearly pension to the valew of 10 librae per annum, if he hold them for one yeare looseth his place.
p. 335 13. Mr Knyghtylye's lecture to be read in Latine.
14. Three books of statutes, one with the warden, one with the

[1] Cf. Merton Coll. Mun. 2.22, Book of Leaves of Absence (1738–60).

subwarden and one to be chayned to the library for the use of the fellowes.

15. The parishioners comminge to the chappell are to have a distinct day for their communions.

16. The chaplens are to follow the rubricks of the Booke of Common Prayre for Gloria Patri, the hymmes etc.

17. Noe masters of arts to proceede next yeare nor till my Lord's Grace give allowance.

18. All wood sales to be registered in a booke of accounts for that purpose and the receipts, deductions and disbursments to be registered.

19. All the college evidences to be putt into the college treasury and to be ordered into severall boxes. And none to be taken out for the college, but after subscription of him that shall take any out, in a booke to be kept for that purpose.

20. The weekly accompts to be made on fridy, betweene one and five in the afternoone. Each bursar to make his accompt within a month after his third part of the yeare and to make his aeque within two months after that. And the generall accompts to be made betweene the first and seventh of November, 'sub poena expulsionis' to any faylinge, and to any absent that is bound to be there.

21. The moneyes of Bodlye's and Reade's chest to be made up by those that lent them, if they be livinge; if they be dead by the warden and fellowes.

22. The colledge not to be at charge of furnishinge above two roomes in London for the use of the warden or fellowes.

23. Mr Iacob is to chuse his owne author, and to sett up his bill the day before his lecture.

24. The fellowes to sitt on one side of the tables in the hall, and none to be called to any other table, but such as may be by statute or custome and the chaplens to sitt at a table alone.

25. The statutes to be read 3 times in the yeare accordinge to statute and use.

26. The fellowes to go in habitu clericali, noe colours, bootes, cuff linkes, large bands etc.

27. No doble beare or ale to be in the colledge.

28. The postmasters not to pay for their commons frydayes or saturdays.

29. The postmasters to be chosen fellowes before others 'caeteris paribus'.

30. Noe money to be taken for a postmaster's place, 'sub poena expulsionis' where noe penalty is here imposed, the penalty to be arbitrary and to be imposed by the warden and in his absence the subwarden, and in his absence his lieuetenent or the senior master and this only to continue untill the iniunctions shall be sent under seale.

Mr Newman never to beare office but may be lecturer or preacher.

A new deane to be chosen for mr French.

Mr Nevill senior put a fortnight out of commons 'cum monicione'.

Mr Burton put out of commons a month. Mr Gibbes put out of commons a month.

Lambeth October 19th 1638. W. Cant.

Hisce edictis addita sunt postmodo alia quaedam edicta ex speciali iussu reverendissimi patroni expresso per literas datas ad doctorem Turner et in praesentia sociorum publicatas ix^{bris} 4to et 18, X^{bris} 2° et 9°.

1. That henceforth none of the postmasters of Williot's foundation be chosen or nominated, but according to their founder's ordination,
p. 336 namely by the warden, the principall and the three simply seniors, which shall be present at the colledge at the time of the election.

2. Divinity disputations are to begin from the senior masters and so to descend to the juniors till the course be gone round, and then to begin againe at the seniors, and so 'in orbem'.

3. Such of the fellowes as live constantly abroade as domestique servants to any nobleman or bishop, and so cannot attend the constant and continued exercise of the colledge shall not be tyed to come home 'toties quoties' as they may have a turne for disputations, but yet notwithstandinge when any business of the colledge of their owne shall call them home they shall then take the next turne whose ever it be, and then the turne to goe on againe.

4. If any man be absent upon private occasions, when it shall fall to his turne to come into Divinity Disputations the next to him shall take the turne, with this proviso that whosoever shall be absent one or more turnes when he returnes to the colledge, he shall supply as many turnes as in his absence he hath missed; which if he refuse or neglect to doe, he shall forfeit to the use of the library for every turne in answeringe omitted 10s., for every turne in opposinge 6s. 8d., this mulct to be exacted by the subwarden or in his absence the senior fellowe, and by him to be applyed to the use of the library.

5. Noe election to be made of fellowes, officers or postmasters or leases

let during his Grace's Visitation, without his Grace's consent to it first had and obtayned.

Decembris 17. Habita est commemoratio fundatoris, lecta statuta, initumque de more scrutinium, dominus custos significavit detrita iam linea suppelectile in hospitio suo, se mappas, et mensalia Londoni coemisse in usum hospitii viliori ut putabat pretio, quam quo isthic comparari potuissent, cuius rei arbitrium penes bursarium esse volebat.

Eodem etiam tempore ad socios retulit de expensis magistri Doughty in lite circa decimas de Lapworth, cumque ex priori decreto haec expensae inter collegium et magistrum Doughty ex aequo partiendae forent, ipsarum examen, vicecustodi, seniori decano, seniori bursario et principali portionistarum permittendum censuit, qui cum ipsas sub examen revocassent, in hoc tandem convenerunt ut expensis omnibus tum prioribus tum praesentibus in unam summam redactis de semisse summae decideretur quod iamdudum solverat collegium, quod reliquum foret magistro Doughty numeraretur.

Decembris 19, 20, 21. Inchoatus est computus magistri Hinton Imi bursarii et sequenti die continuatus, sed non consummatus propter varia intervenientia impedimenta ante diem huius mensis 21um.

Decembris 31. Habitum est de more scrutinium in quo tribus illis solennibus a bursario propositis, 1, de moribus servientium, 2, de numero portionistarum, 3, de electione hortulani; in hortulanum electus est magister Newman, consensum est ut numerus portionistarum idem est qui prius.

[1639]

Ianuarii 11. Convenimus in hospitio ubi dominus custos literas hasce a reverendo patrono sibi missas sociis communicavit.

According to statute and the ancient practise of the colledge there shall be made a cista oeconomiae to be placed in the chequer under the subwardens custodye with two keyes to it one to be kept by the bursar the other by the senior fellowe. In this chest all rents and receiptes of the college are to be putt untill they amount to a summe of 100 librae or more, fitt to be carryed up to the treasury for the safer custody of it. None of these rents or other receipts to be received by the bursar (under paine of losinge his office) but 'sub testimonio vicecustodis' as the statutes require.

W. Cant. Lambeth, Ianuarii 3 1638/9

p. 337 Eodem tempore unanimi consensu decretum est ut in posterum magister Carpenter in locum magistri Hannes qui cerevitiarii munere defungi desierat substitueretur.[1]

Februarii 11°, de consensu reverendissimi patroni per literas datas (Februarii 1° ac rursus Februarii 7°) significato, admissi sunt in numero magistrorum dominus [*sic*] Owen, Broad, Clark, Allen, Scriven. Eodem tempore cum magistro Hinton dispensatur, consentiente custode per literas datas Februarii 4°, ut ipsius aeque differatur in 3 septimanas. Eodem etiam tempore admoniti sunt socii, de registro iam parato in quo quisque urbe excedens rediensve, nomen suum inserere, sub poena dupli pro tempore absentiae, tenetur.

Martii 1°. De licentia domini patroni cum consensu custodis per literas significato, principalis et tres simpliciter seniores in electione domi praesentialiter existentes in aula convenientes, processerunt ad eligendum portionistam in locum portionistae magistri Richardi Nevill, modo vacantem. Et electus est communibus suffragiis Ed' Martin et statim admissus per doctorem Turner, seniorem.

7°. Magister Hinton confecit aeque suum.

25°. Hoc ipso die oportebat eos qui ad beneficia ecclesiastica a collegio praesentati fuerant (prout ipsis optionem permiserat dominus patronus) palam pronuntiare, utrum beneficiis suis an iuri in societate renuntiaturi essent. Dominus custos igitur, sociis in apodyterium convocatis statim a precibus matutinis, a singulis exquirit, quod apud se statuissent.

Magister Fisher, 1° in loco interrogatus, respondet se societati huius collegii renuntiare et vicariae Sancti Petri in oriente adhaerescere. Hac tamen cautione quod in integram restitui expectet, si dominus patronus iniunctionem de uberiori revocaverit.

Loco magistri Gibbs absentis, magister Corbet ipsius (ut videtur) proxeneta respondit nondum exactum esse annum ipsius gratuitum, haud aequum igitur videri, ut priusquam dies cesserit, societati vel beneficio renuntiare cogatur.

Responsum est non requiri vel illico renuntiet, sed ut statim pronuntiet utrum, exacto anno gratuito, beneficio vel societate cessurus sit. Respondit igitur ab ipso magistro Corbet, decretum ipsi esse societati suae, exacto anno gratuito (qui finitur Aprilis 21°) renuntiare et

[1] In a different hand.

rectoriae de Gamlingay adhaerescere. Magistro Woodcock vicario de Elham non permissa fuerat optio a domino patrono; ideoque dominus custos pronuntiavit, iam inde ab hoc die ipsum pro socio non amplius reputandum.

Eodem tempore magister Fisher (inchoato iam ante paucos dies termino administrationis suae in officio bursariatus) aequum putavit ut ipse substitutum deputaret, qui vice sua illud officium administraret. Res aliquam diu agitata tandem communibus suffragiis ad dominum patronum refertur.

Additamentum de 400 ovium pascuis, insertum indenturae Sherwood, sociorum consensu firmatur.

Vidua Smyth permittitur domum extruere ex adverso domus quam iam incolit in Holywell, hac tamen cautione, ut ne receptaculum pauperculis extruat, qui paroeciae onerosi esse possint, ne ut tenentem admittat contra consensum custodis et sociorum.

26°. Magister French subrogatur loco magistri Chennell bursarii Williot.

Aprilis 1°. Convocatis in aulam magistris per dominum custodem, loco magistri Burton (exacto iam anno ipsius gratuito) subrogatus est magister Howson, senior decanus qui prius fuerat medius, et sic provecto ibidem iuniore decano, in locum iunioris decani suffectus est magister Owen.

7°. Habita est pro more commemoratio fundatoris postridie.

8°. Lecta sunt statuta, et initum scrutinium, in quo magister Richardus Nevill subrogatus est loco magistri Fisher in munere bursarii. Conventum est de maiore et balivis Cantabrigiensibus in ius vocandis, ob negatum reditum annum xx s.

Magister Sanbach in ius vocandum esse, si batella filii sui (quae a retro sunt) solvere porro recuset.

Consensum est de domino Iacobo Leviston, baronetto, mensae sociorum adhibendo.

Variationes magistri Howson (eo quod decanus hoc anno foret) in proximum annum differendas.

Maii 6°. Cum electio vicecustodis, loco magistri Gibbs cedentis, frustra tentata fuisset, Aprilis 22° tandem dominus patronus super hac re consultans literas misit ad doctorem Turner, quibus eum rem sibi gratam facturum significavit, si in semanas vicecustodis recipere in animum suum induceret, non ut suffragiis magistrorum designatus sed ut a se nominatus, idque ipsum in acta mittendum et registro inserendum fore. Ille igitur honoratissimi patroni voluntatis morem gerens munus illud in re quam lubentissime recepit. Ac mox sibi literis honoratissimi patroni monuit socios quotquot presentes aderant, exigere dominum patronum, ut iuxta edictum suum omnes dehinc portionistae eligantur, secundum ordinacionem Williot. Ac insuper edictis sive ordinationibus suis, hoc adiciendum mandasse.

Addition to his grace's orders

1. That the principale of the postmasters shall have but one single voice (as the rest of the electors) in the choice or nomination of the common postmasters, lately wont to be chosen by the principale alone. And if it happen that the principale of the postmasters at any such election be one of the three seniors he shall not give one voice as principale and another as senior, but the next senior shall be taken in as an elector ea vice.

p. 338 2. That no postmaster shall hold his place after that he hath gotten his grace to be a graduate in the university but 'ipso facto' it shall be voide, and another chosen in his roome.

Iuxta haec edicta seu ordinationes iniunxit dominus patronus vicecustodi, ut, si qui tales in portionistarum numero forent, eorum loca ipso facto vacua esse pronuntiaret, simulque ad eligendos alios in ipsorum aliorumque (si quae fuerint) loca vacantia procederet. Id quod a vicecustode factum est, et loco Iames, qui gratiam suam in domo congregationis obtinuerat, electus est filius magistri Morly olim socii huius collegii, a domino patrono commendatus, simulque monitus magister Corbet, ut loco magistri Greaves (qui itidem gratiam suam obtinuerat) alium de consensu patroni nominandi licentiam procuraret.

Deinde, de consensu patroni, portionistae, occasione magistrorum cedentium, transferendi vel eligendi, secundum ordinem cessionis, in magistros quibus proximum ius competebat, translati vel electi sunt. Magistri Eduardi Nevill portionista translatus est ad magistrum Newman. In locum portionistae magistri Fisher, ex nominatione magistri Howson de consensu patroni electus est Antonius Morgan. Magistri Woodcock portionista translatus est ad magistrum Wright. In locum portionistae magistri Gibbs, nominatus est a magistro Iacob, [*space for Christian name*] Nethersall, et electus de consensu custodis, principalis et trium simpliciter seniorum etc.

[Maii ?] 18°. Literae a domino, patrono ad vicecustodem datae sunt, quibus socios quorum interest moneri iubet, se, prae mole negotiorum quae ipsi in absentia regiae maiestatis incumbet, ad tempus a se praestitutum (ineunte scilicet Iunio) collegii nostri negotiis ulterius audiendis vacare non posse. Sibi igitur in animo esse conventum prius indictum prorogare usque ad initium proxime sequens termini Michaelis. Tum demum coram se compararent quorum interesset.

Iulii 16[to]. De consensu custodis et sociorum indentura de Thorncroft magistro Nevill sigillanda decernitur et magistro Owen atturnatus noster constituitur, ad tradendum ipsi possessionem dicti manerii.

Viduae Neale, cuius fortunae domus suae repentino misere nuper attritae fuerant, decreta est symbola xis. ex aeque dividenda inter collegium et socios, quorum partio a liberatura proximi anni subtrahenda est.

De consensu reverendissimi patroni dominus custos, principalis et tres simpliciter seniores elegerunt in portionistam magistri Newman, Mathiam Caldecott.

20°. Habita solenni commemoratione fundatoris lecta sunt postmodum statuta, et initum pro more scrutinium.

Praediorum locationes anni MDCXXXVIII/IX[1]

A° Di MDC 39, regis Caroli XV, custodis Brent XVIII p. 339

Magistri in artibus

1. Petrus Turner, M.D.
2. Ioannes French
3. Ioannes Greaves
4. Edwardus Corbet
5. Ranulphus Domvill
6. Guilelmus Berkly
7. Richardus Nevill
8. Richardus Newman
9. Nicolas Howson
10. Franciscus Wright
11. Henricus Iacob
12. Rogerus Brent
13. Gulielmus Owen
14. Franciscus Broade
15. Georgius Clerk
16. Edwardus Allen
17. Ioannes Scriven

[1] See below Table 1.

Praedia, Fundi & Tenementa	Firmarii	Tempus Indenturae		Habendum	Tempus Redintegratum	Finis	Licent' Alienat'	
		Concessae	Sigillatae				Concessae	Sigillatae
2^{dus} domus in Holywel	Maenwaring	Augusti 7°	ix^{ris} 28°	A 13° Maii per spatium 40 annorum	12 anni post 28	vi li. xiiis. ivd.	Aug. 8°	ix^{ris} 28°
Farleigh, praedium	Hawtree	viii^{ris} 4° 1638	ix^{ris} 28°	A 4° viii^{ris} 1638 per spatium 21 annorum	7 anni post 14	lx li.[1]		ix^{ris} 28°
Farleigh, sylvae	Hawtree	viii^{ris} 4° 1638	ix^{ris} 28°	A 4° viii^{ris} 1638 per spatium 21 annorum	7 anni post 14			ix^{ris} 28°
Stillington & Seton Carewe semessis 1°	Hartburn	viii^{ris} 4° 1638	ix^{ris} 28°	A 4° viii^{ris} 1638 per spatium 21 annorum	8 anni post 13	60 li. in sigill' indent', 60 in festo S. Thomae 1639 per obligationem		
Stillington & Seton Carewe semessis 2°	Morpeth	ut supra	ut supra	ut supra	ut supra	ut supra		
Mill Hill cum molendino, in Essex	Bennet	viii^{ris} 4° 1638	Augusti 15° 1639	A 4° viii^{ris} 1638 ad 30 annos	24 anni post 6	xiii li. vis. viiid.		
Merton Hall in Cantabrig'	Sherwood	viii^{ris} 9° 1638	Martii 26° 1639	A 29° vii^{ris} 1638 ad 21 annos	5 anni post 16	vi li. xiiis. ivd.		
Portio vacivi fundi in Holywell e regione tenementi n° 22^{di}	Ingelsby	x^{ris} 10° 1638	19 Februarii 1638/9	A 29° vii^{ris} 1638 ad 40 annos	nunc primum elocata	o, o, o	26 Martii 1639	30 Martii 1639
Portio vacivi fundi in Holywell e regione xvi tenementi	Winkle	ut supra	ut supra	ut supra	ut supra	o, o, o		
Domus in Knight Rider Street	vidua D^{ris} Hawly							28 Martii 1639
Wolford	Oakely						25 Martii 1639 ad annos xi	29 Martii 1639
Chedington	Guilielmus Mayne	19 Apr. 1639	30° Apr. 1639	A 29° vii^{ris} 1638 ad 21 annos	4 anni post 17	x li. in sigill' indent', x li. 25 Martii 1640		

Table 1. Praediorum locationes Anno MDCXXXVIII/IX[2]

[1] A bracket in the MS. indicates that this fine was for both Farleigh leases.
[2] The MS. has a table with grid lines simlar to the above; some abbreviations have been retained to facilitate printing.

Baccalaurei in artibus

1. Edwardus Coply
2. Radulphus Burton
3. Ioannes Priaulx
4. Robertus Sayer
5. Christophorus Fowle
6. Georgius Loveioye

Capellani

1. Ioannes Brent
2. Ioannes Rainolds

Augusti 1mo. In solenni conventu custodis et sociorum in alta aula, post resignatas officiariorum claves custos una cum 5 simpliciter senioribus, reliquis ad tempus secedere iussis, ad novorum officiariorum electionem processit. Quae tamen, quia rata esse non poterat, nisi per reverendissimum patronum nostrum approbata, cumque alias de designandis seniore decano et bursario haud satis conveniret, res domini patroni arbitrio permissa est, qui officiarios, partim a nobis designatos, partim a se, nunc in modum constituit:
vicecustos, doctor Turner.
decani, magistri Howson, Broad, Clark.
bursarii, magistri Nevill, Wright, Owen.
principalis portionistarum, magister French; bursarius Williot, magister Allen; exhibitionarius Hamsterly, magister Earles; exhibitionarius Bodly,[1] magister Nevill, magister Brent, capellanus; capellanus capellae, magister Iacob; lectores, linguae Graecae, magister Button, grammaticae, magister Scriven; custodes cistarum Reade, 3 decani; [cistae] Bodly, [magistri] Brent, Allen, Scriven.

Eodem tempore data est magistro Raye de Kibworth licentia diruendi partem domicilii sui ibidem quo commodius ipsam reaedificet.

Decernitur procuratorium sigillandi praesentibus bursariis ad exigendos reditus, sive insolutos, sive ab hominibus dubiae fidei solvendos.

Progressus decernitur ad visitandos fundos et praedia in comitatibus, Oxon', Buckingham, Surry, Essex'; Cantii nulla facta fuerat mentio; illuc tamen defleximus, sed frustra. Nam apud Newington magister Trafford, quamvis per literas custodis praemonitus quo tempore illic appulsuri essemus, nullus comparuit. Ideoque coacti sumus, post confecta illo ipso die 40 milliaria, ingruente iam nocte in mediis tenebris et pluvia progredi Sittingbornum usque. Magistri Nevill, Hinton, Hewson et Wright, prius a domino patrono nominati, modo designantur pro anno sequente ad informandum dominum patronum quomodo ordinationes ipsius observentur a singulis.

[1] *recte* 'Bickley'.

5° [Augusti]. De consensu domini patroni Benson et Duncomb admittuntur in numerum portionistarum per custodem, tres simpliciter seniores et principalem.

15°. Magister Nevill, 3ius bursarius computavit, una hebdomade anterius quam decreta requirunt; et discessit aeque. Praesentatio magistri Hinton ad vicariam de Maldon sigillatur. Tunc etiam sigillata est indentura ventimolae in Essex, locatae Isaac Bennet.

17°. Dominus patronus, dum bursariorum computa prioris anni ad se missa percurreret, notaverat forte aliquas expensas collegio imputatas nomine litis quae magistro Doughty intercedet cum domino Thoma Holt circa decimas de Lapworth. Literis igitur ea occasione ad dominum custodem datis, districte vetuit, ne quis in posterum a collegio ad beneficium quodcunque promotus, lites occasione beneficii sui motas collegii sumptibus prosequatur citra expressum patroni consensum.

In iisdem etiam litteris alteram exhibitionem Bickly, quae in festo Sancti Petri ad Vincula in magistrum Hinton collata fuerat, in magistrum Brent capellanum transfert, quia inter socios nemo erat qui capax foret.

In iisdem etiam literis licentiam concedit locandi fundos quosdam et tenementa firmariis Redhead, Franklin et tenentibus nonnullis in Holywell.

25°. Occasione literarum in quibus dominus patronus lecturam grammaticae in magistrum Scriven conferebat, dominus custos consentientibus sociis quotquot aderant in apodyterio statim a vespertinis precibus, quoad lecturas grammaticae et Graecae sic ordinavit. uterque lector bis singulis septimanis in termino legat, grammaticae hora 10a antemeridiana, alter hora 3a postmeridiana diebus martis et iovis. Repetitiones utriusque lecturae habendae iisdem horis die saturni.

Septembris 2°. Unanimi consensu custodis et sociorum cautum est, ne quis tenens in manerio nostro de Bilby, magistro Pricket, firmario nostro ibidem citra consensum ipsius obtrudetur in posterum per collegium. Haec cautio, registro inserta si minus ipsi satisfecerit, inter conditiones indenturae iuxta pacta conventa inserenda est.

Decembris 18°. Habita est commemoratio fundatoris, lecta statuta, initumque pro more scrutinium, et prorogatum ad usque pridie Kalendas Februarii

19°. Magister Owen bursarius 1mus computavit.

31°. Habitum est pro more scrutinium, in quo tria solennia proponebantur, mores servientium, numerus portionistarum; et electio hortulani. Mores servientium referuntur ad officiarios, numerum p[ortio]nist[arum] idem esse oportere, qui prius, censuerunt. Electus est in hortulanum magister Howson.

[1640]

A° Di MDC39/40, regis Caroli xv/xvi Martii 27°, custodis Brent xiix/xix Martii 20° p. 340

Ianuarii 8°. De licentia domini patroni Robertus Petty admissus est in numerum portionistarum, per custodem, tres simpliciter seniores et principalem.

De consensu domini patroni, indicta prius electione futura intra paucos dies, post accuratum et sincerum examen candidatorum.

Electi sunt in suum annum probationis dominus Lee, Sarisburiensis dioeceseos, dominus Hill, [*blank*] dioeceseos, dominus Whistler, dioeceseos [*blank*], dominus Iones, Menevensis dioeceseos, contribuent singuli versus bibliothecam collegii, 3 li. 6s. 8d. praeter dominum Iones, qui xxxiiis. ivd. contribuet.

11°. In conventu custodis et sociorum in hospitio, consensum est de curia iudicanda apud Gamlingay, ut quidam Lander unus e custumariis tenentibus copiam suam alteri transcribat. Finis, x librae. Ibidem decernitur solvendas esse magistro Doughty 13 libras pro semisse expensarum in lite cum domino Thoma Holt, a termino Michaelis 1638 exclusive, ad terminum Michaelis 1639 inclusive.

20°. Sex seniores baccalaurei, dominus Coply, Button, Pryaulx, Sayre, Fowle, Loveioye, impetrata prius licentia a domino patrono, admissi sunt in numerum magistrorum. In quorum admissione pars illa iuramenti ab ipsis praescribandi de lectionibus suis ordinariis, ex decreto custodis et 8 seniorum hunc in modum immutata est.

Item tu iurabis, quod leges ordinaria continuo per biennium a festo Sancti Michaelis proximo post tuam inceptionem ita quod primo anno legas quemlibet librum Physicorum Aristotelis, vel alterius cuiusvis libri Naturalem Philosophiam secundo vero anno legas aut mathematica aut metaphysica. Leges autem librum distinctum ab eo, quem seniorum tuorum quivis elegerit; etiam horis distinctis per custodem et 5 seniores assignandis, legendo ad minus omni termino bis in singulis septimanis, nisi aliter tecum dispensatum fuerit.

Eodem tempore dominus Lee, dominus Hill, dominus Whistler, dominus Iones, admissi sunt in annum probationis.

Ibidem item consensere custos et socii de 20 libris obsonatori nostro mutuo dandis ex aerario collegii, modo idoneum fideiussorem adducat, qui una secum sub syngrapha sua caveat de restituendis his pecuniis intra triennium. Ita ut primam portionem solvat (scilicet 6 li. 13s. 4d.) in festo Michaelis 1640, reliquas duas in festis Michaelis 1641 et 1642.

Februarii 13°. Magister Owen 1us bursarius dissolvit pedem computus sui; et sic aeque.

29°. In conventu custodis et sociorum in apodyterio statim a precibus vespertinis decernitur 50s. erogandos esse in reparando cubiculo equisonis. Postea tamen aucta est summa ex consensu ad 4 libras.

Martii 1°. In conventu custodis et sociorum in apodyterio statim a precibus vespertinis lecta sunt informationes, quas ab informatoribus supra memoratis receperat reverendissimus patronus, ab ipso demum ad dominum custodem missae, et coram sociis publicarentur.

4°. In conventu custodis et sociorum in hospitio, de consensu ipsorum magister Bernard iurisconsultus per magistrum Brent seneschallum nostrum deputatur ad curias leet et Baron tenendas apud Gamlingay, ad usum supra memoratum Ianuario 11°.

15°. Dispensatum est cum magistro Allen, ut ultra quadrantem anni a collegio abesse liceat; quin nuper ecclesiasticum beneficium consequutus frequenter absentiae occasiones habet.

23°. Magister Raye, firmarius noster de Kibworth querebatur apud custodem et socios se in computo suo onerari reditu quodam, qui alias per indenturam collegio solveretur. Id cum evidenter nobis constaret, decretum est reditum illum, e reditu assisae in computo ipsius expungendum esse.

Idem magister Raye ad collegium aduxerat equum quendam, cui ut errori manum iniecerat intra manerium nostrum de Kibworth, quem cum collegii usibus idoneum indicarent plerique, strictiori ipsius custodiae in posterum hoc decreto consultum inerunt, ne bursarius equum publicum cuiquam utendum ducet, praeterquam obeunti collegii negotia, citra consensum custodis, sive absente vicecustodis, aut (utroque absente) senioris socii et decani qui domi praesentes fuerint.

28°. Habita est commemoratio fundatoris lecta statuta, initumque pro more scrutinium. In eo conventu concessum est magistro Gardner firmario nostro de Thorncroft ut indenturam suam 3 vitarum mutet in indenturam 21 annorum.

30°. Sigillata est indentura praedicta de Thorncroft magistro Edmundo West de Mussworth in comitatu Buck', armigero ut fiducisario possessori nomine ipsius Gardner.

Aprilis 24°. Nota bene magister Wright bursarius secundus computavit, tota hebdomada posterius quam oportuit; quia tempore debito computum reddere non potuit prae absentia unius auditorum NB.

Maii 30°. De consensu domini patroni dispensatum est cum magistro Owen ut sacris ordinibus initiaretur, ante finitam regentiam, ut capax redderetur beneficii quod ipsi donaverat amicus quidam.

Iunii 6°. De consensu custodis et sociorum 6 li. pars symbolae annuae ad reparandum fanum divi Pauli Londini, quas magistrum Gibbs solvisse oportuit cum postremum bursarius foret (recepta scilicet per ipsum de Maine pro 20 ovibus) solvendae sunt ex aerario collegii et a magistro Gibbs exigendae quam primum solvendo fuerit.

Eodem tempore cum magistro Gibbes liberaturam suam (utcunque maximam partem anni sui gratuiti extra collegium egeret) & alia emolumenta sibi a collegio deberi contenderet, socii super ea re consulti unanimes censuerunt nihil ipsi collegio deberi.

11°. Magister Wright dissolvit pedem computus sui et discessit aeque.

14°. Dominus custos per literas consulet socios, an lis intentanda sit magistro Sheres ob arreragia Hensington, qui unanimes assensere. Eodem tempore de allocatione facienda magistro Domevill peregrinanti. Consultus dominis patronus respondit, sibi non placere ut allocatio annua cuivis peregrinanti facta solvatur ante finem cuiuslibet anni durante tempore peregrinationis.

Eodem etiam tempore dominus patronus consultus de dispensatione quam sibi concedi praebant magister Clark et magister Loveioye ut sacris ordinibus initiarentur ante finitam regentiam, respondit sibi non placere, ut cum regentibus dispensetur ante finitam regentiam, in casu vero promotionis oblatae, quae actu vacet, licere dispensationem concedere.

21°. Dominus custos per literas consulit socios, num in causa Dodd potestatem sibi permitterent cum ipso paciscendi conditionibus minime collegio damnosis; quo post longas legis ambages adigi tandem nos posse sciscebant veri iuris consultissimi. Assensere igitur socii unanimes, ea lege ne quid in preiudicium collegii fieret.

p. 341 Eodem tempore de consensu custodis et sociorum concessa est licentia alienandi magistro West loco magistri Gardener de Thorncroft, et postmodo sigillata Iunii 25°.

Iulii 20°. Habita est commemoratio fundatoris, lecta statuta, initumque pro more scrutinium.

Quoniam firmarius noster de Holywell magister Napper tenetur ex pacto convento plus foeni quotannis foenili nostro importare, quam cui consumendo pares forent equi, quos illic collegii sumptibus pasci oportet, si ex fide equariam annonam tractasset nuperus equiso; cuius annonae residuum, quo in fine anni supererat, publicis collegii usibus vindicari multo iustius videbatur, quam totum ab equisone devorari. Doctor Turner igitur, inita apud se ratione, qua expensae istius pars aliqua ab equisone averti, et in usum bibliothecae nostrae detineri posset (scilicet, si ipsi permitteretur in equili collegii binos equos alere, numerato quotannis pretio, quo sex foeni vehes collegio constarent, et bibliothecae usibus applicato) quod sibi in mentem venerat reverendissimo patrono exponit; simul rogans, ut illud, si sibi probaretur, cum domino custode (qui tum Londini agebat) communicare dignaretur. Reverendissimus igitur patronus, re cum domino custode communicata, et ab utroque ipsorum approbata, literis datis ad doctorem Turner (quas ille coram custode et sociis, 20° Iulii scrutinii tempore recitavit) approbationem suam significavit simulque ordinationem hanc suam registro inseri mandavit: scilicet licere doctori Turner binos equos in equili collegii alere quoad vellet, sub conditione superius memorata.

Eodem tempore publicatae sunt iniunctiones reverendissimi patroni, quas ille nuper sub sigillo suo confirmatas in praesentia domini custodis, vicecustodis et senioris decani, ac bursarii ad collegium transmiserat.

[Iulii] 25°. Dispensatum est cum magistro Loveioye, ut sacris ordinibus initiaretur ante finitam regentiam, quo donationi cuiusdam capax redderetur, ab episcopo Norwicensi sibi donati, actuque vacantis, prout ille sancto affirmabat coram custode et sociis.

Praediorum locationes anni MDC39/40[1]

AD MDC40/41,[2] regis Caroli xvi/xvii, Martii 27°, custodis Brent xix/ xx, Martii 20° p. 342

1. Petrus Turner, doctor medicinae

Magistri in artibus

1. Ioannes French
2. Ioannes Greaves
3. Edwardus Corbet
4. Ranulphus Domvill
5. Gulielmus Berkly
6. Richardus Nevill
7. Richardus Newman
8. Nicolas Howson
9. Franciscus Wright
10. Henricus Iacob
11. Rogerus Brent
12. Guilelmus Owen
13. Franciscus Broade
14. Georgius Clerke
15. Edwardus Allen
16. Ioannes Scriven
17. Edwardus Coply
18. Radulphus Button
20. Ioannes Priaux
21. Robertus Sayer
22. Christophorus Fowle
23. Georgius Loveioye

Baccalaurei in artibus probationarii

1. Ioannes Lee
2. Guilelmus Hill
3. Daniel Whistler
4. Thomas Iones

Capellani

1. Ioannes Brent
2. Ioannes Rainolds

Augusti 1°. In solenni conventu custodis et sociorum in alta aula post resignatas officiariorum claves, custos una cum 5 simpliciter senioribus, reliquis ad tempus secedere iussis, ad novorum officiariorum electionem processit, qua postea a reverendissimo patrono approbato (nisi quod ipsius iussu, in literis ad custodem datis, in locum magistri Coply 2^di^ bursarii magister Scriven suffectus est) electi sunt in annum sequentem officiarii:
vicecustos, magister Greaves.
decani, magistri Nevill, Wright, Button.
bursarii, magistri Brent, Clerke, Scriven.
principalis portionistarum, magister Howson; bursarius Williot, magister Broad; exhibitionarii Hamsterly, magister Nevill; Bickley, magister [*blank*], magister Brent, capellanus; lectores linguae Graecae magister [*blank*]; grammaticae et capellanus

[1] See below Table 2.
[2] Deleted

Praedia, Fundi & Tenementa	Firmarii	Tempus Indenturae		Habendum	Tempus Redintegratum	Finis	Licent' Alienat'	
		Concessae	Sigillatae				Concessae	Sigillatae
Holywell fundus vacivus repondens reditus n° vii^{a}	Ioannes Price	vii^{ris} 2°	viii^{ris} 5°	40 anni a festo Michaelis 1639	xxii anni	00, 00, 00		
[Ibid.] e regione tenementi, n° xxix	Guilelmus Hartly	vii^{ris} 2°	viii^{ris} 5°	40 anni a festo Michaelis 1639	nunc primum elocati	00, 00, 00		
Holywell domus. Tenementum n° xix	Vidua Holt	vii^{ris} 2°	viii^{ris} 5°	40 anni a festo Michaelis 1639	xix anni	02, 00, 00	vii^{ris} 2°	viii^{ris} 5°
Fundi novissime perquisiti in Hensington	Guilelmus Redhed	vii^{ris} 2°	viii^{ris} 8°	21 anni a festo Annuntiationis 1639	x anni	06, 13, 04		
Stillington	Morpeth						x^{ris} 2° Maii 27°	x^{ris} 3° Maii 29°
Ibston ventimola	Edmundus Simons	vii^{ris} 2°	vii^{ris} 3°	21 anni a festo Annuntiationis 1639	x anni			
Thorncroft	Edmundus West	Martii 28°	Martii 30°	21 anni a festo Michaelis 1639	21 anni vice 3 vitarum	00, 00, 00	Junii 20°	Junii 25°

Table 2. Praediorum locationes Anno MDC39/40[1]

[1] The MS. has a table with grid lines similar to the above; some abbreviations have been retained to facilitate printing.

capellae, magister Scriven, quo, suo iure, spontanee cedente, ea munera in magistrum Coply collata sunt; custodes cistae Read, tres decani; [cistae] Bodly, magistri Scriven, Priaux, Sayer.

Cum magistro Newman dispensatum est pro sequentis anni absentia.

3°. Magistro Edwardo Nevil septem arbores assignatae sunt e fundo ... ea tamen cautione, ut eis ad reparandas aedes suas bona fide utatur, neque dolo malo in alios usus convertat.

Ne pecuniae cistarum Reade et Bodly, in posterum negligentia officiariorum, ad quos ea cura spectat, immunerentur aut abraderentur, sancitum est, ut singuli socii, priusquam pecunias mutuo inde accipiant, datis syngraphis, poena dupli teneantur, nisi statim post discessionem a societate, pecuniis numeratis, nomina sua liberaverint. Eadem lege socii etiam obstringuntur, qui pecunias inde iamdudum acceperunt. Ab eis vero qui relicta societate nondum cistis fecerunt satis, pecuniae illae per custodem repetendae sunt, quos si solvere abnuerint, in ius extemplo vocandi sunt.

9°. Finitis lectionibus primi anni cum magistris regentibus dispensatum est pro secundi anni lecturis. Magister Howson et magister Brent hoc anno tenentur variare.

25°. Magister Nevil tertius bursarius computavit, et discessit aeque.

Septembris 8. Magister Broad lector theologiae catechisticae a custode, sociis consentientibus in tres sequentes annos decernitur.

Eodem tempore decretum est de coemendis 12 manuariis tormentis, cum pari numero hastarum, ut bello ingruente, si qui forte palantium militum in collegium irrumpere, eiusve bona depraedari, tentarent melius repellerentur.

[Septembris] 14. Computus generalis totius anni absolvitur.

Magister Greaves vicecustos a reverendissimo nostro patrono lector Linacri inferior declaratur.

Cum carbonarius breve multum de grave lignorum precio, et sumptuosa carbonum vectura quereretur, planeque muneri suo renunciaret, visum est vicecustodi, decano seniori et bursariis, ad quos id negotium a custode sociisque relatum est in annum sequentem experiri, an non magis e re collegio foret carbones fossiles coemere atque in eam sententiam post a reliquis sociis itum est.

Decembris 16°. Magister Scriven primus bursarius computavit et discessit aeque.

18°. Commemoratio fundatoris habita est, lecta statuta, et initum pro more scrutinium q[uod]que ad pridie Kalendas Ianuarii et quemlibet diem citra prorogatum est.

p. 343 Decembris 31°. Habitum est pro more scrutinium in quo tria solennia proponebantur, mores servientium, numerus portionistarum, et electio hortulani. Mores servientium referuntur ad officiarios, numerum portionistarum eundem qui prius esse oportere censuerunt, magister Wright electus est in hortulanum.

[1641]

Ianuarii 23°. Dominus Ioannes Lee, dominus Guilelmus Hill, dominus Daniel Whistler, dominus Thomas Iones, consensu sociorum prius habito, admissi sunt a domino custode in perpetuam societatem huius domus.

Aprilis 17°. Commemoratio fundatoris habita est, lecta statuta, et initum pro more scrutinium quod usque ad Kalendas Maii, et quemlibet diem citra prorogatum est.

22°. Magister Clarke 2us bursarius computavit.

Idem soluto pede computi sui discessit aeque.

Iulii 3°. Magister Clarke de consensu magistri Brent, cui id munus incumbebat, in his quaestionibus variavit:

An {
Deterior sit qui irae fraena dat, quam qui voluptati. Affirmavit, contra Aristotelem, lib' 7 Ethic' capitulo 7°.
Omnes virtutes connectantur in prudentia. Negavit, contra Aristotelem, Ethic' lib' 6, capitulo 13°.
Superiora unico motu moveantur, inferiora omnibus. Negavit, contra Aristotelem lib' 1 de Coelo, capitulo 3°.
}

Finitis variationibus dispensatum est cum eo pro secundis variationibus.

11°. Sociis per vicecustodem in altam aulam convocatis, cum magistro Howson absente dispensatum est pro omissis praesentis anni variationibus, causa assignabatur, et sua et matris aegritudo Londini.

22°. Commemoratio fundatoris habita est, lecta statuta et initum pro more scrutinium, quod usque ad Kalendas Augusti et quemlibet diem citra prorogatum est.

31°. Convenientibus, custode et sociis in apodyterium post preces vespertinas magister Fisher comparuit, et in societatem admitti postulavit. Contendentibus vero vicecustode, et doctore Turner, eum istius modi beneficii esse minime capacem, nisi prius reverendissimi patroni nostri acta, quibus excludebatur, vel pari vel maiori authoritate, rescindantur; re ultro citroque agitata, et incalescentibus paululum hinc inde animis, illi dicam ei impingunt contumaciae et spretae authoritatis patroni, is in illos litem uberioris beneficii regerit. Dum haec aguntur, custos inconsultis et silentibus sociis, magistrum Fisher ad omnia collegii emolumenta restituit, donec in comitiis parliamentariis, de causae ipsius aequitate[1] constiterit.

Hoc anno pecuniis, quas Bibliothecae nostrae donaverat magister Allen, vir eruditione morumque probitate, spectatissimus, et huius collegii quondam socius, empti sunt libri Ebraei, Graeci, Latini, Arabici et Persici.

Praediorum locationes anno MDCXL/XLI[2]

Magister Greaves a longinqua peregrinatione domum reversus, vacante portionistae sui loco, quem ante octo annos contulerat, ius suum vindicat; rogati, custos et tres simpliciter seniores una cum distributore de ea re sententias, unanimes aequum postulari, iure postliminis iudicarunt.

A' D'I MDCXL1/2, Regis Caroli 17/18, Martii 27, custodis Brent 20/ p. 344
21, Martii 20.

Magistri in artibus

1. Ioannes French
2. Alexander Fisher
3. Ioannes Greaves
4. Edwardus Corbett
5. Ranulphus Dunvill
6. Gulielmus Berkley
7. Richardus Nevill
8. Richardus Newman
9. Nicolas Howson
10. Franciscus Wright
11. Henricus Iacob
12. Rogerus Brent
13. Guilielmus Owen
14. Franciscus Broade
15. Georgius Clerke
16. Edwardus Copley
17. Radulphus Button
18. Iohannes Priaux
19. Robertus Sayer
20. Christophorus Fowle
21. Georgius Loveioy

Baccalaurei in artibus

1. Iohannes Lee
2. Daniel Whistler
3. Thomas Iones

[1] 'vel indignitate' deleted. [2] See below Table 3.

Praedia, Fundi & Tenementa	Firmarii	Tempus Indenturae		Habendum	Tempus Redintegratum	Finis	Licent' Alienat'	
		Concessae	Sigillatae				Concessae	Sigillatae
Gamlingay Avenells	Dr Ioannes Iacob, eques	Aug. 2°	Apr. 2° 1641	21 a festo Michaelis 1640	xi anni	£50		
Sylva Mertonage	Dr Ioannes Iacob	vii^{bris} 3°	vii^{bris} 26° 1640	21 a festo Michaelis 1639	xvii anni	£50		
Tenementum in Kibworth	Margareta Standin	Aug. 2°	Aug. 4° 1640	21 a festo Annuntiationis 1640	xiii anni	£50	Aug. 2°	Aug. 4°
Beilby	Marmaducus Pricket	Aug. 2°	Aug. 4° 1640	21 a festo Annuntiationis 1640	viii anni	00		
Tenementum in Holywell n° viii	Augustinus Boxly	Aug. 2°	x^{bris} 15° 1640	21 a 15 x^{bris} 1640	xii anni	00		
Portio fundi vacivi prope Smithgate n° xxiv	Civitas Oxon'	Aug. 2°	Aug. 13° 1640	40 a festo Annuntiationis 1640	xx anni	00		
Portio fundi vacivi in Holywell n° xxvii	Vidua French	Aug. 2°	Aug. 10° 1640	40 a festo Annuntiationis 1640	xv anni	00		
Portio fundi vacivi in Holywell n° xxxv	Vidua French	Aug. 2°	Aug. 10° 1640	40 a festo Annuntiationis 1640	xv anni	00		
Portio fundi vacivi in Holywell n° xlvii	Vidua Iddens	Aug. 2°	Jan. 23 1640	40 a festo Michaelis 1640	iii anni	00		

Table 3. Praediorum locationes Anno MDCXL/XLI[1]

[1] The MS. has a table with grid lines similar to the above; some abbreviations have been retained to facilitate printing.

Capellani
1. Iohannes Gergainy 2. Franciscus Crofts

Augusti 2°. Conventum est pro more in altam aulam hora nona antemeridiana ubi post resignatas officiariorum claves, reliquis sociis hoc tempus secedere iussis, custos una cum quinque simpliciter senioribus sequentis anni officiarios inhunc modum designavit:
vicecustos, magister Corbett.
decani, magistri Clerke, Copley, Priaux.
bursarii, magistri French, Owen, Button.
principalis portionistarum, magister Wright; bursarius Williot et capellanus capellae, magister Brent; exhibitionarius Hampster', magister Loveioy; custodes cistae Reade, tres decani; [cistae] Bodley, magistri Iacob, Brent, Sayer; lectores linguae Graecae, magister Foule, grammaticae, magister Sayer; bursarius itinerans, magister Wright.

Eodem tempore magister Greaves omne ius societatis magistro Fisher denegavit, virtute iniunctionis cuiusdam Lambethanae, qua quicunque a collegio beneficiatus erit, a societate movebitur, contraque illum protestatus est. Pari modo magister Fisher omne ius societatis magistro Greaves denegavit virtute statuti fundatoris quo nemo collegium et uberius beneficium simul retinebit, eoque nomine contra illum protestatus est. Re hinc inde paulum agitata dominus custos hoc modo in praesenti litem composuit, utriusque iura approbando, donec honoratissimus domus parliamenti de illorum causis, sicut de caeteris collegii gravaminibus iudicaverit. Dispensatum est cum magistro Newman pro sequentis anni absentia, cui nihilominus comeduntur emolumenta collegii liveratura sua et fines ut qui multum iniuriae passus est, nec atque satisfactionem accepit. Dominus Hill ad uberiorem fortunam in patria sua promotus, societatem nostram in quam paulo ante admissus erat, reliquit. Eaque de causa et quia annum gratiae non desideravit, et quia vita et studiis optime collegio sese approbavit, consensu domini custodis et sociorum triginta libras obtinuit.

3°. Dispensatum est cum magistris regentibus pro secundi anni [*damage*] lecturis.

Magister Brent et magister Owen hoc anno tenentur variare; monuit p. 345
dominus custos bursarios inquirere de pecuniis ad cistas Reade et Bodley spectantibus. Progressus decernitur hoc anno ad visitandos fundos et praedia collegii in comitatibus Oxon', Buckm', Cantabr' etc.

7°. Coquo seniori conceditur finis Astill, 6 li. 13s. 4d. nec postea tenebitur quadranguli minoris aream componere. Magister Copley accepto plussagio pedis computi discessit aeque.

Septembris 28. Convenientibus in scaccarium domino custode sociisque habitus est computus generalis superioris anni.

Octobris 12°. Sociis in hospitio custodis convenientibus concessae sunt domino

Conopio Graeco duae librae annuatim quamdiu in academia moram fecerit, quorum dimidium, aerarium, alterum vero dimidium socii solvent.

Licentia alienandi tenementum Abrahami Chamber conceditur Richardo Morpeth.

Ad reparationem pontem prope Whately 30 solidi conceduntur.

[Octobris] 13. Sigillata est licentia Richardi Morpeth.

Assignatus est magister Wright ad vendendas arbores apud Barkby tempore quo charius vendi possunt ut cum maiori collegii emolumento..

[Octobris] 16. Ordinatum est in hospitio custodis, quod 9 socii seniores sese praebebunt sponsores principali pro batellis portionistarum propiorum. Portionistae vero Aetonenses et tres (ut loquuntur) communes in admissione sua ibidem fideiussionem praestent quam principalis approbabit, quam etiam portionistae 9 dare tenebuntur, ipsorum magistris collegium deferentibus. Consensere dominus custos et socii de 20 li. mutuo dandis promo Ianes, modo sub syngrapha sua, caveat de restituendis his pecuniis ante computum praesentis bursarii.

Ibidem decernitur duas libras erogandas esse in reparando cubiculo superiori domini Iones, ipsum vero persolvere si quid amplius erogatur.

[Octobris] 20. Decernitur ut platea ante equile collegii lapidibus de novo sterneretur; et ut inferior pars bibliothecae intestino ornaretur.

[Octobris] 28. Cum lites contra Shires et Holt nulla non cura indigebat, socii in hospitio custodis dederunt hoc negotium domino custodi, et magistro Fisher.

Decernitur procuratorium sigillandum bursariis ad exigendos reditus insolutos et arreragias.

Cognitio curiae apud Gamlingay refertur ad prudentiam domini custodis.

Licentia extruendi domum in Holliwell conceditur Richardo Maude, modestalis extruatur quae plateae ornamento sit.

Novembris VI. Visitatio Mertonensis tres annos et dimidium nata, et quae Troianam obsidionem duratione minabatur hoc die providentia divina extinguitur: visitatio omnium iniustissima et peior pessima. p. 346

[Novembris] 16. Consensu sociorum in aula convenientium mutuo datur tractatus Dyonisii de hierarchia Angelorum doctissimo primati Hiberniae et xix ix[bris] alter tractatus de [*blank*] eiusdem authoris, quos intra septimanam honoratissimus vir restituit collegio. Eodem etiam tempore mutuo datur Villapandus magistro Greaves. Conceduntur Henrico Sayr 2 li. 6s. 4d. pro feoudo ballivi 7 annis insoluto, et tamen conditione ut pecunias restituat, et officium resignat si ita visum fuerit domino custodi. Licentia alienationis conceditur Gulielmo Hutchins et Rosae Idens executoribus viduae Idens.

Decembris XVIII. Habita est pro more commemoratio fundatoris, lecta statuta, initum scrutinium quod prorogatum est in primum diem Martii et quemlibet diem citra.

Eodem conventu ordinavit dominus custos ut quilibet bursarius, liberaturam et fines et caetera emolumenta collegii tradant omnibus qui possessione societatis fruuntur donec comitia parliamentaria otium sortiantur ut de collegii querelis aliquid statuant. Consensere dominus custos sociique de venditione Bilby, si quod aliud manerium ad collegii quietem et beneficium plus conducens poterit comparari. Ordinatum est ut magister Howson xi Ianuarii sequentis redderet rationem variationum tot annis neglectarum, ut magister Iacob ostenderet quo iure societatem una cum officii bedelli retineat, ut dominus Iones articulis nonnullis a magistro Nevillo seniori decano contra illum exhibitis, respondeat.

[Decembris] XXXI. Habitum est pro more scrutinium in quo tria solennia proponebantur, mores servientium, numerus portionistarum et electio hortulani. Mores servientium referuntur ad officiarios; numerum portionistarum eundem esse oportere qui prius censuerunt; electus est in hortulanum magister Iacob.

Eodem tempore ianitor collegii reus declaratur irreverentiae, linguae procacis erga magistrum Greaves, ea qua de causa, officii emolumentis pro septimana privatur.

[1642]

Ianuarii X. Decretum est unanimi consensu domini custodis et omnium sociorum praesentium (et novendecim praesentes erant) electionem sociorum numero paucorum fieri, et decimo novo Ianuarii
p. 347 examen eorum habendum esse. / Conceduntur ex aerario et sociorum crumensis 2 li. 10s. ad sublevandum eorum miserias quos flammarum crudelitas apud Marson afflixit.

Conceditur Francisco Sayer licentia extruendi caminum in domo viduae Idens.

Domino custode et sociis in magna aula convenientibus in memoriam magistri Howson revocatur iuramentum de variationibus intra duos annos post susceptum magisterii gradum praestandis, qui quandoque valetudinem praetendens, quandoque culpam suam aliorum (ut sibi videbatur) consimili culpa diluere tentans tandem clementia domini custodis in mandatis habuit, variationis partes legere ante festum Pentecostes proxime aut collegii emolumentis carere, donec eo munere fungeretur.

Eodem tempore magister Iacob multa proferebat ad ius societatis stabiliendum, quae cum non satisfacerent (tum quod officium superioris bedelli in theologia uberius beneficium credebatur, tum quod incongruum socio Mertonensi aestimabatur, tum aliis de causis) dominus custos precibus vicecustodis et magistri Greaves indulsit illi annum gratiae expiraturum eodem die mensis quo primum in officium bedelli admissus fuerat ipsumque ex nunc pro ut ex tunc et extunc ut ex nunc pronuntiavit non socium.

Eodem conventu dominus Iones scriptis respondit querelis magistri Nevill, ea ratione ut aequum videretur domino custodi sociisque ipsum 50s. (quos nomine poenae inflixit illi decanus) a bursario recepturum; nihilominus tamen propter verba nonnulla et domus disciplinam, quae a bacchalaureo requirit obedientiam erga decanum iniusta imperantem corrigitur prima admonitione et tenetur collectanea ex Ciceronis, de Oratore, libris transcribere eaque in manus domini custodis aut vicecustodis ante festum Pascatis tradere.

Eodem tempore dominus Iones oneravit magistrum Nevill gravibus accusationibus, quibus respondere tenetur magister Nevill quam primum illas in scriptis acceperit. Hoc conventu magister Copley decanus probavit dominum Lee contumaciae reum, et disciplinae incuriosum, eaque de causa accepit dominus Lee primam admonitionem, privatur allocatione et communiis pro septimana, et in mandatis habuit flores ex tribus posterioribus libris Institutionum Quintiliani colligere eosque domino custodi, aut vicecustodi ante festum Paschalis tradere. Has censuras egit dominus custos consensu sociorum quas propria authoritate se posse praestare professus est.

[Ianuarii] XVII. Scripta de reipublicae negotiis, a serenissimo rege Carolo ad academiam publicanda missa, legit dominus custos coram sociis et scholaribus collegii quod munus saepe profecit postea vicecustos.

XIX/XXI. Post sincerum examen candidatorum die xix° electi sunt die p. 348
xxi dominus Martin, dominus Wood, dominus Lydall, Oxoniensis dioeceseos, dominus Kettlewell, Wintoniensis dioecesos et decretum erat omnes admittendos esse primo die termini paschalis.

Eodem die sociis in hospitio custodis convenientibus hora nona matutina, cum iam in eo essent, ut ad electionem sociorum se accingerent interveniens doctor Turner in haec verba protestatus provocavit: 'I protest concerningue ye nullitie of your proceedings in this election of fellowes; and therefore ore tenus I appeale to our visitor, my Lorde's Grace of Canterbury, or in case the visitor's power be suspended I appeale to the King's M'tie from the greivance which mr Warden offers ye colledge[1] in proceedinge to an election of fellowes, contrary to ye college statutes, contrarie to ye visitor's iniunctions, and by makinge use of ye votes of such as have no right of votinge in any collegiat act. P. Turner'.

Februarii I. Convenientibus domino custode sociisque in apodyterio immediate post preces vespertinas concessae sunt magistro Corbett in transmarinas partes profecturo, 20 librae annuae in biennium. Contribuent dominus Wood et dominus Lydall in usum bibliothecae collegii 5 marcas, dominus Martin vero et dominus Kettlewell 26s. 8d. Sigillata est indentura magistro Wilcoxson et procuratorium magistro Sumner de decimis Elham, nisi magister Woodcock ante festum Anuntiationis debita collegio solvat. Conceditur [*sic*] equisoni 40 solidi pro pallio. Magister Button, primus bursarius dissolvit pedem computi et discessit aeque.

[1] 'Statutes' deleted.

Aprilis 2°. Divina fecimus pro fundatore, legimus statuta et habuimus scrutinium quod prorogavimus in primum diem Iunii et quemlibet citra

Magister Wright auspicatus est lecturam clarissimi viri magistri Knightley.

[Aprilis] XX. Admissi erant dominus Martin, dominus Wood, dominus Lydall, dominus Kettlewell in annum probationis.

Variavit magister Brent defendens suas theses:

1. [*blank*]
2. [*blank*]
3. [*blank*]

Magister Howson variavit in has theses: [*blank*]

p. 349 [? Maii] XII. Dispensatum est cum magistro Howson et magistro Brent pro secundis variationibus.

XII/XIII. Doctor Turner presentibus magistris French, Greaves, Howson, Wright, Owen, Iacob mutuo accepit manuscriptum Aristoxeni ex archivis bibliothecae.

XV. Finito gratiae anno qui magistro Iacob indulgebatur dominus custos per literas ad vicecustodem monuit, ut magister Iacob allocationem et communas in futurum amitteret, nec illo postea collegio beneficio iure socii frueretur.

XXX. Hoc anno tenebatur magister Owen variare sed propter rationes a domino custode approbatas dispensationem obtinuit. Munus illud variatoris in sequentem annum transferendi

Iulii VIII. Suprema parliamenti curia declarationes quasdam aliaque de reipublicae salute scripta ad academiam misit ut publicarentur, quae domino vicecancellario per singula collegia et aulae commendante, vicecustos coram sociis et scholaribus Mertonensibus publicavit.

XX. Commemoratio fundatoris habita est, lecta etiam statuta, ac initum de more scrutinium, quod continuatum est ad 10m Augusti.

XXII. Dominus custos computavit et accepto plussagio discessit aeque.

XXVI. Susanna, uxor Gulielmi Wiblin, rogatu ipsius Gulielmi, obtinuit a collegio, ut pari iure cum marito tam in indentura quam in licentia alienationis frueretur.[1]

[1] *Margin,* 'G Wiblin'.

Praediorum locationes anno MDCXLI/XLII [1]

[*blank*][2] p. 350

[1643]

Martii XXIV°. Cum nulla, vel incerta spes esset, custodem atque vicecustodem (qui fere sex abhinc menses Londinum secesserant) brevi reversuros, visum est serenissimo regi Carolo, per literas privato ipsius sigillo signatas, iubere, ut socii novum vicecustodem eligerent, cui pro more antiquo collegii regimen mandaretur. Convenientibus igitur quinque senioribus, electus est in vicecustodem magister Greaves. p. 351

Exemplar literarum serenissimi regis Caroli
Charles Rex
Trusty and wellbeloved we greete you well. Whereas in the absence of Sir Nathaniel Brent, the warden of Merton College, and of mr Corbet, the subwarden, the said college hath been left destitute, of the statutable and usual way of government, the fellowes of themselfes, without the concurrence of these, being disabled to make, or execute any collegiate act, our will and pleasure therefore is, that the five seniours shall nominate, and elect, according to the custome of the said college, a sub-warden to continue till the first of August next. At which time if the warden be not present, the five seniors, as they were formerly wont, shall proceede to the election of their annual officers. And the sub-warden both now, and then to be elected, shall have full power, with the coassistance and consent of the maior part of the company at home, to dispose of the revenues, fines, profits and other emoluments of the said college, and to perform all other acts, conformable to the true purpose and intention of their founder. Given at our court at Oxford, the 22th [*sic*] day of March 1642.

To our trusty and well-beloved the warden, sub-warden and in their absence to the five senior fellowes of Merton College.

[1] See below Table 4.

[2] Warden Brent, who had been found backward in stirring Merton to subscribe to the royal loan of July 1642 had gone to London with subwarden Corbet by October 1642 [HUO, iv. 695]. In September the senior fellow, Dr. Peter Turner, had volunteered to join the king but was captured en route to doing so [Ibid. 697]. College business devolved on to the five senior fellows until a new subwarden was elected. This blank page was left for business transacted after July 1642, but was never filled in.

Praedia, Fundi & Tenementa	Firmarii	Tempus Indenturae		Habendum	Finis	Licent' Alienat'	
		Concessae	Sigillatae			Concessae	Sigillatae
Margaret Stratton parsonage	Franciscus Kemble	Aug. 3	Oct. 20	21 a festo Michaelis 1641	£120		
Signum Rosae in Watford	Iohannes Leonard	Aug. 3	Nov. 4	21 a festo Michaelis 1641	£30	Aug. 30	Nov. 4
Canes in West Tilbury	Dominus I. Boteler	Aug. 3	Feb. 9	21 a festo Michaelis 1641	£40		
Tenementum in Holiwell	Willielmus Wibl[in] et Susanna uxor	Aug. 3 Iulii 30	Apr. 23 1641 Iulii 30 1642	21 a festo Michaelis 1641	£2 10s. & 3 capones annuatim		Iulii 30
Tenementum in Hampton Poil	W. Astill	Aug. 3	Oct. 16	21 a 16° Aug. 1641	£6 13s. 4d.	Ian. 10	
Tenementum in Holywel	Ricardus Maude	Aug. 7	Apr. 23	40 a festo Michaelis 1641	duo capones per annum	Ian. 10	Apr. 23

Table 4. Praediorum locationes Anno MDCXLI/XLII[1]

[1] The MS. has a table with grid lines similar to the above; some abbreviations have been retained to facilitate printing.

[Martii] XXV°. Commemoratione fundatoris habita, lecta sunt statuta et initum pro more scrutinium.

XX° Aprilis. Hoc die vicecustos ad socios retulit, quid statuendum censerent de eis quos dominus custos, repugnantibus licet doctore Turner et magistro Greaves, frustraque reverendissimi patroni nostri acta violari conquerentibus, in annum probationis admiserat. Illi re pensitata, habitaque proventuum collegii ratione, aerisque alieni, quod nuper contractum est, nequaquam inpraesentiarum in perpetuam societatem admittendos esse iudicarunt. Ne tamen omnis in posterum eis praecipue domino Lydal, qui solus aderat, spes abscinderetur, rem integram arbitrio patroni relinquerunt.

Iunii V°. Cum magistro Coply 2do bursario dispensatum est, quod p. 352 elapsis octo septimanis, a tempore quo primo rationem exhibuit, nondum suum aeque absolverat. Praetendebat enim se plus expendisse, quam acceperat.

A quinque senioribus magister Nevil decanus electus est, in locum magistri Button, qui octo menses continuos a collegio abfuerat.

Iussu serenissimi regis Caroli omnia emolumenta, quae doctori Turner iure socii debebantur, eidem absenti ab officiariis, quibus id munus incumbit, eroganda sunt. Cum magistris, qui hoc anno variare tenebantur, dispensatum est.

Acceptis literis a serenissimo rege nostro, vicecustos socios consuluit, qua ratione regiae maiestati, quae dominum Woodes et dominum Lydall in perpetuam societatem admitti iussit, satisfacerent, et antiquis collegii institutis simul prospicerent, quibus cautum est ut baccalaurei, scholasticis exercitiis nulla gratia aut relaxatione impetrata, fungantur. Responsum est, et regiae maiestati, et collegio, satisfactum iri, si termino Michaelis proxime sequenti in societatem admittantur, ea lege, ut scholastica exercitia praestent, et disciplinam a maioribus traditam, sed hominum, temporumque, vitio collapsam, subeant.

Commemoratio fundatoris habita est, lecta statuta, et initum pro more scrutinium quod ad Kalendas Augusti, et quemlibet diem citra prorogatum est.

Golding tonsor a parochia Divi Petri in Oriente consensu sociorum prius habito, a vicecustode in tonstrinam admittitur.

p. 353 I° Augusti. Officiarii sequentis anni qui, absente custode, a quinque senioribus electi sunt:
vicecustos, magister Greaves.
decani, magistri Brode, Sayer, Loveioy,
bursarii, magistri Howson, Wright, Fowles.
principalis portionistarum, magister Nevil; bursarius Williot, magister Brent; capellanus capellae, magister Nevil; lector Linacri inferior, doctor Greaves e collegio Omnium Animarum; lector linguae Graecae, magister Priaulx; lector grammaticae, magister Owen; exhibitionarius Hamsterly, magister Owen.

IV Augusti. Sociis ob reditus insolutos rerum omnium inopia laborantibus, aliis rusticatum ire coactis, aliis peregre proficisci, totaque academia morbo castrensi afflicta, vicecustos caeterique socii qui domi aderant, consensuerunt omnia collegii emolumenta, quae pacatis temporibus, singulis numerari solent, quem primum pace restituta, fieri possit, eis aeque absentibus, ac praesentibus, esse eroganda.

XIV Novembris. In superiorem Linacri lecturam vacantem ob mortem clarissimi doctissimique viri, domini Iohannis Bainbrigii, medicinae doctoris, et in academia Oxoniensi publici astronomiae professoris, qui paulo ante cum summo omnium eruditorum desiderio, et luctu, e vivis excesserat, dominus Edovardus Greaves e collegio Omnium Animarum, medicinae doctor, unanimi sociorum consensu electus est. In inferiorem Linacri lecturam dominus Sambatch, medicinae doctor olim collegii alumnus, eisdem approbantibus, suffectus est.

XVI Novembris. Dominus Wood et dominus Lydall in perpetuam societatem admissi sunt.

[1644]

II Februarii 1644. Dominus Lee et dominus Whistler, completo quadriennio a prima eorum admissione, in numerum magistrorum asciti sunt.

p. 354 [*blank*]

p. 355 Anno Domini MDCXLIIII, regis Caroli XX, custodis Brent XXIII.-Septembris 26. Magister Ricardus Nevill vicecustos tabe absumptus desideratus est.

Octobris 1. Magister Howson in eius locum suffectus est vicecustos.

Novembris 26. Magister Whistler veniam impetravit peregre proficiscendi ad duos annos, atque eodem tempore assensum est ut allocatio viginti librarum illi a collegio annuatim debeatur, numeranda ubi collegium solvendo fuerit.

Decembris 17. Dispensatum est cum magistro Lee ut sacris ordinibus initiaretur, etsi biennium non compleverat.

Decembris 18. Commemoratio fundatoris habita est, atque initum scrutinium cum lectione statutorum dispensatum est. Scrutinium in primum diem Martii, et quemlibet diem citra prorogatum est.

Decembris 20. Magister French computavit.

[1645]

Ianuarii 27. Sede metropolitana Cantuariensi vacante, eoque iure patronatus collegii in regias manus devoluto, rege tunc temporis occasione belli plus quam civilis Oxoniae in Aede Christi residente, circa horam undecimam antemeridianam tradita sunt vicecustodi a regia maiestate missae literae ad societatem Mertonensium. Quibus acceptis vicecustos, re sociis significata, indictoque ad horam primam postmeridianam conventu, praestituto tempore omnes socii domi existentes convenerunt. Eodemque tempore literae serenissimi regis a vicecustode palam factae recitataeque sunt.

Tenor regiarum literarum

To our right trustie and welbeloved the subwarden and
ffelowes of Merton Colledge in Oxford,

Charles Rex

Trustie and welbeloved wee greete you well. Whereas Sir Nathaniel Brent Knt your warden of Merton Colledge hath long since adhered and contributed to ye rebells now in armes against us and hath notoriusly taken / upon him the office of judge marshall, or other p. 356
commission to that effect among them, and hath contemptuously refused to repaire to our Royall Person, and besides for almost these three yeares last past hath neglected his attendance and office of wardenship, and during all this time or any part thereof he hath not expressed any act of industrie or diligence either in respect of the government or discipline of ye said colledge which by your statutes he ought to have done; and att this present continues still absent from the same your colledge standing in much need att this time of ye industrie, care and diligence of a warden, whic as it is by notorietie of the fact well knowne, soe we also have been ascertained by three of you the fellowes of the said colledge of this his absence and neglect, our

pleasure and command therefore is to displace and put out, and wee doe displace and put out the said Sir Nathaniel Brent as a man unworthie and no longer capable of that imployment from that his wardenship and from all right and interest therein and from all benefitt and priviledge any way by him to be claimed hereafter of or by the same. And our further pleasure and command is that you the subwarden with such of the fellowes as are now present, or can speedily be called together, without delay proceed to the election and nominacion of three men (as your custome hath been) unto us. One of which three thus electe and nominated we intend for the peace and good of your college to appoint and constitute ye warden in the stead of the said Sir Nathaniel Brent. And so wee bid you farewell. Given at our court att Oxon, this 24th day of January 1644.

This is according to your majestie's command.
Hertforde

His literis lectis consultatus est de tempore conveniendi ad electionem nominationemque novi custodis, atque unanimiter visum est rem ultra horam nonam crastinae diei non ampliandam, ne quinquam enim expectandum obsessis undequaque infestisque militibus viis, aut nuntium perferri, aut absentes socios tutum ad collegium receptum habere posse. Consequenter etiam statutum fundatoris quod ad electionem novi custodis pertinet a vicecustode lectum, viz. De custode autem cum ibi ponendus fuerit hoc modo provideatur. Septem de provectioribus et discretioribus dictae domus assignentur ad inquirendum a singulis scholaribus et itaque septem seniores assignati sunt, viz. magister Howson, vicecustos, doctor Turner, magister French, magister Fisher, magister Greaves, magister Brent, magister Sayer ad inquirendum a singulis sociis et scholaribus, si quos in spiritualibus et temporalibus sive de dicta domo, sive aliunde discretos et exercitatos noverint, ut ex iis qui per dictos scholares nominati fuerint, aut aliis si liquido magis expedierint, tres quos magis idoneos, et domui nostro necessarios intelligerent regiae maiestati nominarent.

Conventum est etiam eodem tempore, ut vicecustos sede vacante, septimanatim percipiat integram allocationem mensae domini custodis factam usque ad realem novi custodis inductionem.

[Ianuarii] 28. Convenerunt hora praestituta socii ad electionem nominationemque novi custodis, ubi septem seniores, consultis prius interrogatisque sociis et scholaribus, iisque secedentibus, hos eximios viros nominabant:

magistri Sayer, Brent, Greaves, Fisher nominabant doctorem Harvey, doctorem Hinton, magistrum Sellar.
Magister French nominabat doctorem Higges, doctorem Earles, magistrum Hales.
Doctor Turner nominabat magistrum Hales, magistrum Morley et seipsum.
Vicecustos nominabat doctorem Harvey, magistrum Morley et magistrum Seller.
Facta nominatione doctorTurner, magister French et magister Greaves omnium consensu deputati et assignati sunt, ut nominationem ita factam serenissimae regis maiestati repraesentarent.

[Ianuarii] 29. Instrumentum nominationis hora prima pomeridiana in p. 357
conventu sociorum collegii sigillo munitum est.

May it please your most excellent maiesty. In humble obedience to your maiestie's commands we ye subwarden and fellowes of Merton college, havinge convened our present company for ye election and nomination of a warden in this present vacancy of ye place, having first consulted with ye junior fellowes, and observed al things required by our statutes, the seven seniors delivered their votes in this manner, the junior fellow first deliveringe his voice.
Mr Sayer, mr Brent, mr Greaves, mr Fisher nominate doctor William Harvey, doctor Hinton, mr Sellar.
Mr French nominates doctor Higges, doctor Earles, mr Hales.
Doctor Turner nominates mr Hales, mr Morley and himself.
The subwarden nominates doctor Harvey, mr Morley, mr Sellar.

Having in all humility and obedience to your maiesties commands represented to your sacred majesty these our nominations, in testimony thereof we have applied our common seale. Datum 29 Ianuary Anno Domini 1644 et regis Caroli vicesimo.

Eodem die magister French et magister Greaves instrumentum nominationis regi praesentabant. Doctore Turner id muneris detrectante dominus rex electionem suam novi custodis suspendit. Doctor Turner suas exceptiones contra sociorum nominationem in pet[it]ione ad regem exponit.

Petitio ad regem doctoris Turner

To the king's most excellent ma'tie the humble petition of Peter Turner, ffellow of Merton College in Oxon'

Most humbly sheweth,

That upon your maiestie's letters lately directed to the subwarden and ffellowes of Merton College, declaring the office of that warden of that college to be voyd, and requiring the ffellowes to proceed to the nomination of a new according to statute, the ffellowes have accordingly proceeded, but in so undue and unstatuable manner as that their nomination is questionable in divers respects. Ffirst that one of the suffragantes hath been avered (as tis probable) by a charge of felony, as to petition against his unkle Sir Nathaniel Brent, so to give his vote to a stranger. Secondly that one (who had been putt out of his fellowship by my Lord of Canterbury above six yeares since, and was after three yeares restored to it by Sir Nathaniel Brent meerly in despight and affront to my Lord of Canterbury being then oppressed by the rebels) was sent for to make a party and admitted to vote in the nominations, lastly that whereas the statutes of the college require that the seaven seniors should name three to the visitor they have named eight.

May it therefore please your sacred ma'tie to suspend your choice upon so questionable a nomination untill oure visitor (hereafter to be named by your mai'tie) may take the business into his consideration and your petitioner shall as in duty bounde ever pray etc.

p. 358 Sequitur relatio honoratissimi Marchionis Hertford regi facta post examinationem petitionis.

According to your maiesties commands I have this day called doctor Turner together with the subwarden and the rest of the ffellowes of Merton College (now resident) before mee, and in the presence of them all caused to be read the petition hereunto annexed, being the said doctor Turner's petition to your maiestie to suspend the choice of a new warden until your Maiestie shall be pleased to name a visitor; in which petition I find three obiections sett forth by doctor Turner why that petition already made (in pursuance of your maiesties commands) is so undue and unstatuable, as that their nomination is questionable (viz't)

1. That one of the suffragens hath been (probably) averred by a charge of felonie, as to petition against his uncle Sir Nathaniel Brent, so to give his vote for a stranger. This obiection I found to be grounded on no proofes but bare assertion.

2dly. That one who had been putt out of his fellowship by my Lord of Canterbury above six yeares since and was after three years restored to it by Sir Nathaniel Brent meerely in despight and affront of my lord of Canterbury (then opposed by the rebells) was sent for to make a partie and admitted to vote in the nomination. This obiection was answered by magister Greaves who said that he would averre that he being in London since the partie meant in the petition was so readmitted and waiting upon my Lord of Canterbury (amongst other things), some mention being made of this party his lordship replyed that he had been misinformed (or words to that effect) and liked it well that he was restored to his fellowship againe.

3dly. Whereas the statutes of the college require that the seaven seniors should name three to the visitor they have named eight.

To this they said that doctor Turner was the onely ffellow amongst them that proposed a greater number than three. And in generall to that part of the petition which chargeth them with an undue and unstatuable proceeding they all saide they might elect doctor Harvey because the very worde of their statutes were 'sive de dicta domo sive aliunde discretos et exercitatos noverint', which statutes being called for and read I founde the expresse word.

To this doctor Turner framed several replies but especially that ye archbishopps had been visitors of that college by the space fo 300 yeares, and in all that time neither of them (except one Matthew Parker archbishopp) had nominated any stranger and whether your mai'tie for that one president would give the wardenshippe to a stranger he humbly left to your maiestie's consideration. The sub-warden and ffellowes pretending not to know any such thing and insisting on the words of their statutes humbly entreated your maiestie not to suspend ye choise of a warden, but to give them a head whereof (they say) they stood in present necessitie.

All which I, humbly leave to your maiesties great wisdome.

7 February 1644

Februarii 14. Magister French bursarius discessit aeque.

Martii 30.Habita est fundatoris commemoratio, initum scrutinium, dispensatum cum lectione statutorum.

Eodem tempore dispensatum est cum magistro Owen et magistro Brode pro suis variationibus pro hoc anno, eo quod dimissis baccalaureis, inde in disputationibus baccalaureorum prout consuetum est habere non possent.

p. 359 Anno Domini MDCXLV, regis Caroli xxi°, doctoris Harvey custodis 1°.

Aprilis 8. Dominus doctor Harvey vicecustodi significavit se acceptisse regias literas ad collegium nostrum directas, quibus serenissimus rex illum custodem renuntiabat. Itaque cupere ut socii proximo die hora octava matutina ad admissionem suam obsolvendam in ecclesia convenirent, consequenter admoniti sunt socii a vicecustode ut loco et tempore praedictis praesto adessent circiter horam 7^{am} matutinam doctor Turner resignationem suam registro inserendam hisce verbis misit vicecustodi.

Resignatio doctoris Turner

Anno Domini 1645 Aprilis 9°. Ego Petrus Turner modo socius collegii Mertonensis, totum illud ius quod hactenus habui habeove in dicta societate, sponte et deliberato resigno. In cuius rei fidem uberiorem chirographum meum praesentibus apposui. Petrus Turner.

Hora octava matutina clarissimus vir doctor Gulielmus Harvey et omnes socii domi existentes in choro ecclesiae Sancti Iohannis Baptistae conveniunt, ubi doctor Harvey praesentibus hisce amplissimis viris qui honoris causa illuc deducebant, viz. doctore Stuart, decano Sancti Pauli, doctore Fell, decano Aedis Christi, doctore Morris, linguae Hebraicae regio professore, doctore Clayton, regio medicinae professore, et domino Thoma Rives, regi advocato, et tradidit vicecustodi has serenissimi regis et honoratissimi Marchionis Hertforde literas quarum exemplaria sequuntur, quae palam et publice recitatae sunt.

To our trustie and welbeloved the subwarden and ffellowes
of Merton College in Oxon'.

Charles Rex.

Trustie and welbeloved we greett you well, whereas we have chosen, and by these our letters thought fit to signifie unto you that we doe choose our wel beloved servant doctor William Harvey, one of our principall physitians, to be your warden of our house or college in Oxon' called Merton College, being one of those w'ch according to your statutes you have elected, and nominated unto us for the wardenship thereof; our will and command therefore is that according to your accustomed manner you forthwith receive and admitt the said doctor William Harvey (alreadie sworne by our command before our right trustie and wel beloved cozen and countrollour, the marquesse of Hertford, chancellour of our universitie of Oxon' as well to our royal authoritie as to observe the statutes and customes of the said college, according to the foundation thereof to be your warden of our said house or college in the stead of Sir Nathaniel Brent deservedly removed by us from that place, to have and enjoy the wardenship of ye said house or college, withall the rights emoluments and profitts thereunto belonging, in as ample and beneficiall manner as the said Sir Nathaniel Brent or any of your wardens heretofore have had or enjoyed the same as by the foundation and statutes of the said college he or they had, or ought to have had or enjoyed, straitly charging and commanding you and every of you, to give him, the said doctor William Harvey, obedience in all respects as to your warden doth of right appertaine and belong. Given att our court att Oxon' this seaventh day of Aprill 1645.

Subscribed by his Maiesties command, Hertforde

William Marquesse and Earle of Hertford, Viscount Beauchamp, Lord Seymour, one of his maiesties most hon'ble privie councell and chancellour of the universitie of Oxon', to the warden and ffellowes of Merton College in Oxon' aforesaid and all others whom it may concerne, greeting.

According to his maiesties command, signified to me in writing under his signe manuall, I have caused Sir William Harvey one of his maiesties principall physitians to be sworne (before mee) warden of Merton College aforesaid, to observe ye statutes and customes of ye said college according to the ffoundation of the same. Given under my hand and seale at Oxon' the 8th day of Aprill anno domini 1645.

Hertforde

Admissio custodis

Lectis litteris vicecustos authoritate, qua in hac parte fungitur dominum doctorem vero Gulielmum Harvey, sic admissit custodem, viz. secundum hanc formam; 'Insignissime domine, quod felix faustumque sit, quod sacratissimis pulveribus illustrissimi fundatoris Gualteri de Merton gratum accidat, quod universae Mertonensis societatis bene vortat, librum hunc statutorum prudentissimi fundatoris, necnon clavem maximae portae collegii insignia regiminis custodiaeque vestrae magis nosmet ipsos [lu]bentes gratantesque in vestras manus dedimus. / Peracta admissione, ad preces matutinas p. 360
discessum est, quibus finitis domus custos singulos socios amplexus, itidem ab iisdem, prosequentibus praefatis amplissimis viris ad

hospitium custodis deductus est, ubi nihil commoratus, in altam aulam ascensum est, ubi dominus custos lauto cupediarum apparatu, symposioque tum praefatos amplissimos viros, tum socios excepit. Post epulas discedentibus amplissimis viris dominus custos ad hospitium suum, socii ad cameras suas se receperunt.

Aprilis 11°. Dominus custos convocatis in altam aulam socios haec verba [*two words crossed out*] ad illos fecit, forsitan predecessores custodiam collegii ambivere ut exinde sese locupletarent, se vero longe alio animo victurum, et collegii lucro et emolumento potius foret, simulque socios ut concordia amicitiaque inter se solerent, sedulo solliciteque hortatus est.

17°. Magister French bursarius computavit.

Maii 9° Dispensatum est cum magistro Sayer ut vicaria quadam in agro Somersetensi in sese nuper collata, una cum collegio donec pax regno restituatur frueretur, licet excederet iuxta regii codicis estimationem valorem octo librarum annuatim. Quin et insuper indultum est ut pace regni restituta optionem haberet, vel collegio vel beneficio renuntiandi.

Iunii 12°. Magister French bursarius discessit aeque.

Iulii 20°. Habita est fundatoris commemoratio initum scrutinium quod ad 1^mum^ diem Augusti et quemlibet diem citra prorogatum est (cum lectione statutorum dispensatum)

Anno Domini 1645°, regis Caroli 21°, domini doctoris Harvey custodis 1°

A note or inventory of such goods and household stuffe which were in the Warden's Lodging of Merton Colledge or disposed of by mr John Greaves there with note or inventory were given by Avis Smith who was left in trust with ye lodgeing goods by Sir Nathaniel Brent.

In ye Kitchin
Spitts 4
Kettles 2
Brasse Potts 2
Skimmers 2
dishes 12
Chargers 2
Cleaver 1
Mincing knife 1
ffrying pan 1
Skilletts 2
Tinning dripping pans 3
Morter & pestle 1
Gridiron 1

William Noble Cooke acknowledgth these things to be for ye use of ye Lady of Northampton

In ye Lady Cobham lodgings

Peeces of hangings 5 John Browne

Turky worke Chaires & Stooles 10

In ye parlour, and about ye house

Turky worke stooles and Chaires 20

Tables 2

Stripe carpetts 2

Rugges 4

Blanketts 6

Featherbedds 8

Bolsters 8

Pillowes 3

Candlesticks 8

Chamber potts 4

Basons 2

One old woolebedd & bolster 1

Coverletts 3

Anthony Harsey servant to ye Countesse of Northampton did acknowledge this housholdstuffe to be in her possession.

A note of ye warden's linnen in ye vestry p. 361

Diaper Tablecloathes 3 old & 7 new 10

Two breadth Tablecloathes 10

whereof mr Greaves hath had 4 & 2 single flexon ones with 1 breadth

Tablecloathes for ye Servants 6

Of dammaske Tablecloath 1

Towell 1

Cupboardcloath 1

Long diaper Towells 3

Flexon Towells 17

Foure dozen & one of broad dowlasse Napkins whereof mr Greaves had 2 dozen

& 2 dozen of holland diaper Napkins

Foure dozen & 10 napkins of narrow dowlasse whereof mr Greaves had 2 dozen

Three dozen of old flexon Napkins

Five old Flexon napkins more

Ten old dammaske Napkins sutable to ye Cloath

Three dozen & 3 Napkins of old diaper

Three dresser Cloathes

Five paire of old Canvase Sheetes for ye Servants

Eight paire of new strong Sheetes for ye Servants

Three paire of old Flexon Sheetes

Five paire of Holland Sheets whereof mr Greaves had 3 paire which were old thother 2 new.

Five paire of pillowbeares whereof mr Greaves had 3 paire

One Lawne Cupboard Cloath.
All these are in ye 2 chests except those which mr Greaves hath received.

John Browne

More belonging to ye Lodging
The little Chamber at ye South end of the Gallery hanged with Coarse Arras
One Bed & bolster bedsteed with greene silke Curtaines & Vallance two blanketts and one silke greene quilte

All which at ye Queen's comming were disposed of by mr Greaves except ye hangings

In ye Gallery
Two great Turky workd Chaires
Twelve Turky worked Chaires
Twelve Stooles of ye same
One Long drawing Table
Two side boards Tables
One Court Cupbord

In ye Drawing Chamber
Arras hangings. Two Tables Two Turky worke Carpetts A Court Cupboard with a Turky worke Covering A paire of brasse Andirons

In ye little Chamber where ye Cooke lay
One halfe headed bedsteed. A bed bolster one blankett & blew rugge One round table.

In ye Vault Chamber
One bedsteed bed & bolster 2 pillowes 3 blanketts a Counterpane which shee will deliver
A high blue Chaire 2 blew Stooles 2 blew low stooles one round Table one Court Cupboard with blew sutable Coverings
A paire of iron doggs. Course Arras hangings like those in ye Chamber on ye South end of ye Gallary

In ye little Chamber ioyning to it over ye Vault
One Bedsteed with striped Curtains and Vallance A Bed Bolster two Blanketts 1 greene rugge

In ye Dineing roome where ye Queene lay
A drawing Table with a Turky worke Carpett a Court Cupboard A side Table all with suteable Turky worke Carpetts One great Turky

worke Chaire 12 Turky-worke backt Chaires 2 paire of brasse Andirons

In ye Chamber over ye Parlour

Arras hangings ye best in ye lodging

1 bedstead 1 mattresse a bed 1 bolster 2 downe pillowes 1 holland quilte 3 blanketts Curtaines Vallance and Counterpane of Orange Tawny lawn, a Table, Court Cupboard with Covering of ye same, one great Chaire 2 low Chaires 2 low Stooles of ye same

In ye Parlour

One Ovall Table 12 old Turky worke Chaires & Stooles together An old striped carpet a Court Cupboard a side Table with old striped Covering

In ye great hall

A long Table a long forme A still

In ye great Parlour

was ye furniture of young mr Brent now used by mr Willowby vizt A bedsteed bed bolster pillow 3 blanketts, a blue rugge 3 Irish stitchd Chaires a paire of Andirons with brasse topps

In ye Kitchin

three dozen & a halfe of Pewter dishes wheof ye Countesse has a dozene, mr Greaves 2 dozen the rest being old left with Hawkins.

More in ye Kitchin p. 362

Two brasse potts 2 kettles 2 Skilletts 3 or 4 Spitts a Jacke a Cleaver & mincing knife A frying pan, & brasse ladles 2 Tin dripping pans

The 5 bedds with yeir furniture disposed by mr Greaves

The Countesse of Northampton hath 7 ffeather bedds with bolsters blanketts.

Twenty one paire of Sheets wheareof she putt up sixteene in ye Chest 5 she gave to mr Greaves whereof 2 were fine Holland & one of ye paires had 3 breadths in a sheet

To mr Greaves 6 pillowbeeres

To mr Greaves 2 Diaper Table Cloathes Two suteable side boarde Cloathes 2 dozen of Diaper Napkins 2 dowlasse Table Cloathes with 2 breadths in a Cloath

Two suteable side board Cloathes 2 dozen of broad Dowlasse Napkins 2 flaxen TableCloathes with 2 breadths in a Cloath 2 dozen of narrow dowlasse Napkins new

June ye 11th 1645

All these was taken from ye mouth of Avis Smith in ye presence of doctor Harvey ye Warden & us

Francis Brode
Charles Scarborough
The marke of Avis Smith.

[*Added later*] Avis Smith hath of ye College Goodes – One Sylver Salt seaven sylver spoones, whereof one broken, another crack'de.

[*Added later*] Memorandum that this silver salt and these 7 spoones above written were by consent of ye Warden and fellows changed into 12 new silver spoones.

p. 363 Anno Domini MDCXLV, regis Caroli xxi°, doctoris Harvey custodis 1°.

Magistri in artibus

1. Iohannes French
2. Alexander Fisher
3. Iohannes Greaves
4. Edvardus Corbet
5. Gulielmus Berkley
6. Nicolaus Howson
7. Ranulphus Donvile
8. Franciscus Wright
9. Rogerus Brent
10. Gulielmus Owen
11. Franciscus Broade
12. Georgius Clark
13. Edvardus Coply
14. Radolphus Button
15. Iohannes Pryaulx
16. Robertus Sayer
17. Christophorus Fowle
18. Georgius Loveioye
19. Iohannes Lee
20. Daniel Whistler
21. Thomas Iones

Domini

1. Martin
2. Wood
3. Lydall

Capellani

1. Iohannes Gurgaine
2. Franciscus Crofts

Augusti 1°. Sociorum collegii nostri numerus satis amplus suprascribitur hisce vero difficillimis temporibus domi aderant tantum quinque videlicet magister French, magister Howson, magister Brent, magister Coply, magister Lee quibus in bibliotheca convenientibus (neque domini hospitium custodis aut aula alta nobis de tempore usui fuerunt) dominus custos praefatus est, accepisse secundum solemnem et antiquam consuetudinem fuisse collegii nostri in festo Sancti Petri ad Vincula novos collegii officiarios eligendos esse. Quibus (pro more) sustentandis, neque res satis ampla collegii aut numerus sociorum sufficerunt. Itaque custos una cum quinque sociis praesentibus secundum regis rescriptum datum Oxoniae 22[do] Martii anno domini 1642 sequentis anni officiarios designarunt et eligerunt, viz. magistrum French vicecustodem, magistrum Coply, principalem portionistarum, magistrum Lee, bursarium, pro toto anno insequente.

Eodem die sancitum est per custodem et socios quaecunque in registrum collegii inserenda fuerint, prius literis scriptis per vicecustodem conciperentur et coram custode et sociis publice in conventu recitarentur. Cum ratione civilium motuum per universum Magnae Britanniae grassantium proventus collegii et reditus annui per firmarios minus diligenter solvantur quibus / provideretur necesariis repar- p. 364
ationibus collegii et sustentationi sociorum praesentium, per dominum custodem et socios consensum est, quod centum librae nomine custodis et scholarium collegii de Merton mutuo acciperentur ad facta lecta conferanda et victum custodis et sociorum. E quibus pecuniis hebdomadatim in quolibet die veneris custos recipiet viginti solidos pro portione sua, et quilibet socius praesens octo solidos. Prima solutio incipiet in primo die Augusti qui est dies veneris.

Decretum est insuper literas attornatus communi sigillo collegii muniendas esse, virtute quarum potestas fiat magistro Coply colligendi arreragias pro decimis Cirencestrensibus a domino Gulielmo Masters debitas, necnon locandi decymas praedictas pro anno sequenti.

Cum quidem Robertus Symons, et Georgius Symons possessionem terrarum nuper perquisitarum in Hensington delyneant et earum reditus non omnino solvant per socios tum praesentes huius negotii tractatio demandata est domino custodi et vicecustodi. Prorogatur scrutinium ad festum Michaelis et quemlibet diem citra.

Magister Broad nuper secessit rusticatum [*sic*] ut cubiculus [*sic*] iam vacuus fuerit, coram custode et sociis magister Brent promisit, si magister Howson illi clavem dicti cubiculi traderet, se in adventu magistri Broade sursum redditurum dictum cubiculum magistro Broade.

Quinto Augusti convenimus in bibliotheca, ubi vidua Holt exhibuit supplicem libellum, coram domino custode et sociis, qui cum quaestionem in eis conti[n]uebat; responsum est per custodem et socios, se cum consilio iurisperitorum deliberaturos, et ut occasio postularet eidem responsuros.

Eodem die Thomas Clark et Franciscus Sayre una sursum reddiderunt indenturas domus cuiusdam in Holliwell nuperrime constructae. Quas indenturas de novo dymitti petierunt cuidam Ioannae Coxe in mynore aetate, degenti in eadem parochia. Huic petitioni consenserunt socii. Nomine finis quadraginta solidi sunt memorandi in die sigillationis pro spatio viginti unius annorum incipiente in termyno Michaelis proxime sequenti.

Electus est magister Howson bursarius Williot pro anno sequente.

p. 365 Literae attornatus sigillatae fuerunt communi sigillo collegii magistro French, magistro Lee, Thomae Appleby obsonatori collegii et Gulielmo Thomas equisoni collegii ad petendos redditus insolutos et arreragias redituum necnon alia negotia peragenda in dictis literis specificata.

Vicesimo nono Augusti magister French computavit pro ultimo termino huius anni coram domino custode, magistro Howson, magistro Brent et magistro Lee, cui computo subscripsit magister Howson, Nicolaus Howson loco vicecustodis qui eo tempore senior socius erat, in audiendo computo. Istam superscriptionem non propria authoritate factam sed ex suo mandato in registrum inseri iussit dominus custos.

Decimo sexto Octobris magister French in praesentia domini custodis et sociorum decessit aeque, cui magister Howson ut supra subscripsit.

Eodem die cum consensu custodis et sociorum globus terrestris et caelestis e bibliotheca collegii mutuo dantur duci Eboracensi degenti in aula regia quae tum erat in Aede Christi Oxon', quos magister Carolus Maye tuto reponi fidem fecerat domino custodi. Eodem die magister Gurgaine, capellanus senior, petiit a domino custode et sociis, ut allocationes et stipendia sibi debita a collegio aut numerarentur, aut sub chirographis officiariorum collegii attestarentur. Magister Lee, bursarius huic ratiocinio destinatur. Querela tum incidit quod magister Gurganie capellanus tantum, oblationes collegii debitas sibi assumpserat, custode et vicecustode inconsultis, necnon feoda quorundam matrimoniorum in ecclesia nostra celebratorum, magistro Lee bursario harum rerum examinatio mandatur.

Vicesimo septimo Octobris virtute decreti in cancellaria magister Lee, bursarius petiit possessionem terrarum nuper perquisitarum apud Hensington in comitatu Oxon' necnon reditus collegio debitos.

Novembris 27° convenimus in bibliotheca collegii ubi secundam
p. 366 ordinationem dominorum adversus obsidionem / (quam Deus avertat)

ratio habenda fuerat necessiorum victualum pro octo sociis et in hunc modum providebatur vizt duae quarteriae tritici et duo modii, quatuor sucidiae casei pondo centum et dimidium, salis modius et dimidium, orizae viginti pondo, carnis bovinae duo pectora, horum omnium provisio a magistrum Lee referebatur, et ut asseruit ipse omnia haec in tuto repondebantur.

Eodem die decretum est per custodem et socios ut rami arborum in parte occidentali collegii amputarentur.

Decimo octavo Decembris celebrantur divina pro commemoratione fundatoris.

Scrutinium eo die habitum erat. Et differebatur sive prorogabatur ad 1um diem Ianuarii et quemlibet diem citra.

Decimo nono die magister Lee, bursarius computavit pro 1° termino.

Ex decreto domini custodis et sociorum omni meliori modo et iuris forma postulandi fuerunt reditus tenentium nostrorum qui secundum tenorem indenturarum eos non solverunt. Eaque de causa magistro Lee bursario collegii et magistro French et aliis sigillatae fuerunt literae attornatus ad eundem effectum.

Vicesimo die Septembris postulabantur reditus rectoriae de Woolford a magistro Ioanne Oakly inter horas quintam et septimam eiusdem die in aula collegii per magistrum French, praesentibus magistro Brent, socio, et Iohanne Browne, clerico, ad istud testificandum requisiti.

Eodem die similiter postulati sunt reditus de Cheddington ab magistro Maine, iisdem praesentibus ad eundem effectum.

Octobris 26to postulabantur similiter redditus de Ibston a Wilmot per magistrum Lee, praesentibus Nathaniele Iones, Augustino Boxly.

Eodem die postulabantur redditus pro ly Falcon in Gamlingay a Charnock, praesentibus Nathaniele Iones et Augustino Boxly.

Novembris septimo postulabantur redditus de Newington in comitatu Kantii a magistro Trafford, praesentibus Nathaniele Iones et Augustino Boxly.

Novembris 8° postulabantur reditus a Peirs alias Noone pro Basingstoak in agro Hantonensi, praesentibus Iones et Boxly.

Novembris 9° postulabantur reditus de silvis Mertonage a domino Iohanne Iacob, praesentibus Nathaniele Iones, Augustino Boxly.

p. 367 Novembris decimi sexto postulabantur reditus de West Tilbury a domino Iohanne Botiler in aula communi collegii intra horas quintam et 6^{tam}, praesentibus Nathaniel Iones et Augustino Boxley.

Novembris 23°. A domino Iohanne Iacob similiter pro Gamlingay Avenells in agro Cantabrigiensi, praesentibus Nathaniele Iones et Thomas Hawkins.

Decembris 13°. Magister Howson et magister Owen designantur ad inquirendem [*sic*] de valore annuo domus nostrae in parrochia Sancti Aldati et ad aestimandum quantum incommodi tenens passus est per incendium.

[1646]

Sexto Ianuarii. Convenimus in bibliotheca ubi lectae sunt literae a serenissima regis maiestate ad collegiorum et aularum praefectos, quas in registrum inseri custodi et sociis visum est, ut posteri sciant quantae curae fuerit serenissimo regi divinam maiestatem votis et ieiuniis poscere ut calamitatem ecclesiae et magnae Britanniae regno imminentem averteret. Literarum examplar sequitur.

Charles Rex

Trustie and welbeloved wee greet you well. Oure expresse will and pleasure is that you take speciall care that divine service established by lawe bee read daily morning and evening as nowe it is in youre respective howses. And wee further command that upon all Wednesdayes and Fridayes you make choice of some fit times both in ye morning & evenyng (besides those imployd in the common lyturgie) wherein you are to use one of those formes lately set out for private use, soe that in those dayes you shall meet fower times at divine service. And although wee doe not enjoyne the use of those formes oftner than on Wensdayes and Frydayes, yet wee shall bee well pleased yt you do the like on other days as your occasions shall permit, and your devotions shall persuade you. And this course wee require you to continue during these sad times. And for Frydaies you shall take speciall care yt neither flesh nor fish bee prepared for youre severall companies untill five of ye clock at soonest in ye afternoone when ye evening service hath binne first performed, and this you shall observe more and at all times
p. 368 hereafter according to ye example of ye Primitive Christians. Given at our court at Oxon' the 28th daye of December 1645.

By his Maiesties Command
Edward Nicholas.

Ordinatum est desuper quod formulae privatae orationum a bursario sumptibus collegio procurentur, et quod quolibet die mercurii et veneris inter horas decimam et undecimam ante meridiem et secundam et tertiam post meridiem celebrentur divina durante hoc tempore calamitoso.

Decimo Ianuarii relatum est ad custodem et socios per magistrum Owen et magistrum French magnas ruinas fecisse incendium in parochia Sancti Aldati ubi tenementum habemus vocatum Bull-Hall quod pene consumptum erat per incendium, rogante itaque Abele Parmer qui possesssor erat dicti tenementi renovatae sunt indenturae pro quadraginta annis qui finem quinque librarum solvere tenetur, vizt quinquaginta duos solidos in sigillatione indenturae et 52 solidos anno sequente, quo tempore cautum est ut reparationes fierent quam cito fieri possint.

Decimo tertio Februarii. Magister Lee in praesentia custodis et sociorum decessit aeque.

Magister Owen electus est bursarius pro termino tertio vizt a festo Annuntiationis ad festum Sancti Petri ad Vincula.

Renovatum est decretum quod bursarius non recipiet pecunias collegii nisi in praesentia vicecustodis aut socii senioris et eas aut in cista oeconomiae aut cistam iocalium reponet.

Decimo nono Martii. Celebrantur divina pro commemoratione fundatoris, quo die dispensatum est cum lectione statutorum, prorogatur scrutinium ad primum diem Maii et quemlibet diem citra.

Vicesimo quarto die Martii. Sigillata est obligatio nonaginta et quatuor librarum communi sigillo collegii pro solutione quadraginta et septem librarum in usum Georgii Hilliard lanii cui obsonator Applebee oberatus erat pro carnibus in usum collegii, vicecustode, magistro Greaves, bursariis magistris Howson, Wright, Fowles.

Dies pro solucione pecuniarum productarum apponitur vicesimas octavas dies Martii in anno domini 1648°, praesentes erant cum sigillum apponebatur doctor Harvye, custos, magister French, vicecustos, magister Brent, Loveioy, Lee, dominus Lydall, socii.

[*blank*] p. 369

p. 370 Anno Domini MDCXLVI, regis Caroli XXII, doctoris Nathanaelis Brent XXV.[1]

Socii

Magistri in artibus

1. Ioannes French
2. Alexander Fisher
3. Ioannes Greaves
4. Ranulphus Domvill
5. Gulielmus Barkley
6. Nicholas Howson
7. Franciscus Wright
8. Rogerus Brent
9. Gulielmus Owen
10. Franciscus Brode
11. Georgius Clarke
12. Eduardus Copley
13. Rodolphus Button
14. Ioannes Pryaulx
15. Robertus Sayer
16. Christophorus Fowle
17. Georgius Loveioy
18. Ioannes Lee
19. Daniel Whistler
20. Thomas Iones

Baccalaurei in artibus

1. dominus Martin
2. dominus Woode
3. dominus Lydall

Capellani

1. Magister Ioannes Gurgayny
2. Magister Franciscus Crofts

Octobris 19. Desaeviente tandem, summa Dei bonitate, bello civili, quod per annos complures universam afflaverat Britanniam, etiam domino custode sociorumque plerisque ad collegium reversis, visum est, pro more, licet tempore inassueto, electionem officiariorum inire. Sed quum nulli essent in collegi baccalaurei, rari scholares numerus etiam magistrorum infrequens esset, placuit unum tantum decanum, unumque bursarium in annum sequentem designare. Convenientibus igitur domino custode et sociis in hospitio (nec enim in aula licebat, quae iacebat situ et ruinis squalida) iunioribus secedere iussis, per custodem et quinque simpliciter seniores, more consueto in annum sequentem.

Electi sunt:

vicecustos, magister Fisher.

decanus, magister Copley.

bursarius, magister French.

principalis portionistarum, magister Howson.

bursarius Willyott, capellanus capellae, et exhibitionarius Hamsterley, magister Brent.

[1] In the hand of Alexander Fisher.

Quo eodem tempore magistro Fisher vicariam Sancti Petri resignante ea vicaria in magistrum Lee tunc praesentem unanimi custodis et sociorum consensu, collata est. Cum vero magistrorum plurimis nondum variassent, nec iam in disputationibus baccalaureorum, quae nullae erant, variare possent, cum iis omnibus dispensatum est, donec domino custodi et sociis aliter videretur.

Novembris 16. Dominus Lydall admissus est in numerum magistrorum, sed sub hac conditione, ut nullum inde preiudicium domino Martin, qui tunc aberat, iure senioritatis factum intelligatur.

Cum magistri Gurgany senioris capellani, turbulentis hisce temporibus per quadrennium, et quod excurrit, nulla ratio, ut aiebat, habita fuisset, adeo ut neque communias neque stipendia, neque exhibitionem Bickley (cuius onera solum se sustinuissse caussabatur) i[n] toto hoc tempore recepissest, gravem de hac sive iniuria sive neglectu apud dominum custodem querelam instituit. Atque is aequum postulari iudicans, per literas significavit, admodum sibi placere, ut ratio aliqua iniretur, qua magistro Gurgany damna haec quoquo modo resarcirentur. Re igitur multum diuque agitata, socii tandem unanimes consenserunt in quinquaginta octo libras, novem solidos, novem denarios, ei pro tempore concedenda [*sic*]. Sed quum praesens collegio status huic summae dissolvendae ob aerarii inopiam non sufficeret, placuit duabus obligationibus, quibus summa praedicta comprehendebatur, eius securitati prospicere. Atque hae obligationes ex unanimi consensu communi sigillo collegii munitae sunt, et tempus solutionis assignatum, festum Sancti Thomae quod futurum est, Anno Domini 1647.

Novembris 30. Dominus Martin admissus est, primo in perpetuam societatem huius domus, (quod ei ob absentiam nondum contigerat). Deinde in numerum magistrorum, consuetis iuramentis utrobique prius praestitis.

Eodem tempore magister French loco magistri Owen tertii bursarii anni superioris, computavit, et discessit in plussagio.

Decembris 17. Habita est commemoratio fundatoris, deinde lecta sunt statuta, et scrutinium initum quod prorogatum est in calendas Ianuarii.

Eodem die magister French computavit pro primo termino huius anni.

Decembris 18. Confectus est computus generalis a festo Sancti Petri ad Vincula anni domini 1641, usque ad idem festum 1642, nescio cuius incuria ante omissus.

Decembris 26. A sociis consensum est (voluntate domini custodis ante per literas significata) ut aulaea quae orientalem capellae partem olim adornabant, sed iam in apodyterio inter impedimenta iacebant in hospitium transferentur, ad instruendam et ornandam cameram, quae altae aulae contingua est.

p. 371 Quo tempore magister Button, magistrum Greaves iure societatis excidisse protestatus est, eo quod praelector Astronomiae Savilianus iam per biennium extitisset. Eum insuper accusavit, quod magnum supellectilis, qua in hospitio erat partem intervertisset, vel in suum, vel in amicorum suorum usum, necdum restituisset.

Decembris 31. Habita est de more scrutinium in quo tria illa solennia proposita sunt, 1. Mores servientium, 2. Numerus portionistarum, 3. Electio hortulani. Servientes, resumptis clavibus, quae prius resignaverant, ad officiarios remissi sunt. Placuit ut idem numerus esset portionistarum qui annis superioribus. In hortulanum electus est magister Copley.

In hoc scrutinio magister Iones accusavit magistrum Greaves, libros quosdam ante aliquot annos, se praesente e bibliotheca desumpsisse, necdum restituisse. Libri erant Eusebius, Scaligeri, Villapandus, alii.[1]

Eodem tempore concessae sunt equisoni duae librae pro pallio.

[1647]

Februarii 17. Magister French confecit aequum suum pro 1mo termino huius anni. Et computus magistri Copley, 2^{di} bursarii anni domini 1642, antea quidem confectus, sed (ut tempora ferebant) tumultuario et confuso more, ex domini custodis mandato a sociis in examen revocatus est. Et allocatis allocandis, discessit in plussagio 135 li. 8s. 6d. ob. quae summa et aliquanto maior cerevisiario, pistoribus, obsonatori, aliisque. Anno Domini 1642 debita erat, sed non soluta ob aerarii inopiam.

Februarii 26. Concessae sunt a sociis (voluntate domini custodis ante per litteras intellecta) magistro Iones in Gallias iter meditanti 20 librae in annum sequentem. Concessum etiam est ut frueretur liberatura praesentis anni cuius maiorem partem vel in collegio exegerat, vel exigere voluit, si per bellum et pestem licuisset.

[1] Presumably Merton Coll. Libr. 84.K.4, Eusebius Pamphilus, *Thesaurus temporum: opera et studio Jos. Justi Scaligeri, cum eiusdem notis* (Leyden, 1606) and ibid. 85 hh 1–3, J. B. Villalpandi et Hier. Pradi, *In Ezechielem explanationes, et apparatus urbis ac templi Hierosolymitani commentariis et imaginibus illustratus* (3 vols., Rome, 1596–1605).

Eodem tempore computus magistri Brode tertii bursarii, anno domini 1642/1643 examini subiectus est, eodem prorsus modo, et ob easdem rationes quae computum magistri Copley 2^di^ bursarii eodem anno, examini subiecerant. Et allocatis allocandis discessit in plussagio 113 li. 14 s. 6d. qa.

Martii 27. Magister Powell suffragiis omnium sociorum qui tunc in collegio commorabantur (consensu custodis ante impetrato) electus est in rectorem ecclesiase parochialis de Ibston cuius praesentatio post biduum sigillata est.

Aprilis 12. Dispensatum est cum magistro French ob auditorum paucitatem, ut computum suum in unam alteramve septimanam differre posset.

Aprilis 20. Consensum est a sociis (custodis assensu per litteras ante significato) in praesentationem magistri Blickard, pro-capellani, ad rectoriam[1] nostram de Maldon. Quae praesentatio die 23 eiusdem mensis sigillata est.

Aprilis 21. Magister French computavit pro 2do termino huius anni, et discessit in plussagio.

Maii 10. Sigillatum est procuratorium vicecustodi, bursario, et decano, una cum obsonatore et equisone, ad arreragia collegii, quae plurima erant, exigenda. Quo eodem tempore consensum est, ut vicecustos Londinum proficisceretur, ad illud, et alia collegii negotia procuranda. Consensum etiam est, ut magister Wright iure cubiculi sui frueretur ad proximum festum Sancti Michaelis, etiamsi continuo per maiorem anni partem a collegio abfuisset.

Iunii 28. Consensum est ut vicecustos iterum Londini proficisceretur ad arreragia colligenda, et alia collegii negotia procuranda.

Iulii 20. Habita est commemoratio fundatoris, et initum scrutinium, quod in calendas Augusti prorogatum est. Statutorum vero omissa est lectio tum ob custodis et vicecustodis a domo absentiam. tum sociorum tunc domi commorantium paucitatem.

[1] 'vicariam' deleted.

p. 372 Anno Domini MDCXLVII, regis Caroli XXIII, domini Nathanaelis Brent XXVI.

Socii
Magistri in artibus

1. Iohannes French
2. Alexander Fisher
3. Iohannes Greaves
4. Ranulphus Domvill
5. Gulielmus Barkley
6. Nicolaus Howson
7. Franciscus Wright
8. Rogerus Brent
9. Gulielmus Owen
10. Franciscus Brode
11. Georgius Clarke
12. Eduardus Copley
13. Rodolphus Button
14. Iohannes Priaulx
15. Robertus Sayer
16. Christophorus Fowle
17. Georgius Loveioy,
18. Iohannes Lee
19. Daniel Whistler
20. Thomas Iones
21. Gulielmus Martin
22. Richardus Lydall

Capellani

1. Magister Iohannes Gurgany
2. Magister Franciscus Crofts

Augusti 1°. Domino custode iam ad collegium reverso, et sociorum plerisque omnibus domi praesentibus, conventum est post preces vespertinas in apodyterio, et quia dies erat dominicus, eoque secularibus negotiis tractandis haud idoneus iudicaretur de prorogando scrutinio actum est, quod in calendas Septembris prorogandum censuerunt.

Augusti 2do.Convenimus pro more, in alta aula, hora nona antemeridiana ubi magister Fowle ex mandato domini custodis ab omnibus collegii emolumentis exclusis est, donec summae curiae parliamenti, in quam arma sumpsisse ferebatur, aliter visum esset, quod etiam de magistro Loveioy, qui in eadem causa erat censebat. Deinde per custodem, et quinque simpliciter seniores, caeteris ad tempus secedere iussis, electi sunt in officiarios anni sequentis:
vicecustos, magister Fisher.
decani, magistri Brent, Owen, Sayer.
bursarii, magistri Howson, Brode, Copley.
principalis portionistarum magister French; bursarius Williot et capellanus capellae, magister Lee; exhibitionarius Hamsterley, magister Owen; praelector grammaticae, magister Lidall; custodes cistae Reade, tres decani; custodes cistae Bodleigh, magistri Lee, Whistler, Lydall; bursarius itinerans, magister Brent. Quo eodem tempore renunciati

sunt in proximum triennium doctor Whistler, superior Linacri praelector, inferior, magister Lydall.

Augusti 4°. Decretum est, quod magistri Lee, Whistler, Iones, Martin, Lydall, pecuniam bibliothecae quam in socios eligerentur debitam dissolverent, atque ut summa eorum cuique imposita et arreragiis termino magistri Brode 1643 debitis decideretur. Quum ante per dominum custodem et socios consensum fuisset, quod omnia vel sociis vel servientibus eo termino debita, quam primum huic rei aerarium sufficeret, solverentur.

Augusti 9no. Quum ex portionistis aliqui, vel saltem ii qui in eorum absentium loca suffecti erant, batellis non solutis a collegio saepius discesserant, unde non leve in principales portionistarum damnum redundare necesse erat, decretum est ut in posterum magistrorum singuli, quibus ius ad portionistam competebat, ad portionistae sui batella dissolvenda, si ipse hoc praestare negligeret, tenerentur. Principali ipso ad hoc idem obligato. Eorum ratione, quos ipse in portionistarum numerum elegerat. Reliqui vero (i.e. Aetonenses) non admitterentur, nisi prius vel a sociorum aliquo, vel alio non dubiae fidei homine, de batellorum eius solutione cautum esset.

Augusti 18. Sociis in hospitium convocatis dispensatum est cum magistro French, qui febre tunc laborabat ut computum suum in aliquot septimanas differre posset.

Eodem tempore consensum est, ut stipendium olim solutum Haukins (viz quinque librae annuae) sed per aliquos annos intermissum, ei in posterum a bursariis solveretur.

Consensum etiam est, ut terminus Nevill loco Fowle 1^{mi} bursarii anno domini 1643 in examen revocaretur, ut unusquisque tum sociorum, tum servientium, quaecunque iis clare debitae erant, ubi primum solvendo esset, aerarium reciperet.

Septembris 8. Magister French computavit pro tertio termino anni superioris et discessit in plussagio.

24. Dominus custos computavit in scaccario, et discessit in plussagio.

Octobris 11. Sociis in hospitium a domino custode convocatis decretum est, quod magistri Owen et Brode, hoc anno variare tenerentur, etiamsi nullae essent baccalaureorum disputationes, cum reliquis magistrorum, qui nondum variaverant, eodem tempore dispensatum est.

Magister Sayer eodem tempore praelector Graecae linguae a domino custode constitutus est.

p. 373 Perlecta etiam sunt eodem tempore littera magistri Gulielmi Clarke patris magistri Clarke huius collegii socii, quibus significavit se, iuxta munus sibi a collegio demandatum, terras illas in Radipole, in agro Dorsettensi, ex quibus viginti librae annuae ad portionistarum sustentationem ex dono doctoris Iesoppe exire debebant invisisse; atque arreragia efflagitasse, quas iam ad centum et viginti libras excreverant; hoc vero responsum tulisse a magistro Baynarde qui fundorum illorum possessor erat, se pecunias illas nullo modo numeraturum, quum nullus (ut prae se ferebat) ad eum per aliquot annos ex terris illis proventus redierit. Nec existimare se in posterum huic annuae pensionis solvendae obligatum. Decretum igitur est, ut arreragia haec dolo malo detenta, iure recuperaremus, et ius nostrum in posterum stabiliremus. Cui negotio, aliisque obeundis consensum est vicecustodem Londinum, termino Michaelis mittendum, ut domino custodi in collegii negotiis, quae turbulentis hisce temporibus plurima erant, praesto esset.

Octobris 14. Magister Gibbs omne ius suum ad medietatem rectoriae de Gamlingay publice resignavit, confecto hac de re authentico instrumento, quod coram sociis in aula congregatis perlectum est.

Octobris 15. Sigillata est praesentatio magistri Iohannis Wilson ad eandem medietatem rectoriae de Gamlingay.

Novembris 1mo. Sigillata est praesentatio magistri Francisci Barret ad vicariam de Dodington, in quam custos et socii unanimes consensere.

Decembris 15. Dispensatum est cum magistro Copley, ut computum suum in duas septimanas differre posset, ob graves quae sociis praesentibus necessariae videbantur, rationes.

17. Sacra in memoriam fundatoris, pro more fecimus, post lecta sunt statuta, et scrutinium initum quod in ultimum diem Decembris prorogatum est.

30. Iterum dispensatum est cum magistro Copley, ut computum suum ulterius in duas septimanas differre posset.

31. Habitum est, de more scrutinium, in quo tribus illis solennibus propositis, 1mo de moribus servientium, 2do de numero portionistarum, 3° de hortulano eligendo; placuit ut mores servientium ad officiarios corrigendi remitterentur, ut numerus portionistarum idem sit, qui

annis superioribus. In hortulanum electus est magister Button, deinde scrutinium in festum Purificationis prorogatum est.

[1648]

Ianuarii 12. Magister Copley, 1^{mus} bursarius computavit in scaccario.

15. Confectus est ibidem computus generalis anni 1642/1643.

27. Magister Copley 1^{mus} bursarius confecit suum aeque.

Quo eodem tempore consensum est, ut vicecustos Londinum proficisceretur ad arreragia colligenda, et alia collegii negotia procuranda.

Concessum etiam est, ut magister Clarke ius ad societatem retineret, quamvis uberiori beneficio in praesens frueretur, tum ob incertas vices temporum, tum ob litigia, quae suboriri posse non vane causabatur.

Etiam magistro Iones in Italia peregrinanti 20 libras in alterum annum concessae sunt. Quibus omnibus dominus custos consensum suum per literas, quae coram sociis lectae sunt, significavit.

Martii 16to. Consensum est (domino custode iam ad collegium reverso) ut nova suppellex, praesertim linea, in usum hospitii pararetur, vetere vel detrita, vel maxima parte perdita; sed sub conditione ut diligens fieret inquisitio, cuius incuria vel culpa potius hoc in collegium damnum inundaverat ut ratio aliqua iniretur, qua in delinquentis caput dispendium hoc recideret, et collegium indemna, quantum fieri posset, praestaretur.

23. Confectus est in scaccario computus anni 1643/1644 et anni 1644/1645.

25. Divina fecimus in memoriam fundatoris, post lecta sunt statuta, et scrutinium initum quod in calendas Maias prorogatum est.

28. Convenimus in hospitio, ubi consensum est:
1mo. De progressu huius anni continuando, ita ut maneria collegii in comitatibus Essex, Kent, Surrey visitarentur; et sylvae apud Canes in comitatu Essex in usum sociorum divenderentur. Quibus negotiis obeundis delecti sunt vicecustos, et magister Brent, bursarius itinerans, huius anni.
2do. De arreragiis de Radipoole, Knowle Parke et Shaftesbury, quae per 7 iam annos insoluta erant, iure repetendis, si aliter fieri non posset; quod idem placuit etiam de arreragiis de Hensington repetendis a magistro Sheires.

3°. Consensum est ut novi plutei in sociorum musaeis, qui turbulentis hisce temporibus avulsi et disiecti erant, collegii sumptibus resarcirentur.

p. 374 April 5to. Decretum est, quod officiarii, quorum muneris hoc esset, i.e. decanus senior et bursarius dispicerent quid in hospitii suppellectile necessarium deesset, ut Londini quanto fieri poterat collegii compendio, mox emeretur.

Consensum etiam est eodem tempore, per dominum custodem et socios quod sociorum unusquisque, sive absens a collegio eo tempore, sive praesens fuisset, decem libras reciperet pro portione sibi debita termino magistri Howson anno domini 1644, ita ut in quibus nihil penitus eo termino solutum erat, totam hanc summam reciperenti; caeteris vero, qui quamcunque summae huius partem, iamdudum receperant, adderetur quicquid deerat ad decem libras explendas, sub hac conditione, ut si quid collegio quocumque nomine, deberet sociorum quispiam, tantum huic devaderetur, quantum debito huic solvendo sufficeret.

Aprilis 11mo. Ad collegium accessit honoratissimus Pembrochiae comes, Academiae Cancellarius, ibique per tres dies commoratus est quem in ipso collegii vestibulo magister Button procurator designatus, eleganti oratione excepit. Ad quem mox salutandum praetor, aldermanii et ballivi civitatis accedentes, lictores suos cum officii sui insignis praeuntes habuerunt, sed petita prius et obtenta a custode et sociis venia, ne quid praeiudicii iuri et libertatibus nostris inde factum intelligeretur.

Aprilis 17. Cum magister Greaves, quem sociorum aliquot ut reum damni domus accusaverant, quamvis saepius vocatus, et a clerico summonitus non tamen comparaverat, dominus custos eum ut contumaciae reum ab omnibus collegii emolumentis excludi iussit, donec in his quibus onerabatur, caussam suam probasset. Mandavit etiam ne qua parte arreragiorum sibi annis superioribus debitorum frueretur, priusquam de hospitii suppellectile, de bibliothecae libris, et de collegii precuniis, quas intervertisse ferebatur, satisfecisset. Hoc autem ubi primum effectum daret, iussit ut in integrum restitueretur.

Aprilis 20. Magister Brode 2^{dus} bursarius computavit.

Iulii 20. Divina fecimus in memoria fundatoris, post lecta sunt statuta, et initum, de more, scrutinium, quod in calendas Septembres prorogatum est.

Praedia et tenementa hoc anno locata [i.e. in the college year 1647–8]
Augusti 2do [1647]. Dimissum est manerium de Callowland Gulielmo Woolley pro termino 21 annorum inchoandorum ad festum Michaelis proximum. finis 60 librae, una cum licentia alienacionis.

Dimisimus manerium nostrum de Barkby Iohanni Mennell pro termino viginti et unius annorum, una cum licentia alienacionis. Finis 13 li. 6s. 8d.

Dimisimus manerium nostrum de Merton Hall in Cantabrigia Iohanni Sherwoode pro termino 21 anorum. Finis 13 li. 16s. 8d.

Martii 3° [1648]. Elocata est rectoria de Wolford Eduardo[1] Oakley pro termino vitae eiusdem Eduardi, Margaritae Barry, et Eduardi Warren. Finis 200 li. Quarum pars prior solvenda ad indenturae sigillationem, posterior, decimo die Maii anno domini 1649, una cum licentia alienandi.

Atque haec omnia, diversis temporibus, sed anno sequente, 1648, sigillata sunt.

Anno Domini MDCXLVIII, regis Caroli XXIIII, domini Nathanaelis Brent custodis XXVII.[2] p. 375

Socii Collegii
Magistri in artibus

1. Iohannes French,
2. Alexander Fisher
3. Ioannes Greaves
4. Ranulphus Domvill
5. Gulielmus Berkley
6. Nicolaus Howson
7. Franciscus Wright
8. Rogerus Brent
9. Georgius Clarke
10. Eduardus Copley
11. Rodolphus Button
12. Robertus Sayer
13. Christopherus Fowle
14. Georgius Loueioy,
15. Daniel Whistler
16. Thomas Iones
17. Gulielmus Martin
18. Ricardus Lydall

Capellani
[*blank*]

Augusti 1mo. Convenimus pro more, in aula, hora nona antemeridiana, ubi resignatis clavibus officiariorum superioris anni, per dominum custodem, et quinque simpliciter seniores presentes, (reliquis ad tempus secedere iussis) electi sunt in annum sequentem:

[1] 'Johanni' deleted. [2] In the hand of Alexander Fisher.

vicecustos, magister Fisher.,
decani, magistri French, Howson, Button.
bursarii, magistri Brent, Martin, Lydall.
principalis portionistarum, magister Copley; bursarius Williot, magister Sayer; exhibitionarius Hamsterley, magister Wright; capellanus capellae, magister Fisher.

Quo tempore decretum erat, quod omnia emolumenta ex pane provenientia (etiam ex battellis portionistarum) in posterum bursario cederent; principali vero portionistarum qui antea, de more, ea percipiebat, octo librae annuae ex aerario (huius dispendii loco) numerarentur.

Augusti 5°. Consensum est ut ex reditu Gulielmi Obbard, firmarii de Farleigh debito ad festum Sancti Iohannis Baptistae, qui ad 46 li. 2s. 8d. excreverat, viginti una librae, duo solidi, et octo denarii deciderentur, eique condonarentur ob taxationes, militares depraedationes, aliaque onera, quae plurima ultimo hoc biennio perpessus erat.

Augusti 7°. Concessi sunt viduae Moore et viduae Chittenden duodecem denarii in singulas septimanas, durante utriusque vita naturali; quod datum est partim earum paupertati, partim maritorum memoriae, qui per annos complures in collegii servitio serverant.

Consensum etiam est ut vicecustos et magister Copley ad Cirencestriam proficiscerentur, ad arreragia decimarum, quae ibi ex dono magistri Thomas Masters olim socii et saepius vicecustodis collegii, nobis obvenerent, exigendam; easdemque decimas domino Gulielmo Masters, donatoris nepoti, vel alteri cuicunque elocandas. Deinde ut ad Cricklade proficiscerentur, ad arbores, quae in fundis nostris ibi succrescebant, visendas; easdemque, si e re collegii videretur vendendas.

Consensum etiam est ut iidem ad Teuxsburiam in agro Glocestrensi mitterentur, ad clausuras nostras in Walton visendas quas autem annos complures, magister Hartford, olim collegii socius nobis donaverat, et quarum plenum ius intra triennium, et quod excurrit, nobis obventurum erat, prioribus indenturis iam ad exitum vergentibus.

Eodem tempore computavit dominus custos, et discessit aeque.

Confectus etiam est computus generalis anni 1645/1646.

Augusti 24. Magister Howson 3us bursarius anni superioris computare incepit quo eodem die confectus est computus generalis anni 1646/1647.

Augusti 25. Dispensatum est cum magistro Howson, ut computum suum ad aliquot dies differre posset.

Augusti 30. Magister Howson 3^{ius} bursarius computavit, quo tempore decretum est, quod magister Copley et magister Sayer hoc anno variare tenerentur; cum reliquis, qui nondum variaverant, dispensatum est.

Electi sunt eodem tempore custodes cistae Bodley, magistri Copley, Sayer, Lydall.

Custodes autem cistae Read erant ex antiqua consuetudine tres decani.

Septembris 25. Computavit dominus custos pro annis 1642/1643, p. 376
1643/1644, 1644/1645 et 1645/1646. Et discessit in plussagio.

Septembris 27. Consensum est per dominum custodem et socios in electionem quarto die mensis sequentis instituendum, ad supplendum numerum sociorum qui admodum pauci erant.

Septembris 30. Decretum est ut firmariis nostris de Bielby in agro Eboracensi, quorum omnium indenturae vel exierant, vel ad exitum vergebant, novae concessiones fierent per magistrum Pricket (qui id sibi iuris arrogabat) sed sub his conditionibus quod fines collegio cederent, et unuscuiusque indentura, communi sigillo collegii muniretur, et hoc demum facto confirmata intelligeretur, quod ipsi tenentes unice expetebant.

Octobris 9. Visum est aequum tenentes nostros in Holywell hoc in posterum levare incommodo, ne ulterius totam regiam viam lapidibus sternere tenerentur, ad quod unusquisque, qui particulam aliquam vacivi illius, quod fossae de Holywell conterminum est, possidebat antea obligatus erat, quod nostris in non leve preiudicium cedebat, dum tenentes collegii de Wadham ab hoc onere liberi interim existerint.

Octobris 10. Convenimus in hospitio, ubi post longum et serium examen, quod per tres dies duravit, consensum est in hosce sex baccalaureos, in annum probationis admittendos viz. dominum Eduardum Wood e diocesi Oxoniensi, dominum Edmundum Dickenson e diocesi [*blank*], dominum Richardum Francklin e diocesi [*blank*], dominum Iosephum Hervy, dominum Richardum Trevor, et dominum Thomam Franke.[1] Atque hos approbarunt, et in socios futuros designarunt, custos et socii unanimes; elegerunt vero visitatores ad academiam reformandam a Parliamento constituti, qui ius illud sibi

[1] All the names are followed by 'e diocesi [*blank*]'.

competere contendebant ex authoritate Parliamentaria. Quo eodem tempore decretum est, quod eorum singuli ad usum bibliothecae 3 li. 6s. 8d. exsolverent.

Consensum etiam est quod vicecustos Londinum proficisceretur termino proximo, eoque munimenta quaedam spectantia ad quietos reditus de Cantabrigia, et tenementi vocati Ramshead in Fanchurch Street, London, secum deferret, quorum necessarius futurus erat usu, si ius nostrum, lite intentata, vindicare cogeremur.

Octobris 11. Concessae sunt ex consensu custodis et sociorum quadraginta librae magistro Gibbs nuper socio collegii ad resarciendos sumptus (qui ad 80 libras et supra excreverant) quos in reparando cancello ecclesiae de Gamlingay fecerat. Atque hoc partim eius gratiae, partim necessitati datum erat, non ut res in exemplum transiret, ac si collegium ad huiusmodi sumptus faciendos vel ibi vel alibi teneretur.

Conventum etiam est cum coquo iuniore, ut is, acceptis a bursario viginti sex libris, carbones in usum culinae per totius anni curriculum suppeditaret.

Octobris 26. Magister Howson 3us bursarius confecit suum aeque.

Novembris 6. Admissi sunt in annum probationis dominus Wood, dominus Dickenson, dominus Francklin, dominus Hervy, dominus Trevor, dominus Franke.

Decembris 17. Sacra fecimus in memoriam fundatoris, sed quum is dies in dominicum incideret, lectio statutorum in diem sequentem dilata est; quo tempore initum etiam est scrutinium, et in ultimum diem Decembris prorogatum.

Decembris 20. Magister Lydall 1^{mus} bursarius computare incepit, sed ob graves, quae auditoribus patebant, rationes, dispensatum cum eo est, ut computum suum in unam septimanam differre posset.

Decembris 27. Ulterius dispensatum est cum magistro Lydall, ob easdem rationes, ut computum suum ad duas vel tres septimanas differret.

Decembris 31. Habitum est, de more, scrutinium, in quo tribus illis sollenibus propositis, viz. 1, moribus servientium, 2, numero portionistarum, 3, electione hortulani; electus est in hortulanum magister Sayer; placuit ut idem numerus esset portionistarum, qui annis superioribus; servientes ad officiarios remissi sunt pro meritis suis corrigendis. Deinde scrutinium prorogatum est in festum Purificationis.

[1649]

Ianuarii 4. Consensum est, ut decimae manerii de Archbalds iuxta Ciceter in comitatu Glocestriae donatae a magistro Thoma Masters, olim collegii socio dimitterentur domino Gulielmo equiti aurato, eius nepoti, sub anno reditu septem librarum, cum antea octo librae annuae ab eodem per aliquot annos persolverentur, cuius diminutionis causa erat amissio quorundam ly-sheepe-walks in eodem manerio a [*blank*] iure recuperatorum.

Ianuarii 18. Magister Lydall 1^{mus} bursarius computavit.

Quo tempore consensum est de arreragiis de Newington et Granchester, quae plurima erant, iure a magistro Trafford, firmario ibidem repetendis, si aliter fieri non posset. Cui negotio, aliisque procurandis consensum est ut vicecustos Londinum proficisceretur.

Februarii 26. Consensum est ut curia per annos complures intermissa in manerio nostro de Tracyes in parochia de Newington in agro Cantiano, post festum Paschalis haberetur, et ut vicecustos huic negotio obeundo domino custodi comes esset.

Martii 18. Habita est commemoratio fundatoris, post lecta sunt statuta, et scrutinium initum quod in calendas Maii prorogatum est.

Martii 22. Magister Lydall 1^{mus} bursarius aeque suum confecit.

Martii 24. Magister Copley principalis portionistarum longa tabe obsumptus placide in domino obdormivit. In cuius locum suffectus est magister French.

Maii 24.[1] Magister Lydall loco magistri Martin 2^{di} bursarii computavit. p. 377

Quo eodem tempore confectus est computus generalis anni 1647/1648.

Iulii 6. Magister Sayer variavit in his quaestionibus:

An { iuvenis sit idoneus auditor moralis philosophiae. Affirmavit contra Aristotelem libro 1mo Ethic', capitulo 1mo.
detur scientia. Negavit contra Aristotelem libro 1mo Posteriorum Analyticorum, capitulo 2do.
sensus possit errare circa proprium obiectum. Affirmavit contra Aristotelem libro 2do de Anima, capitulo 6to. }

Finis disputationibus dispensatum cum eo est pro secundis variationibus.

Iulii 19. Magister Lydall loco Martin confecit aeque suum.

[1] In the hand of Alexander Fisher.

Iulii 20. Divina fecimus in memoriam fundatoris post lecta sunt statuta et scrutinium initum. Quod in calendas Septembris prorogatum est.

Iulii 28. Dominus custos computavit in scaccario.

Iulii 31. Fines a magistro Prickett impositi tenentibus nostris de Beilby, a custode et sociis approbati sunt; eorumque indenturae sigillo collegii munitae.

Praedia et tenementa hoc anno locata [i.e. in the college year 1648–9]

Augusti 2do [1648]. Medietas rectoriae de Gamlingay dimissa est Iohanni South, pro termino unius et viginti annorum. Finis 50 li. quarum pars prior solvende ad sigillationem indenturae, altera ad festum Annuntiationis proximum. Concessa est etiam eidem licentia alienandi.

Elocatum est tenementum in Salisbury-Ally-London Richardo Preston pro spatio 40 annorum. Finis 80 li. quarum una pars solvenda ad sigillationem indenturae, alteras ad festum Michaelis 1649, una cum licentia alienandi.

Dimisimus maneria nostra de Canes et Norton Mandevill magistro Eduardo Spranger et magistro Isaaco Davis pro triennio viginti et unius annorum. Finis 250 li. quarum magister Spranger solveret 147 li. 10s., magister Davis 102 li. 10s.

Eodem tempore vendidimus sylvas nostras caeduas apud Canes, una cum 100 ly saplins magistro Spranger, pretium 150 li. quarum pars solvenda ad festum Sancti Iacobi proximum, altera pars ad idem festum anno revoluto. Vendidimus etiam magistro Davis ex sylvis nostris in Norton Mandevill quantam ad 40 li. exsurgeret.

Dimisimus molendinum in Norton Mandevill Isaaco Bennet pro 30 annis. Finis 2 li. 10s.

Dimissum est tenementum in Holywell Gulielmo Smith pro termino 40 annorum una cum licentia alienandi. Finis duo capones.

Dimissum est tenementum in Abbots Langley Gulielmo Ewer pro 21 annis. Finis 3 li. 6s. 8d.

Elocavimus sylvas nostras caeduas apud Callowland Gulielmo Woolley pro termino viginti et unius annorum, ad annuum reditum trium librarum, una cum licentia alienandi.

Augusti 5°. Dimisimus magistro Philippo Owen utramque medietatem rectoriarum de Emildon et Ponteland pro termino 21 annorum. Finis centum librae solvendae ad sigillationem indenturae.

Dimisimus magistro Iohanni Hether manerium de Farleigh et sylvas ibidem pro termino viginti et unius annorum. Finis 50 li. una cum licentia alienandi.

Dimissum est tenementum in Holywell Avisiae Smith pro 40 annis. Finis duo capones.

Elocavimus sylvas nostras de Ibston pro 21 annis viduae Willmott. Finis o.

Dimissum est tenementum nostrum in Pennyfarthinge street vocatum Bull hall Arthuro Dimmock pro 40 annis. Finis 10 li. una cum licentia alienandi.

Dimisimus Gulielmo Hartley pro 40 annis eam partem fundi vacivi in Holywell quae obiacet tenemento vocato The Cardinalls Hatt. Finis duo capones.

Augusti 7mo. Dimisimus manerium de Cuxham magistro Edmundo Gregory pro termino 21 annorum. Finis centum et decem librae, quarum pars prior solvenda ad primum diem Decembris, altera ad festum Annuntiationis 1649.

Dimissum est tenementum vocatum Halswicke in parochia de Chedington Iohanni Seabrooke pro 21 annis. Finis 13 li. 6s. 8d.

Augusti 25. Dimisimus rectoriam de Margarett-Stratton magistro Francisco Kemble pro termino viginti et unius annorum. Finis 80 li.

Dimisimus magistro Richardo Robins clausuras in Cricklade pro termino 21 annorum. Finis 20 li. una cum licentia alienationis. Eidem etiam eodem tempore vendidimus tantum de sylvis nostris ibi succrescentibus, quantum ad quinquaginta libras excresceret.

Augusti 26. Dimisimus manerium de Ibston viduae Willmott pro 21 annis. Finis 60 li.

Octobris 4°. Dimisimus manerium de Kibworth magistro Roberto Ray pro spatio viginti et unius annorum. Finis 40 li. una cum licentia alienandi, et iure balivatus sibi et filio Gulielmo.

Dimisissum est tenementum Sunnings in parochia de Ibston Adriano Barney pro termino 21 annorum. Finis 10 li.

Atque haec omnia suis temporibus sigillata sunt.

p. 378 Anno Domini MDCXLIX, domini Nathanielis Brent custodis XXVIII.

Socii Collegii

Magistri in artibus

1. Ioannes French
2. Alexander Fisher
3. Ioannes Greaves
4. Ranulphus Domvill
5. Gulielmus Berckley
6. Nicolaus Howson
7. Franciscus Wright
8. Rogerus Brent
9. Georgius Clarke
10. Rodolphus Button
11. Robertus Sayer
12. Christophorus Fowle
13. Georgius Loueioy
14. Daniel Whistler, doctor medicinae
15. Thomas Iones
16. Gulielmus Martin
17. Richardus Lydall

Baccalaurei in anno probationis

1. dominus Woode
2. dominus Dickenson
3. dominus Francklin
4. dominus Hervey
5. dominus Trevor
6. dominus Francke

Capellani

1. Magister Georgius Lort
2. Magister Beniamin Cooper

Primo die Augusti nulla novorum officiariorum (secundum statuta et consuetudinem) electio facta est. Sic enim placuit commissionariis authoritate parliamentaria ad academiam ordinandam et reformandam constitutis, qui decreverant veteres anni superioris officiarios retinendos, donec aliter sibi videretur.

Augusti 4o. Decretum est per dominum custodem et socios, gravi prius habita deliberatione seu baccalaureos, quam primum annum probationis finiretur, qui ad sextum diem Novembris exiturus erat, statim in numerum magistrorum huius collegii admittendos fore; nisi interim quid admitterent, quod eos hac gratia indignos redderet.

Atque hoc, quamvis exemplo careret, fieri placuit ad praevertenda plurima aliter quae ingruere timebantur collegio mala, praesertim cum res statutis non adversaretur.

Augusti 8°. Consensum est de remittendo centrum libras magistro Trafford, firmario nostro de Thracies et Thrognolds in parochia de Newington in agro Cantiano, et molendini Grandchester in comitatu Cantabrigiensi, ob taxationes et alia onera quae plurima per aliquot annos, gliscente bello civili sustinuerat. Cautioni tamen atque adeo obligatione data, de solvendo sexaginta octo libras, novem solidos quatuor denarios, quae eius ultima arreragia erant. Idem etiam factitatum magistro Richardo Morpeth ratione firmae nostrae de Stillington et Ceton-Carewe, cui remisimus septuaginta libras. Et viduae Hartburne etc. remisimus etiam tertiam partem arreragiorum firmae de Basingstoke cuidam Hunt et Temple.

Augusti 20. Consensum est per dominum custodem et socios quod magister Lydall in episcopatum Dunelmensem se mitteretur ad arreragia de Stillington et Ceton-Carewe exigenda, et res ibi ordinandas. Ad quae conficienda procuratorium ei, et Henrico Sayre (qui comes ei additus) sigillatum est.

Consensum etiam est, quod vicecustos, una cum magistro Brent bursario proficisceretur ad Basingstoke ad arreragia requirenda et sylvas ibi visendas, atque inde ad Radipoole et Shaftesbury in agro Dorsettensi, ubi reditus collegii debiti per aliquot annos insoluti remanserant.

Cum autem palam esset magistrum Fisher iniuria exclusum fuisse a societate omnibusque collegii emolumentis anno domini 1639, atque hanc iniustam exclusionem durasse a festo Annuntiationis eiusdem anni ad primum diem Augusti 1641 (quo tempore in integrum restitutus erat) hoc est per biennium, anni trienti', et quod excurrit aequum visum est, adeoque ab omnibus consensum quod 70 li. quo damna haec resarcirentur, ei numerarentur viz. iuxta 30 li. in annos singulos.

Consensum etiam ut magistro Iones, qui nuper ex peregrinatione redierat, decem librae numerarentur ratione commemorationis suae semestris, ultra biennium, in partibus transmarinis.

Etiam consensum quod residuum arreragiorum magistri Gurgainy, non ita pridem senioris capellani a collegio solveretur, non, quod fieri solebat, a domino custode; quia per ea tempora quorum ratione haec arreragia vendicabat, collegio inservierat, non custodi, qui absens erat.

Atque his confectis scrutinium prorogatum est in calendas[1] Decembris.

Augusti 23. Magister Brent 3us bursarius computavit. Quo tempore conventum est cum coquo iuniori, de carbonibus, ab eo suppeditandis in usum culinae per annum sequentem, quod in se recepit, modo viginti octo librae ei a bursariis numerarentur. Concessae etiam sunt viduae Smith pauperculae 12 denarii in singulas septimanas durante

[1] 'ultimum diem' deleted.

vita eius naturalis, ob c[onsi]derationes propter quas eadem gratia viduae Moore et viduae Chittenden anno superiore indulta erat.

Cum vero custodi et sociis compertum esset, quod ei reditus quos magister Button Londini receperat ab anno 1642 ad 1646 inclusive, ab eo iamdudum collegio solutis fuissent, et quod continebantur in iis arreragiis quam iampridem custos et socii receperant, aequum est visum ut hoc, ad eius instantiam registro insereretur.

p. 379 Octobris 4°. Magister Brent 3us bursarius confecit suum aeque.

Octobris 8. Convenimus in hospitio, ubi consensum est, quod magister Loueioy triginta librae solverentur, loco omnium arreragiorum, quae ullo modo vindicare posset.

Novembris 6to. Dominus Woode, dominus Dickenson, dominus Francklin, dominus Hervey, dominus Trevor, dominus Franke, anno probationis iam finito, admissi sunt in numerum sociorum; ac statim post in numerum magistrorum huius collegii, secundum ordinationem a domino custode et sociis factam 4° Augusti. Prius tamen utrobique consueta iuramenta praestiterunt, iis solum omissis, quae in admissione in socios superflua fuerunt, iis qui statim in numerum magistrorum erant admittendi.

Novembris 19. Consensum est ut vicecustos Londinum proficisceretur ad collegii negotia, quae plurima erant, procuranda.

Decembris 17. Habita est commemoratio fundatoris, sed ob absentiam custodis et vicecustodis, qui prope diem expectabantur, dilata est lectio statutorum et scrutinium in diem vicesimum primum mensis.

Decembris 21. Lecta sunt statuta et scrutinium initum, quod in calendas Ianuarii prorogatum est.

Dominus custos ante triduum ad collegium accesserat partim ad novos officiarios, qui hactenus deerant, substituendos, partim ad sententiam commissionatiorum Oxoniensium (qui ante aliquot septimanas undecem socios viz. quatuor magistros, et septem baccalaureos, una electione et voto in collegium cooptant) executioni demandandam. Restiterat quidem ille, quantum in se erat, huic sententiae, tanquam domui onerosae, et prorsus novae, atque adeo, appellatione facta, querelam apud commissionarios Londini commorantes, instituerat, sed frustra.

Decembris 22. Reversus igitur ad collegium duos de quatuor magistris viz. magistrum Petrum Nicolls, et magistrum Iohannem Powell; qui soli se praesentes stiterant, admisit in numerum magistrorum, praestitis prius ab iis consuetis iuramentis.

Decembris 24. Convenimus pro more in alta aula, hora nona antemeridiana ubi resignatis clavibus officiariorum superioris anni (qui per hunc etiam anni trientem officia sua retinuerant) per dominum custodem et quinque seniores praesentes, electi sunt in residuum anni sequentis:
vicecustos, magister Fisher.
decani, magistri Iones, Dickenson, Francklin.
bursarii, magistri Nicolls, Hervey, [*blank*].
principalis portionistarum, magister Powell; bursarius Williot, magister Woode; exhibitionarius Hamsterley, magister Nicolls; capellanus capellae, magister Iones; custodes cistae Read, 3 decani; custodes cistae Bodley, magistri Brent, Powell, Woode.

Eodem tempore consensum est, quod magister Iones una cum equisone proficisceretur ad Basingstoke, ad sylvas nostras ibi vendendas.

Facta etiam est potestas doctori Higgs, olim socio collegii, novos fiduciarios in demortuorum locum substituendi, quorum nomina indenturae eius de rectoria de Dodington praefigerentur.

Consensum etiam est, quod unusquisque recens electorum, sive magister esset, sive baccalaureus, solveret 3 li. 6s 8d in usum bibliothecae.

Decreta etiam sunt eodem tempore domino custodi, viginti librae, quo damna sua, et sumptus in molesto hoc et litigioso negotio factos, resarciret.

Datae etiam sunt eius amanuensi Gulielmo Newhouse tres librae.

Decembris 27. Dispensatum est cum magistro Brent 1mo huius anni bursario, ut computum suum unam alteramve septimanam differre posset.

Decembris 31. Initum est de more scrutinium, in quo tria illa sollemnia proposita sunt, 1, Mores servientium, 2, Numerus portionistarum, 3, Electio hortulani. Atque in hortulanum electus est doctor Whistler; placuit ut idem sit numerus Portionistarum qui prius; servientes vero ad officiarios remissi sunt. Quo facto, prorogatum est scrutinium in festum Purificationis.

[1650]

Ianuarii 1mo. Admissi sunt in annum probationis, secundum decretum commissionariorum dominus Sterry, dominus Maunde, dominus Hully, dominus Pavier, dominus Hurst, dominus Willoughby, praestitis prius consuetis iuramentis.

Ianuarii 5to. Admissus est in annum probationis eodem iure, eodemque modo, quo illi sex priores dominus Cripps.

p. 380 Ianuarii 9no. Magister Brent 1^{mus} bursarius computavit.

Ianuarii 12. Confectus est computus generalis anno 1648/1649.

Februarii 27. Admissus est in numerum sociorum, atque adeo magistrorum Iohannes Arnold in medicina baccalaureus, praestitis prius consuetis iuramentis. Factum hoc est ex decreto commissionariorum Londini commorantium ad collegium misso.

Aprilis 6. Divina fecimus in memoriam fundatoris, post lecta sunt statuta, et scrutinium initum, quod in calendas maias prorogatum est.

Aprilis 19. Magister Hervey 2^{dus} bursarius computavit.

Maii [*blank*]. Dominus Sterry cuius annus probationis nondum exierat ex decreto et mandato commissionariorum in socium atque adeo in magistrum collegii promotus est, qui in admissione sua consueta utrobique iuramenta praestitit.

Iunii 10. Consensum est a sociis (domino custode voluntatem suam per litteras significante) ut praesentatio ad medietatem rectoriae de Gamlingay magistro Esdrae Marshall (qui eam iampridem authoritate parliamentaria possidebat) sic petenti sigillaretur.

Iunii 17. Magister Hervey 2^{dus} bursarius confecit suum aeque; quo tempore sigillata est praesentatio magistri Nicholls, ad vicariam Sancti Petri in Oriente.

Iulii 20. Habita est commemoratio fundatoris, post lecta sunt statuta, et scrutinium initum quod in calendas Augusti prorogatum est.

Iulii 31. Dominus custos computavit, et discessit in plussagio.

Praedia et tenementa hoc anno locata [*i.e. in the college year 1649–50*]

Augusti 2 [1649]. Dimissae sunt clausurae in Walton (sed earum vetere censu prius redacto ad ratas pecuniae, tritici et brasei portiones) magistro Eduardo Aly pro spatio viginti unius annorum. Finis 40 li. una cum licentia alienandi.

Elocatum est tenementum in Holywell (olim vocatum The Cardinalls Hatt, nunc in computis collegii, domus Bust), magistro Iohanni Elborrowe, pro spatio 40 annorum. Finis 12 li. una cum licentia alienationis.

Augusti 3. Dimissum est manerium de Thorncroft magistro Gualtero Rogers pro 21 annis inchoandis ad festum Michaelis proximum. Finis 66 li. 13s. 4d. una cum licentia alienandi.

Augusti 8. Dimissum est manerium de Thracyes et Thrognolds in parochia de Newington, in agro Cantiano, et molendinum de Grandcester in agro Cantabrigiensi, magistro Iohanni Trafford pro spatio viginti et unius annorum. Finis utriusque 350 li. Quarum prima pars solvenda ad sigillationem indenturae, altera ad festum Michaelis anno domino 1650, una cum licentia alienationis utriusque.

Augusti 17. Dimissa est medietas de Stillington et Ceton-Carewe magistro Richardo Morpeth pro spatio 21 annorum. Finis 100 li. quarum pars prior solvenda ad sigillationem indenturae, altera ad festum Michaelis anno revoluto. Eidem etiam 18vo Octobris concessa est licentia alienandi.

Dimissus est hortus culinaris (qui adiacet domui nostrae in Knightriders-street London') Elizabethae Feildinge, viduae, pro spatio 21 annorum. Finis 4 li.

Dimissum est tenementum in Holywell Thomae Hawkins pro 21 annis. Finis duo capones.

Concessa est licentia alienationis in annos 12 tenementi Woolsack in Bread-streete London', Gulielmo Sherman. Finis o.

Octobris 11. Dimissa est rectoria de Elham in agro Cantiano executoribus ultimae voluntatis dominae Elizabethae Sedley, durante vita naturali Caroli Sedley, domini Gulielmi Sedley, baronetti, et Iohannis Harison filii Richardi Harison, armigeri. Finis sexcentae librae, una cum littera, quam vocant, atturnatus, ad eos in possessionem eiusdem rectoriae immittendos.

Octobris 18. Dimissa est altera medietas de Stillington et Ceton Carewe magistro Thomas Barnes pro spatio viginti et unius annorum. Finis 100 li. quarum prima pars solvenda ad sigillationem indenturae, altera calendis Novembris 1650, una cum licentia alienandi.

Octobris 26. Dimissa est firma de Basingstoke Gulielmo Temple pro 21 annis. Finis 40 li. quarum pars prima solvenda ad sigillationem indenturae, altera eodem tempore anni sequentis.

Decembris 24. Dimissae sunt duae virgatae terrae cum dimidia in Hensington aldermanno Whistler pro spatio viginti et unius annorum, ad annum valorem quindecem librarum. Finis o.

Dimissae sunt sylvae de Thorncroft magistro Rogers pro spatio 21 annorum, ad annuum valorem 6 li. 13s. 4d., qui reditus initium sumere intelligeretur ad festum Annuntiationis 1651, soluto interim pro reditu anni proximi, uno grano piperis. Concessa etiam est licentia alienationis. Finis o.

Iulii 30 [1650]. Sigillata est indentura decimarum vicariae de Elham magistro Henrico Hannington, qui illa[m] vicariam, vacantem per eiectionem magistri Woodcocke, iampridem obtinuerat authoritate Parliamentaria.

Ac caetera etiam omnia suis temporibus sigillata sunt.

p. 381 Anno Domini MDCL, domini Nathanaelis Brent, custodis, XXIX.

Socii Collegii
Magistri

1. Iohannes French
2. Alexander Fisher
3. Rogerus Brent
4. Daniel Whistler, medicinae doctor
5. Thomas Iones
6. Gulielmus Martin
7. Richardus Lydall
8. Iohannes Powell
9. Petrus Nicolls
10. Edwardus Woode
11. Edmundus Dickenson
12. Richardus Francklin
13. Iosephus Hervey
14. Richardus Trevor
15. Iohannes Arnold
16. Nathaniel Sterry
17. Thomas Franck

In anno probationis

1. dominus Cripps
2. dominus Maund
3. dominus Hully
4. dominus Pavier
5. dominus Hurst
6. dominus Willoughby

Capellani

1. Magister Lort
2. Magister Cooper

Augusti 1mo. Convenimus, pro more, in alta aula, hora nona antemeridiana, ubi resignatis clavibus ab officiariis superioris anni, et sociorum reliquis ad tempus secedentibus, a domino custode, et

quinque simpliciter seniores qui aderant, hii officiarii in annum sequentem electi sunt:
vicecustos, magister Fisher.
decani, magistri Lydall, Woode, Francke.
bursarii, magistri Iones, Dickenson, Trevor.
principalis portionistarum, magister Powell; bursarius Williot, magister French; exhibitionarius Hamsterley, magister Nicolls; capellanus capellae, magister Nicolls; custodes cistae Read, tres decani; custodes cistae Bodley, magistri French, Powell, Nicolls; praelector Graecae linguae, magister Hervey; praelector grammaticae, magister Sterry.

Quo tempore doctor Whistler et magister Lydall electi sunt praelectores Linacri, in alterum triennium a domino custode, et sociis, quibus id iuris competebat.

Consensum etiam est, quod utrique praelectores linguae Graecae, et grammaticae in posterum quinque libras perciperent annuatim.

Iniunctum etiam est doctori Whistler et magistro Iones ut hoc anno in disputationibus baccalaureorum variarent. Cum caeteris magistris dispensatum est.

Augusti 2do. Consensum est quod quadraginta librae hisce quatuor (qui olim portionistae erant, sed tempore belli civilis per aliquot annos a collegio secesserant) viz. Munday, Woode, Rider, Dickenson, ex aerario solverentur, loco omnium arreragiorum sibi a collegio debitorum, ratione huius absentiae.

Aequum etiam visum est, atque adeo consensum per dominum custodem, et socios quod viginti librae viduae Moore solverentur, loco maioris summae ei debitae (quae ad triginta fere libras excreverat) a magistro Eduardo Nevill, et magistro Domvill, quum ante annos complures principales erant portionistarum. Atque hoc partim aequitati, partim, paupertati eius datum est, sub hac tamen cautione ne quid postea sub quocunque debiti praetextu, a collegio flagitaret.

Augusti 14. Datae sunt Henrico Sayre, ballivo nostro de Barkby, quinque librae tanquam munus hororarium.

Consensum etiam est quod 3 li. 13s. 4d. ultra illas decem libras superius concessas solverentur Henrico Munday non ita pridem portionistae.

Augusti 22. Magister Nicolls 3us bursarius computavit.

Augusti 24. E vivis excessit Ioannes Blackham, ianitor, in cuius locum suffectus est Eduardus Bucknell.

Augusti 27. Conventum est inter dominum custodem et socios quod ille omnia emolumenta iure officii sibi per triennium debita, id est annorum domini 1643, 1644, 1645, collegio remitteret, ex altera vero parte, loco compensationis, quod illi nihil ex reditibus de Emildon et Ponteland per eosdem annos collegio debitis exigerent; atque insuper, ut quicquid reliquum erat de iis pecuniis, quas Custos iisdem annis Londini receperat, necdum rationem reddiderat, totum expungeretur.

Consensum etiam est, quod quicquid pecuniarum a magistro Nicolls 3° bursario in aerarium inducendum erat, inter dominum custodem et socios divideretur, ita ut dominus custos triginta, sociorum quilibet viginti libras perciperet; ad quam summam supplendam si pecuniae illae inducendae non sufficerent, reliquum ex aerario suppeditaretur.

p. 382 Augusti 30. Consensum est per dominum custodem et socios de admittendis in collegium communariis (ita tamen ut eorum numerus ultra sex non excresceret) sub his condicionibus

1. Quod nulli admitterentur nisi equitum auratorum filii, vel armigerorum aut generosorum filii natu maximi.
2. Quod eorum quilibet poculum argenteum collegio donaret, cuius pretium infra quinque libras non subsideret.
3. Quod eorum tutores ad communias et batella solvenda tenerentur, viderentque ne quid detrimenti collegium inde caperet.
4. Quod per singulas septimanas eorum quilibet octo denarios solveret pro decrementis.
5. Quod disputationes, et caetera collegia exercitia obirent, et praelectores diligenter audire tenerentur.
6. Quod principalis portionistarum regimini subessent, cui 1d. ob. per septimanam eo nomine solverent.
7. Quod hortum magistrorum non intrarent, nisi aliquem ex numero magistrorum sibi comitem haberent.

Quo eodem tempore conventum est cum coquo iuniore quod is carbones in usum culinae suppeditaret in annum sequentem, quo nomine triginta libras a bursariis reciperet. Consensum etiam est de stipendio lotricis augendo, ita ut in posterum viginti solidos a quolibet bursario reciperet.

Electus est eodem tempore magister Powell in alteram exhibitionum Bickley, vacantem per resignationem magistri Nicholls.

Septembris 5. Magister Nicolls 3us bursarius confecit aeque suum.

Decembris 17. Habita est commemoratio fundatoris, post lecta sunt statuta, et scrutinium initum, quod in calendas Ianuarii prorogatum est.

Decembris 18. Magister Trevor 1^{mus} bursarius computavit.

Decembris 31. Initum est de more scrutinium, in quo tribus illis solemnibus propositis, 1mo de moribus servientium, 2° de numero portionistarum, 3^{tio} de electione hortulani. Servientes ad officiarios remissi sunt; placuit ut idem numerus esset portionistarum, qui prius; in hortulanum electus est magister Iones. Quo facto prorogatum est scrutinium in festum Purificationis.

[1651]

Ianuarii 2. Admissi sunt in perpetuam societatem huius domus dominus Maund, dominus Hully, dominus Pavier, dominus Hurst, dominus Willoughby, praestitis prius consuetis iuramentis quibus obligantur admittendi in socios.

Ianuarii 6. Admissus est in perpetuam societatem dominus Cripps, iisdem iuramentis prius praestitis.

Februarii 9. Magister French postquam per aliquot menses decubuisset, placida morte a vivis excessit, moriens decem libras legavit ad libros coemendos in usum bibliothecae collegii.

Februarii 12. Magister Trevor 1^{mus} bursarius confecit aeque suum.

Martii 23. Sacra fecimus in memoria fundatoris, sed quum is dies in Dominicum incideret delata est statutorum lectio in diem sequentem.

Martii 24. Lecta sunt statuta et initum scrutinium, quod in primum diem Iunii prorogatum est.

Martii 25. Dominus Master commendatus a commissionariis, authoritate parliamentaria constitutis, ad Academias ordinandas admissus est in annum probationis, praestitis consuetis iuramentis.

Aprilis 7. Convenimus in hospitio ubi consensum est quod illae centum librae a magistro Simonson (non ita pridem socio huius domus) ultimo istius testamento collegio legatae, in pocula argentea converterentur quae custodis et sociorum usui deservirent.

Quo eodem tempore, quum appareret, arreragii quaedam insoluta esse et necessarium videretur ad debita quaedam recuperanda iure experiendum esse, consensum est quod vicecustos Londinum proficisceretur ut domino custodi in his, aliisque rebus collegium spectantibus praesto esset.

Aprilis 17. Magister Dickenson 2^{dus} bursarius computavit.

Iunii 7. Magister Dickenson confecit aeque suum. Dominus Whitehall ab iisdem commendatus a quibus dominus Master admissus est in annum probationis, praestitis prius consuetis iuramentis.

Iulii 10. Magister Iones variavit in hisce quaestionibus:

An {
1. Mundus sit ingenerabilis et incorruptibilis. Negat: contra Aristotelem libro 1mo de Caelo, capitulis 9, 11.
2. Responsio platonica sit omnibus aliis anteferenda. Affirmat: contra Aristotelem 2do Politic', capitulis 1, 2, 3, 4 etc.
3. Mores animi sequantur temperamentum corporis. Affirmat: contra Aristotelem 1mo Politic', capitulo 5to.

Finitis disputationibus dispensatum est cum eo pro 2^{dis} variationibus.

Iulii 11. Doctor Whistler variavit in hisce variationibus:

[*blank*]

Quibus peractis dispensatum cum eo est pro 2^{dis} variationibus.

p. 383 Iulii 20. Habita est commemoratio fundatoris, sed quum is dies in Dominicum incideret statutorum lectio et scrutinium in diem sequentem dilata sunt.

Iulii 21. Lecta sunt statuta, et scrutinium initum, quod in 1^{mum} Augusti diem prorogatum est.

Iulii 28. Dominus Eyre ab iisdem commendatus a quibus dominus Master et dominus Whitehall, admissus est in annum probationis praestitis prius consuetis iuramentis. Eodem die dominus custos computavit, et discessit in plussagio.

Praedia et tenementa hoc anno locata [*i.e. in the college year 1650–1*]

Augusti 2do [1650]. Dimisimus tenementum vocatum The Rose in Watford magistro Antonio Knightbridge pro spatio viginti unius annorum. Finis 30 librae. Cui paulo post concessimus licentiam alienationis.

Dimisimus etiam manerium de Elshage in parochia de Chedington magistro Roberto Mayne pro spatio 21 annorum. Finis 60 librae. Una cum licentia alienandi.

Augusti 7. Dimissae sunt duae virgatae terrae in Hensington Aldermanno Whistler pro spatio 21 annorum. Finis 0.

Dimissae sunt ly Swaythes in Kibworth Richardo Burdett pro spatio 21 annorum. Finis 15 librae [*whole entry later crossed through*].

Dimisimus manerium de Gamlingay Merton magistro Henrico Kerseley durante vita naturali Henrici Iacob, et Francisci Iacob filiorum domini Iohannis Iacob Equitis Aurati, et Henrici Kerseley filii eiusdem Henrici Kerseley. Finis centum librae.

Dimisimus manerium de Gamlingay Avenells eidem Henrico Kerseley pro spatio 21 annorum. Finis 50 librae.

Dimisimus etiam sylvas Mertonagii eidem Henrico, pro spatio viginti et unius annorum. Finis 20 librae, quorum omnium summarum pars solvenda ad sigillationem indenturarum, altera pars anno revoluto.

Concessimus etiam eidem postea licentiam alienandi manerium de Gamlingay Merton.

Dimisimus etiam eodem tempore Dorotheae Hawley, viduae, alteram partem domus vocatae Stonehouse in Knightrider Street, London, pro spatio 40 annorum una cum licentia alienationis. Finis 50 librae.

Augusti 14. Dimissae sunt decimae de Burmington in agro Warwicensi magistro Iohanni French durante vita eius naturali.

Dimissum est tenementum vocatum ye White Lyon in St John's streete, London, Roberto Makin pro spatio 40 annorum. Finis 0.

Augusti 27. Dimissum est tenementum in Hampton Poyle Gulielmo Astill, pro spatio viginti unius annorum, una cum licentia alienandi. Finis 6 li. 13s. 4d.

Dimisimus tenementum e regione Sancti Martini Isabellae Pawlinge, viduae, pro spatio 40 annorum. Finis 40 librae.

Dimisimus firmam de Holywell, et rectoriam de Wolvercott et Holywell magistro Edmundo Napper durante vita naturali Gulielmi Napper, Georgii Napper et Francisci Napper filiorum eiusdem Edmundi.

Demisimus etiam molendinum de Holywell et Regium Carolo Napper, filio eiusdem Edmundi pro spatio quadraginta annorum. Finis utriusque indenturae quadringentae quinquaginta librae, quarum 250 librae solvendae ad sigillationem indenturarum, et ex unanimi consensu dividendae inter custodem et socios. Earum autem quae superant ducentarum librarum consensum est quod pars prior solveretur ad festum Michaelis Anno Domini 1651, altera ad idem festum 1652.

Demisimus tenementum in Holywell Augustino Boxley pro 21 annis. Finis, duo capones.

Eodem tempore consensum est de dimittendis fundis nostris in Lapworth, vocatis Heinseleyes, magistro French, sed iure tantum fiduciario, quo expeditius, eiecto quodam magistro Lovell, qui ea per annos complures occuparat, nec reditus quicquam solverat, collegium ius suum recuperaret.

Martii 24 [1651]. Dimissae sunt decimae de Burmington magistro Fisher durante vita eius naturali.

Martii 25. Dimissum est tenementum vocatum Leaden-Porch Edmundo Eton pro 40 annis una cum licentia alienandi. Finis octoginta librae, quarum pars prior solvenda ad sigillationem indenturae, altera eodem tempore anno revoluto.

Aprilis 7mo. Dimisimus tenementum vocatum The Flower-de-Luce et Aulam Portionistarum una cum horto ei adiacente Mariae Woode, viduae, pro spatio 40 annorum.[1] Finis 30 librae, quarum altera pars solvenda ad sigillationem indenturarum, altera annno revoluto. Concessa etiam est licentia alienandi utrumque tenementum.

Atque haec omnia suis temporibus sigillata sunt.

p. 384 Anno Domini MDCLI, domini Nathanielis Brent custodis XXXmo.

Socii Collegii
Magistri

1. Alexander Fisher
2. Daniel Whistler, medicinae doctor
3. Iohannes Powell
4. Petrus Nicolls
5. Thomas Iones
6. Richardus Lydall
7. Eduardus Wood
8. Edmundus Dickenson
9. Richardus Francklin
10. Iosephus Hervey
11. Richardus Trevor
12. Iohannes Arnold
13. Nathaniel Sterry
14. Thomas Francke

Baccalaurei

1. dominus Cripps
2. dominus Maund
3. dominus Hully
4. dominus Pavier
5. dominus Hurst
6. dominus Willoughby

[1] *Margin*, 'hortus locatus est pro termino 27 tantum annorum'.

In anno probationis

1. dominus Master
2. dominus Whitehall
3. dominus Eyres

Capellani

1. Magister Georgius Lort
2. Magister Beniamin Cooper

Augusti 1. Convenimus in aula hora nona antemeridiana, ubi de more, resignatis clavibus officiariorum superioris anni, per dominum custodem et quinque simpliciter seniores praesentes (reliquis interim sociorum secedentibus) electi sunt in annum sequentem:.
vicecustos, magister Fisher.
decani, magistri Iones, Hervey, Sterry.
bursarii, magistri Powell, Francklin, Arnold.
principalis portionistarum, magister Lydall; bursarius Willyot, exhibitionarius Hampsterley et capellanus capellae, magister Nicolls; praelector Graecae linguae, magister Dickinson; praelector grammaticae, magister Woode; custodes Cistae Read, tres decani; custodes Cistae Bodleigh, magistri Lydall, Francklin, Arnold.

Quo eodem tempore electus est in alteram exhibitionum Bickley, magister Woode, vacantem per resignationem magistri Fisher.

Consensum etiam est ut praelector Logicae quatuor libras annuas a bursariis in posterum reciperet.

Necessarium etiam visum est ut progressus hoc anno iniretur, ad visitanda maneria de Cuxham et Ibston in agro Oxoniensi, et maneria de Kibworth et Barkby in agro Leicestrensi cui rei conficiendae designatus est bursarius itinerans doctor Whistler. Cum vero longo ambitu, et saepius iteratis petitionibus instarent tenentes nostri apud Barkby, aliique de vicinia, ut sibi per nos liceret fundos suos (qui sparsi confusique in agris iacebant) segregare et fossis saepibusque includere et munire, ex quo magna sibi emolumenta pollicebantur, sine alterius cuiusquam iniuria: aequum est visum ut sociorum aliquis eo mitteretur, ad rem inspiciendam tractandamque. Quam provinciam in se suscepit magister Lydall.

Augusti II. Suffectus est magister Thomas Cole in locum Iohannis Brent, collegii seneschalli, nuper defuncti, sub iisdem prorsus conditionibus quibus alter ille, hoc munere fruebatur.

Augusti IV. Consensum est quod salinum argenteum vetustate corruptum et cochlearia quaedam argentea confracta et contusa mutarentur in duodecim cochlearia nova, quae usui hospitii deinceps inservirent.

Augusti XXII. Magister Iones, 3us bursarius, computavit.

Quo tempore consensum est per dominum custodem et socios ut pecuniae a bursario in aerarium inducendae quae ad quadringentas et triginta libras excreverant, sic dividerentur ut custos triginta, sociorum vero quilibet viginti libras perciperet.

Septembris XXX. Vicecustos et magister Lydall (qui vices doctoris Whistler in progressu ad Kibworth et Barkby suppleverat) domum reversi ad custodem sociosque retulerunt quid a se in negotio illo de Barkby actum est, nimirum consensisse se, nomine collegii, in agrorum ibidem, ut vocant inclusionem sed certis sub conditionibus (quibus ecclesiae praesertim et pauperibus cautum erat) quae nisi impleantur, rem adhuc esse integram. Condiciones postea lectae sunt et unanimi consensu approbatae.

Eodem tempore consensum est in divisionem centum et quinquaginta librarum inter custodem et socios, sed hac adhibita cautione, ut si quis pecunias bibliothecae debitas nondum solvisset tantundem ex his pecuniis ei detraheretur in usum bibliothecae.

p. 385 Septembris XXX. Decretum est quod praedia illa et fundi (quae quum revera in collegii peculio censenda essent, sub alienis tamen nominibus, iure fiduciario, adhuc censerentur) in collegii ius et nomen transirent, quod ut quam celerrime fieret iurisperitos consulendo censuerunt.

Octobris II. Consensum est quod magister Powell et magister Nicolls variare non tenerentur modo duas conciones sacras eorum uterque haberet in templo Beatae Mariae vel in privata collegii capella, quum ad hoc officium obeundum a domino custode vel, eo absente, a vicecustode rite admonerentur.

Atque eodem tempore ordinatum est quod magister Lydall et magister Wood hoc anno variarent; cum reliquis magistrorum dispensatum est.

Consensum est de indentura fiduciaria in quinquennium conficienda vicecustodi terrarum nuperrime perquisitarum apud Hensington, partim ad recuperanda arreragia quae per aliquot annos insoluta erant, partim ad eiiciendum Gulielmum Redhead iuniorem (qui invito patre Gulielmo Redhead seniore firmario nostro tenementum illud cum fundis annexis possidebat) id quod pater unice expetere videbatur.

Quo eodem tempore magister Iones 3us bursarius confecit aeque suum.

Novembris XXVII. Dominus Nathaniel Brent eques auratus praefectura huius domus (quam per annos triginta circiter summa fide et cura administrarat) ultro se Londinis abdicavit.

Decembris IX. Dominus Ionathan Goddard, medicinae doctor, ad collegium accessit, ad eiusdem regimen (per spontaneam resignationem domini Nathanielis Brent iam vacuum) capessendum: ad quod munus ad honoratissimis commissionariis authoritate parliamentaria ad academias ordinandas et reformandas constitutis, designatus erat. Venientem comitabantur dominus doctor Greenewood, vicecancellarius, dominus doctor Langbane, dominus doctor Wilkins, aliique complures. Quibus obviam in ipso collegii vestibulo se stiterunt vicecustos, sociique et scholares universi. Ubi dominus doctor Goddard instrumentum quoddam (ordinationem vocant) vicecustodi porrexit, quod in haec verba scriptum erat: subscriptum vero variis commissionariorum praefatorum nominibus:

Novembris 27 anni domini 1651.

At ye committee for Reformation of the universityes.

Whereas this committee have this day receyved a resignation under ye hand of Sir Nathaniel Brent, Warden of Merton College in ye university of Oxon', which this committee doth accept; and whereas this Committee have not yet declared ye sayd college to be in a capacity of makinge theire Elections in a Statutable way, This Committee having receyved satisfactory testimony of ye piety and true worth of Jonathan Goddard, Doctor of Physicke and of his fitnesse for that place, doe order that ye said doctor Goddard be Warden of Merton College aforesaid in ye roome and place of ye said Sir Nathanie(l) Brent, and hereby ye said Doctor is constituted and appoynted Warden of ye said College, to all intents and purposes, and shall from henceforth receive all and singular Profitts and Priviledges to ye same annexed, or in any wise belonginge. And ye Subwarden or Senior Fellowe of ye said College is hereby required to Admitt ye said Doctor accordingly. And all Fellowes, Schollers, Members and Officers of ye said College are hereby enioyned to take notice hereof, and to conforme and subiect themselves to ye said Doctor Goddard, as Warden of ye sayd College.

Haec quum perlegissset, palamque recitasset, vicecustos, novo custodi librum statutorum et collegii clavem (quibus si quis in muneris sui possesionem de more mittebatur) in manus cum praefatiuncula, tradidit, confestimque magister Sterry hanc orationem habuit.

Oratio magistri Sterry.

Salve, dignissime praeses, quin et faveas musis nostris, alacri velut penna, et modesto calami triumpho, ad pedes vestros advolantibus. Novum scilicet confidenter sibi praesagiunt, et generosum magis ex tanto vestigio Helicona. Absint demum lachrymae nostrae et suspiria, soloecismi isti pietatis. Est hoc praesentiae vestrae beneficium, ut optimorum (quotquot hinc discesserint) praesidum memoria liceat serena frui, et superstitioso gemitu imperturbata. Enimvero expressas in vestra fronte istorum omnium imagines gratissima contemplatione percurrimus. Saepius lilia docuisti, quomodo in vitro mercuriali velut ex proprio funere renascerentur, eandemque sibi urnam haberent et incunabula. In te ipso hodie deprehendiumus Bicklium, Savilium, Bodleium ex suis cineribus gloriosius reflorescentes. Sparsas quippe horum et per varia capita dispensatas virtutes in unum colligis, ex isto porro compendio fortiores. Severam Savilii maiestatem miscuisti humanitate Brentiana, et in suaviora commercia temperasti. Talem vero decuit nobis esse praesidem. Ingenuae enim sunt musae, et honestioris indolis; quam constringit nimius imperii rigor, premitque generosos impetus. Ecquid regnum appellitamus, an, pro praesenti genio, rempublicam literariam in qua tamen non pavidi securos, non fasces, circumferuntur qualicunque cypresso funestiores. Nolito ob haec in nobis suspicari aequioris legis, et verecundi fraeni impatientiam. 1mo vero per fundatoris nostri manes, per musas et Apollinem veneramur, ut sanctissima tibi nostra sit disciplina; illa, quae a sacro suo capite, per tot annorum Maeandros, et ludibria desilientis saeculi, syncera ad te derivatur et inviolata. Tantiae, obsecro, fuerit Mertonenses nostros prae ipso Nerone sacros audire; ut idcirco istius disciplinae velut arterias laxarent, quae a tenerrima itis infantia, ad hoc quicquid est, aetatis pariter ac gloriae praeiverit? Ignoscas, insignissime vir, si ad haec te sollicitem, quae interim fatemur a pientissimo ingenio anteverti. Obvium illud erat umbram vestris encomiis, et latebras quaerenti. Ita enim indulgemus quantum par est, verecundiae vestrae; quam laedunt manifestiores laudes, magisque velut in aprico lucentes. Alia vero lege neutiquam dissimulassem sensa nostra, et laetissimos instinctus qui illud altius insinuant, nihil nobis de institutis maiorum, de literarum fastigio periturum, quousque tu in vivis fueris, aut saltem Cromwellus. Atque hoc nomine mihi prolubium erat ruentem orationem sufflaminasse; ut si faelicitatis et votorum, etiam esset et sermonis periodus. Verum militare nomen,

ac si suas etiam insidias didicisset, adoritur[1] ex opaco, improvisamque in me suffundit dicendi copiam. Macte demum dux augustissime, invictissime Caesar. Caesarem dixi? Fateor contumeliam tituli. Neque enim ad huius sive nomen, sive praesentiam: (quod ad Caesaris olim fecit in Catonem) concidet examinata philosophia: sed surget, sed efflorescat, sed ad exemplares patroni sui triumphos alludat innocentiori aemulatione. Non horrebimus amplius ad importunos arietes; qui etiamsi Athenas hasce aliquando demoliti fuerint; novas illico Cromwellus conderet, uti suas Thebas Amphion, doctae vocis architectonica; conditas quasi faecundaret, deductis ex proprio pectore scientiarum coloniis. Istius vero miraculi favorem quo minus experturi simus, ipse efficies; orbis scilicet literarii praesentius columen. Quo titulo liceat a nobis diutius censeri. Ubi vero ad maiora te provocaverit seu reipublicae, seu fatorum / necessitas, nomen nobis delegabis, et p. 387
memoriam; nomen quidem constans ad aeternitatem; perinde ac perennes apud Romanos faces, quanquam inter cineres demum tuos et sera sepulchra, illud tamen non exibit e sua luce: memoriam vero, qualem poetae suam voluere, nempe quae nova musarum soboles se mox sit exdutura nepotibus.[2]

Perorantem excepit dominus custos, suumque in collegium studium et in munere obeundo futuram diligentiam hisce verbis testatus est:

Viri ornatissimi, et collegae charissimi,

Quod nobis visus fuerim in collegium vestrum structura magnificum, et, quod maius, insigni alumnorum doctrina percelebre, tam honorifice excipiendus, a me, ad munus oratorium natura vel arte minime comparato, eoque nomine longe impari, oratoris vestri consummatissimi oratione dignum referendo responsum, atque ad tale quicquam, in hoc genere moliendum impraesentiarum prorsus imparato; orandi estis, ut mihi sufficiat unico verbo, gratias quantas possum maximas ex animo retribuere; simulque spondere, omni me gratitudinis et observantiae officio, aestimationem apud vos, quam potuero plurimam consequi fovere ac tueri, summa virium mearum contentione, daturum operam; sicut custodem oportet collegii faelicitatis dignitatisque studiosissimum, vobisque omnibus affectu sincero exoptantem omnia fausta.

[1] 'mihi' deleted.

[2] *Margin*, 'Haec oratio habita est quo tempore de bonis Academiarum publicandis rumor increbuit, cuiusmodi consiliis ne executioni mandarentur, istam (exercitus id temporis imperatione) se opposuisse simul accepimus'.

His confectis dominum custodem ad hospitium deduxerunt, ubi aliquamdiu commorati, et convivio, ut moris est, recepti, omnes ad sua se receperunt.

Decembris XVII. Habita est commemoratio in memoriam fundatoris, post lecta sunt statuta, et scrutinium, de more, initum, quod in calendas Ianuarii prorogatum est.

Eodem tempore dispensatum est cum magistro Arnold 1mo bursario ut computum suum in tres septimanas differre posset.

Decembris XXXI. Initum est scrutinium in quo tria illa sollennia proposita sunt: 1. Mores servientium; 2. Numerus portionistarum; 3. Electio hortulani, et in hortulanum electus est magister Lydall; placuit ut idem esset portionistarum numerus, qui annis superioribus, servientes ad officiarios remissi sunt, pro meritis suis castigandi. Deinde scrutinium prorogatum est in festum Purificationis.

[1652]

Ianuarii VII. Confectus est generalis computus anni 1650/1651. Consensum etiam est a domino custode et sociis qui plerique omnes aderant, in aliam divisionem (cui aerarii sufficere videbatur) quadringentarum et triginta librarum, ita ut custodi triginta, sociorum unicuique viginti librae obvenirent.

Eodem tempore magister Arnold 1^{mus} bursarius computavit.

p. 388 Anno Domini 1651, doctoris Goddard custodis 1°.

Nomina Sociorum, in adventu Goddard custodis

Magistri

1. Alexander Fisher
2. Daniel Whistler, medicinae doctor
3. Iohannes Powell
4. Petrus Nichols
5. Thomas Iones
6. Richardus Lydall
7. Edwardus Wood
8. Emundus Dickenson
9. Richardus Franklin
10. Iosephus Hervey
11. Richardus Trevor
12. Iohannes Arnold
13. Nathaniel Sterry
14. Thomas Frank

Baccalaurei

1. dominus Crips
2. dominus Maund
3. dominus Hulley
4. dominus Pavier
5. dominus Hurst
6. dominus Willoughbey

In anno probationis

1. dominus Master
2. dominus Whitehall
3. dominus Eyre

Capellani

1. Magister Georgius Lort
2. Magister Beniamin Cooper

In adventu Goddard custodis status collegii in praesentia officiariorum inventus est ut sequitur:.

In pecuniis numeratis in cista iocalium 466 li. 12s. 6d.
In pecuniarum summis super obligationibus collegio debitis 235 li.
Summa 701 li. 12s. 6d.

Vasa argentea in Cista iocalium.

1 sylver basen gilt.
2 flagons.
1 communion cup with a cover gilt.

Vasa argentea in Hospitio Custodis.

A piece of plate with a cover, given to ye college by magister Stafford.
2 of ye tankards given by magister Symondson, marked 2.4.
12 spoons.

Vasa argentea in promptuario.

18 tankards given by magister Symondson marked on ye covers 3, 5, 6, 7, 8, 9, 10, 11, 12, 13, 14, 15, 16, 17, 18, 19, 20.
1 tankard given by magister Skip.
1 tankard given by magister Southcoat.
1 tankard given by magister Abdey.
1 tankard given by magister Gwinn.
1 tankard given by magister Gregory.
1 tankard with ye college arms and no other mark.
6 spoons knopt, marked with the college arms.

Lintea in usum Hospitii.

2 pair of Holland sheets.
4 pair of flaxen sheets.
12 Holland pillowbeares.
6 pair of canvas sheets.
7 pair of old coarse flaxen sheets.
1 olde long damask tablecloath.
3 olde long diaper tablecloaths.
1 diaper tablecloath for ye communion table.

6 new douglasse tablecloathes.
5 olde douglas tablecloaths.
3 new canvas tablecloaths.
4 old canvas tablecoaths.
1 damask cupboard cloath.
5 old diaper cupboard cloaths.
2 old long diaper towells.
5 old damask napkins.
6 old diaper napkins.
11 dozen of douglas napkins.
2 dozen of olde douglas napkins.
12 towells.

Alia Suppelex in usum Custodis.

In ye chamber next ye south end of ye gallery, hung round with coarse arras.
a bedstead.
a feather bed.
2 bolsters.
1 pillowe.
p. 389 1 pair of blankets.
olde curtains, valens and a counterpane of blew cloath.
a round folding table.
a blew cloath carpet.
1 olde blew chair.
4 olde blew stooles.
a pair of dogs.
a fireshovell.
a pair of tongues.

In ye Gallery.

a table.
a long green cloath carpet, fringed.
18 Turkey work chairs.
1 great old Turkey work chair.

In ye chamber at ye north end of the Gallery.

4 pieces of old Arras hangings.
a bedstead with purple serge curtains and valens laced and fringed.
a down bed.
2 bolsters.
1 pillow.

a pair of blankets.
an orange coloured rug.
a counterpaine sutable to ye curtains.
a little square table.
a carpet sutable to ye bed.
an elbow chair and 4 back chairs, all sutable to ye bed.
a pair of brasse Andirons.
a fire shovell and tongues.
a pair of window curtains of blew shaded striped stuff.

In ye little garret over ye staircase.
a little bedstead with green curtains.
2 feather beds.
a bolster.
a pair of new blankets.
2 olde blankets.
a little table.
a little blew carpet.

In ye Chamber over ye Parlour.
5 pieces of olde Arras hanging.
a bedstead.
4 curtains with double valens, a counterpain, a great elbow chair, 2 low chairs, 2 low stools, and 2 carpets, all sutable of orange tawney serge trimmed with blew silk lace and fringe.
a feather bed.
a bolster.
a course mattresse.
an Holand quilt.
2 down pillowes.
a pair of blankets.
a table.
a court cupboard.
a close stool and pan.
2 window curtains of striped stuff.
2 olde green velvet cushions.
1 pair of brasse andirons.
2 pair of creepers.
a fireshovel and tonges.
a pair of bellowes.

In ye upper closet next ye stairs.
a little table with a blew carpet.
a turkey work old chair.

In ye Dining room.
a long drawing table.
a court cupboard.
a sideboard table.
a long carpet, a cupboard cloth and side-board cloth, all of Turkey work, a great elbow chair, with 12 back chairs, all of a sute, of Turkey work.
2 window curtains of striped stuff.
a pair of great brass andirons.
a pair of dogs.
a fireshovell and tongues.
Lord Burleigh's picture.

In ye vault chamber.
2 small pieces of olde hangings.
4 pieces of rich Arras hangings.
a large featherbed.
a canvas mattresse.
a bolster of ye bed.
2 down pillows.
1 pair of fine blankets.
a counterpain of skarlet.
4 curtains with double valens of scarlet, lined with taffata.
a bedstead.
a close stool and pan.
a carpet and a sideboard cloth of scarlet.
a table.
a little sideboard.
an elbow chair, 2 low chairs and 2 low stools, all of scarlet.
a pair of brasse andirons.
a fireshovell and tongues.

In Sever's chamber.
3 feather beds.
2 bolsters.
3 pillowes.
2 old blankets.
1 green rug.

1 bedstead.
5 old strip'd curtains with valens.
1 old blew rug.
1 old striped carpet.
a long green carpet to ye dining room table.
a short green carpet.
an olde Turkey work carpet.
a table. p. 390
an old fourm.
a pair of dogs.
a fire shovel and tongues.

In ye room behinde Sever's chamber.

2 old fether beds.
a fether bolster.
a flock bolster.
an half-headed bedstead.
an old blanket, carpet and coverlid.
a chest.

In ye olde studie.

a crimson velvet Communion table Carpet trimmed with golde lace, and silk and golde fringe: together with a Cushion sutable to it.
a feather bed.
a bolster.
a blanket.
a red rug.
an olde carpet.
an olde bedstead.
2 olde tables.

In ye Servants' chamber over ye olde Cellar.

2 fether beds.
2 fether bolsters.
a flock bolster.
2 olde coverlids.
an olde rug.
2 half headed bedsteads.
an olde table.
an olde desk.
an olde presse.

In ye olde Parlour next to ye olde Hall.
a table.
an old cupboard.

In ye new Parlour.
1 great olde Turkey work chair.
12 Turkey work olde chairs.
6 olde Turkey work stools.
6 olde Cushions of blew satin with starres in a square table with leaves to turn up (golde).
a side table.
a court cupboard.
an olde green Couch.
2 olde Carpets and a Cupboard cloth of green.
a pair of window curtains of strip'd stuff (cloth).
a pair of brasse andirons.
a pair of dogs.
a fireshovel and tongues.
a pair of bellowes.

In ye Hall.
a table.
3 fourms whereof 2 belonging to ye chappel.
a still.
a Court cupboard.
a pair of Andirons.

In ye Servants' dining room.
a table.
a fourm belonging to ye chappell.
a chest.

In ye Kitchin to ye Warden's Lodgings.
Pewter.
18 larger dishes.
7 smaller dishes.
7 sallet dishes.
12 larger trencher plates.
20 smaller trencher plates.
2 py plates.
2 basons.
5 chamber pots.
1 flagon.

10 porrengers.
7 saucers.
6 candlesticks.

Brasse.

1 candlestick.
2 kettles.
3 skillets.
2 potts.
2 skimmers with iron handles.
a warming pan.
9 spoons tinned over.

Lattine.

a colender.
9 candlesticks.
2 drippin panns.
an apple roaster.

Iron.

a jack with ye appurtenances.
4 spits.
a pair of pot hooks.
2 pot hangers.
a rack for spits.
a frying pan.
a gridiron.
a pair of Andirons for burning seacoal, with iron barres, in ye vestry.
a little fork.
a pair of tongues.
a range.

Other Utensils.

a pair of bellowes.
a movable choping dresser.
2 old yellow velvet cushions.

In ye College Treasure room.

a round table.
a green carpet.
6 leather stooles.
1 leather chair.

In ye College Buttery.
a bread bin with 2 lids.
a great dish with a drawer.
a wicker basket to carry plate and bread into ye Hall.
a wainscot preasse with 2 cupboards underneath.
3 pieces of wainscot with benches joyned to them.
7 pewter salts, 18 pewter spoons (for ye Hall).
6 old napkins to make clean ye plate withall.
an olde settle with a Candle box.

p. 391 *In ye College Kitchin.*
Pewter.
1 great charger.
3 middle chargers.
8 biggest sort of dishes.
13 of ye 2[d] sort of dishes.
28 of ye lesser sort of dishes.
6 sallet dishes.
26 porrengers.
14 sawcers.
1 pye plate.
Brasse.
3 potts.
2 kettles.
2 panns.
4 skillets.
1 skummer.
1 ladle.
1 colender.
Iron.
9 spits.
2 racks.
a range before ye fire.
a frying pan.
a cleaver.
a mincing knife.
a setting perl.
a fine perl.
3 pair of pot hooks.
3 pot hangers.

a gridiron.
a trivet.

Other utensils.

a great desk.
2 salt tubs.
a powdering tub.
a salt box.
a grater.

In ye Manciples room.

a safe.
a shelf with brackets.

In ye inner Kitchin.

an iron mortar and pestle.
an iron before ye fire.
2 racks.

In ye Porters room.

Table cloths:
- 3 for ye Masters table.
- 3 for ye Bachellours table.
- 2 for ye upper Commoners table.
- 2 for ye under Commoners table.
- 2 for ye Postmasters table.
- 2 for ye Servants table.
- 1 for ye crosse table.

7 dozen and 7 napkins.
4 long towells.
2 great brasse candlesticks.
14 lesser brasse candlesticks.
2 tinne candlesticks.
3 pewter Salts.
12 pewter spoons.
a brasse bason to wash in.
2 iron grates for ye Hall fire.
a large fireshovel.
an olde cupboard.

In ye Porters lodge.

a piece of old arras.
a little bason for ye barber.

In ye Chappel and Vestry.
a fair standing desk all of brasse.
3 olde folio bibles.
24 fourmes.
2 back fourmes.
1 longer and 2 shorter clothes of white and green cope work with golde.
1 cloath of blew sattin with starres in golde.
a pulpit cloath of purple velvet with sylver and blew fringe.
a pulpit Cushion of blew velvet wrought in golde.
2 long blew sattin Cushions wrought in golde with starres.
6 square cushions of ye same sattin work.
an Organ in pieces.
2 olde Cushions of Velvet wrought in golde.
a Font of black marble.
a Communion table.
2 desks before ye 2 Chaplins.
8 fair long desks before ye seats of ye Commoners and Postmasters.

p. 392 Ianuarii XX. Robertus Griffin coquus iunior diem obiit, in cuius locum suffectus est Iohannes Griffin defuncti filius.

Ianuarii XXIX. Consensum est per dominum custodem et socios, quod vicecustos Londinum profisceretur ad collegii negotia procuranda. Consensum etiam est in quadraginta ulmos, magistro Ray concedendas, ad ventimolam apud Kibworth, quae ruinam minitabatur, reficiendam; sed ea condicione ut earum pleraeque ex ipsius fundis desumerentur, caeterae supplerentur ex aliorum tenentium copiis.

Februarii XXI. Consensum est, quod opus intestinum (quod in cubiculo suo magister French ante aliquot annos propriis sumptibus crescerat) ab executoribus eius a collegio redimeretur (iusto pretio ab harum rerum peritis prius posito). Atque ut in posterum inter collegii bona, at [*sic*] illud cubiculum pertinentia, censeretur.

Consensum etiam, quod quicquid deficeret in cubiculo magistri Franke, ad explendas tres libras, id a collegio suppeditaretur.

Februarii XXVIII. Cum superius cautum esset ne communariorum numerus ultra sex excresceret, iam visum est domino custodi et sociis hanc condicionem relaxare, nec ullum omnino numerum definire; aequum etiam visum est, ut eorum unusquisque tres denarios in singulas septimanas principali portionistarum in posterum solveret.

Iniecta etiam est mentio de aliis, sed inferioris subsellii communariis; sed quibus sub condicionibus in collegium admitterentur eo tempore non est consensum.

Martii XVI. Dominus Rood a commissionariis ad academias ordinandas constitutis commendatus, in annum probationis admissus est, praestitis prius consuetis iuramentis.

Martii XIX. Consensum est inter dominum custodem et socios in has condiciones:

1. Quod socii in posterum suis communiis contenti essent; omnibus vero appientantiis, exequiis, carni aprugnae, vino ad carnem aprugnam, et ly-sheepe-money renunciarent.

2. Quod dominus custos hisce omnibus renunciaret, atque insuper ly-sowcark, in quod nihil iuris sibi in posterum competere pronuntiaret.

3. Quod domino custodi compensationis loco, singulis annis allocarentur triginta librae ratione rununtiationis ly-sowcark-1 li. 17s. 6d. pro appietantiis, 40s. pro carne aprugna, 20s. pro exequiis, et 10s. pro ly-sheep money, quae summae (una cum nova allocatione quae est 13 li. 17s. 4d. per annum, et allocatione Elae Comitissae et Leech, quae est 1 li. 14s. 8d. per annum, et coenis quadragesimalibus, quae sunt 6 librae per annum) excrescunt ad 56 li. 19s. 6d. Atque ut haec summa in posterum in custodis computo, nomine allocationis novae insigniretur, et singulis annis allocationi veteri, quae est 23 li. 2s. 2d. coniungeretur.

4. Quod sociorum unuicuique compensationis loco, cederent duo solidi in singulas septimanas, probationariis et capellanis unus solidus et quatuor denarii, servientibus sex denarii.

5. Quod si quis sociorum vel probationariorum absens a collegio fuerit, ei per singulos absentiae suae dies decem denarii subtraherentur, quinque vero ratione absentiae a coena vel prandio. Capellano vero iuniori octo denarii, si per totum diem absens fuerit; vicecustodi autem, seniori capellano et servientibus nihil subtrahatur.

6. Quod allocatio haec initium sumeret[1] a termino tertii bursarii inchoante, duraretque ad festum Sancti Petri ad Vincula, quod futurum est anno domini 1653; quo tempore rursus dispiceretur, an collegium huic oneri ferendo par esset. Cum vero hanc appietantiarum abolitionem coquo seniori damnosam esse constaret, consensum est quod tres librae annuae veteri eius stipendio adderentur, ad damnum hoc, quoquo modo, resarciendum.

[1] This word was deleted then interlined.

Martii XXV. Admissus est dominus Master in perpetuam societatem huius collegii, praestitis prius consuetis iuramentis.

Aprilis X. Habita est commemoratio fundatoris, post lecta sunt statuta, et scrutinium initum quod in decimum diem Maii prorogatum est. Quo tempore dispensatum est cum magistro Francklin 2do bursario, ut computum suum in unam alteramve septimanam differre posset; et postea in duas alteras septimanas.

Maii XIII. Magister Francklin 2^{dus} bursarius computavit.

Iunii V. Cum plurima collegii negotia Londini essent transigenda, consensum est quod vicecustos eo proficisceretur ad ea procuranda.

Iunii XXIIII. Dominus Whitehall admissus est in perpetuam societatem huius domus praestitis consuetis iuramentis.

Iulii VIII. Magister Wood variavit in hisce quaestionibus:

An {
- Peregrinatio sit utilis. Negat contra Aristotelem, libro 1mo Rhetorices, capitulo 4, textu 18vo.
- Ars superet naturam. Affirmat contra Aristotelem, libro 2do, Physicorum, capitulo 2, textu, 22.
- Vita activa sit praestantior speculativa. Affirmat contra Aristotelem, libro 10mo, Ethic', capitulo 7mo.

Finitis disputationibus, dispensatum est cum eo, pro 2^{dis} variationibus.

p. 393 Iulii IX. Magister Lydall variavit in hisce quaestionibus:

An {
- Voluptas sit summum bonum. Affirmat contra Aristotelem libro 1mo Ethic', capitulo 3°.
- Desiderium scientiae sit hominibus naturale. Negat contra Aristotelem, libro 1mo Metaphysicorum, capitulo 1mo.
- Sanguis sit humor nutritius. Negat contra Aristotelem, libro 2do, De partibus Animalium, capitulo 3°.

Finitis disputationibus cum eo dispensatum est pro 2^{dis} variationibus.

Iulii XX. Habita est commemoratio fundatoris, post lecta sunt statuta et scrutinium initum, quod in ultimum diem Augusti prorogatum est.

Iulii XXVIII. Dominus Eyres admissus est in perpetuam societatem huius collegii praestitis prius consuetis iuramentis.

Praedia et tenementa hoc anno locata [*i.e in the college year 1651–2*]
Septembris 30 [1651]. Dimisimus Ly Swaythes in Kibworth Richardo Burdett, pro spatio viginti et unius annorum. Finis 5 librae.

Dismissae sunt tres virgatae terrae in Kibworth, nuper in tenura Margaretae Standen, Rodulpho Guy, pro spatio viginti et unius annorum. Finis 35 librae, una cum licentia alienationis.

Dimisimus firmam de Barkby Iohanni Mennell pro spatio viginti et unius annorum. Finis 0, quod partim eius gratiae, partim paupertati datum est. Eidem etiam concessimus licentiam alienandi.

Dimissa est domus in Py-Lane magistro Iohanni Bull pro spatio quadraginta annorum, una cum licentia alienationis. Finis 10 librae. Cautione tamen prius data ne quid inde praeiudicii cuidam Iohanni Smith, eiusne liberis (qui, ius in tenementum hoc, vel maiorem eius partem sibi vindicabant) crearetur. Obligatione etiam data, 40 librarum qua Iohannes Bull se obstrinxit collegium hoc in negotio indemne praestiturum.

Octobris 2do. Dimissum est tenementum in Turfeild Thomae Simons pro spatio 21 annorum, finis 5 librae.

Dimissa est ventimola in Ibston Edmundo Simons pro 21 annis.

Finis 2 librae.

Novembris 13. Dimissi sunt fundi in Pockrilsston Iohanni Prattant pro 21 annis, Finis 40 librae, quarum prima pars solveretur ad indenturae sigillationem, altera eodem tempore anni revoluti.

Iulii 24 [1652]. Dimissa est medietas de Stillington et Ceton-Carewe magistro Samueli Rawlinge, pro spatio viginti et unius annorum, (sed facta prius resignatione eiusdem a magistro Richardo Morpeth, omnibusque arreragiis solutis, et damnis resarcitis), finis 20 librae quae summa satis idonea videbatur, ad redimendum duos annos et dimidium, qui de veteri indentura elapsi erant, concessa est etiam illis licentia alienationis.

Iulii 26. Sigillata est indentura decimarum Cirencestrensium (quae ante aliquot annos confecta erat) domino Gulielmo Master equiti aurato.

Iulii 31. Dimissa est firma de Ibston Gulielmo Wilmot pro 21 annis. Finis 10 librae.

Eidem etiam dimissae sunt sylvae de Ibston pro 21 annis. Finis 0.

Eodem tempore dimissum est manerium de Beilby magistro Marmaduko Prickett pro spatio viginti et unius annorum. Finis 0.

Dimissa est firma et molendinum in Beilby Georgio Butler, armigero pro 21 annis. Finis 6 li. 13s. 4d. Solvit etiam 15 li. pro arreragiis huius tenementi.[1].

Eidem etiam dimissum est tenementum Weekes in Beilby pro spatio unius et viginti annorum. Finis 10 librae.

Atque hae duae indenturae a magistro Prickett, firmario et ballivo nostro de Beilby prius sigillatae sunt, deinde communi collegii sigillo confirmatae et munitae, ut illius manerii consuetudo fert.

Aliae vero omnes suis quaeque temporibus sigillatae sunt.

p. 394 Anno[2] domini MDCLII, doctoris Goddard custodis 1mo.

Socii Collegii

Magistri

1. Alexander Fisher
2. Daniel Whistler, medicinae doctor
3. Ioannes Powell
4. Petrus Nicolls
5. Thomas Iones
6. Ricardus Lydall
7. Eduardus Wood
8. Edmundus Dickenson
9. Ricardus Francklin
10. Iosephus Hervey
11. Ricardus Trevor
12. Iohannes Arnold[3]
13. Nathaniel Sterry
14. Thomas Francke

Baccalaurei

1. dominus Crips
2. dominus Maund
3. dominus Hully
4. dominus Hurst
5. dominus Willoughby
6. dominus Master
7. dominus Whitehall
8. dominus Eyres

In anno probationis

1. dominus Rood

Capellani

1. Magister Georgius Lort
2. Magister Beniamin Cooper

Secundo Augusti, primus enim dies in dominicum inciderat, convenimus, pro more, in aula, hora nona antemeridiana, ubi resignatis clavibus officiariorum superioris anni per dominum custodem, et quinque simpliciter seniores, sociorum reliquis interim secedentibus, electi sunt in annum sequentem:
vicecustos, magister Fisher.

1 'debitis annis domini 1644 and 1645' interlined.
2 In the hand of Alexander Fisher.
3 'Thomas Francke' deleted.

decani, magistri Powell, Hervey, Trevor.
bursarii, magistri Lydal, Wood, Sterry.
principalis portionistarum, magister Iones; bursarius Williot, exhibitioniarius Hampsterley capellanus capellae, magister Nicholls; custodes cistae Read, tres decani; custodes cistae Bodleigh, magistri Iones, Wood, Sterry; praelector linguae Graecae, magister Dickenson; praelector grammaticae, magister Francklin.

Quo tempore decretum est, quod magister Dickenson et magister Francklin hoc anno in disputationibus baccalaureorum variare tenerentur. Cum reliquis magistrorum dispensatum est. Cum progressus hoc anno necessarius videretur ad maneria collegii visitanda, electus est bursarius itinerans, qui custodem comitaretur, magister Powell.

Augusti XXVI. Magister Powell 3us bursarius computavit.

Quo tempore consensum est quod lotrici collegii in posterum solverentur ab unoquoque bursario 1 li. 6s. 8d. partim ad resarciendum damnum quod sustiniuit ob sublatas appietantias anno superiori, partim ad stipendium quod minus aequo caussabatur, augendum.

Septembris I^mo^. Conventum est cum Iohanne coquo iuniore quod is carbones in usum culinae suis sumptibus suppeditaret ab hoc die ad I^mum^ Septembris qui futurus est, 1653, quo nomine a bursariis reciperet triginta quinque libras, non numeratis interim in hoc conventu iis carbonibus, quos bursarius iunior in usum collegii emerat initio termini sui, quorum ad tria circiter plaustra adhuc reliqua erant.

Novembris VI. Dominus Nathaniel Brent eques auratus, collegii Mertonensis per annos complures custos vigilantissimus, dignissimusque, et curiae praerogativae Canturariensis iudex sive praeses supremus, dierum et honorum iam satur, Londini placide in domino obdormivit.

Novembris XII. Admissi sunt in numerum magistrorum ex consensu custodis et sociorum quibus id iuris competebat, dominus Crips, dominus Maund, dominus Hully, dominus Hurst, dominus Willoughby, dominus Master, dominus Whitehall, dominus Eyres, praestitis prius consuetis iuramentis, sed quibusdem condicionibus annexis, quibus se volentes subiecerunt. Harum praecipue erant.

1. Quod computis hebdomadalibus in aula interessse tenerentur, saltem eorum quatuor, sub poena 3s. 4d. decano seniore in delinquentes irroganda.

2. Quod eorum unusquisque disputationibus baccalaureorum non tantum interesse teneretur, sed et respondentis et opponentium vices subire, sub poena 10s. in respondentem, 5s. in opponentem si deliquerit, infligenda; quam mulctam si decanus iunior, qui disputationibus ea vice moderari tenebatur irrogare negligeret, ipse eandem subiret, a custode, vel in eius absentia, a vicecustode infligendam.
3. Quod eorum nemo, durante termino, a collegio absens esset nisi venia prius petita et impetrata a custode, vel eo absente a vicecustode, et eo decano cui moderatoris munus illa septimana incumbebat.
4. Quod hae condiciones usque ad publica sequentis anni comitia durare intelligerentur.

p. 395 Eodem tempore consensum est, quod vicecustos Londinum proficisceretur ad collegii negotia, quae plurima erant, procuranda.

Novembris XIII. Magister Powell confecit aeque suum in aula coram sociis.

Decembris XVI. Magister Sterry, 1^{mus} bursarius computavit.

Decembris XVII. Divina fecimus in memoria fundatoris, post lecta sunt statuta et scrutinium initum, quod in calendas Ianuarii prorogatum est.

Decembris XX. Confectus est computus generalis anni 1651/1652.

Decembris ultimo. Habitum est scrutinium, in quo tria illa solennia proposita sunt: 1. Mores servientium, 2. Numerus portionistarum, 3. Electio hortulani. Et in hortulanum electus est magister Wood, placuit ut idem numerus portionistarum esset, qui prius; servientes vero ad officiarios remissi sunt, prout res exigeret, corrigendi. Quibus peractis scrutinium prorogatum est in ultimum diem Ianuarii.

[1653]

Februarii XXI. Consensum est quod decem librae Pococke, quondam portionistae solverentur, ob easdem rationes, quae ad eandem summam aliis etiam portionistis solvendam voluerant anno domini 1650, Augusti 2do.

Martii XVI. Dominus Rood admissus est in numerum sociorum, praestitis prius consuetis iuramentis.

Aprilis II. Habita est commemoratio fundatoris, post lecta sunt statuta, et scrutinium initum, quod in calendas Maias prorogatum est.

Aprilis XIV. Magister Wood 2^{dus} bursarius computavit.

Maii IV. Consensum est quod vicecustos Londinum proficisceretur ad procuranda collegii negotia.

Iulii VII. Magister Francklin variavit in hisce quaestionibus, vel potius has theses proposuit et defendit contra Aristotelem:

Anima humana non est tabula rasa sed picta. Contra Aristotelem, libro 3°, De Anima, capitulo 4to, textu 14.
Deterior est qui irae fraena dat, quam qui voluptati, contra Aristotelem, libro 7mo, Ethicorum, capitulo 7mo.
Sapienti nihil, aut non multum scribendum, contra Aristotelem, libro De Poetica, capitulo 8vo.

Finitis disputationibus dispensatum est cum eo pro 2^{dis} variationibus.

Iulii VIII. Magister Dickenson in disputationibus baccalaureorum has theses defendit contra Aristotelem:

Vitia sunt laude digna, contra Aristotelem, libro 2, Ethic' capitulo 4, textu 14.
Solitudo societate multo potior, contra Aristotelem, libro 1mo, Politic', textu 17.
Auditus visu praestantior, contra Aristotelem, libro 1mo Metaphysic' capitulo 1mo.

Finitis disputationibus cum eo etiam dispensatum est pro 2^{dis} variationibus.

Iulii XX. Habita est commemoratio fundatoris, post lecta sunt statuta, et scrutinium initum, quod in ultimum diem Augusti prorogatum est.

Praedia et tenementa hoc anno locata [i.e in the college year 1652–3]
Septembris 1mo [1652]. Dimisimus tenementum in Holywell olim Eduardi Turley, Iohanni Dickenson pro spatio viginti et unius annorum, una cum licentia alienationis. Finis 40s.

Dimisimus etiam tenementum in Holywell nuper Iohannis Hauks Roberto Harper pro 40 annis, una cum licentia alienationis. Finis – 40s.

Octobris 3°. Dimissum est tenementum in Holywell nuper viduae Hore et Williams, Gulielmo Ball pro 40 annis. Finis 10 librae. Eidem etiam concessa est licentia alienandi.

Octobris 20mo. Dimissum est manerium de Canes magistro Eduardo Spranger pro 21 annis. Finis, 40 librae.

Eodem tempore dimissae sunt sylvae de Canes Susannae Spranger, viduae, pro 21 annis sub annuo reditu decem librarum. Consensum etiam est quod omnes arbores in iisdem sylvis crescentes eidem

Susannae cederent, sub condicionibus in indentura comprehensis, ob quas 70 libras collegio solveret.

Februarii 21mo [1653]. Dimissum est tenementum in Holywell in vacivis ibidem iam extructum viduae Kidwell pro spatio 40 annorum. Finis, 3 librae.

Dimissum est aliud tenementum in iisdem vacivis Gulielmo Hartley pro 40 annis. Finis 40s.

Dimissum etiam est tenementum in Holywell Iohanni Selwood pro 40 annis. Finis 5 librae.

Mai 4to. Dimissum est stabulum sive tenementum in Holywell nuper Richardi Maud Francisco Sayre pro 40 annis. Finis 2 li. 10s.

Dimissum etiam est tenementum in Holywell, nuper Roberti et Catharinae Smith, Iohanni Bates pro spatio 40 annorum. Finis, 2 li. 10s.

Atque haec omnia suis temporibus sigillata sunt.

p. 396 Anno Domini MDCLIII, doctoris Goddard custodis 2do.

Socii Collegii

Magistri

1. Alexander Fisher
2. Daniel Whistler, medicinae doctor
3. Iohannes Powell
4. Petrus Nicolls
5. Thomas Iones
6. Richardus Lydall
7. Eduardus Wood
8. Edmundus Dickenson
9. Richardus Francklin
10. Iosephus Hervey
11. Ricardus Trevor
12. Iohannes Arnold
13. Nathaniel Sterry
14. Thomas Franck
15. Robertus Cripps
16. Clinton Maud
17. Robertus Hully
18. Henricus Hurst
19. Carolus Willoughby
20. Gulielmus Master
21. Robertus Whitehall
22. Henricus Eyres

Baccalaureus

1. dominus Rood

Capellani

1. Magister Georgius Lort
2. Magister Beniaminus Cooper

Augusti 1mo. Convenimus in aula hora nona antemeridiana ubi, quum officiarii superioris anni claves suas resignassent, perlectae sunt a vicecustode litterae domini custodis Londini tunc commorantis quas nuper receperat in haec verba scriptas:

Mr Subwarden.

I do nowe finde, that I cannot handsomely, or indeed without great preiudice, as it may fall out, come to Oxford against ye time I intended, for it is not free for any in my Relation to goe into ye country without askinge leave of ye House, and that may occasion an accompt of ye businesse callinge me away about which I am not convinced that comminge is so urgent, as not to be dispenced withall, and therefore can lesse expect Others should thinke it so. The businesse of your Election, I doubt not, may be as well don in my absence by ye five Seniors whom I desire to proceede thereto, accordinge to ye Custome of ye College, and what Officers ye maior part of them shall pitch upon, I am confident I shall have no cause to be dissatisfyed in. There can be no worke for Deanes this yeare, but about Presentations and Accompts, and therefore One may very well serve, and I am sure ye College hath neede enough of savinge unnecessary Stipends. The businesse of treatinge and agreeinge with any Tennants comminge to Renewe, I shall also referre unto you, according to ye directions in my last letter.

Your very respectfull freind, Jonathan Goddard.
London, 28th of July 1653.

Hisce perlectis litteris sociorum reliquis secedentibus per quinque seniores unanimi consensu electi sunt hi officiarii in annum sequentem, viz:

vicecustos, magister Fisher.
decani, magistri Iones, Maund.[1]
bursarii, magistri Hervey, Trevor, Cripps.
principalis portionistarum, magister Nicolls; bursarius Wilyott et capellanus capellae, magister Francklin; exhibitionarius Hamsterley, magister Hully; praelector Graecae linguae, magister Whitehall; praelector grammaticae, magister Hurst; custodes cistae Reade, tres decani; custodes cistae Bodleigh, magistri Nicolls, Hurst, Whitehall.

Quo tempore electi sunt praelectores Linacri in proximum triennium, magister Lydall et magister Dickenson.

Decretum etiam est quod magister Hervey et magister Trevor hoc anno variare tenerentur, cum caeteris magistrorum dispensatum est.

[1] *Margin*, 'hunc binarium decanorum numerum, tanquam collegio necessarium hoc anno, per alias litteras approbavit dominus custos'.

Augusti 8vo. Convenimus in hospitio ubi decretum est quod camerae (quae complures erant in area ut vocant baccalaureorum) quae nec sociorum, nec capellanorum, nec clericorum propriae erant, communariis elocarentur in usum collegii. Cuius rei cura seniori decano et principali portionistarum demandata est.

p. 397 Augusti 15. Consensum est in litteram atturnatus, ut vocant, mittendam magistro Gulielmo Newhouse tunc Dunelmi commoranti, qua ei potestas fieret, arreragia nostra apud Stillington et Seton Carewe recuperandi. Consensum etiam est quod magister Eyres proficisceretur in agrum Dorsettensem ut breve, quod sub poena vocant, in magistrum Thomam Baynard, qui reditum de Radipoole, nisi sub certis conditionibus solvere recusabat, curaret infligendum. Ei etiam demandatum est, ut arreragia de Knowle-Parke et tenementum in Shaftesbury exigeret.

Augusti 24. Dominus custos computavit, et discessit inplussagio.

Augusti 25. Magister Lydall, 3us bursarius computavit.

Septembris 12. Consensum est, quod indentura viduae Hartburne fiduciaria, ante aliquot annos facta cuidam Thomae Barnes, nunc in eiusdem viduae patrem magistrum Georgium Menyll, resignatione prius ab eodem Thoma Barnes facta devolveretur.

Decembris15. Dispensatum est cum magistro Cripps, 1° bursario, ut comptum suum in unum mensem differre posset ob graves quae a senioribus approbates sunt rationes.

Decembris 17. Habita est commemoratio fundatoris, post lecta sunt statuta, et scrutinium initum, quod in calendas Ianuarii prorogatum est.

Decembris 31. Initum est scrutinium in quo tria illa sollemnia de more proposita sunt,1.de moribus servientium, 2. de numero portionistarum, 3. electio hortulani.

Et in hortulanum electus est magister Dickenson; placuit ut idem esset numerus portionistarum qui annis superioribus; servientes vero ad officiarios remissi sunt, pro meritis suis corrigendi[s]. Quibus peractis scrutinium in ultimum diem Ianuarii prorogatum est.

[1654]

Ianuarii 12. Ulterius dispensatum est cum magistro Cripps 1mo bursario, ut computum suum in alteram septimanam differre posset.

Ianuarii 19. Magister Cripps primus bursarius computavit.

Ianuarii 23. Confectus est computus generalis anni 1652/1653.

Februarii 18. Conventum est in hospitio, ubi per dominum custodem, et septem seniores dispensatum est cum magistris regentibus ne ulterius ad praelectiones in aula de more legendas hoc anno tenerentur. Causas complures huius indulgentiae in medium attulerunt regentes, quae custodi et senioribus graves et iustae, ut res tunc erant, videbantur.

Eodem tempore decretum est quod in posterum nullus commensalis vel batellarius in collegium admitteretur, nisi cautione idonea prius data, qua obsonator et promus indemnes praestarentur. Idonea vero cautio videbatur, si commensalis superioris ordinis 6 li. 13s. 4d., inferioris vero 5 li. Alii quadraginta solidos, in bursarii manus traderent, ab eodem adservanda, vel in cistam oeconomiae reponenda, quamdiu in collegio moram traxerint.

Februarii 20. Convenimus in hospitio, ubi promo iniunctum est, quod p. 398
antequam praesentis bursarii terminus exitum haberet, syngrapham cum idoneis stipulatoribus exhiberet qua in trecentis libris obligaretur, pocula argentea, et reliquam collegii supellectilem ei commissam, una cum pane et potu ante annos complures ei concredito, sarta tecta conservare, nisi usu quotidiano et necessario quicquam detritum esset. Hoc nisi quam ocyssime faceret ab officio amoveretur vel saltem ad tempus suspenderetur, praesertim cum ad hoc praestandum saepius sed frustra interpellatus fuisset.

Iniunctum est etiam coquo iuniori, cuius id officium erat, ut diligentiorem circa carbones in culina cura adhiberet, nec summam praescriptam, quae quadraginta librarum erat, excederet, si secus fecerit, ipse sine ulla compensationis spe, damnum lueret.

Eodem tempore consensum est quod vicecustos proximo termino Londinum proficisceretur ad collegii negotia procuranda.

Martii 16. Magister Cripps 1^{mus} bursarius confecit aequum suum.

18. Habita est commemoratio fundatoris, post lecta sunt statuta, et scrutinium initum, quod in calendas Maii prorogatum est.

23. Sigillata est indentura de Heinsleyes in Lapworth magistro Lovell, quae duraret quamdiu ipse rectoria de Lapworth frueretur. Prius ante arreragia per aliquot annos collegio debita solvit, et sub chirographo

cavit de refundendis expensis, si quas collegium in lite circa hos fundos fecisset.

Aprilis 20. Dispensatum est cum magistro Trevor 2do bursario ut computum suum in tres septimanas differre posset, ob graves, quae senioribus approbatae sunt, rationes.

Maii 9. Ulterius cum eo dispensatum est per alias tres septimanas, ob easdem rationes etc.

Maii 29. Dispensatum est cum magistris regentibus per dominum custodem et seniores, ut eorum unusquisque in sua facultate publice profiteri posset, etiamsi biennium suae regentiae nondum complevissent, nec adhuc variassent.

Iulii 5. Magister Trevor variavit in hisce duabus quaestionibus, cum moris esset in tribus variare, sed duae sufficere videbantur, quum duo tantum decani essent, qui suum Aristotelem defenderent. Quaestiones erant:

[*blank*].

Finitis disputationibus cum eo dispensatum est pro 2^dis^ variationibus.

Iulii 7. Magister Hervey variavit in hisce 2^bus^ quaestionibus:

An { Barbaris politiorum imperium non admittentibus bellum inferri possit, iure naturali. Negat contra Aristotelem libro 1mo Politicorum, capitulo 8vo.
Civitas sit a natura. Negat contra Aristotelem libro 1mo Politicorum, capitulo 2do.

Finitis disputationibus cum eo etiam dispensatum est pro 2^dis^ eius variationibus.

Iulii 20. Divina fecimus in memoriam fundatoris, post lecta sunt statuta et scrutinium initum, quod in calendas Septembres prorogatum est.

Iulii 25. Magister Trevor 2^dus^ bursarius computavit.

Iulii 26. Consensum est de dimittendis illis quinque aut circiter iugeribus in Elham, (quae olim sylva erat caedua, sed impraesentiarum dumiet[or]um) magistro Henrico Hannington sub annali reditu viginti solidorum, collegio ab ipso solvendorum quamdiu is vicaria de Elham frueretur, quam eo tempore authoritate parliamentaria obtinebat.

Tenementa et praedia hoc anno elocata [*i.e in the college year 1653–4*]
Augusti 3 [1653]. Dimissum est tenementum in Holywell, quod nuper

a magistro Atwoode possidebatur, Rogero Gill, pro spatio 40 annorum, una cum licentia alienationis. Finis 7 li.

Eodem tempore dimissum est tenementum in Holywell Thomas Clarke pro spatio 40 annorum. Finis 5 li.

Dimissum etiam est Ioannae Cox tenementum pro spatio 21 annorum. Finis, decem solidi quos statim pauperculae cuidam in Holywell, ex consensu largiti sumus.

Augusti 3. dimissum est Carolo Winckle lanioni stabulum vel laniena p. 399
in Holywell pro spatio 40 annorum, finis duo capones.

Februarii 6 [1654]. Concessa Iohanni Sellwoode licentia alienandi domum suam in Holywell quam anno superior ei dimiseramus.

Martii 27. Dimissum est tenementum hoc quod Iohannes Sellwood iam alienaverat Iohanni Bates pro spatio 40 annorum, una cum licentia alienacionis. Finis duo capones.

Martii 28. Dimissum est tenementum in St Albans magistro Richardo Iennings pro 21 annis, una cum licentia alienacionis. Finis, 10 li.

Martii 29. Dimissum est tenementum Partridge in Holywell Gulielmo Smith pro spatio 40 annorum, quo nomine collegio solvit 25 li., quantum quinque solvit pro fine, reliquas vero ob gratiam ei factam in clausulae cuiusdam inductione, qua sumptus non mediocres in domum hanc aedificandam in veteri indentura tenebatur. Haec autem viginti librae ex consensu inter custodem et socios divisae sunt.

Maii 1mo. Dimissum est tenementum in Holywell viduae Couch pro spatio 40 annorum, una cum licentia alienacionis. Finis, 16 li.

Iulii 31. Dimissum est manerium de Merton Hall, Cantabrigiae Mariae Sherwoode viduae et relictae Iohannis Sherwood (per annos complures ibidem firmarii) pro spatio 21 annorum a festo Michaelis proximo inchoandorum. Finis 13 li. 6s. 8d.

Atque haec omnia variis, ut res ferebat, temporibus sigillata sunt.

p. 400 Anno Domini MDCLIV, doctoris Goddard custodis 3°.

Socii Collegii

Magistri

1. Alexander Fisher
2. Daniel Whistler, medicine doctor
3. Iohannes Powell
4. Petrus Nicolls
5. Thomas Iones
6. Ricardus Lydall
7. Eduardus Wood
8. Edmundus Dickenson
9. Ricardus Francklin
10. Iosephus Hervey
11. Ricardus Trevor
12. Nathaniel Sterry
13. Thomas Franke
14. Robertus Cripps
15. Clinton Maund
16. Robertus Hully
17. Henricus Hurst
18. Carolus Willoughby
19. Gulielmus Master
20. Robertus Whitehall
21. Henricus Eyres

Baccalaureus

1. dominus Roode

Capellani

1. Magister Georgus Lort
2. Magister Beniamin Cooper

Augusti 1mo. Convenimus in aula hora nona antemeridiana, ubi resignatis clavibus officiariorum superioris anni, clavibus item bibliothecae coram prolatis, per dominum custodem et quinque simpliciter seniores (reliquis interim secedentibus) electi sunt in annum sequentem hi officiarii:
vicecustos, magister Fisher.
decani, magistri Wood, Dickenson, Willoughby.
bursarii, magistri Nicolls, Sterry, Eyres.
principalis portionistarum, magister Powell; bursarius Williot et capellanus capellae, magister Francklin;exhibitionarius Hamsterley, magister Hully; praelector linguae Graecae, magister Whitehall; praelector grammaticae, magister Master; custodes cistae Read, tres decani; custodes cistae Bodley, magistri Powell, Nicolls, Sterry.

Eodem tempore decretum est quod magister Sterry et magister Franke (qui tunc a collegio aberat) ante annum revolutum variare tenerentur in disputationibus baccalaureorum, quae per dominum Rood, et quotquot ex communariis baccalaurei erant, de more observabantur, cum reliquis magistrorum dispensatum est.

Augusti 18. Confirmata sunt denuo unanimi domini custodis et sociorum consensu, ea omnia quae annis superioribus circa allocationes tum custodis tum sociorum ordinata erant. Cum vero sociorum hebdomadalis allocatio, quae ex tritici et brasei pretio, magnam partem exurgebat, ob eorum praesentem vilitatem infra iustum subsidere videretur, adeo ut loco appietantiarum, carnis aprugnae, ly-sheepe money etc. (quae collegio illi remiserant) nulla compensatione in praesens fruerentur, ad damnum hoc quoquo modo resarciendum.

Decretum est quod si quis sociorum per integram septimanam a collegio abesset nihilominus tres solidos et sex denariorum nomine allocationis reciperet, si per integrum diem sex denarios, unius autem refectionis nomine, sive prandii sive coenae tres denarios. Sed hac adhibita cautione, ut ii tantum hac indulgentia fruerentur, quibus liberatura debita erat anno superiore, reliqui vero, si qui essent, penitus excluderentur. Sed quum nihil hinc emolumenti vicecustodi accresceret (cuius sive praesentis sive absentis eadem erat et stata allocatio, viz. 2s. 6d.) aequum visum est atque adeo unanimi consensu decretum, ut huic summae sex denarii singulis septimanis adderentur.

Decretum etiam est, quod allocatio senioris capellani, quae hactenus erat unius solidi et octo denariorum, in posterum ad duos solidos, et quatuor denarios excresceret, similisque additio fieret iuniori capellano, ut quatuor solidos deinceps singulis septimanis perciperet.

Augusti 24. Dispensatum est cum magistro Hervey, 3° bursario ut computum suum differre posset in duas septimanas, ad quam dispensationem necessario adigebantur, ob tenentium quorundam in reditibus solvendis tarditatem.

Septembris 7. Magister Hervey 3us bursarius computavit. p. 401

Octobris 23. Magister Hervey 3us bursarius confecit suum aeque.

Decembris 13. Dispensatum est cum magistro Eyres 1mo bursario ob rationes quae senioribus approbatae sunt, ut computum suum in tres septimanas differre posset.

Decembris 17. Habita est commemoratio fundatoris, sed quum dies is in Dominicum incideret, delata est lectio statutorum in diem sequentem.

Decembris 18. Lecta sunt statuta et scrutinium initum, quod in calendas Ianuarii prorogatum est.

Decembris 31. Habitum est de more scrutinium, in quo tria illa solemnia proposita sunt, 1. Mores servientium, 2. Numerus portionistarum, 3. Electio hortulani. Et servientes remissi sunt ad officiarios; placuit ut idem numerus esset portionistarum qui prius; in hortulanum vero electus est magister Francklin.

[1655]

Ianuarii 4. Ulterius dispensatum est cum magistro Eyres ut computum suum differre posset in aliam septimanam.

Ianuarii 11. Magister Eyres 1^mus^ bursarius computavit.

Ianuarii 22. Consensum est in praesentationem sigillandam magistro Hurst ad vicariam de Ponteland, vacantem per mortem naturalem doctoris Thomas Gray quum interim magister Humfredus Bell inscio et invito collegio eam occupasset.

Martii 7. Magister Wood unanimi custodis et sociorum, qui in aula comparuerant, consensu designatus est ad munus procuratorium in academia quod secundum rationes cycli procuratorii in nostrum collegium hoc anno revolutum erat.

Aprilis 7. Habita est commemoratio fundatoris, post lecta sunt statuta, et scrutinium initum, quod in calendas Maii prorogatum est.

Aprilis 9. Consensum est de indentura fiduciaria manerii de Thracyes et Thrognolds in parochia de Newington in agro Cantiano, dimittenda magistro Hervey in triennium proximum, ut sic iure experiremur, si necesse esset, cum magistro Trafford, qui reditus ibi debitos solvere detractarat.

Aprilis 19. Dispensatum est cum magistro Sterry 2do bursario ut computum suum differe posset in mensem, ob graves, quae senioribus approbabantur, rationes.

Maii 17. Ulterius dispensatum est cum magistro Sterry 2do bursario ut computum suum in mensem alterum differre posset ob easdem rationes.

Maii 22. Magister Wood senior collegii decanus et academiae procurator iunior, summo sui relicto desiderio e vivis excessit: in cuius locum ex domini custodis nominatione (cui id iuris per leges cycli procuratorii competebat) suffectus est magister Francklin.

Iunii 12. Consensum est ut vicecustos Londinum mitteretur, ut in collegii negotiis procurandis domino custodi adesset et adsisteret.

Iuniii 18. Dispensatum est cum magistro Sterry, ne hoc anno variare teneretur ob rationes quae domino custodi, et sociis approbatae sunt, praesertim quia munus pro procuratoris in proximis comitiis, alias fortasse vacaturum, in se susceperat.

Iunii 19. Dispensatum est cum eodem, ut computum suum ulterius differre posset, ob easdem quae supra rationes, praesertim ob redituum iamdiu collegio debitorum, sed nondum a tenentibus quibusdam solutorum, defectum.

Iulii 20. Habita est commemoratio fundatoris, post lecta sunt statuta, dein scrutinium initum de more, quod in calendas Septembres prorogatum est.

Praedia et tenementa hoc anno locata [*i.e in the college year 1654–5*] p. 402

Augusti 1mo [1654]. Dimissum est manerium de Barkby Iohanni Iohnson pro spatio 21 annorum una cum licentia alienacionis. Finis 20 li. Qui finis solito longe maior ei impositus (tres enim annos tantum redimerat) partim quia novus [*sic*] ibi inquilina erat, partim alias ob causas quae collegio aeque videbantur.

Augusti 2. Dimissa est rectoria de Margaret-Stratton magistro Thomae Kemble pro spatio 21 annorum. Finis 80 li., quarum prima pars solvenda ad sigillationem indenturae, altera ad festum Annuntiationis proximum.

Eodem tempore dimissum est stabulum sive laniena in Holywell Francisco Sayre lanio (quae anno superiore elocata erat Carolo Winckle) pro spatio 40 annorum, Finis 0. Eique concessum, ut stabulum hoc in tenementum commutaret, modo in illud aedificandum centum libras insumeret, quod syngrapha data se intra biennium facturum collegio obligavit.

Augusti 7. Dimissae sunt duae virgatae terrae in Hensington aldermanno Whistler pro spatio 21 annorum inchoandorum ad festum Michaelis proximum, Finis 0.

Dimissae etiam sunt eidem aliae duae virgatae terrae cum dimidio ibidem pro spatio 21 annorum ab eodem termino inchoandorum. Finis 0.

Eodem tempore dimissum est manerium de Thorncroft magistro Waltero Rogers pro spatio 21 annorum. Finis 30 li., quarum prima pars solvenda ad sigillationem indenturae, altera ad festum Annuntiationis 1655. Una cum licentia alienacionis.

Augusti 15. Dimissa est firma de Basingstoke Gulielmo Temple, pro spatio 21 annorum, una cum licentia alienacionis. Finis 20 li. quarum prima pars solvenda ad sigillationem indenturae, altera ad festum Annuntiationis proximum.

Augusti 30. Dimissa sunt molendina de Grandchester magistro Bing pro 21 annis, una cum licentia alienacionis. Finis 30 li.

Eodem tempore dimisimus utramque medietatem rectoriarum de Emildon et Ponteland magistro Philippo, pro spatio 21 annorum. Finis 120 li.

Et consensum est quod anno revoluto eandem indenturam pro eodem temporis spatio de novo sigillatam haberet gratis.

Octobris 21. Dimissum est tenementum in Holywell viduae Wiblin pro spatio 40 annorum, una cum licentia alienacionis. Finis 10 li. Qui finis solito maior, ideo excreverat quia 40 anni iam ei dimissi sunt, quum superiores dimissiones unius tantum et viginti annorum essent.

Eodem tempore dimissae sunt sylvae apud Thorncroft magistro Waltero Rogers pro spatio 21 annorum, una cum licentia alienacionis. Finis 0.

Aprilis 9 [1655]. Dimissum est tenementum in Holywell quod olim erat magistri Hopper, sed in tria tenementa, iampridem dispertitum, una cum horreo e regione istius domus, pro spatio 40 annorum hisce quatuor, 1, magistro Walker; 2, magistro Ellis; 3, magistro Bayly et Mariae Ashley tanquam fiduciariis nepotis magistri Boone nuper defuncti; horreum vero Gulielmo Harris. Finis omnium 20 li. Concessa etiam est licentia alienacionis horum unicuique.

Dimissum est tenementum in Holywell, quod olim erat Iohannis Chandler, aldermanno Whistler pro spatio 40 annorum, una cum licentia alienacionis. Finis 10 li.

Aprilis 26. Dimissum est tenementum in Holywell quod ante annos aliquot Iohannes Chandler e fundamentis extruxerat, dominae Annae Vesey uxori Roberti Vesey armigeri, pro 40 annis una cum licentia alienacionis. Finis 15 li.

Maii 11. Dimissum est tenementum in Holywell, quod prius erat viduae Holt, magistro Antonio Nicholas pro spatio 40 annorum, una cum licentia alienacionis. Finis-3 li.

Eodem tempore dimissum est aliud tenementum in Holywell quod nuper erat Augustini Boxley, Iohanni Royston, pro spatio 21 annorum. Finis 4 li.

Atque heec omnia variis, ut res ferebat, temporibus sigillata sunt.

Anno Domini MDCLV, doctoris Goddard custodis 4to. p. 403

Socii Collegii
Magistri

1. Alexander Fisher
2. Daniel Whistler, medicinae doctor
3. Iohannis Powell
4. Petrus Nicolls
5. Thomas Iones
6. Richardus Lydall
7. Edmundus Dickenson
8. Richardus Francklin
9. Iosephus Hervey
10. Richardus Trevor
11. Nathaniel Sterry
12. Thomas Franke
13. Robertus Cripps
14. Clinton Maund
15. Henricus Hurst
16. Carolus Willoughby
17. Gulielmus Masters
18. Robertus Whitehall
19. Henricus Eyres

Baccalaureus

1. dominus Rood

Capellani

1. Magister Georgius Lort
2. Magister Beniamin Cooper

Augusti 1mo. Convenimus in aula hora nona antemeridiana, ubi resignatis clavibus ab officiariis superioris anni, biblothecae etiam clavibus coram prolatis, a domino custode, et quinque simpliciter seniores [*sic*], reliquis sociorum interim secedentibus, electi sunt in annum sequentem:
vicecustos, magister Fisher.
decani, magistri Lydall, Francklin, Master.
bursarii, magistri Iones, Dickenson. Maund.
principalis portionistarum, magister Nicolls; bursarius Williott et capellanus capellae, magister Hervey; exhibitionarius Hamsterley, magister Nicolls; praelector Graecae linguae, magister Whitehall; praelector grammaticae, magister Willoughby; custodes cistae Read, tres decani; custodes cistae Bodley, magistri Nicolls, Hervey, Hurst; praelectores Bickley, magister Cripps, magister Hurst (electi ab eis quibus id iuris competebat, qui succederent magistro Powell, qui muneri huic publice renunciarat, et magistro Wood qui nuper fato functus erat).

Eodem tempore consensum est in progressum hoc autumno ad maneria de Cuxham, Ibston, Kibworth et Barkby, et bursarius itinerans designatus est magister Nicolls.

Augusti 3. Consensum est per dominum custodem et socios, quorum multo maior pars adfuit, ut magistro Trevor in Galliam et Italiam peregrinaturo viginti librae annuae concederentur in proximum triennium, si ei in transmarinis partibus tam diu commorari contigerit. Consensum etiam est ut liberatura omnibusque finibus socio debitis frueretur durante hoc peregrinationis tempore.

Augusti 9. Magister Sterry 2^{dus} bursarius computavit.

Augusti 23. Dispensatum est cum magistro Nicolls 3° bursario, ut computum suum differre posset in unam septimanam.

Augusti 25. Dominus custos computavit in scaccario et discessit in plussagio.

Augusti 26. Ordinatum est quod magister Sterry et magister Franke, qui anno superiore variare tenebantur, hoc anno variarent; cum caeteris magistrorum dispensatum est.

Augusti 27. Consensum est per dominum custodem et socios, quod aldermanno Whistler (cui anno superiore dimissae erant duae virgatae terrae in Hensington) potestas fieret demoliendi toftum quoddam in Woodstocke vulgo appellatum The Dove-house, quod illarum virgatarum particula erat, et eadem indentura comprehensum, quae tamen indentura nondum sigillata erat. Causa huius concessionis erat quod ruinam minitabatur, nec per annos plus minus quadraginta, ut accolae testabantur, ulli inserviisset usui, nisi ad pauperes et errones recipiendos, unde viciniae damnosum et onerosum extitit.

Augusti 30. Dispensatum est ulterius cum magistro Nicolls 3° bursario, ut computum suum in tres, quatuorve septimanas differre posset.

Septembris 27. Magister Nicolls 3us bursarius computavit.

Octobris 11. Magister Sterry 2^{dus} bursarius anni superioris confecit aeque suum.

p. 404 Octobris 17. Illa sacelli nostri pars, quae turri contigua meridiem versus in lucum prospectat, ingenti cum fragore corruit, nemine tamen laeso, quum ad noctis horam circiter nonam ruina haec contigisset, caelo sereno et imperturbato.

Novembris 2. Concessa est et sigillata licentia magistro Samueli Rawlinge firmario nostro unius medietatum de Stillington, qua potestas ei facta est, atque adeo ei iniunctum, ut per indenturam dimitteret Thomae Lambe et Richardo Lynne (pro spatio quindecem annorum) duas trientes firmae illius, quas per aliquot annos obtinuerant possederantque ex vi testamenti cuiusdam Roberti Lambe, quam possessionem cancellaria decreto suo ante aliquot menses emisso, ratam firmamque esse iussit. Sed sub hac conditione concessio haec facta est, ut Thomas ille et Richardus obligatione quinquagentarum librarum tenerentur, nullum se hinc emolumentum ulterius percepturos, si testamentum illud Roberti Lambe irritum (quod vidua Maltby eiusque filius sibi spondebant) pronunciaretur.

Novembris 13. Magister Nicolls 3us bursarius confecit aeque suum.

Novembris 20. Dominus Rood, (concessa ei prius venia a domino custode mediandi apud 7 seniores domi existentes, iisque approbantibus) admissus est in numerum magistrorum praestitis prius consuetis iuramentis.

Decembris 17. Habita est commemoratio fundatoris, post lecta sunt statuta, et scrutinium initum quod in calendas Ianuarii prorogatum est.

Decembris 19. Dispensatum est cum magistro Maund 1mo bursario, ut computum suum differre posset in tres septimanas, ob graves, quae senioribus approbates erant rationes.

Decembris [*blank*]. Initum est de more scrutinium, in quo illa tria solemnia proposita fuerunt, 1. Mores servientium, 2. Numerus portionistarum, 3. Electio hortulani. Et in hortulanum electus est magister Hervey; placuit ut idem numerus esset portionistarum qui prius; servientes autem ad officiarios remissi sunt etc.

In hoc scrutinio, magistrorum nonnulli obsonatorem et coquum seniorum proterviae petulantiaeque accusarunt, et quod minus decenter erga socios sese gessissent. Qui comparentes cum sese non satis expedirent, aequum visum est, ut in poenam unius septimanae communiis et allocationibus excluderentur; eiusque rei cura ut in effectum daretur, seniori decano et praesenti bursario demandata est. Deinde scrutinium prorogatum est in ultimum diem Februarii.

[1656]

Ianuarii 10. Ulterius dispensatum est cum magistro Maund, ut computum suum in septimanam differre posset, ob easdem, quae supra, rationes.

Ianuarii 17. Magister Maund 1^{mus} bursarius computavit.

Martii 13. Magister Maund confecit aeque suum.

Martii 29. Habita est commemoratio fundatoris, post lecta sunt statuta, et scrutinium initum quod in calendas Maii prorogatum est.

Aprilis 16. Dispensatum est cum magistro Dickenson 2do bursario ut computum suum in mensem differre posset, ob rationes quae senioribus approbabantur.

Maii 9. Concessa est et sigillata licentia magistro Samueli Rawlinge, qua ei potestas facta est dimittendi alteram trientem firmae cuiusdam in Stillington, Margaretae Maltby viduae, pro toto temporis residuo, quod ipse in indentura sua ibidem obtinebat, id est pro annis octodecem.

Maii 12. Ulterius dispensatum est cum magistro Dickenson 2do bursario, ut computum suum differre posset in alterum mensem, ob easdem rationes quae supra, id est ob tenentium quorundam in reditibus suis solvendis tarditatem.

Iunii 16. Dispensatum est cum magistro Sterry, ne hoc anno variare teneretur perlectis prius domini custodis literis, qui hanc illi gratiam indulgendam censuit.

Iulii 20. Habita est commemoratio fundatoris, post lecta sunt statuta, et scrutinium initum, quod in ultimum diem Augusti prorogatum est.

Praedia et tenementa hoc anno locata [*i.e in the college year 1655–6*]
Augusti 2 [1655]. Dimissum est manerium de Kibworth Gulielmo Ray filii [*sic*] Roberti Ray nuper defuncti, pro spatio 21 annorum, una cum licentia alienacionis. Finis 40 li., quarum viginti solvendae ad sigillationem indenturae, reliquae viginti ad festum Michaelis, 1656.

p. 405 Augusti 2. Dimissa est medietas rectoriae de Gamlingaye Iohanni South pro spatio 21 anorum una cum licentia alienacionis. Finis 20 li. Qui finis solito minor erat, eo quod eodem tempore arreragia, quae nomine taxationum detinuerat, iam collegio solvit, promissione etiam adhibita in futurum se totum reditum, sine ulla taxationum deductione, constanter soluturum.

Augusti 3. Concessum est magistro Gulielmo Wilmott ut partem quandam firmae de Ibston alienare posset in decennium.

Augusti 4. Dimissum est manerium de Cuxham magistro Edmundo Gregory pro spatio 21 annorum. Finis 60 li., quarum prima pars solvenda ad sigillationem indenturae, altera ad festum Annuntiationis proximum.

Augusti 11. Dimissum est tenementum (vocatum Cranes) in West Tilbury Philippo Butler, armigero, pro spatio 21 annorum. Finis 30 li.

Augusti 25. Dimissa est altera pars domus vocatae Stonehouse in Knightrider Street, London, viduae Feildinge pro spatio 40 annorum. Finis 70 li.

Augusti 27. Dimissae sunt duae virgatae terae in Hensington (non ita pridem perquisitae a Iohanne Mead) Gulielmo Redhead seniori de Ludwell pro spatio 21 annorum. Finis 10 li.

Eodem tempore dimissum est tenementum in Holywell (quod nuper erat Roberti Smith) Iohanni Philips pro spatio 40 annorum una cum licentia alienationis. Finis 6 li. 13s. 4d.

Concessa est etiam licentia Francisco Sayre ut tenementum suum in Holywell, ante biennium ei dimissum, et ab eo nuper a fundamentis fere extructum, alienare posset. Eodem etiam tempore tenementum in vico Sancti Iohannis, London, vulgo vocatum The White Lyon, dimissum est Magaretae Mackernesse, viduae, pro spatio 40 annorum. Finis 3 li.

Dimissus est etiam murus stabuli Smoote magistro Thomae Egerley pro spatio 40 annorum. Finis duo doliola ostrearum.

Ianuarii 7 [1656]. Dimissum est manerium de Norton Mandevill magistro Gulielmo Stanes pro spatio 21 annorum, una cum licentia alienacionis. Finis, 60 li.

Eodem tempore dimissum est stabulum in Holywell (quod antea erat Gulielmi Ingoldsby) eiusdem relictae Elizabethae Ingoldsby pro spatio 40 annorum, una cum licentia alienacionis. Finis 40s.

Dimissimus etiam Thomae Billingsley hortum in Holywell (qui nuper erat magistri Bayly) pro spatio 40 annorum. Finis duo porcelli. Eique concessum ut domum ibi extrueret, modo centum ad minimum libras in eam aedificandam insumeret, quod syngrapha data se facturum obligavit. Postea ei concessa est licentia alienationis.

Martis 22. Dimissa est altera pars fossae in Holywell Abrahamo Watson pro spatio 40 annorum, et simul duo vaciva in Holywell pro eodem spatio. Finis omnium 8 li. Postea vero, viz. 12mo Iulii, eo iam defuncto, consensum est quod hae tres indenturae in duas contraherentur, eodem reditu servato atque ut eiusdem relictae Sarae Watson demitterentur.

Aprilis 17. Dimissa est altera pars fossae in Holywell magistro Thomae French pro spatio 40 anorum una cum licentia alienacionis. Finis 7 li. Dimissa etiam sunt eidem pro eodem spatio dua vaciva ibidem. Finis 3 li.

Eodem tempore dimissum est tenementum in Holywell cum horto eidem adiacente (quem super a magistro Thoma French redemerat) Aviziae Smith, viduae, pro spatio 40 annorum, una cum licentia alienacionis. Finis duo capones, et duo porcelli.

Maii 10. Concessa est licentia Gulielmo Readhead, ut tenementum et duas virgatas terrae in Hensington, quae nuper ei dimissa[e] erant, alienare posset.

Atque haec omnia, suis quaeque temporibus, hoc anno sigillata sunt.

p. 406 Anno Domini MDCLVI,[1] doctoris Goddard custodis V^to^.

Socii Collegii

Magistri

1. Alexander Fisher
2. Iohannes Powell
3. Petrus Nicolls
4. Thomas Iones
5. Richardus Lydall, medicinae doctor
6. Edmundus Dickenson, medicinae doctor
7. Richardus Francklin
8. Iosephus Hervey
9. Richardus Trevor
10. Nathaniel Sterry
11. Robertus Cripps
12. Clinton Maund
13. Henricus Hurst
14. Carolus Willoughby
15. Gulielmus Masters
16. Robertus Whitehall
17. Henricus Eyres
18. Edoardus Rood

Capellani

1. Magister Georgius Lort
2. Magister Beniamin Cooper

Augusti I^mo^. convenimus pro more in alta aula hora nona antemeridiana, ubi resignatis clavibus ab officiariis anni superioris (reliquis sociis ad tempus secedere iussis) custos una cum 5 simpliciter senioribus sequentis anni officiarios hunc in modum designavit:
vicecustos, magister Iones.
decani, magistri Hervey, Hurst, Whitehall.
bursarii, magistri Powell, Francklin, Cripps.
principalis portionistarum, magister Nicolls; bursarius Williot et capellanus capellae, magister Rood; exhibitionarius Hamsterly, magister Nicolls; praelector linguae Graecae, magister Willoughby; praelector grammaticae, magister Masters; custodes cistae Read, tres decani; custodes cistae Bodleigh, magistri Nicolls, Francklin, Cripps.

[1] A new hand, possibly that of subwarden Thomas Jones.

Quo tempore praelectores Linacri in alterum triennium electi sunt, Richardus Lydall et Edmundus Dickenson, medicinae doctores.

Quo die decretum est ut magister Sterry (cui variandi munus ab uno vel altero anno incumbebat at ex speciali custodis et sociorum gratia cum eo in hunc usque diem indultum est) ante annum revolutum variare teneret, cumque magistrum Francke (ad idem munus ante designatum) collegium penitus deseruisse crederetur aequum visum est ut magister Cripps eius loco suffectus ad variandum in disputationibus baccalaureorum ante anni exitum teneretur.Cum reliquis magistrorum dispensatum est.

Necessarium etiam visum est ut progressus hoc anno iniretur ad visitanda maneria de Gamlingay, de Merton Hall in Cantabrigia, de Canes et Norton Mandevill in agro Essexiensi, de Farleigh, de Thorncraft in comitatu Surriensi cui res conficiendae designatus est bursarius itinerans magister Iones.

II°. Consensum est per dominum custodem et socios in praesentationem Ioannis Love ad vicariam de Maldon, quae per spontaneam resignationem magistri Blickard vacua videbatur.

VI^{to}. Dispensatum est cum doctore Dickenson, 2° bursario, ut computum suum in unam septimanam differre posset, ob graves, quae a senioribus approbatae sunt, rationes.

XIII°. Consensum est a domino custode caeterisque sociis in praesentationem magistri Rood ad medietatem rectoriae de Gamlingay quae morte magistri Marshall ultimi rectoris vacua cedebat.

XV°. Magister Prickett, firmarius noster de Beilby computavit in scaccario et discessit aeque.

Quo tempore dominus custos computavit in scaccario et discessit in plussagio.

Doctor Dickenson 2^{dus} bursarius anni precedentis computavit.

Dispensatum est cum magistro Iones ut computum suum in sex septimanas differre posset ob rationes a senioribus approbatas.

XXVI^{to}. Decreto cautum est a domino custode sociis, ad quos id spectat, consentientibus ut nulli equi, praeter eos quos collegii sumptibus pasci oportet, in collegii equili alantur nisi uniuscuiusque dominus ante festum Michaelis duo saltem faeni plaustra in nostrum faenile importaret.

p. 407 Anno Domini MDCLVI, doctoris Goddard custodis V^{to}.

Augusti XXVI. Quo tempore coram domino custode et sociis in communarios quosdam deferebantur querelae, quod hi sese in sociorum sodalitia ingerebant, et ad mensam, quam vocant sociorum accedentes, cum sociis ad epulandum mixtim concumbebant, unde id mali collegio evenerit quod dum socii sermones ad mensam miscentes de publicis collegii negotiis agitabant hi convivae collegii a consiliis evadunt quae res tum domino custodi tum sociis gravis et absona videbatur. Quare decretum est communarios cuiuscunque sunt ordinis vel gradus a magistrorum mensa in posterum abstinere.

Septembris XXVI°. Magister Iones 3^{tius} bursarius computavit.

Octobris VII. Consensum est unanimiter a sociis ut ex curiarum rotulis novissimae mutuo darentur domino Holloway iurisconsulto, quarum testimoni inserviret in decisione litis nuperrime subortae inter tenentes nostros de Cuxham, de quarum restitutione vicecustodi fidem oppignoravit, quem post aliquot dies liberavit.

XI°. Consensum est ut doctor Dickenson et magister Maund proficiscerentur ad sylvas vendendas apud Cuxham.

Quo tempore decretum est ut vicecustos (postquem collegii negotia Londinum expediretur) ad Farleigh una cum obsonatore se transferat, ut sylvas (si quae caeduae forent) venum exponeret, ubi 70 arbores firmario nostro domino Hether vendivit a quo 70 libras (quasi iustum tot arborum pretium) numerata pecunia recepit quas collegio remisit ut evidenter liqueat ex libro rationum.

Eodem die doctor Dickenson soluto pede computi discessit aeque.

Eodem tempore magister Iones 3^{ius} bursarius fecit aeque suum.

Quo die computus generalis totius anni factus est.

Decembris XVII. Habita est commemoratio fundatoris, post lecta sunt statuta et scrutinium initum est, quod in calendas Ianuarii prorogatum est.

Eodem tempore dispensatum est cum magistro Cripps, 1mo bursario, ut computum suum in unum mensem differre posset.

XXXI. Initum est de more scrutinium in quo illa tria proposita fuerunt, 1. Mores servientium, 2. Numerus portionistarum, 3. Electio hortulani. Et in hortulanum electus est magister Sterry; placuit ut idem numerus esset portionistarum qui prius; servientes autem ad officiarios remissi etc.

In eodem scrutinio obsonator ad examen revocatus tanta petulantia se in conventu magistrorum gessit. Aequum visum est omnibus ut unius mensis communiis (tanquam in penam suae maledicentiae) aliisque allocationibus excluderetur eiusque res cura ut in effectum daretur seniori decano et praesenti bursario demandata est. Deinde scrutinium prorogatum est in ultimum diem Februarii.

[1657]

Ianuarii III^{tio}. Consensum est ut sylvae caeduae apud Gamlingaye Avenells domino Henrico Kersly (qui tunc praesens aderat, hancque gratiam a collegio expetebat) honesto proposito pretio venum darentur. At cum de arborum valore partes satis diu altercarentur utrimque tandem conventum est, ut dominus Kersley (facta prius indentura contractus, quam vulgo vocant 'bargaine and sale') ducentas viginti libras collegio, pro sylvis caeduis apud Avenells numeraret, quarum 120 li. ad sigillationem caeterae inita obligatione, ad 1um Augusti debitae veniant.

Dispensatum est cum magistro Rood ut sacris ordinibus initiaretur ante finitam regentiam ut vicariae de Gamlingay ad quam a serenissimo protectore erat promotus capax videretur.

Dimissum est diploma seu potius literae patentes firmario nostro domino Nicolae Herleston, quarum virtute ballivi officio fungi oportet, tum ad reditus assisae colligendos, tum alia ballivatus munera obeunda in manerio nostro de Thracies et Thrognolls iuxta Newington.

V^{to}. Cum de hebdoma[da]li capellanorum allocatione nihil certi adhuc definiebatur an stata semper maneret, an ad pretium tritici braseive cresceret caderetve compertum est (toto negotio allocationum retexto et quasi ad calculos revocato) capellanorum allocationem de sedecem denariis (quae illis loco appietantiarum cedit[ur]) infra iustam proportionem subsidere, quare decretum est a sociis, domino custode per literas / suffragante, ut capellani xx denarios compensationis loco per p. 408
septimanam perciperent eo tamen pacto, ut eorum allocatio uti illa sociorum, ex tritici et brasei pretio magnam partem exurgeret.

Ianuarii XI. Convenimus in hospitio, (ubi lectis literis a domino custode receptis) Magister Rood hanc gratiam a sociis expetivit, ut loco anni gratuiti (qui sociis collegium deserentibus more solito indulgeri solet) certam summam pecuniae reciperet; quoniam officii sui ratio postulabat, ut in vicaria sua de Gamlingay continuo commorari obstringeretur. Re itaque a sociis serio pensitata, tandem itum est in hanc sententiam uti triginta librae ipsi statim a bursario numerarentur sub hac conditione ut ex nunc prout ex tunc omni iure quod habere possit in collegio (beneficio anni gratuiti) penitus renunciaret, et ab eo penitus excluderetur.

Quo tempore cum eo dispensatum est quod pecunias bibliothecae debitas, necnon illas, quas a cista Bodleigh sub obligatione mutuo accepit, non redderet solutas ante festum Michaelis proxime sequentis.

Decretum est unanimi sociorum consensu (domino custode per literas mandante assensum suum) ut quinque campanae a fusoris aeramentarii manu (cum per multos annos squallore obsita tacite iacebant) igni tradantur ut inde vocales magis et loquaces resurgant, in cuius sumptus (ne aerarium collegii hoc onere nimis praegravetur custos et socii summam [*blank*] librarum contulerunt, de qua summa magister Fisher sponte sua decem libras obtulit. Insuper dominus Woode, firmarius noster, quinque libras in campanarum fusuras dono dedit.[1]

Februarii XXVII. Quo tempore aequum visum est, ut nostrae campanae ad stateram revocarentur, antequam fusor aeramentarius fraudulentas manus in eas iniiceret; huic muneri (ad quod a sociis erat designatus) operam dedit vicecustos, qui uniuscuiusque pondus post exactam trutinationem testimonio fretus ipsius aeramentarii hunc in modum definiebat. Pondus, 1^{ae} – 6 c., 3 qua., 14 lib.;[2] 2^{dae} – 10: 2: 14; 3^{tiae} – 11: 2: 14; 4^{tae} – 23: 2: 0; 5^{tae} – 32: 1: 14. Par est ut Henrici de Abingdon (huius collegii olim custodis) munificentiam posteritati commendarem, qui campanam ordine quintam at nulli secundam amplam satis et sonoram ex aere prope dixerim Corinthiaco confectam, collegio dedit, quae iam (necessitate id postulante) communem sortem subiens in octavam transformatur.

Martii XX°. Habita est commemoratio fundatoris; post lecta sunt statuta et scrutinium initum quod in calendas Maii prorogatum est.

XXII°. Quo tempore nostri metalli massa (ad 87 centennarios et 87 libras exurgens) a fusore aeramentario, cuius fidei concredabatur in 8 campanas digeritur, quibus ad libellam expensis inventa est: 1^{a} – 4 c., 3 qua., 14 lib.; 2da – 5: 0: 26; 3^{tia} – 6: 0: 14; 4ta – 6: 3: 0; 5ta – 8: 1: 11; 6ta – 10: 0: 25; 7^{a} – 13: 2: 3; 8^{a} – 19: 3: 6. Sic omnes aggregatim sumpta non appendunt ultra 74 c., 3 qua., 15 lib. ita ut fusor iste sublestae fidei sit

[1] *Margin*, 'Maud [?] Wood vidua'.

[2] i.e. hundredweights, quarters, and pounds.

in aere collegii 8 c., 2 qua., quam summam sub obligatione 200 librarum (interposito etiam fideiussore) collegio reddere tenetur.

Aprilis XIV. Hisce, (quae ad campanas spectant) rite compositis, campanistae saepius experiundo comperierunt, funes campaniles ad 30 ulnarum distantiam attractos in incertum vagari, adeo ut campanarum pulsus ad modum harmonicum reducere desperarunt. Quare socii (domino custode per literas non refragante) decreverunt ut novum tabulatum a campanario ad xv ulnas dissitum excitaretur (spatium omnium 30 ulnarum a summo tabulatu ad solum usque intercipitur) ostiumque illi pateret campanilis parte perfossa, qua iter ducit ad campanarium, idemque huic novo tabulatus inserviret, ne caterva campanistarum frequentia sua ecclesiam perturb[abat]. In huius sumptus dominus Wilmott, firmarius noster de Ibston, viginti libras et dominus Gregory, firmarius de Cuxham, 5 li. ultro contulere.

Aprilis XVI. Magister Cripps soluto pede computi confecit suum aeque.

XXV. Magister Francklin 2^{dus} bursarius computavit.

Iulii IV. Magister Cripps variavit in hisce questionibus:

An {
1. Dilectio sui prae aliis sit licita. Negat contra Aristotelem 9° libro Ethic', capitulo 8°.
2. Mundus fuerit ab aeterno. Negat contra Aristotelem 2° libro de Caelo, capitulo 1°.
3. Deterior sit, qui irae fraena dat, quam qui voluptati. Affirmat contra Aristotelem 7mo libro Ethic', capitulo 6to.
}

Finitis disputationibus cum eo dispensatum est pro 2^{dis} variationibus. p. 409

Quo tempore consensum est ut liber, quem vulgo vocant curiarum rotulus, mutuo daretur magistro Holloway in lite promovenda contra Crooke.

Iulii XII. Magister Sterry variavit in hisce duobus quaestionibus, cum non nisi duo essent decani:

{
An praestet legem imperare, quam virum. Negat contra Aristotelem Politicorum libro 3, capitulo [*blank*].
An forma praestantes debeant caeteris imperare. Negat contra Aristotelem, Politicorum libro 1, capitulo 5.
}

Finitis disputationibus cum eo dispensatum est pro 2^{dis} variationibus.

XX. Divina fecimus in memoriam fundatoris, post lecta sunt statuta et scrutinium initum est, quod in calendas Septembres prorogatum est.

Tenementa et praedia hoc anno elocata [i.e in the college year 1656–7]

Augusti I° [1656]. Dimisimus manerium de Basingstoke domino Knight pro spatio viginti unius annorum una cum licentia alienationis. Finis X li.

II°. Dimissum est manerium de Callowland Gulielmo Woolley pro termino 21 annorum una cum licentia alienacionis. Finis 30 li.

VII. Dimissum est manerium de Thracies et Thrognolls iuxta Newington Nicolao Hurleston una cum licentia alienacionis. Finis 66 li. 13s. 4d.

Quo tempore terrae nuper perquisitae apud Newington elocatae sunt Nicolao Hurleston una cum licentia alienationis. Finis o.

Dimissum est manerium de Ibston Gulielmo Wilmot una cum licentia alienacionis. Finis X li.

XIII. Elocatum est tenementum in Holywell viduae Hastings una cum licentia alienationis. Finis XVI li.

Eodem tempore dimissa est domus in Holywell Dickenson pro termino 40 annorum facta ei prius alienandi potestate. Finis 5 li.

Concessa est licentia alienandi domino Napper.

Ianuarii III° [1657]. Dimissae sunt sylvae caeduae apud Gamlingay Avenells Henrico Kersley pro termino 21 annorum. Finis 30 li.

Eidem dimissae sunt sylvae de Gamlingay Mertonage, Finis Nihil.

Martii XXIX. Dimissa est domus in vaciva de Holywell Cotterell pro termino 40 annorum una cum licentia alienacionis. Finis duo porcelli et duo capones.

Aprilis I°. Dimisimus domum in vaciva de Holywell cuidam Hartley, cum licentia alienacionis. Finis 5s.

XV°. Dimissum est manerium de Chedington Untono Crooke pro termino 21 annorum una cum licentia alienationis. Finis 40 li.

Maii I°. Dimissa est domus in vaciva de Holywell cuidam Bates pro termino 40 annorum una cum licentia alienacionis. Finis Nihil.

XXIII°. Dimissa est domus in vaciva de Holywell domino Such pro termino 40 annorum una cum licentia alienationis. Finis duo porcelli et duo anseres.

Iulii XI°. Dimissa est medietas Stillington et Ceton Carew Rodolpho Iennison pro termino 21 annorum. Facta ei alienandi potestate. Finis 60 li.

Atque haec omnia variis, ut res ferebat, temporibus sigillata sunt.

Anno Domini MDCLVII,[1] doctoris Goddard custodis 6to. p. 410

Socii Collegii
Magistri

1. Alexander Fisher
2. Iohannes Powell
3. Petrus Nicolls
4. Thomas Iones
5. Richardus Lydall, medicinae doctor
6. Edmund Dickenson, medicinae doctor
7. Richardus Francklyn
8. Iosephus Hervey
9. Richardus Trevor
10. Nathaniel Sterry
11. Robertus Cripps
12. Clinton Maund
13. Henricus Hurst
14. Carolus Willoughby
15. Gulielmus Master
16. Robertus Whitehall
17. Henricus Eyre
18. Edvardus Rood

Capellani

1. Magister Georgius Lort
2. Magister Beniamin Cooper

Augusti 1mo. Convenimus in aula, hora nona antemeridiana, ubi (pro more) resignatis clavibus officiariorum anni superioris, bibliothecae etiam clavibus coram prolatis, per dominum custodem, et quinque simpliciter seniores (reliquis sociorum interim secedentibus) electi sunt in annum sequentem hi officiarii:
vicecustos, magister Powell.
decani, doctor Dickenson, magistri Sterry, Cripps.
bursarii, doctor Lydall, magistri Hurst, Willoughby.
principalis portionistarum, magister Hervey; bursarius Williot, capellanus capellae, exhibitionarius Hamsterley, magister Nicolls; praelector linguae Graecae, magister Maund; praelector grammaticae, magister Master; custodes cistae Read, tres decani; custodes cistae Bodleigh, magistri Hervey, Hurst, Willoughby.

Eodem tempore decretum est, quod magister Maund et magister Hurst hoc anno in disputationibus baccalaureorum variare tenerentur. Cum reliquis magistrorum dispensatum est.

Augusti 4°. Consensum est per dominum custodem et socios, ut magistro Trevor in Galliam et Italiam peregrinanti, viginti librae annuae concederentur in proximum biennium abhinc (scilicet in annum post triennium praeconcessum), si ei in transmarinis partibus

[1] Another hand, possibly subwarden John Powell.

tam diu commorari contigerit. Consensum etiam est, ut liberatura, omnibusque finibus socio debitis, frueretur, durante hoc peregrinationis tempore.

Augusti 9no. Magister Prickett, firmarius noster de Beilby, computavit in scaccario, et discessit aeque.

Augusti 10°. Magister Francklyn 2^{dus} bursarius anni superioris confecit aeque suum.

Augusti 19mo. Consensum est per dominum custodem et socios (quorum maior pars adfuit), ut magistro Whitehall in Hyberniam peregrinaturo, viginti librae concederentur, a discessu suo in annum sequentem, si eum tamdiu abfuturum esse contigerit. Consensum etiam est, ut liberatura, omnibusque finibus socio debitis, etiam et camera reservata frueretur, durante hoc peregrinationis tempore. Tot favorum ampliandi causa fuit, quoniam ab honoratissimo viro domino Henrico Cromwellio, Dubliniensis academiae cancellario, literis commendatus fuerat ut ibidem publicis negotiis inserviret.

p. 411 Literae sunt:

These for doctor Jonathan Goddard, Warden of Merton College in Oxford.

Sir, Having lately (from persons of Honour) received a Testimony concerning mr Robert Whitehall, fellow of Merton College in Oxford, which renders him capable of being serviceable and usefull heere amongst us in Ireland, where is a paucity of Schollars, both for Ecclesiasticall and Civill imployments, It is therfore my Request to yourself and the Members of that Society, that he may have a Travellours place conferred upon him, and the full Allowance, arising out of the profitts of his Fellowship, As also his Chamber secured for him during his absence from the College (the like Favour having been granted to severall of other Colleges in Oxford, that are now resident amongst us) and herein you will much oblige.

Your assured ffriend H. Cromwell.

Dublin, June ye 22^{d} 1657.

Eodem tempore consensum est, ut decem arbores, ex manerio de Callowland desumendae, concederentur magistro Croke, ad reficienda tecta manerii de Chedington.

Eodem tempore consensum est, ut pro stipendio priore et novo, e collegii redditibus decem librae contribuerentur uni ex nostris concionanti in ecclesia de Holywell. Attamen sub ea lege, quod incolae contribuerent etiam alteras decem libras annuas, neque nostra diutius quam illorum contributio duratura sit. Item amerciamenta omnia ad curiam nostrum pertinentia, iamdudum neglecta dehinc exigantur.

Eodem tempore consensum est a domino custode et sociis, ut praesentatio ad rectoriam de Farleigh magistro Ieremiae Meere sic petenti sigillaretur.

Augusti 27mo. Dispensatum est cum magistro Powell, ut computum suum in 2 aut 3 septimanas differre posset, ob rationes a senioribus approbatas.

Septembris 17mo. Magister Powell, 3^{tius} bursarius computavit.

Octobris 29no. Ex consensu sociorum (custodis assensu per literas significatos [*sic*]) praesentatio ad vicariam de Emildon conceditur magistro Gulielmo Coxe (filio Guilielmi Coxe olim socii et vicarii, ibidem nuper mortui) et sigillatur. Consensum est, ut vicecustos Londinum mitteretur, ut in collegii negotiis domino custodi assisteret.

Novembris 3^{tio}. Magister Powell 3^{tius} bursarius confecit suum aeque.

Decembris 7°. Quo tempore dominus custos computavit in scaccario, et discessit in plussagio.

Eodem tempore magister Ray, firmarius noster de Kibworth, computavit in scaccario et discessit aeque.

Decembris 17mo. Habita est commemoratio fundatoris, post lecta sunt statuta, et scrutinium initum, quod in calendas Ianuarii prorogatum est. Eodem die computus generalis totius anni factus est. Eodem die magister Willoughby 1^{mus} bursarius computavit.

Decembris 23^{tio}. Magister Iones ex consensu sociorum mutuum accepit a bibliotheca librum viz. Philipi Cluverii, de Italia Antiqua.

Decembris ultimo. Initum es de more scrutinium, in quo illa tria solennia proposita fuerunt, viz. 1°. Mores servientium, 2^{dum}. Numerus portionistarum, 3^{tium}. Electio hortulani. Et in hortulanum electus est magister Crippes. Placuit ut idem numerus esset portionistarum, qui prius. Servientes autem ad officiarios remissi sunt etc., Deinde scrutinium prorogatum est in calendas Martii.

Ioannes Powell socius et vicecustos donavit bibliothecae S.S. Biblia Brytannice translata, fol.

[1658]

p. 412 Ianuarii 4to. Rarum pietatis et charitatis exemplar, Edovardus Corbett, sacrae theologiae doctor, et pastor ecclesiae Haseliensis in comitatu Oxon', quondam huius collegii socius, et deinde gener domini Nathanaelis Brent, olim custodis dignissimi, placide conquievit in domino. Moriens legavit bibliothecae I[acobi] Cuiacii libros 4 vol. Item sociis singulis 20s. viritim, et portionistis et servientibus 10s. viritim.

Februarii 25to. Magister Willoughby 1^{mus} bursarius confecit aeque suum.

Martii 6to. Praesentatio ad vicariam de Emildon, quae iam vacaverat per resignationem magistri Coxe, ex consensu sociorum (custodis etiam assensu significato per literas) conceditur magistro Guilielmo Cawdwell et sigillatur.

Martii 10mo. Convenimus in hospitio, ubi (literis a domino custode receptis, et prius lectis) magister Francklyn hanc gratiam a sociis expetivit, ut loco anni gratuiti (qui sociis collegium deserentibus pro more solet indulgeri) certam pecuniae summam perciperet. Quibus placuerit ut triginta librae ipsi statim a bursario numerarentur, annusque gratiae, sub ipsas Ianuarii calendas inchoatus, per id tempus proxime futurum determinaretur.

Eodem die Robertus Powell, portionista, longa tabe consumptus moritur in collegio, ministri filius unicus, et bonae spei iuvenis, sepelitur in sacelli parte australi.

Aprilis 3^{tio}. Habita est commemoratio fundatoris, post lecta sunt statuta, et scrutinium initum, quod in calendas Maii prorogatum est.

Aprilis 15to. Magister Hurst 2^{dus} bursarius computavit.

Maii 8vo. Praesentatio ad rectoriam de Ibston, quae iam vacaverat per mortem naturalem magistri Powell, ex consensu sociorum (custode prius asentiente per literas) conceditur magistro Davidi Lloyde, et sigillatur.

Maii 29vo. Magister Nicolls resignavit in manus collegii vicariam Sancti Petri in Oriente, Oxon'.

Iunii 10mo. Magister Hurst 2^{dus} bursarius confecit suum aeque.

Iunii 15to. Dispensatum est cum magistro Hurst, ne hoc anno variare teneretur, perlectis prius domini custodis literis, qui hanc illi gratiam indulgendam censuit, quoniam in ecclesia B.Marie coram academicis in ipsa dominica comitiorum vespertinam concionem habiturus esset.

Iulii 6to. Praesentatio ad rectoriam de Lapworth, iam vacans per resignationem magistri Lovell, ex consensu sociorum (custodis etiam assensu significato) magistro Cawdwell sigillatur.

Iulii 9vo. Dispensatum est cum magistro Maund, ne hoc anno variare teneretur quod tunc temporis cum venia custodis et sociorum in Hibernia agebat.

Iulii 17mo. Magister Iones restituit bibliothecae librum P[hilippi] Cluverii, de Italia Antiqua quem mutuatum acceperat.

Iulii 22. Postridie diei gratulationis publicae, habita est commemoratio fundatoris, post lecta sunt statuta, et scrutinium initum, quod in calendas Septembris prorogatum est.

Praedia et tenementa hoc anno locata [*i.e in the college year 1657–8*]
Augusti 3^{tio} [1657]. Dimissum est molendinum in Norton Mandevill Isaaco Bennet pro 30 annis (9 elapsis). Finis 5 marcae.

Augusti 4to. Dimissum tenementum vocatum The Rose in Watford Iosepho Hill et Franciscae uxori pro 21 annis (7 elapsis). Finis 40 marcae una cum licentia alienandi.

Dimisimus magistro Iohanni Heather, manerium de Farleigh pro 21 annis. Finis 40 li. una cum licentia alienationis.

Dimisimus etiam sylvas ibidem eidem magistro Heather pro termino 21 annorum. Finis 60 li. una cum licentia alienandi.

Augusti 7mo. Dimissa est altera medietas de Stillington et Ceton p. 413
Carewe (resignatione indenturae prius facta a magistro Thoma Barns) magistro Richardo Wasse pro 21 annis. Finis 80 li., quarum prior pars, viz. 50 li. solvendae ad sigillationem indenturae, altera 30 li. cum proximis reditibus ad Decembris 23 per obligationem magistri Todd. Indulsimus illi tantos fauores quia ruinosam domum reaedificatam et alia damna sustineret, etiam alienandi licentia concessa est.

Ianuarii 7mo [1658]. Dimissa est domus in Py-Lane Iohanni Prince pro 40 annis. Finis 5 marcae. Et puteus (olim elocatus collegio Corporis Christi) pro annuo reditu octo denariorum una cum licentia alienationis.

Eodem tempore dimissa est Guilielmo Harding domus in Holywell pro 40 annis. Finis 10 li. una cum licentia alienandi.

Eodem tempore dimissa sunt eidem Guilielmo Harding stabula in Holywell cum 2 portiunculis terrae ibidem pro 40 annis. Finis duo capones singulis annis, supra reditus annuos unius solidi et sex denariorum. Eique concessum, ut stabula haec in tenementum commutaret, modo in illud aedificandum centum libras insumeret, quod syngrapha data se intra biennium et anni dimidium facturum collegio obligavit.

Martii 6to. Concessa est licentia alienandi tenementum in Holywell Iohanni Bates.

Aprilis 6to. Dimissa est domus in Holywell magistro Ellis pro 40 annis. Finis 0, una cum licentia alienandi.

Aprilis 17mo. Dimissum est tenementum in Hampton Poyle Guilielmo Osborne pro 21 annis una cum licentia alienandi. Finis 5 li.

Iunii 9no. Dimissum est manerium de Cuxham magistro Edmundo Gregory iuniori pro annis 21. Finis 30 li., quarum pars prior solvenda ad sigillationem indenturae, altera ad festum Annunciationis proximum esset. Item pro suppelectile prius aestimata, et pro tritico, et brasio, et piso, quibuscunque debitis olim per indenturas priores (iuxta precia granorum eorundem in festo Annunciationis novissime lapso) soluturum numeratis pecuniis intra quinquennium, data syngrapha se collegio obligaret.

Concessum est etiam sibi ipsi ius ballivatus ibidem.

Iulii 9no. Dimisimus domum in Holywell Carolo Poole pro 40 annis una cum licentia alienandi. Finis 8 li.

Iulii 22do. Elocatum est tenementum in Holywell cui olim insigne The White Horse, Petro Goddard pro termino 40 annorum. Finis 10 li.

Elocatum est tenementum aliud in Holywell eidem Petro Goddard pro 40 annis. Finis 0, una cum licentia alienandi.

Atque haec omnia sui temporis sigillata sunt.

Anno Domini MDCLVIII, doctoris Goddard custodis 7to. p. 414

Socii Collegii
Magistri

1. Alexander Fisher
2. Iohannes Powell
3. Petrus Nicolls
4. Thomas Iones Iur' doctor
5. Richardus Lydall medicinae doctor
6. Edmundus Dickenson medicinae doctor
7. Iosephus Hervey
8. Richardus Trevor
9. Nathaniel Sterry
10. Robertus Cripps
11. Clinton Maund
12. Henricus Hurst
13. Carolus Willoughby
14. Gulielmus Master
15. Robertus Whitehall

In anno probationis

1. dominus Roberts
2. dominus Iones
3. dominus Francklin
4. dominus Workeman
5. dominus Huntington
6. dominus Turnour
7. dominus Powell

Capellani

1. Magister Lort
2. Magister Cooper

Augusti 2do. Primus enim dies in dominicum inciderat, convenimus in aula, hora nona antemeridiana, ubi quum officiarii superioris anni claves suas resignassent perlecta sunt a vicecustode litterae domini custodis Londini tunc commorantis, quas nuper receperat in haec verba scriptas:

Mr Subwarden,

I did realy intend and promise, to have beene at the College against the solemne time of electing officers for the yeare ensuing; but am prevented uppon the account of his Highnesse service, and commands to attend here; which any, I presume will account a satisfactory excuse, and sufficient dispensation for my absence, though otherwise and uppon any less urgent ocasion, at such a season, I account it not to be easily answered for. I desire at the time there may be a proceeding to election of Officers, by the five Seniors. The buisnesse of renewing leases to any tenants that shall repair to the College, I shall referre to the company; and any other buisnesses, about which there may be application to the College at this time, I shall alsoe referre unto them, for their finall determination, except themselves or ye partys concerned should desire that I take cognisance thereof, in which case they shall speedily receive what I can contribute or offer

therein. I pray present to all the Fellows ye true respects of their and
Your respectfull friend Jonathan Goddard
Gresham College, July 28th 1658.

Hisce perlectis literis sociorum reliquis secedentibus, per quinque seniores, unanimi consensu electi sunt hi officiarii in annum sequentem:

vicecustos, doctor Lydall.
decani, magistri Powell, Hurst, Willoughby.
bursarii, magistri Nicolls, Maund, Whitehall.
p. 415 principalis portionistarum, doctor Dickenson; bursarius Williot, magister Hervey; capellanus capellae, magister Sterry; exhibitionarius Hamsterly, magister Nicolls; praelector grammatice, magister Cripps; custodes cistae Read, tres decani; custodes cistae Bodleigh, doctor Dickenson, magister Maund, magister Whitehall.

Augusti 28vo. Doctor Lydall tertius bursarius computavit.

Eodem tempore computavit dominus custos et discessit in plussagio.

Octobris 24to. Doctor Lydall tertius bursarius aeque suum confecit.

Decembris 17mo. Habita est commemoratio fundatoris, post lecta sunt statuta et scrutinium initum, quod in calendas Ianuarii prorogatum est.

Eodem die magister Whitehall primus bursarius computavit.

Decembris 22do. Post sincerum examen candidatorum die 22do incoeptum, et in 24^{tum} continuatum, electi sunt eodem die, vesperi in annum probationis: dominus Roberts, diocesis Wigorniensis; dominus Iones, Bristoliensis; dominus Francklyn, dominus Workman, dominus Huntington, Glocestrensis; dominus Turnour, Oxoniensis; dominus Powell, Londinensis.

Eodem tempore decretum est ut unusquisqe illorum 3 li. 6s. 8d. in usum bibliothecae persolverent [*sic*].

Decembris 22$^{do.}$ Ordinatum est quod magister Maund variaret, cum caeteris magistrorum dispensatum est.

Magister Wilton unanimi custodis et sociorum consensu electus est bibliothecarius, quo tempore decretum est ut pro stipendio communem cum sociis haberet mensam, et tres solidos septimanatim a collegio acciperet pro potu et pane, et camera iuxta borealem bibliothecae partem posita pro termino vitae perfrueretur.

Decembris 30mo. Initum est de more scrutinium, in quo illa tria solennia proposita fuerunt, 1mo. Mores servientium, 2do. Numerus portionistarum, 3^{tio}. Electio hortulani; et in hortulanum electus est magister Maund; placuit ut idem numerus esset portionistarum qui prius; servientes autem ad officiarios remissi sunt. Deinde scrutinium prorogatum est in calendas Februarii.

[1659]

Ianuarii 17mo. Admissi erant dominus Roberts, dominus Iones, dominus Francklin, dominus Workeman, dominus Huntington, dominus Turnour, dominus Powell.

Martii 15to. Convenimus in hospitio ubi (literis a domino custode receptis et lectis) unanimi fere sociorum consensu decretum est ut triginta librae magistro Eyre a bursario collegii statim numerarentur, eo quod sponte et voluntario, omne ius quod in collegio vel prius habuit, vel in posterum habiturus est exnunc prout extunc penitus renunciabat. p. 416

Martii 26to. Habita est commemoratio fundatoris, post lecta sunt statuta, et scrutinium initum quod in calendas Maii prorogatum est.

Aprilis 16to. Magister Maund 2^{dus} bursarius computavit.

Iunii 20mo. Convenimus in hospitio ubi (litteris a domino custode receptis et prius lectis) consensum est per socios quorum multo maior pars adfuit, ut magister Trevour in Italia iam commoranti, viginti librae annuae in proximum biennium concederentur. Consensum etiam est ut liberatura omnibusque finibus socio debitis frueretur, durante hoc peregrinationis tempore.

Iulii 20. Divina fecimus in memoriam fundatoris, post lecta sunt statuta et scrutinium initum, quod in calendas Septembris prorogatum est.

Iullii [*blank*].[1] Variavit magister Maunde in has quaestiones:

An { Rationalis anima sit definibilis a philosopho. Negat.
Virtutes omnes sint inter se connexae. Negat.

Eodem die dispensatum est cum eo pro 21^{dis} suis variationibus.

Decembris 21mo. Cum vicaria de Wolvercott, per resignationem magistri Nicolls vacaret decretum erat quod magister Parry e collegio Iesu munia et officia istius ecclesiae loco praedicti magistri Nicolls perageret, usque dominus custos et socii collegii Mertonensis alium habilem aptum et idoneum surrogarent.

[1] This entry is added later and out of place, below the entry for 21 Dec.

Praedia et tenementa hoc anno locata [i.e in the college year 1658–9]

Decembris 29no [1658]. Dimissum est tenementum Sunnings in parochia de Ibston Adriano Barney pro termino 21us annorum. Finis, 8 li.

Eodem die praesentatio ad vicariam de Emildon, iam vacuam per resignationem magistri Cawdwell ex consensu custodis et sociorum magistro Hewer sigillata est.

Aprilis 16to [1659]. Clausurae apud Walton demissae sunt magistro Ally pro termino 21us annorum. Finis, 30 li. una cum licentia alienationis.

Eodem tempore concessum est magistro Staines ius ballivatus manerii de Norton Mandevill.

Maii 5to. Firma apud Ibston concessa est magistro Gulielmo Wilmott, una cum licentia alienationis pro termino 21us annorum. Finis 20 li.

Eodem tempore concessae sunt eidem magistro Wilmott sylvae apud Ibston pro termino 21us annorum. Finis o.

p. 417 Maii 23to. Concessa est licentia alienationis viduae Fielding pro domo in Knight-riders Street, London'.

Maii 25to. Dimissum est tenementum in Holliwell olim domus Moore Mariae Coxed, viduae, spatio 40 annorum. Finis 17 li.

Iunii 8vo. Dimisimus rectoriam de Margaret-Stratton magistro Thomae Kemble quo tempore unanimi sociorum consensu mutavimus indenturam pro terminis annorum in indenturam pro terminis vitae, scilicet durante vita naturali Thomae Kemble, Elizabethae et Annae Kemble praedicti Thomae filiarum, dedit etiam idem Thomas pro fine 140 li.

Augusti 4to. Dimisimus sylvas apud Newington magistro Hurlestone pro spatio viginti et unius annorum. Finis 40 li.; eidem etiam concessimus licentiam alienationis.

Iunii 20mo. Pars vaciva in Holiwell muro luci Magdalenensis proximae concessa est magistro Harding pro terminis 40 annorum et dedit pro fine 2os capones.

Augusti 10mo. Dimissum est manerium de Beilby magistro Prickett pro spatio viginti et unius annorum. Finis o.

Eodem tempore decretum est quod magister Prickett singula messuagia in agro praedicto tenentium singulis de novo concederet, eo quod eorum omnium indenturae vel exierant, vel ad exitum vergebant; sed sub his conditionibus, ut fines collegii cederent nec non in maiorem rei confirmationem commune collegii sigillum indenturarum singulis affligeretur.

Septembris 11mo. Dimissum est magistro Lovell ly Hains lease in Lapworth (una cum licentia alienationis) pro termino viginti et unius annorum. Finis 70 li.

Atque haec omnia suis temporibus sigillata sunt.

Anno Domini MDCLIX, regis Caroli secundi XI, doctoris Goddard custodis VIII.[1] p. 418

Socii Collegii
Magistri
1. Alexander Fisher
2. Iohannes Powell
3. Petrus Nicolls
4. Thomas Iones, Iur' doctor
5. Richardus Lydall, medicinae doctor
6. Edmundus Dickenson, medicinae doctor
7. Iosephus Hervey
8. Richardus Trevor
9. Nathaniel Sterry
10. Robertus Crips
11. Clinton Maund
12. Henricus Hurst
13. Carolus Willoughby
14. Gulielmus Master
15. Robertus Whitehall

In anno probationis
1. dominus Roberts
2. dominus Iones
3. dominus Francklyn
4. dominus Workman
5. dominus Huntington
6. dominus Turnour
7. dominus Powell,

Capellani
1. Magister Georgius Lort
2. Magister Beniamin Cooper

Augusti 1mo. Convenimus in aula hora nona antemeridiana, ubi resignatis clavibus officiariorum superioris anni clavibus item bibliothecae coram prolatis, per dominum et quinque simpliciter seniores (reliquis interim secedentibus), electi sunt in annum sequentem hi officiarii:
vicecustos, magister Nicolls.
decani, magistri Hervey, Maund, Whitehall.
bursarii, doctor Iones, magister Hurst, magister Willoughby.
principalis portionistarum, magister Cripps; bursarius Williott et capellanus capellae, magister Powell; exhibitionarius Hampsterley, magister Nicolls; praelector linguae Graecae, dominus Iones; praelector

[1] This entry was evidently made after the Restoration.

grammaticae, dominus Roberts; custodes cistae Read, tres decani; custodes cistae Bodleigh, magistri Cripps, Maund, Willoughby.

Quo tempore electi sunt praelectores Linacri in proximum triennium doctor Lydal et doctor Dickenson. Decretum est etiam quod magister Hurst hoc anno in disputationibus baccalaureorum variare teneretur, cum caeteris magistrorum dispensatum est.

Augusti 3do. Ex consensu domini custodis et sociorum concessa est doctori Lydall summa 30 librarum in compensationem anni gratuitatis inchoandi a festo Sancti Michaelis proxime sequenti.

Eodem tempore concessum est magistro Sterry reipublicae causa perigrinanti ut communiis, finibus, liberatura, caeterisque socio debitis perfrueretur, durante peregrinationis tempore, hac tamen adhibita cautione ut si in Angliam intra semestris spatium reverteretur, haec gratia omnino cessaret.

Augusti 6to. Doctori Lydal 30 librae loco anni gratuiti concessae numerabantur a bursario, quibus acceptis, non ita multo post totum illud ius quod in nostra societate habuit, vel habere potuerit, penitus renunciabat.

Augusti 25to. Computavit magister Nicolls tertius bursarius.

Septembris 22do. Idem soluto pede computi sui discessit aeque.

Octobris 11mo. Concessa est litera atturnatus (ut vocantur) magistro Maund qua rei potesta[s] facta est arreragia nostra apud Pockrilston, Shaftsbury, Knowl Park et Radipoole recuperandi.

Octobris 25to. Convenimus in scacario, ubi absolutus est computus generalis anni 1658/1659.

Eodem tempore habitus est computus domini custodis et discessit in plussagio.

Eodem tempore concessum est procuratorium doctori Iones ad arreragia nostra apud Lapworth, Elam, West Tilbury, exigenda.

Eodem tempore consensum est ut marcidae et senio consumptae arbores in Barkby in collegii usum venderentur. Huiusce rei cura ballivis nostris, Ray et Iohnson demandata est.

Decembris 15to. Computavit magister Willoughby primus bursarius.

Eodem tempore consensum est ut altera medietas finium magistri Kemble et magistri Lovell inter custodem et socios divideretur.

Decembris 17mo. Sacra fecimus in memoriam fundatoris, postmodum lecta sunt statuta, et scrutinium initum, quod in calendas Ianuarii prorogatum est.

Reverendus vir dominus Griffinus Higgs, sacrae sanctae theologiae doctor et ecclesiae Liechfildensis decanus atque nostri collegii olim non minus ornamentum et decus, quam socius, moriens, pie legavit bibliothecae nostrae universam suam suppelectilem librariam, necnon quinquaginta libras, quibus secundum mentem testatoris coemendi sunt libri solum theologiae viz eruditiones critici polemici casuistae, et sacrae scripturae interpretes, iamque intra spatium unius anni a pecunia collegio persoluta inchoandi.

Decembris 31mo. Initum est de more scrutinium, in quo tria illa p. 419
solennia proposita sunt, 1. Mores servientium, 2. Numerus portionistarum, 3. Electio hortulani. Atque in hortulanum electus est magister Hurst. Placuit ut idem sit numerus portionistarum qui prius. In hoc scrutinio decanus senior, aliique socii coquum seniorem proterviae et insolentiae accusarunt, ut quod petulantius erga socios saepius se gessisset. Qua ex criminatione tum sese non potuerit expedire, aequum visum est, ut in poenam maledicentiae suae, unius mensis communiis et allocationibus excluderetur, necnon prima admonitione corriperetur. Quibus peractis, scrutinium in primum diem Februarii prorogatum est.

[1660]

Ianuarii 17mo. Admissi sunt in perpetuam societatem huius domus dominus Roberts, dominus Iones, dominus Francklyn, dominus Workman, dominus Huntington, dominus Turnour, dominus Powell, praestitis prius consuetis iuramentis, quibus obligantur admittendi in socios.

Februarii 7mo. Consensum est a sociis (domini custodis consensu per literas significato) ut magistro Willoughby in partes transmarinas profecturo 20 librae annuae concederentur in proximum biennium, si ei in istis partibus tam diu commorari contigerit. Consensum etiam est ut liberatura omnibusque finibus socio debitis frueretur durante hoc peregrinationis tempore.

Februarii 9no. Magister Willoughby primus bursarius confecit suum aeque.

Februarii 23[tio]. Concessum est magistro Hervey ut una cum caeteris sociis sortiretur partem in liberatura licet (negotiis suis eum averantibus [*sic*]) maiorem anni partem collegio interesse non potuerit.

Aprilis 14°. Habita est commemoratio fundatoris, post lecta sunt statuta, pro more initum est scrutinium, quod in calendas Iunii prorogatum est.

Aprilis 18. Computavit magister Hurst secundus bursarius.

Iunii 11. Concessum est magistro Hurst (domino custode consensum per literas significante) ut loco anni gratuiti triginta librae ei statim numerarentur. Insuper ei indultum est, ut ius societatis non amitteret, modo intra unius anni spatium a pecunia accepta inchoandi praedictas 30 libras bursario rependat.

Iunii 12. Magister Hurst secundus bursarius confecit suum aeque.

Iulii 6. Magister Hurst variavit in hisce quaestionibus:

An { Honores et divitiae sunt per se expetendae. Negat.
Senes et austeri sunt idonei ad amicitiam. Affirmat.

Finitis disputationibus cum eo dispensatum est pro secundis variationibus.

Iulii 7. Acepimus literas ab augustissimo rege Carolo secundo missas in haec verba:[1]

Charles R.

Trusty & welbeloved we greet you well. Wheras ye Wardenship of Merton Colledge in our Universitie of Oxford is void by the death of Sir Nathaniel Brent, late Warden there, and that the provision for the supply of that Headship appertaineth to us, in the vacancy of the Sea of Canterbury, Wee have designed our trusty and well beloved Doctor Edward Reynolds, one of our Chaplaines in Ordinary,for that office and dignity, in consideration of his learneing and other vertues enableing him thereunto, as a person capable of being elected, haveing beene formarly a Fellow of that Society, and doe therefore require you the Fellows of that Colledge, that assembleing your selves in due manner, you proceed forthwith to the election of the said Warden and to the same to name and admitt him the said Doctor Reynolds, and likewise that you performe and put in execution all other thinges which appertaine to you and every of you joyntly and severally for the makeing up and perfecting this our determination. Given at our Court

[1] *Margin*, 'Tenor Regiarum Literarum'.

at Whitehall, the third day of July 1660 in the twelfe yeere of our Reigne.

By his maiesties command
Edward Nicholas.

To ye Subwarden and Fellows of Merton College in
our University of Oxford.

Quibus perlectis, singulisque in iis contentis sedulo pensitatis consensum est ut vicecustos magister Fisher, et magister Hervey Londinum adirent ad hoc negotium procurandum.

Iulii 11. Convenimus (Londinum missi aliique collegii socii) in aedibus domini doctoris Reynolds, ubi re inter ipsum et nos ultro citroque deliberata, tandem itum est in hanc sententiam, viz: orandam esse regiam maiestatem ut nobis liceat in re tam gravis momenti collegiumque tantopere concernente, secundum vim et formam statutorum nostrorum, in quae iurati sumus, procedere.

INDEX

NOTE. Places are assigned to counties as defined before 1974. Forenames in square brackets are supplied by the editor from other sources. Characters in bold type denote the following Merton College posts: (**c**), chaplain; (**f**), fellow; (**s**), servant; (**w**), warden. Other abbreviations include abp., archbishop; Ant., Anthony; Bart., Bartholomew; Benj., Benjamin; bp., bishop; Cath., Catherine; Chas., Charles; Chris., Christopher; coll., college; Dan., Daniel; Edm., Edmund; Edw., Edward; Eliz., Elizabeth; fl., flourished; Geo., George; Gilb., Gilbert; Hen., Henry; Humph., Humphrey; Jas., James; Laur., Laurence; m., married; Marg., Margaret; Mat., Matthew; Mic., Michael; n., note; Nat., Nathaniel; Nic., Nicholas; Oxf., Oxford; Phil., Philip; Ric., Richard; Rob., Robert; Rog., Roger; Sam., Samuel; Sim., Simon; Steph., Stephen; Thos., Thomas; Tim., Timothy; univ., university; w., wife; Wal., Walter; Wm., William.